HEBREW FORMS OF ADDRESS

ANCIENT NEAR EAST MONOGRAPHS

Editors
Jeffrey Stackert
Juan Manuel Tebes

Editorial Board
Angelika Berlejung
Jeffrey L. Cooley
Roxana Flammini
Tova Ganzel
Daniel Justel Vicente
Lauren Monroe
Emanuel Pfoh
Stephen C. Russell
Andrea Seri

Number 31

HEBREW FORMS OF ADDRESS

A Sociolinguistic Analysis

by
Young Bok Kim

Atlanta

Copyright © 2023 by Young Bok Kim

All rights reserved. No part of this work may be reproduced or transmitted in any form or by any means, electronic or mechanical, including photocopying and recording, or by means of any information storage or retrieval system, except as may be expressly permitted by the 1976 Copyright Act or in writing from the publisher. Requests for permission should be addressed in writing to the Rights and Permissions Office, SBL Press, 825 Houston Mill Road, Atlanta, GA 30329 USA.

Library of Congress Control Number: 2023949870

To Su Hyeon, Gunn, and Joon
אשת חיל ונחלת יהוה
αὐτῷ ἡ δόξα εἰς τοὺς αἰῶνας, ἀμήν

Contents

Preface xiii

Abbreviations xv

Transliteration xxi

Introduction 1

1. Exploring Forms of Address: Insights from Sociolinguistic Studies 3

    1.1. Statement of the Problem 3
    1.2. Previous Studies 6
    1.3. Methodological Considerations 16

2. Free Forms of Address: Internal Structure 27

    2.1. Introduction 27
    2.2. Previous Studies 28
    2.3. Grammatical Categories 29
    2.4. Semantic Categories 45
    2.5. Conclusion 56

3. Free Forms of Address: Social Dynamics 57

    3.1. Introduction 57
    3.2. Theoretical Frameworks 58
    3.3. Data 66
    3.4. Analysis 68
    3.5. Conclusion 113

4. Free Forms of Address: Position and Function 115

    4.1. Introduction 115
    4.2. Previous Studies 116
    4.3. Method 126
    4.4. Analysis 131
    4.5. Conclusion 148

5. Bound Forms of Address 149
    5.1. Introduction 149
    5.2. Internal Structure of Indirect Forms of Address 152
    5.3. External Syntax of Indirect Forms of Address 154
    5.4. Social Dynamics of Indirect Forms of Address 159
    5.5. Conclusion 169

6. Conclusions 171

Appendix A: Text and Translation (1 Kings 22:1–28) 177

Appendix B: Free Forms of Address: Grammatical Classification ... 181

Appendix C: Free Forms of Address: Semantic Classification 191

Appendix D: Indirect Addresses: Semantic Classification 199

Bibliography 201

Ancient Sources Index 215

Modern Authors Index 231

Subject Index 235

LIST OF FIGURES

Figure 3.1. Brown and Gilman's Power and Solidarity Semantic 60
Figure 3.2. Brown and Ford's Linguistic Universal in Abstract Terms 62
Figure 3.3. Typology of Face-Threatening Acts (FTAs) 64
Figure 3.4. The Use of APNs and HPNs in the Hebrew Bible 84
Figure 3.5. The Use of ATs and HTs in the Hebrew Bible 102
Figure 3.6. The Use of Address Terms in Biblical Hebrew 114
Figure 4.1. Word Order of the Preface Elements in the C-unit 128
Figure 4.2. Word Order of the Body Elements in the C-unit 131
Figure 6.1. The Social Dynamics of Free Forms of Address 173

LIST OF TABLES

Table 1.1. Ahab's Use of Forms of Address in 1 Kgs 22:1–28 4
Table 1.2. Jehoshaphat's Use of Forms of Address in 1 Kgs 22:1–28 4
Table 1.3. Prophets' Use of Forms of Address in 1 Kgs 22:1–28 5
Table 1.4. Number of Hebrew Forms of Address Surveyed 18
Table 1.5. Positive and Negative Politeness 24
Table 2.1. Nominal Forms of Address and the Definite Article 35
Table 2.2. Nominal Forms of Address without the Definite Article in Prose ... 36
Table 2.3. Combinations of Two Appositional Addresses 40
Table 2.4. Semantic Types of Free Forms of Address in Biblical Hebrew 45
Table 2.5. Simple/Complex Addresses to Human(s) 46
Table 2.6. Compound Addresses to Human(s) 50
Table 2.7. Simple/Complex Addresses to Divine Being(s) 52
Table 2.8. Compound Addresses to Divine Being(s) 54
Table 2.9. Addresses to Inanimate Object(s) 55
Table 3.1. Data Table for Address Forms 67
Table 3.2. Number of APNs and HPNs in Each Book of the Hebrew Bible 70
Table 3.3. APNs and HPNs Used by Superiors to Inferiors 71
Table 3.4. APNs Used between Close Equals 77
Table 3.5. APNs and HPNs Used by Inferiors to Superiors 80
Table 3.6. ATs and HTs in Each Book of the Hebrew Bible 85
Table 3.7. ATs Used by Inferiors to Superiors 86
Table 3.8. HTs Used by Inferiors to Superiors 92
Table 3.9. The Distribution of נביא and איש האלהים in the Hebrew Bible 95
Table 3.10. The Distribution of נביא and איש האלהים in the Elijah-Elisha Narrative. 96
Table 3.11. ATs Used by Superiors to Inferiors 97
Table 3.12. KTs Used in Reference in the Hebrew Bible 104
Table 3.13. AKTs and HKTs in Each Book of the Hebrew Bible 106
Table 3.14. AKTs and HKTs Used Literally 107
Table 3.15. Ascending AKTs and HKTs Used by Inferiors to Superiors 109
Table 3.16. AKTs Used between Equals 110
Table 3.17. AKTs and HKTs Used by Superiors to Inferiors 112

Table 5.1. Indirect Addresses to Humans.. 153
Table 5.2. Indirect Forms of Address Beginning with T or Ascending KT..... 161

Preface

This book is the culmination of a decade-long research project exploring the intricate usage of forms of address in Biblical and Epigraphic Hebrew. Various aspects of this research were presented at annual meetings of the Society of Biblical Literature in 2020, 2021, and 2022. I am deeply grateful for the valuable feedback provided by colleagues and friends, which played a crucial role in refining my ideas and contributing to the overall development of this project.

I extend my special appreciation to Jeffrey Stackert for his encouragement to publish this work in the Ancient Near East Monographs series, and to Nicole L. Tilford for her valuable contributions in curating the project with SBL Press. I am also deeply thankful for the invaluable feedback and meticulous observations provided by two anonymous reviewers, which greatly enhanced the quality of the manuscript and shaped its final version.

I am immensely grateful to my esteemed former teachers, who provided me with exceptional instruction in the fields of philology and linguistics. Their expertise and guidance have been invaluable in shaping my academic journey. I extend my sincere gratitude to the following individuals for their remarkable contributions to my education: Dennis Pardee, Rebecca Hasselbach-Andee, Lenore Grenoble, the late Norman Golb, David Scholen, Stuart Creason, Michael Sells, Kay Heikkinen, Stephen Kaufman, Samuel Greengus, the late David Weisberg, Miles Van Pelt, John Currid, Alastair McEwen, and Stephen Voorwinde. Their teachings have left a lasting impact on my scholarly pursuits, and I truly appreciate their dedication and wisdom.

To my dear friend, Chip Hardy, I wholeheartedly extend my appreciation for being a constant source of encouragement and unwavering support since my arrival in Chicago. His presence in my life has been invaluable. I'm also deeply appreciative of Benjamin Noonan for his friendship and encouragement throughout the journey of this book. Our countless conversations in the Klau Library at Hebrew Union College in Cincinnati, OH, are cherished memories. I would also like to give special thanks to Lee and Mary Ann Cope, who have gone above and beyond their duty, exemplifying the essence of true Christian friendship since my family and I arrived in the United States. Their kindness and support have meant the world to us.

To my parents, Sung Soo Kim and Ae Soon Kwon, and my parents-in-law, Hee Sung Kang and the late Hye Ri Cho, I am deeply thankful for their boundless love and unwavering support throughout my life. Their unconditional care and affection are a testament to God's perfect love. I am forever grateful for the nurturing and guidance they have provided, which have shaped me into the person I am today. Their love has been a constant source of strength and inspiration, and I am truly blessed to have them in my life.

My deepest gratitude goes to my beloved wife, Su Hyeon Kang, and my cherished sons, Gunn and Joon, for their unceasing love and support throughout this journey. They have stood by my side through twelve challenging years of my graduate studies, demonstrating incredible patience and understanding. Their love and encouragement have been a constant source of strength for me, and I am truly grateful for their unwavering dedication. This volume is dedicated to my loving family as a testament to the profound impact they have had on my life and the unending support they have provided. I am humbled and blessed to have them by my side, and I am forever grateful for their love, patience, and belief in me.

Above all, I thank my Lord and my God, who, in His divine plan, predestined me, called me, justified me, and glorified me. I acknowledge that every step of this journey has been guided by His grace and providence. To Him alone belongs all the glory.

Soli Deo Gloria.

ABBREVIATIONS

The interlinear morpheme-by-morpheme linguistic glosses in this book generally adhere to the standard abbreviations and conventions established by the Leipzig Glossing Rules, developed by the Max Planck Institute.

1	first person
2	second person
3	third person
ACC	the object marker ʔe*t*
ADJ	adjective
AKT	address forms composed of a kinship term alone
APN	address forms composed of a personal name alone
ART	definite article
AT	address forms composed of a title alone
C	common gender
CSTR	construct state
F	feminine gender
FTA	face threatening act
H	hearer
HKT	compound address forms headed by a kinship term
HPN	compound address forms headed by a personal name
HT	compound address forms headed by a title
IMP	imperative
INF	infinitive
INTER	interrogative
KT	kinship term
M	masculine gender
N	noun
NEG	negation, negative
O	object
P	predicated
PC	prefix conjugation
PL	plural

PN	personal name
POL	politeness marker (*naʔ*)
PRO	pronoun
PTCP	participle
REL	relative clause
S	subject
SG	singular
T	title
V	verb
v	verse
VOC	vocative
X	any clausal constituent other than the subject, verb, or object
AA	*American Anthropologist*
AAL	*Afroasiatic Linguistics*
AB	Anchor Bible
ABD	Freedman, David Noel, ed. *Anchor Bible Dictionary*. 6 vols. New York: Doubleday, 1992.
AfO	*Archiv für Orientforschung*
AION	*Annali dell'Istituto Orientale di Napoli*
A.J.	Josephus. *The Antiquities of the Jews*. Translated by William Whiston. Nashville: Nelson, 1998.
ALH	*Acta Linguistica Academiae Scientiarum Hungaricae*
ALLCB	*Association for Literary and Linguistic Computing Bulletin*
ANES	*Ancient Near Eastern Studies*
ANET	Pritchard, James B., ed. *Ancient Near Eastern Texts Relating to the Old Testament*. Princeton: Princeton University Press, 1969.
AnL	*Anthropological Linguistics*
AP	*American Psychologist*
ARM	Archives royales de Mari. Paris: Geuthner, 1950–
BASOR	*Bulletin of the American Schools of Oriental Research*
BBR	*Bulletin for Biblical Research*
BDB	Brown, Francis, Samuel R. Driver, and Charles A. Briggs. *The Brown-Driver-Briggs Hebrew and English Lexicon*. Peabody: Hendrickson, 2003.
BFL	*Bulletin of Faculty of Letters*
BHS	Elliger, Karl, and Wilhelm Rudolph, eds. *Biblia Hebraica Stuttgartensia*. Stuttgart: Deutsche Bibelgesellschaft, 1984.
BHHB	Baylor Handbook on the Hebrew Bible

BHRG	Merwe, Christo H. J. van der, Jacobus A. Naudé, and Jan H. Kroeze. *A Biblical Hebrew Reference Grammar*. Sheffield: Sheffield Academic, 1999.
BHRG²	Merwe, Christo H. J. van der, Jacobus A. Naudé, and Jan H. Kroeze. *A Biblical Hebrew Reference Grammar*. New York: Bloomsbury T&T Clark, 2017.
BL	Bauer, Hans, and Pontus Leander. *Historische Grammatik der hebräischen Sprache des Alten Testamentes*. Hildesheim: Olms, 1962.
BT	*The Bible Translator*
CBQ	*Catholic Biblical Quarterly*
CBQMS	Catholic Biblical Quarterly Monograph Series
CLS	*Chicago Linguistic Society*
ConBOT	Coniectanea Biblica: Old Testament Series
CSL	Contributions to the Sociology of Language
CTU	Dietrich, Manfried, Oswald Loretz, and Joaquín Sanmartín, eds. *The Cuneiform Alphabetic Texts from Ugarit, Ras Ibn Hani and Other Places*. Münster: Ugarit-Verlag, 1995.
COS	Hallo, William W., and K. Lawson Younger Jr., eds. *The Context of Scripture*. 4 vols. Leiden: Brill, 1997–2016.
DCH	Clines, David J. A., ed. *The Dictionary of Classical Hebrew*. 9 vols. Sheffield: Sheffield Academic, 1993–2014.
EA	El-Amarna tablets. According to the edition of Anson Rainey. *The El-Amarna Correspondence*. Boston: Brill, 2015.
EB	Byalik, Mosad, ed. *Encyclopedia Biblica*. 9 vols. Jerusalem: Byalik Institute, 1950–1982.
EncJud	Skolnik, Fred, and Michael Berenbaum, eds. *Encyclopedia Judaica*. 2nd ed. 22 vols. Detroit: Macmillan Reference USA, 2007.
FAT	Forschungen zum Alten Testament
FGS	Functional Grammar Series
GKC	Gesenius, Wilhelm. *Gesenius' Hebrew Grammar*. Edited by Emil Kautzsch. Translated by Arthur E. Cowley. 2nd ed. Oxford: Clarendon, 1910.
HALOT	Koehler, Ludwig, Walter Baumgartner, and Johann J. Stamm. *The Hebrew and Aramaic Lexicon of the Old Testament*. Translated and edited under the supervision of Mervyn E. Richardson. 2 vols. Boston: Brill, 2001.
HAR	*Hebrew Annual Review*
HKM	Alp, Sedat. *Hethitische Keilschrifttafeln aus Maşat-Höyük*. Ankara: Türk Tarith Kurumu Basimevi, 1991.

HS	*Hebrew Studies*
HSM	Harvard Semitic Monographs
HUCA	*Hebrew Union College Annual*
HUCM	Monographs of the Hebrew Union College
IBHS	Waltke, Bruce K., and Michael O'Connor. *Introduction to Biblical Hebrew Syntax*. Winona Lake: Eisenbrauns, 1990.
ICS	*Intercultural Communication Studies*
IDB	Buttrick, George A., ed. *The Interpreter's Dictionary of the Bible*. 4 vols. New York: Abingdon, 1962.
IEJ	*Israel Exploration Journal*
JANES	*Journal of the Ancient Near Eastern Society*
JAOS	*Journal of the American Oriental Society*
JASPs	*Journal of Abnormal and Social Psychology*
JBL	*Journal of Biblical Literature*
JCCP	*Journal of Cross-Cultural Psychology*
JETS	*Journal of the Evangelical Theological Society*
JLg	*Journal of Linguistics*
JNES	*Journal of Near Eastern Studies*
JNSL	*Journal of Northwest Semitic Languages*
JoP	*Journal of Pragmatics*
Joüon	Joüon, Paul *A Grammar of Biblical Hebrew*. Translated and revised by Takamitsu Muraoka. Rome: Pontifical Biblical Institute, 2005.
JPSP	*Journal of Personality and Social Psychology*
JPT	*Journal of Pentecostal Theology*
JSOTSup	Journal for the Study of the Old Testament Supplement Series
JE	Singer, Isidore, ed. *The Jewish Encyclopedia*. 12 vols. New York: Funk & Wagnalls, 1901–1906.
JSS	*Journal of Semitic Studies*
KUSATU	*Kleine Untersuchungen zur Sprache des Alten Testaments und Seiner Umwelt*
LA	Linguistik Aktuell/Linguistics Today
LiS	*Language in Society*
LHBOTS	The Library of Hebrew Bible/Old Testament Studies
NLLT	*Natural Language and Linguistic Theory*
LR	*Language Research*
LSAWS	Linguistic Studies in Ancient West Semitic
LXX	Septuagint
MS	*Mediaeval Studies*
MT	Masoretic Text
NAC	New American Commentary

NIBCOT	New International Biblical Commentary on the Old Testament
NICOT	New International Commentary on the Old Testament
NIDB	Sakenfeld, Katharine D., ed. *New Interpreter's Dictionary of the Bible*. 5 vols. Nashville: Abingdon, 2006–2009.
NIDOTTE	van Gemeren, Willem A., ed. *New International Dictionary of Old Testament Theology and Exegesis*. 5 vols. Grand Rapids: Zondervan, 1997.
OTL	Old Testament Library
OTS	Oudtestamentische Studiën
P&BNS	Pragmatics and Beyond New Series
RS	Ras Shamra
SAA	State Archives of Assyria. Helsinki: Helsinki University Press, 1987–
SHBC	Smyth & Helwys Bible Commentary
SL	*Studia Linguistica*
SN	*Studia Neophilologica*
SP	*Studies in Philology*
TCS	Texts from Cuneiform Sources
TDOT	Botterweck, G. Johannes, and Helmer Ringgren, eds. *Theological Dictionary of the Old Testament*. Translated by John T. Willis et al. 8 vols. Grand Rapids: Eerdmans, 1974–2006.
TLOT	Jenni, Ernst. *Theological Lexicon of the Old Testament*. With assistance from Claus Westermann. Translated by Mark E. Biddle. 3 vols. Peabody, MA: Hendrickson, 1997.
UCLA Hist. J.	*UCLA Historical Journal*
UF	*Ugarit-Forschungen*
VAT	Vorderasiatische Abteilung Tontafel. Vorderasiatisches Museum, Berlin
VT	*Vetus Testamentum*
VTSup	Supplements to Vetus Testamentum
WAW	Writings from the Ancient World
WBC	Word Biblical Commentary
ZAW	*Zeitschrift für die alttestamentliche Wissenschaft*

TRANSLITERATION

a. CONSONANTS

א	ʔ		ח		ḥ		פ	ף	p
בּ	b		ט		ṭ		פ	ף	p̄
ב	ḇ		י		y		צ	ץ	ṣ
גּ	g		כּ	ךּ	k		ק		q
ג	ḡ		כ	ך	ḵ		ר		r
דּ	d		ל		l		שׁ		š
ד	ḏ		מ	ם	m		שׂ		ś
ה	h		נ	ן	n		תּ		t
ו	w		ס		s		ת		ṯ
ז	z		ע		ʕ				

b. VOWELS (with ב as a dummy consonant)

בַ	ba		בֲ	bᵃ
בָ	bɔ		בֳ	bᵓ
בֶּי, בֵּ	bɛ		בֱ	bᵋ
בֵּי, בֵּ	be		בְּ	bə (vocal)
בִּי, בִּ	bi			
בֹּ, בּוֹ	bo			
בֻּ, בּוּ	bu			

Note: vowel letters (ה, ו, י) and silent schwa are not transliterated.

INTRODUCTION

Forms of address play a vital role in language, constituting "a sociolinguistic subject par excellence" (Philipsen and Huspek 1985, 94) that reveals the social background of both the speaker and the addressee more prominently than other aspects of language. When referring to the addressee, speakers carefully evaluate their relationship within the social context and choose the most appropriate address form from the available options. What is particularly intriguing is that speakers are not confined to using a single address form throughout a conversation but often switch between different forms.

Address forms exhibit remarkable variation across languages. For instance, many European languages employ distinct second-person pronouns like *tu*/*vous* in French and *du*/*Sie* in German, which convey varying levels of formality, social distance, familiarity, or politeness towards the addressee. In contrast, Modern English has been regarded as "the most weakly socially encoded European language" (Mühlhäusler and Harré 1990, 134) due to its use of the second-person pronoun 'you' without conveying social distinctions. However, English compensates by employing functional equivalents such as first names or honorific titles like *sir* or *ma'am* to indicate different attitudes towards the addressee. Similarly, Biblical Hebrew and epigraphic Hebrew share similarities with English in terms of limited social encoding, manifested in their four different forms of second-person independent pronouns (אתה *ʔattɔ* [MS]; את *ʔatt* [FS]; אתם *ʔattem* [MP]; אתן/אתנה *ʔatten*/*ʔattenɔ* [FP]). Nevertheless, these languages employ other nominal forms of address to indicate various social relationships between the speaker and the addressee.

This book examines the forms of address used in the prose sections of the Hebrew Bible and the epigraphic Hebrew letters. Drawing on theories and methodologies from modern sociolinguistics, this study investigates the distribution and usage patterns of address forms in Biblical Hebrew and Epigraphic Hebrew, aiming to uncover underlying rules governing their usage and identify instances where these rules are broken. By combining sociolinguistics and Hebrew studies, this research offers two contributions: (1) shedding light on Hebrew social structure and illustrating the exegetical significance of address variations, and (2) providing sociolinguists with an opportunity to test assumptions and conclusions drawn from their analysis of modern languages.

Previous attempts to describe the use of address forms in Biblical Hebrew and Epigraphic Hebrew have been limited in number and scope. Furthermore, the application of sociolinguistic studies' definitions and categories of forms of address to Biblical Hebrew and Epigraphic Hebrew has been inadequate. This book addresses these issues and fills the gaps in the existing literature.

The book is structured into six chapters. Chapter 1 provides a review of previous studies on forms of address in Hebrew and other languages, highlighting methodological insights relevant to the study of Biblical Hebrew and Epigraphic Hebrew forms of address and discussing sociolinguistic methodological considerations. Chapter 2 delves into the internal structure of free forms of address in Biblical Hebrew, exploring the semantic classification of these forms into categories such as personal names, kinship terms, titles, patronymics, et cetera, along with their respective usage patterns. The classification framework used is based on Friederike Braun's (1988, 9–11) work on modern languages, with necessary modifications for the context of this study. Chapter 3 investigates the social dynamics of free forms of address, drawing upon Roger Brown, Albert Gilman, and Marguerite Ford's (Brown and Gilman 1960; Brown and Ford 1961) address theory and Penelope Brown and Stephen C. Levinson's (1987) politeness theory. This chapter explores the sociolinguistic aspects of address usage, examining how social relationships and politeness norms influence the selection and usage of specific address forms. Chapter 4 focuses on describing the external syntax of free forms of address, aiming to identify correlations between the position and function of these forms within a sentence. The analysis seeks to uncover syntactic patterns or dependencies related to the usage of address forms. Chapter 5 delves into the classification and analysis of bound forms of address, which differ from free forms as they are attached to other linguistic elements. Finally, chapter 6 concludes the book by summarizing the findings and exploring the broader implications of the analysis conducted throughout the study. Through this organizational structure, the book aims to provide a comprehensive understanding of Hebrew address usage, encompassing its internal structure, social dynamics, external syntax, and the usage patterns of both free and bound forms of address.

1.
EXPLORING FORMS OF ADDRESS:
INSIGHTS FROM SOCIOLINGUISTIC STUDIES

This chapter presents a theoretical framework for the study of Hebrew forms of address. It begins by examining the fascinating phenomenon of address switching within dialogues in the Hebrew Bible, presenting a compelling case study that sheds light on this intriguing aspect (§1.1). Next, it conducts a synthesis and evaluation of previous studies that have explored address forms in Hebrew and other languages, providing valuable insights into their findings and establishing a foundation for further analysis (§1.2). Lastly, the chapter outlines essential methodological considerations for conducting research in this field, emphasizing the importance of a rigorous and comprehensive approach to the study of address forms (§1.3). By offering a solid framework and drawing upon various sources of evidence, this chapter paves the way for a deeper understanding of the complexities and dynamics of address forms in Hebrew.

1.1. Statement of the Problem

When a proficient speaker of a language interacts with his addressee, he carefully assesses the nature of their relationship and the social context in which they find themselves. Based on this evaluation, he chooses the most appropriate address form from the available options. What makes it intriguing is that they are not bound to using a single form of address throughout a conversation. Instead, they often switch between different forms.

An example from the Hebrew Bible can shed light on this phenomenon. In 1 Kgs 22:1–28, we encounter a story involving Ahab, the king of Israel, and Jehoshaphat, the king of Judah, as they seek divine counsel from Yahweh before going to war against Aram.[1] At Jehoshaphat's request, Ahab gathers around four hundred prophets to inquire whether they should engage in battle against Ramoth

---

[1] The text and translation of 1 Kgs 22:1–28 can be found in appendix A. Ahab's name does not appear until v. 20. Instead, he is designated with the title "king of Israel." It is worth noting that his name is used at the beginning of the parallel passage in 2 Chr 18:2.

Gilead. These prophets unanimously give Ahab the green light to proceed. However, Jehoshaphat remains skeptical and urges Ahab to consult another prophet of Yahweh. Reluctantly, Ahab summons Micaiah, the son of Imlah, who has always delivered unfavorable prophecies concerning him. As anticipated, Micaiah delivers a foreboding message: Ahab will meet a gruesome death in the battle.

Upon examining this passage, we observe that the participants in the dialogue—Ahab, Jehoshaphat, Micaiah, and the prophets—employ various forms of address. Ahab, for instance, consistently addresses his conversation partners using second-person references, whether expressed through verbs (i–iii, v) or pronominal suffixes (vi–vii), as presented in table 1.1 below. However, when Ahab initiates the conversation with Micaiah, he directly calls him by his name (iv). Why does Ahab address him by name? Is it merely to identify him or get his attention? Does Ahab's choice of this specific form of address hold any social significance?

Table 1.1. Ahab's Use of Forms of Address in 1 Kgs 22:1–28

#	V	Addressee	Text	Analysis	Translation
i	3	his servants	ידעתם *yḏaʕtɛm*	PC 2MP	"*you* know"
ii	4	Jehoshaphat	תלך *tēlek*	PC 2MS	"*you* go"
iii	9	his officer	מהרה *mahⁱrɔ*	IMP MS	"*(you) bring quickly!* "
iv	15	Micaiah	מיכיהו *miḵɔyǝhu*	PN	"***Micaiah***"
v	16	Micaiah	תדבר *tǝḏabber*	PC 2MS	"*you* speak"
vi	16	Micaiah	ךּ *kɔ*	PRO 2MS	"*you*"
vii	18	Jehoshaphat	ךּ *kɔ*	PRO 2MS	"*you*"

As can be seen in table 1.2 below, Jehoshaphat consistently addresses Ahab using the second-person reference (i–ii). However, in a conscious effort to refrain from speaking unfavorably about the prophet Micaiah, Jehoshaphat shifts his address form to the third person, specifically referring to Ahab as "the king" (iii). This raises the question: What prompted Jehoshaphat to change his address form at this particular point? Is there a specific reason behind Jehoshaphat's deliberate shift in addressing Ahab?

Table 1.2. Jehoshaphat's Use of Forms of Address in 1 Kgs 22:1–28

#	V	Addressee	Text	Analysis	Translation
i	4	Ahab	ךּ *kɔ*	PRO 2MS	"*you*" (3x)
ii	4	Ahab	דרש *dǝrɔš*	IMP MS	"*(you) seek!*"
iii	5	Ahab	המלך *hammɛlɛk*	N	"***the king***"

The four hundred prophets likewise alter their form of address for Ahab, transitioning from the second-person reference to the nominal term "the king," as shown in table 1.3 below (i). The prophet Micaiah follows a similar pattern in addressing Ahab (ii). However, from that point forward, Micaiah consistently employs the second-person address (iii–v). In employing these distinct forms of address, do the prophets intend to convey specific messages about their attitudes towards Ahab, or do they simply employ different forms for the sake of stylistic variation?

Table 1.3. Prophets' Use of Forms of Address in 1 Kgs 22:1–28

#	V	Addressee	Text	Transliteration	Analysis	Translation
i	6, 12	Ahab	עלה ... המלך	ʕᵘle ... hammɛlek	IMP MS N	"(*you*) *go up* ... *the king*."
ii	15	Ahab	עלה ... המלך	ʕᵘle ... hammɛlek	IMP MS N	"(*you*) *go up* ... *the king*."
iii	19	Ahab	שמע	šəmaʕ	IMP MS	"(*you*) *hear!*"
iv	23	Ahab	ך	kɔ	PRO 2MS	"*you*" (2x)
v	28	Ahab	תשוב	tɔšub	PC 2MS	"*you* return"

Understandably, traditional grammars of Biblical Hebrew hardly deal with the questions raised above since the choice of address forms is not solely determined by morpho-syntax. Instead, social factors such as participants' status, gender, age, and context play a significant role in shaping address behavior. To tackle these inquiries, sociolinguistics offers paradigms and models for cross-linguistic comparison, providing valuable insights into the subject matter.

Since the 1960s, sociolinguists have conducted extensive research on address forms in various languages, aiming to uncover the underlying rules that govern their usage. Although most studies have focused on contemporary languages, an increasing number of scholars have recently attempted to apply their findings to older texts, including Shakespearean plays and ancient Greek literature. Consequently, it is worthwhile to explore how modern research on address can contribute to our understanding of address usage in Biblical Hebrew and Epigraphic Hebrew.

This book utilizes the theories, methodologies, and insights of modern sociolinguistics to describe and analyze the systems of address in Biblical Hebrew and Epigraphic Hebrew. The primary objective is to provide a comprehensive understanding of the various forms of address, examining their distribution and patterns of usage, in order to identify the underlying rules that govern address usage. Also, it acknowledges the unique complexities posed by biblical and epigraphic texts as subjects of sociolinguistic analysis. By combining sociolinguistics with biblical studies, this approach offers two potential benefits: shedding light on the social structure of Hebrew society and demonstrating the exegetical significance of address variations.

1.2. Previous Studies

1.2.1. Scholarship on Hebrew Forms of Address

To date, there have been relatively few studies focusing on Hebrew forms of address, and the existing ones have often been limited in terms of both corpus and scope. In the following sections, I will not only identify the weaknesses and limitations of previous studies on terms of address but also provide insights into the methodology employed in this book. The review will be presented in chronological order, following the sequence of publication dates.

1.2.1.1. Cynthia L. Miller[2]

In a section entitled "Social Relationships of Speech Participants," Miller (2003, 269–81) briefly discusses terms of address and deferential language in the prose portions of Genesis through 2 Kings and epigraphic Hebrew letters. Regarding terms of address, she provides several examples of kinship terms and titles that indicate equality (e.g., אחי *ʔoḥi* "my brother") and inequality (e.g., אדני *ʔᵃdoni* "my lord"), noting that kinship terms can be used for nonfamily members to indicate intimate relationships. Concerning deferential expressions, she classifies them into four types based deictic orientation: (1) speaker-based deference (the first-person pronoun for speaker and אדני *ʔᵃdoni* "my lord" for addressee; e.g., אל יחשב לי אדני עון *ʔal-yaḥᵃšob-li ʔᵃdoni ʕowon* "May *my lord* not hold *me* guilty" in 2 Sam 19:20); (2) addressee-based deference (עבדך *ʕabdəkɔ* "your servant," אמתך *ʔᵃmoṭekɔ* "your maidservant," or שפחתך *šipḥoṭəkɔ* "your maidservant" for speaker and the second-person pronoun for addressee; e.g., אל תזכר את אשר העוה עבדך *ʔa- tizkor ʔeṯ ʔᵃšer heʕwɔ ʕabdəkɔ* "May *you* not remember how *your servant* did wrong" in 2 Sam 19:20); (3) combined (עבדך *ʕabdəkɔ* "your servant," אמתך *ʔᵃmoṭekɔ* "your maidservant," or שפחתך *šipḥoṭəkɔ* "your maidservant" for speaker and אדני *ʔᵃdoni* "my lord" for addressee; e.g., בי אדני ידבר נא עבדך דבר באזני אדני *bi ʔᵃdoni yəḏaber nɔʔ ʕabdəkɔ ḏɔḇɔr bəʔozne ʔᵃdoni* "Please, *my lord*, let *your servant* speak in the ears of *my lord*" in Gen 44:18); (4) distanced/anaphoric (עבדו *ʕaḇdo* "his servant" or the third-person pronoun for speaker and המלך *hammɛlɛḵ* "the king" or the third-person pronoun for addressee; e.g., אל ישם המלך בעבדו דבר *ʔal yɔśem hammɛlɛḵ bəʕaḇdo ḏɔḇɔr* "let not *the king* accuse *his servant* of any matter" in 1 Sam 22:15).

Miller's linguistic description of terms of address and deferential forms is concise and well-organized. However, it is not without issues. Firstly, Miller's definition of "terms of address" is ambiguous. According to Braun (1988, 7), the term *address* denotes "a speaker's linguistic reference to his/her collocutor(s)."

---

[2] Miller's work is reviewed first because there is minimal difference in content between the section entitled "Social Relationships of Speech Participants" in her monograph (2003, 269–81) and the corresponding section in her dissertation (1992, 214–23).

Therefore, it includes not only kinship terms and titles, but also names, patronymics, and various noun phrases. However, Miller (2003, 270) does not seem to consider names as terms of address when she states that "in most of the Arad letters, terms of address are lacking." In fact, there are twenty-five terms of address in the Arad letters, eighteen of which are names.[3] Additionally, Miller's (270) statement that "no terms of address are used by a superior in addressing an inferior" highlights her exclusion of names as terms of address, since names are commonly used to address equals or inferiors in Biblical Hebrew (e.g., Elijah calls his disciple Elisha by his name in 2 Kgs 2:4).

Secondly, Miller's focus is limited to a linguistic description of deferential forms, emphasizing how speaker and addressee are linguistically represented. Politeness theory, which could be helpful in describing deferential phenomena, is not employed. Sociolinguistic issues, such as the reasons for the speaker's use of a particular deferential form at a specific moment, the relationship between the speaker and addressee, and variations in deferential forms in a given dialogue, are not taken into consideration. Consequently, the social dynamics of deferential forms are largely overlooked.

Lastly, Miller's (2003, 280) conclusions concerning deferential expressions are problematic. She rightly argues that the narrator's ideology ultimately influences the use of deferential language, with which no one would disagree. However, her further statement "as a result, no deferential language is used... by Moses and Aaron in speaking to Pharaoh" is incorrect, since Moses uses the title Pharaoh to address Pharaoh deferentially (Exod 8:25).[4]

Overall, while Miller's linguistic analysis of terms of address and deferential forms is informative, there are shortcomings in her definition, the inclusion of sociolinguistic aspects, and her conclusions.

1.2.1.2. Ernest J. Revell

In his monograph *The Designation of the Individual*, Revell (1996) conducts a synchronic analysis of designations used for individual characters in the books of Judges, Samuel, and Kings (excluding poetic passages). Recognizing that

---

[3] Terms of address in the Arad letters are as follows: (1) Name: Elyashib (1:1; 2:1; 3:1; 4:1; 5:1; 6:1; 7:1; 8:1 [partial]; 10:1 [partial]; 11:1; 12:1 [partial]; 14:1 [partial]; 16:2; 18:1–2 [following the title "my lord"]; 24:1–2 [partial]); Nahum (17:1); Gedalyahu (21:1–2 [preceding a patronymic "son of Elyair"]); Malkiyahu (40:3); (2) Title: my lord (18:1–2 [preceding name "Elyashib"]; 21:3; 21:4 [partial]; 26:2; 26:4; 40:6; 40:10 [partial]). For more information, see Pardee et al. 1982.

[4] Moses uses the title "Pharaoh" twice to address Pharaoh in this verse. One of them has a textual variant, but the other does not. The same title is used by a chief cupbearer and Joseph as a deferential expression (Gen 41:10; 16, 25 [2x], 28 [2x]; 32, 33, 34, 35). For more information, see Longacre 2003, 131–33.

narration and speech are two different text types with distinct conventions, he discusses the designations used in each type separately. The forms of address are naturally examined while analyzing character designations within direct speech.

Revell approaches the subject of terms of address from a sociolinguistic perspective, examining how characters are addressed, the relationship between the speaker and addressee, the context in which an address term is used, and the speaker's attitude toward the addressee. He observes various patterns of terms of address and identifies several expressive usages that may have exegetical significance, such as Michal's ironic use of the title "king of Israel" (מלך ישראל *mɛlɛḵ yiśrɔʔel*) in 2 Sam 6:20. After carefully analyzing all the designations in narration and speech, Revell (361) concludes that "the usage studied is self-consistent" despite the composite nature of the text.

Revell's treatment of terms of address is much more detailed than Miller's. Many of his findings are convincing and provide exegetical insights. However, two issues can be pointed out. First, Revell's corpus is rather limited, consisting of only three historical books. Therefore, many of his observations may not hold true outside his selected corpus. For instance, Revell's (333) statement that "the personal name is the only form of vocative which God is shown ... as using to humans" is contradicted in the book of Ezekiel, where God exclusively addresses Ezekiel as בן אדם *bɛn ʔɔḏɔm* "son of man." This problem calls for a comprehensive analysis of an expanded corpus of Biblical Hebrew and Epigraphic Hebrew to test the universality or idiosyncrasy of Revell's conclusions in Biblical Hebrew and Epigraphic Hebrew.

Second, since Revell aims to cover all the designations in the text, the forms of address are only briefly discussed. Sometimes, only verse lists are provided without any analysis, and at other times, Revell makes assertions without supporting data. Moreover, the discussions on terms of address are fragmented and scattered throughout the book, with various components of bound forms of address being treated in several chapters as part of broader discussions. Consequently, it becomes extremely challenging to perceive a coherent and comprehensive picture of address usage. Despite these issues, Revell's work stands the best example of sound methodology and analysis concerning Hebrew forms of address to date.

1.2.1.3. Bryan D. Estelle

In his dissertation and a subsequent article based on that dissertation, Estelle (2001; 2012) examines deferential language in Aramaic and in the book of Esther. Employing Brown and Levinson's (1987) politeness theory, Estelle (2001, 41–51) identifies five common deferential strategies found in the corpus: (1) the vocative use of titles; (2) the substitution of third-person forms for second and first-person forms; (3) the deferential use of prepositions (Aramaic קדם *qʔḏɔm* or מן קדם *min qᵊdɔm* "before" and Hebrew לפני *lip̄ne* "before"); (4) the use of indefinite or unspecified agents; (5) the employment of the majestic passive. The first and second strategies directly relate to forms of address, so as Estelle discusses these two strategies in the book of Esther, he naturally touches upon the topic of address usage.

However, Estelle's understanding of deferential language appears incomplete. He claims that "there is only one deferential vocative in the book of Esther," referring to Esther addressing King Xerxes as המלך *hammɛlɛḵ* "O king" in Esth 7:3 (2012, 12). Yet, he fails to discuss the two deferential vocatives used by King Xerxes to address Esther (אסתר המלכה *ʔɛster hammalkɔ* "Queen Esther" in Esth 5:3; 7:2). As Brown and Levinson (1987, 178) note, deferential terms can also be employed by a superior to convey mutual respect.[5]

1.2.1.4. Benjamin Thomas

Thomas (2009) conducts an examination of ancient Hebrew letters to explore the utilization of politeness strategies. He astutely observes that when a letter is directed to a superior, politeness is conveyed through the inclusion of conventional *praescriptio* (address, greeting, and blessing) and the use of deferential terms (אדני *ʔᵃdoni* "my lord" and עבדך *ʕaḇdᵊkɔ* "your servant"). However, Thomas's (2009, 38) statement that "if it is an inferior who is addressed, neither greeting nor term of address accompanies the personal name" creates a misleading impression that personal names are not considered part of terms of address.

1.2.1.5. Raffaele Esposito

Esposito (2009) undertakes an analysis of the semantic significance of kinship terms in the Hebrew Bible. He compiles all the kinship terms utilized in the Hebrew Bible and determines whether they are employed in a literal or fictive manner. He ultimately concludes that approximately 70 percent of the kinship terms are used fictively. However, the validity of Esposito's conclusion is questionable because it is challenging to definitively ascertain the literal or fictive usage of kinship terms, particularly in poetry where contextual evidence may be lacking. Esposito includes poetry in his analysis and automatically categorizes kinship terms in these texts as fictive. Yet, how can we be certain that the repetition of "my son" in Proverbs, for example, was not intended to address the author's actual son?[6] In order to accurately determine the semantic value of kinship terms, it would be advisable to focus solely on prose where the social status of the individuals involved can be properly assessed from contextual indicators.

---

[5] O'Connor (2002, 24), who served as Estelle's dissertation reader, also interprets "Queen Esther" as a deferential expression.

[6] Fox (2000, 80) does not dismiss the possibility of the literal meaning of the terms "father" and "son" in Proverbs.

1.2.1.6. Edward J. Bridge

Bridge (2010a) conducts a similar study as Thomas's, but with a specific focus on the Lachish letters, all of which were addressed to social superiors. In his critique of previous studies on ancient letters, which attribute variations in deferential expressions (אדני *ʔᵃdoni* "my lord" and עבדך *ʕabdəkɔ* "your servant") to scribal differences or social distance, Bridge argues for the importance of considering the content or subject matter of a letter when analyzing variation. He highlights that senders had freedom to express their opinions and even criticize the recipients, leading to a reduction in the use of deferential terms.

However, Bridge's study has a limitation in that he relies on a specific text edition without critically examining its accuracy. He exclusively utilizes the texts provided by Frederick W. Dobbs-Allsopp et al. (2005), which often differ from the transcriptions of Dennis Pardee et al. (1982). It is important to note that Pardee et al.'s transcriptions are based on photographs and personal examinations of the documents. These differences should have been acknowledged, particularly given that the central thesis relies on only one edition.[7]

In his dissertation, Bridge (2010b) examines the use of "slave terms," such as עבד *ʕɛḇeḏ* "servant," אמה *ʔɔmɔ* "maidservant," and שפחה *šip̄ḥɔ* "maidservant" in the Hebrew Bible from the perspective of politeness theory. These terms are frequently used by speakers to express self-abasement, indicating that the addressee holds power over them, particularly in the context of making a request. While the opposite term אדון *ʔɔḏon* "lord" is relevant to the purpose of the study, it is only briefly discussed. In contrast to terms denoting servitude, אדן often expresses deference by elevating the status of the addressee. Recognizing these master-servant terms as clear examples of Brown and Levinson's politeness strategy known as "give deference," Bridge argues that speakers strategically employ them to try to achieve their desired outcomes.

One of Bridge's significant contributions is his defense of Brown and Levinson's politeness theory as a suitable tool for analyzing biblical texts. By identifying politeness strategies used by biblical characters, he demonstrates how they are portrayed as (im)polite. For instance, in Num 20:14–21 where Israel requests passage to travel through Edom, Israel is portrayed as very polite, employing various politeness strategies such as *in-group identity markers* ("your brother Israel" in v. 14), *give reasons* (Yahweh's deliverance of Israel from Egyptian oppression in vv. 14c–16), and *minimize the imposition* (staying on the King's highway and refraining from drinking Edom's water in v. 17). In

---

[7] Bridge (2010, 530) argues that "אדני is used less frequently" based on the absence of אדני in Lach 3:6 in Dobbs-Allsopp et al.'s (2005, 309) transcription: *šlḥtʰ ° ʔl ʕbdk*. However, other text editions, including Torczyner (1938, 46–47, 51), Gibson (1971, 44), and Pardee et al. (1982, 84), read: *šlḥ ʔdny lʕbdk*.

contrast, Edom responds bluntly, threatening to fight against Israel. They do not employ any politeness strategies, refusing to be a "brother" to Israel and potentially assuming a superior role. This portrayal aligns with the depiction of Edom as a "bad brother" to Israel/Judah elsewhere in the Hebrew Bible (e.g., Gen 25:29–34 and Amos 1:11–12). Given Bridge's demonstration of the usefulness of politeness theory as a heuristic tool for describing the intentionality of character's speech, particularly regarding the use of deferential terms, I intend to employ it in this book, especially when analyzing kinship terms used as free forms of address in chapter 3.

1.2.1.7. Summary

Previous studies on Hebrew forms of address are, while providing valuable insights, have certain shortcomings in three key areas. First, the understanding and application of the definition and classification of forms of address, along with deferential language, in ancient Hebrew have been inadequate. Second, these studies have been limited in terms of the corpus and scope they cover. Third, text-critical issues have not been adequately addressed prior to the analysis of the text. As a result, there is still a need for a comprehensive sociolinguistic study that systematically examines the use of Hebrew forms of address in diverse social contexts.

1.2.2. Scholarship on Forms of Address in Different Languages

Sociolinguistics is the descriptive study of language in relation to society—a branch of both linguistics and sociology. While the term *sociolinguistics* was coined by Thomas C. Hodson in 1939,[8] the quantitative analysis of language variation was pioneered by William Labov in 1960s.[9] Sociolinguists, in reaction to the Chomskyan assumption that grammars are unrelated to the social lives of speakers, focus on the social motivation of language change.[10] They are concerned with how people with different social background (e.g., age, gender, occupation, race, ethnicity, class, regions, etc.) speak and how their language changes in different social contexts.

Forms of address have been extensively studied in sociolinguistics due to their ability to encode sociolinguistic parameters, such as gender, age, and status of the speaker and addressee. It is generally agreed that Brown, Gilman, and Ford

---

[8] While Hodson uses the term *sociolinguistics* in the title of his five-page article "Socio-Linguistics in India," it does not appear in the body of the article. As Currie (1980, 407) points out, Hodson's sociolinguistic suggestion is limited. It was actually Nida (1949, 152) who first introduced the term in linguistics.

[9] For a more comprehensive examination of Labov's contributions to the field of sociolinguistics, see Watt 2005, 172–75.

[10] For a concise history and overview of sociolinguistics, consult Mesthrie 2001, 1–4.

initiated modern sociolinguistic investigation of address terms. They published three consecutive articles on the development of pronominal and nominal forms of address in European languages, which laid the foundation for further research in this area. The following review provides an overview of sociolinguistic work on address terms in different languages, highlighting methodological insights relevant to the study of Biblical Hebrew and Epigraphic Hebrew forms of address.

1.2.2.1. Albert Gilman and Roger Brown

In an article titled "Who Says 'Tu' to Whom," Gilman and Brown (1958) trace the differentiation of pronominal address (polite vs. familiar) in English, French, German, and Italian back to the fourth century CE. During this time, the Latin plural form *vos* instead of singular form *tu* began to be used to address the Roman emperor. As the use of the plural address spread, two dimensions of pronominal usage developed: (1) a vertical dimension of status, where plural polite pronoun was used for superiors and the singular familiar pronoun was used for inferiors, and (2) a horizontal dimension of status, where the plural pronoun was used among distant equals and the singular pronoun was used among intimate equals. In the past, both dimensions were visible in English with the use of *thou* and *ye*. However, as the horizontal dimension became dominant, Modern English no longer expresses the vertical dimension with different pronouns. Instead, the vertical dimension can be expressed through nominal differentiation, such as first names or title + last name.

In their second article entitled "The Pronouns of Power and Solidarity," Brown and Gilman (1960) further elaborate the concept of pronominal differentiation by introducing the symbols T and V, which represent the putative origin in Latin *tu* and *vos*. In medieval Europe, the usage of T/V was governed by what authors now refer to the "power semantic," where T was used for inferiors and V for superiors, resulting in nonreciprocity and asymmetry. However, between equals, pronominal address was reciprocal: upper-class speakers exchanged V and lower-class speakers exchanged T.

An important observation made by Brown and Gilman is that speakers may spontaneously shift from V to T or vice-versa to express his emotional or attitudinal change towards an addressee. In medieval European literature, a shift from V to T might express contempt and anger towards an addressee, while a shift from T to V might indicate respect and distance.

Since the nineteenth century, another model, the "solidarity semantic," has gradually gained ground. This understanding does not operate based on power distinctions but on the notions of intimacy and like-mindedness. It led to the reciprocal use of T in cases of intimacy and the mutual use of V in cases of distance. As a result, there was an extension of T use (e.g., parents and son exchange T).

A unique contribution of this article to sociolinguistics is that Brown and Gilman employed the modern method of questionnaires to investigate address behavior in French, German, and Italian. After analyzing the answers provided by French, German, and Italian students residing in Boston, they concluded that the German *T* is more readily used for family relations than are the French and Italian *T*.

1.2.2.2. Roger Brown and Marguerite Ford

Brown and Ford's (1961) article entitled "Address in American English" expands on the statement made by Brown and Gilman (1960, 267): "proper names and titles ... operate today on a nonreciprocal power pattern in America." To investigate the use of first names (FN: "John") and titles + last names (TLN: "Mr. Smith"), Brown and Ford collected data through four methods: reviewing American plays, observing address behavior in a Boston business firm, interviewing business executives, and tape-recording children's usage in a midwestern American town. Upon analyzing the data, they identified three dyadic patterns of FN and TLN usage: mutual TLN for acquaintances at the beginning, mutual FN for intimates, and nonreciprocal use of TLN and FN based on age or professional status differences. FN is consistently used for downward social relations (i.e., to equals or inferiors), while TLN designates upward relations (i.e., to superiors). Thus, the distinction in American English between address by FN or TLN functions similarly to the distinction between *T* and *V* in European languages.

Some scholars have argued that the notions of reciprocity/nonreciprocity, power and solidarity, and *T* and *V* proposed by Brown, Gilman, and Ford are sociolinguistically universal.[11] However, their claim has been challenged by other sociolinguists, such as Eleanor Dickey (1996, 257), who discovered the absence of such alleged universal notions in classical Greek.[12] Therefore, Brown, Gilman, and Ford's theories should not be considered absolute universals but rather tendencies. One of the goals of this book is to examine whether Hebrew forms of address align with these proposed cross-linguistic tendencies or demonstrate different patterns.

1.2.2.3. Susan Ervin-Tripp and Others

In addition to the works of Brown, Gilman, and Ford, Ervin-Tripp's (1972) article entitled "On Sociolinguistic Rules" is frequently referenced in literature discussing terms of address. She is well-known for formulating rules of address using a computer flow chart. The flow chart comprises various "selectors" that influence

---

[11] For example, Slobin, Miller, and Porter (1968, 289) assert that "it is a sociolinguistic universal that the address terms exchanged between intimates ... is the same term used in addressing social inferiors, and that the term exchanged between non-intimates ... is also used to address social superiors."

[12] A comparable critique is presented in Braun 1988, 18–24.

the speaker's choice of a variant, such as setting, age, rank, gender, and more. By making a series of binary choices, the speaker ultimately arrives at a specific form of address. Flow charts have been created for the selection of FN and TLN in American English, as well as for *T* and *V* in nineteenth-century Russian, Yiddish, and Puerto Rican Spanish.

Since the publication of Brown, Gilman, Ford, and Ervin-Tripp's articles, numerous works focusing on terms of address in individual languages have emerged.[13] However, the reliability of their data collection methods and analyses has often been called into question (Dickey 1996, 3).

1.2.2.4. Friederike Braun

A large-scale group project conducted at the University of Kiel, titled "Reflections of social structure in natural languages: address behavior," has gathered extensive information on patterns and systems of address in thirty modern languages.[14] The project involved collecting publications on forms of address and conducting interviews with informants using a specially designed questionnaire. This endeavor has resulted in two significant works on terms of address: Braun, Kohz, and Schubert (1986) compiled the most comprehensive annotated bibliography with over 1100 items, while Braun (1988) published the final report of the project, which, in my opinion, offers the best overview of address theory.[15]

Braun's work holds particular importance as it provides clear definitions of essential terms and concepts, classifying address terms based on both word classes and syntax. Address is defined as "a speaker's linguistic reference to his/her collocutor(s)" (Braun 1988, 7).[16] Therefore, terms of address encompass not only pronouns but also verbs and nominal forms used to address the collocutor.[17]

---

[13] For example, Bates and Benigni (1975) conducted a study on pronominal address in Italian by interviewing 117 adults. They found a clear age-class interaction in the overall degree of formality. Similarly, Hwang (1975) focused on Korean pronouns and names, Lambert and Tucker (1976) examined children's pronominal address forms in French and Spanish, Parkinson (1985) investigated Egyptian Arabic address forms including pronouns, kinship terms, and names, and Başoğlu (1987) analyzed Turkish terms of address used in novels and films.

[14] They include Arabic, Chinese, Dari, (Irish) English, Finnish, Georgian, German, Greek, Hausa, Hebrew, Hungarian, Icelandic, Italian, Kazakh, Korean, Kurdish, Mingrelian, Norwegian, Pashto, Persian, Polish, Portuguese, Rumanian, Russian, Serbo-Croatian, Spanish, Swedish, Tigrinya, Turkish, and Twi. See Braun (1988, 2) for more details.

[15] For a comprehensive list of works on address in individual languages produced by the Kiel project, see Braun 1988, 5–6.

[16] This definition is universally accepted among scholars studying terms of address in modern languages. See Kiełkiewicz-Janowiak 1992, 13.

[17] English employs only two types of terms of address: nominal forms ("*Rachel*, how are you?") and pronouns ("Could *you* open the door, please?").

Pronouns of address primarily consist of second-person pronouns (e.g., English *you*, German *du* and *ihr*, and French *tu* and *vous*), although other grammatical persons can also serve as pronouns of address (e.g., German *Sie* [3MP]). Verbal forms of address involve second-person verbs with inflectional elements expressing reference to the collocutor.[18] Nominal forms of address encompass substantives and adjectives that can be categorized into various types, such as personal names, titles, kinship terms, patronymics, and so on.

While terms of address can be classified based on the criterion of parts of speech, they can also be classified according to the syntactic criterion.[19] The same address term may have a different syntactic status as a *bound* or *free* form. Bound forms are integrated into the syntax of a sentence (e.g., "May I talk to *you* for a moment?"), whereas free forms stand outside the sentence structure, not holding a main constituency slot in the clausal syntax; they can appear preceding, succeeding, or inserted into the sentence (e.g., "*You*! Open the window!"). The relevance and applicability of Braun's terminology and classifications to Hebrew forms of address will be demonstrated in detail in §1.3.

1.2.2.5. Eleanor Dickey

Sociolinguists employ five popular methods to collect data on modern languages: introspection, questionnaires, interviews, observation, and text analysis. However, when it comes to ancient Hebrew, the first four methods are not applicable due to the lack of native informants. Nevertheless, text analysis has emerged as a promising approach and has gained popularity even prior to Dickey's groundbreaking work. This method has been particularly utilized by scholars investigating earlier forms of languages, including nineteenth-century Russian (Friedrich 1966), Old French (Bakos 1955), Old English (Waterhouse 1982), Chaucer (Nathan 1959), and Shakespeare (Replogle 1973; Brown and Gilman 1989). It is worth noting that the majority of these studies have focused on relatively recent historical periods.

Dickey's seminal contribution to sociolinguistics lies in her extensive work on forms of address in an ancient language, classical Greek. In her book *Greek Forms of Address*, Dickey (1996) analyzes 13,584 vocatives found in dialogues within a wide range of prose texts authored by twenty-five classical writers from Herodotus to Longus. Thus, the corpus spans over 600 years, providing a comprehensive chronological coverage. Building upon Braun's definition and categorization of terms of address, Dickey presents her findings in two distinct ways. Firstly, she semantically classifies the addresses into categories such as

---

[18] The observation of this phenomenon is most evident in languages where the use of subject pronouns is not obligatory, such as ancient Greek and modern Finnish.

[19] This classification system has proven to be highly valuable in many European languages. See Zwicky 1974; Schubert 1984; Braun 1988; Kiełkiewicz-Janowiak 1992; Dickey 1996; 2002.

personal names, titles, kinship terms, and others, observing the varied usage within these different groups. Secondly, she explores the speakers and addressees, considering social variables such as age, kinship, gender, and rank, to investigate how each group employs different forms of address. By examining address terms from these dual perspectives, Dickey unveils numerous insightful findings about their meanings and the social relations they reflect. For instance, Dickey's (1996, 235–38) research reveals that power differences were prominently manifested in Greek address patterns. In dyads where the addressee held power over the speaker, such as addresses from subjects to monarchs, titles were the customary form of address, while names were considered disrespectful. As demonstrated in chapter 3, this pattern appears to hold true in the context of Biblical Hebrew as well. Although Dickey primarily adopts a synchronic approach, she acknowledges the potential for terms of address to change over time. Surprisingly, Dickey (1996, 249) identifies minimal diachronic changes in the texts she examined. Her work serves as a prime exemplar of sociolinguistic scholarship on terms of address in ancient texts.

1.3. Methodological Considerations

1.3.1. The Nature of the Data

Hebrew forms of address are found in written texts. While analyzing sociolinguistic aspects of written texts has inherent limitations, such as the absence of native speakers providing spoken language data, it has been considered a valid method for gathering information on modern languages (Kiełkiewicz-Janowiak 1992, 36). In fact, analyzing written texts offers certain advantages over other methods that focus on spoken language. For instance, written texts often provide larger and more diverse samples of data compared to those obtained from live speakers (Romaine 1982, 109–11). Additionally, written texts can offer insights into situations that are difficult to observe in real life. Moreover, data from written texts are accessible to other linguists, allowing them to verify the validity of a scholar's conclusions. In contrast, data collected from live informants may need to remain confidential to protect the subjects, making it impossible to fact-check one's assertions based on such data (Milroy 1987, 91).

However, two issues related to the biblical text may pose difficulties in our study. Firstly, the biblical text, that is, the Masoretic Text (MT), is a composite text with a complex history of composition and scribal transmission. As a result, the original linguistic data might have been obscured or altered during this textual history. To address this problem, I will closely examine textual variants and *Kethiv-Qere* alternations. Additionally, while this study primarily adopts a synchronic approach, special attention will be given to linguistic variation reflecting diachronic and dialectal factors.[20]

Secondly, the biblical text is a literary work. Dialogues embedded within the narrative, from which address terms are to be collected, are not exact replicas of original conversations. They were crafted by the author/narrator to fulfill literary objectives. Therefore, our aim is not to reconstruct the actual conversational language of biblical characters, but rather to describe their use of address, which is ultimately controlled by the narrator (Polak 2010, 171).

On the other hand, the literary nature of the biblical text can be advantageous as it provides the contextual backdrop for addressing. As Dickey points out:

> the fact that the language of a literary text was composed by an author rather than produced by informants is a benefit to the researcher, for each word in the text is likely to have a purpose, and the information necessary to understanding that purpose should be given to us by the author. (1996, 37)

Thus, it is crucial for us to examine carefully the literary context of each dialogue to identify literary factors that might affect the speaker's address behavior.

1.3.2. The Corpus

The data for our study are derived from dialogues in the prose sections of the Hebrew Bible and the epigraphic Hebrew letters (Arad [Arad], Kuntillet ʔAjrud [KAjr], Lachish [Lach], Meṣad Ḥashavyahu [MHsh], and Moussaïeff [Mous]). Poetic passages are excluded since poetic usage differs somewhat from prose usage.[21] Moreover, poetic passages often provide little contextual information, making the social relations between speech participants ambiguous.

Table 1.4 presents a comprehensive overview of the address terms in our corpus, totaling 962 terms (682 free forms and 280 bound forms), excluding second- and third-person pronouns used as address terms.[22] These address terms will be subject to exhaustive analysis.

---

[20] This will be considered below (§1.3.2).

[21] For a brief discussion on the linguistic distinctions in reported speech between prose and poetry, see Miller 2003, 20–22.

[22] The title *king* in the phrase "the king's table" in 1 Sam 20:29 is likely a fixed term rather than an address term (compare with 2 Sam 9:13; 2 Kgs 25:29; Jer 52:33). Thus, it is not included in our corpus. Additionally, when determining the total count of bound forms of address, address forms that follow the preposition אל *ʔl* "to" in *praescriptio* within epigraphic letters are excluded. These forms function similarly to second-person pronouns as direct forms of address. Further discussion on the function of these forms can be found in footnote 45 of chapter 3.

Table 1.4. Number of Hebrew Forms of Address Surveyed

Book	Free	Bound	Total	Book	Free	Bound	Total
Gen	55	38	93	Zech	8		8
Exod	9	5	14	Job		1	1
Num	15	7	22	Ruth	12		12
Deut	14	4	18	Esth	5	33	38
Josh	5	1	6	Dan	24	9	33
Judg	24	2	26	Ezra	6	4	10
1 Sam	46	29	76	Neh	11	4	15
2 Sam	62	59	121	1 Chr	30	3	33
1 Kgs	53	31	84	2 Chr	50	8	58
2 Kgs	44	5	49	Arad		9	9
Isa	12		12	KAjr		1	1
Jer	42		42	Lach		25	25
Ezek	142		142	MHsh		1	1
Amos	9		9	Mous		1	1
Jonah	4		4				

There is a general consensus that "Late Biblical Hebrew" exhibits syntactic and lexical differences compared to "Early Biblical Hebrew."[23] Thus, it is

---

[23] Traditionally, scholars have accepted Kutscher's (1984, 12) tripartite division of Biblical Hebrew, which includes: (1) "Archaic Biblical Hebrew" for an earlier stage of Hebrew, (2) "Standard Biblical Hebrew" for preexilic Hebrew, and (3) "Late Biblical Hebrew" for postexilic Hebrew. Additionally, Standard Biblical Hebrew has also been referred to as "Classical Biblical Hebrew" since Hurvitz 1982, 157. However, the debate between Hurvitz and Young in 2003 regarding the linguistic dating of biblical texts has led to wider acceptance of the bipartite division of Biblical Hebrew, which consists of "Early Biblical Hebrew" and "Late Biblical Hebrew" (Young 2003). Late Biblical Hebrew remains the same, while Early Biblical Hebrew encompasses both Archaic Biblical Hebrew and Standard Biblical Hebrew, which is also known as Classical Biblical Hebrew, from the traditional tripartite division. In this study, I follow this bipartite division, excluding archaic poems such as Gen 49, which fall under Archaic Biblical Hebrew.

Although there is no consensus on the specific passages to include in each division, I have created the following corpus by selecting the least debated passages based on Pfeiffer (1948, 296); Radday and Pollatschek (1980, 333); Hurvitz (1982, 170); Rofé (1988, 102); Rooker (1990, 56); Sáenz-Badillos (1993, 56–57); Holmstedt (2010, 20–21); Naudé (2004, 87–102). The corpus of Early Biblical Hebrew includes the Pentateuch, Joshua, Judges, 1 and 2 Samuel, 1 and 2 Kings, Isaiah 1–39, Jeremiah, Hosea, Amos, Obadiah, Micah, Nahum, Habakkuk, and Zephaniah. Late Biblical Hebrew includes Haggai, Zechariah, Malachi, Esther, Daniel, Ezra, Nehemiah, and 1 and 2 Chronicles.

Recently, Young, Rezetko, and Ehrensvärd (2008) have challenged the traditional view that biblical texts can be dated linguistically. However, even they acknowledge that there is a clear distinction in terms of grammar and style between Early Biblical Hebrew and Late Biblical Hebrew.

reasonable to assume that there might be variations in address patterns between two corpora. Special attention will be given to parallel passages between Kings and Chronicles, as their discrepancies may offer insights into diachronic changes.

The data obtained from the Hebrew letters, although limited in quantity, serve as a crucial control for analyzing the Hebrew Bible in two significant ways. First, the letters can be dated to the seventh–sixth centuries BCE, corresponding to the period of composition/redaction of the preexilic sections of the biblical text.[24] Secondly, unlike the biblical texts, the letters represent nonliterary texts, thus providing us with "authentic" language usage with specific times and situations.

1.3.3. Terminology and Concepts

The present study will benefit from many theories and insights of sociolinguistics. Particularly relevant and applicable to the description of the Hebrew address system are Braun's definitions and classifications. Hebrew terms of address refer to words and phrases used to address the collocutor, encompassing not only pronouns but also verbal and nominal forms.[25] Pronouns of address include second-person independent personal pronouns (אתה ʔattɔ [MS]; את ʔatt [FS]; אתם ʔattɛm [MP]; אתן/אתנה ʔatten/ʔattenɔ [FP]), pronominal suffixes (ךָ kɔ [MS]; ךְ k [FS]; כם kɛm [MP]; כן kɛn [FP]), and third-person pronominal suffixes (הו hu, ה oh, ו o, ו w [MS]; ה hɔ, ה ɔh [FS]; הֶם hɛm, ם ɔm [MP]; הן hɛn, ן ɔn [FP]).[26] Verbal forms of address are second-person verbs where the reference to the interlocutor is expressed through inflectional elements.[27] Nominal forms of address consist of substantives and adjectives that can be categorized based on semantic categories, such as personal names, titles, kinship terms, and patronymics. In this book, the primary focus will be on nominal forms of address, as pronouns and verbs carry limited social meaning in Biblical Hebrew and Epigraphic Hebrew.[28]

---

[24] The similarity between the syntax of Biblical Hebrew and Epigraphic Hebrew has been noted by Gogel (1998, 292).

[25] In English, there are only two types of terms of address: nominal forms (e.g., "*Rachel*, how are you?") and pronouns (e.g., "Could *you* open the door, please?").

[26] Third-person pronouns can be used when a deferential title is the antecedent of the pronoun. For example, when Jacob says to Esau (Gen 33:14): יעבר נא אדני לפני עבדו *yaʕʰbɔr nɔʔ ʔʰdoni lip̄ne ʕab̄do* "Let *my lord* pass on ahead of *his* servant."

[27] Theoretically, a third-person verb could also serve as a form of address, as seen in the Amarna example (EA 7:68): [IGI.II] ʻšaʼ a-ḫi-ia li-mu-ra-ma a-ḫu-ú-a li-ik-nu-uk-ma li-še-bi-la "May the [eyes] ʻof' my brother see to it (i.e., gold) and may my brother seal it and may *he* (i.e., my brother) send it." However, to the best of my knowledge, there is no such example in Biblical Hebrew and Epigraphic Hebrew.

[28] Similar to English, Hebrew second-person pronouns and verbs can be used to address anyone, regardless of their social status—superiors, equals, or inferiors. Additionally, as Miller (2003, 275) points out, third-person pronouns are anaphoric rather than deictic. Thus, they are unmarked for social significance.

Hebrew terms of address can also be classified as bound or free forms based on the syntactic criteria. Bound forms are integrated into the syntax of a sentence. For example, in the case of Joseph being addressed by the Egyptians as "my lord," this term serves as the object the preposition, "from," as shown in (1):

(1) לא נכחד מאדני
 loʔ-nəkaḥed   meʔᵃdoni
 not-we.will.hide from=lord.my
 We will not hide from *my lord*. (Gen 47:18)

Free forms, however, refer to those outside the sentence structure, not occupying a main constituent slot in the clausal syntax. They can appear before, after, or be inserted into the sentence. In Hebrew, these free forms are commonly classified as vocatives, which are used by the speaker to either attract the addressee's attention or maintain contact with them. For instance, in the case of Yahweh appearing to Abram in a vision, a vocative is employed, as in (2):

(2) אל תירא אברם
 ʔal-tirɔʔ   ʔaḇrɔm
 not-you.be.afraid Abram
 Do not be afraid, *Abram*! (Gen 15:1)

While many vocatives stand in apposition to the second-person pronoun or verb, as in the example above, they can also stand alone, as seen in (3):

(3) ויאמר אלי מלאך האלהים בחלום יעקב
 wayyoʔmɛr ʔelay malʔak   hɔʔᵉlohim
 and=he.said to=me messenger.of the=God
 baḥᵃlom yaʕᵃqoḇ
 in=the=dream Jacob
 Then the messenger of God said to me in the dream, "*Jacob*!" (Gen 31:11)

This book integrates both classification systems to provide a clearer understanding of the distinct functions of each category.

1.3.4. *Factors Influencing Address Choice*

Sociolinguists have long recognized that address usage is governed by rules that dictate which forms are used in specific contexts (e.g., Philipsen and Huspek 1985, 94; Dickey 1996, 6). Competent speakers are well-acquainted with these rules in order to communicate effectively. Dilworth B. Parkinson (1985, 225) emphasizes the fundamental importance of understanding address rules for successful communication, stating that "knowledge of the proper use of terms of address is ... as important to the overall success of communication as knowledge of the conjugation of verbs would be." Different societies and cultures have their own sets of rules regarding address usage, making it challenging to determine the factors influencing a speaker's choice of addresses (Braun 1988, 304). However, sociolinguists acknowledge two social elements that consistently play a role: the relation between the speaker and addressee and the speech context (Fasold 1990, 1; Dickey 1996, 7).

The speaker-addressee relationship is closely tied with their identities, which encompass various properties such as age, gender, status, kinship, et cetera. These properties significantly influence the speaker's choice of address terms. As Brown and Ford (1961, 375) rightly point out, address usage "is not predictable from the properties of the addressee alone and not predictable from properties of the speaker alone *but only from the properties of the dyad* [emphasis added]."[29] Thus, a person may be addressed using different forms by different speakers. For example, Abraham is addressed by his son Isaac as אבי *ʔɔbi* "my father" (Gen 22:7), while Ephron, who sold his field to Abraham, addresses him as אדני *ʔᵃdoni* "my lord" (Gen 23:11, 15).

The role of the speech context, including the setting and topic of discourse, is also significant in determining address usage. Certain settings may require specific forms of address, such as addressing a judge as "Your honor" in a law court. An example from the Bible that might illustrate this phenomenon is found in 2 Sam 13:24, where Absalom addresses his father David as המלך (*hammelek* "king") instead of using the kinship term אבי (*ʔɔbi* "my father").[30] This choice was likely influenced by the normative use of the title or deferential terms when addressing a king, regardless of the familial relationship with David.

The topic of discourse can also affect address usage. For instance, when a speaker makes a request of the addressee, he may want to use more polite forms of address. Conversely, when he criticizes the addressee, he may opt for less polite forms, as discussed in Bridge's argument (see Bridge's argument above).

As Dickey (1996, 6) points out, address rules are far from inviolable. They can be intentionally broken to achieve powerful discourse-pragmatic effects. One crucial factor for rule-breaking is the speaker's feelings towards to the addressee. Brown and Gilman's study, for example, demonstrates that a medieval European speaker's shift from the *V* form to the *T* form may express contempt and anger towards the addressee. One of the main goals of our study is to identify other factors that influence a speaker's choice of "normal" address forms, enabling us

---

[29] Contrary to Miller (2003, 27), who only mentions "speaker-oriented factors," it should be noted that addressee-oriented factors can also play a crucial role in the speaker's choice of terms of address.

[30] Also, in 1 Sam 19:4, Jonathan addresses his father Saul as המלך *hammelek* "king."

to discern instances where the address rule was intentionally broken to convey the speaker's specific emotions. These cases of rule-breaking hold significance not only socially but also exegetically.

1.3.5. Variations in Rules of Address

The assumption underlying the preceding explanation regarding the factors governing the choice of address forms is that both the speaker and the addressee share a common set of sociolinguistic rules. However, in reality, speakers of the same language may adhere to different norms of address usage due to variations in their sociolinguistic backgrounds, such as social class, education, regional dialect, ethnicity, ideology, religion, and more. All these factors contribute to synchronic variation in address rules. In fact, the social diversity within certain speech communities is so extensive that it is nearly impossible to speak of a single standardized set of address rules (Dickey 1996, 9). For instance, in fourteenth-century England, "the lowest classes would say thou to everybody, even to kings and queens ... because the honorific pronoun [ye] was still outside their repertoire of address pronouns" (Kiełkiewicz-Janowiak 1992, 79). Braun's (1988, 23) comment aptly captures the situation: "variation is not an exception but rather the rule."

Furthermore, address systems may undergo changes over time, leading to diachronic variation. Forms of address suitable for a specific situation in one historical period may not necessarily be suitable for the same situation in another historical period. For instance, the second-person honorific pronoun, *ye*, which was in use in fourteenth-century England, is no longer employed today.

We should anticipate encountering both types of variation in Hebrew. Given that the Hebrew Bible is a compilation of written works authored by diverse individuals, it is reasonable to assume that they employed different address norms to emphasize distinct characteristics of the speakers. Thus, synchronic variation in address patterns might be evident not only between different sources or books but also within the characters of a particular source or book. As mentioned in §1.3.2, diachronic variation in the biblical text is most likely to be observed between Early Biblical Hebrew and Late Biblical Hebrew. Therefore, special attention will be given to examining the differences in address usage between these two groups within the corpus.

1.3.6. Reciprocity/Nonreciprocity

The concepts of reciprocity/nonreciprocity, power/solidarity, and *T/V* proposed by Brown, Gilman, and Ford offer a valuable framework for describing address usage in Hebrew. While Hebrew, like English, does not exhibit an explicit *T/V* distinction within its pronoun system for direct address, the distinction can be achieved through the use of nominal address forms. For instance, when addressing intimates and equals/inferiors, personal names are often employed, as seen in examples like גחזי *geḥªzi* ("Gehazi"; Elisha addressing his servant in 2 Kgs 5:25) or חנה *ḥannɔ* ("Hannah"; Elkanah addressing his wife in 1 Sam 1:8). On the other hand, when addressing nonintimates and superiors, titles are used, as illustrated by אדני *ʔªdoni* ("my lord"; Rebekah addressing a servant of Abraham in Gen 24:18) or המלך *hammɛlɛk* ("king"; Esther addressing Xerxes in Esth 7:3).

1.3.7. Politeness Theory

Some forms of address, including honorific titles, can be employed to convey politeness towards the addressee. Consequently, they have been examined within the framework of politeness studies, which emerged as a prominent subject in pragmatics and sociolinguistics. One of the most comprehensive and influential studies on politeness is presented by Brown and Levinson. According to their theory, all competent adults possess face, which refers to "the public self-image that every member wants to claim for himself" (Brown and Levinson 1987, 61).[31] Face consists of two aspects: positive face, representing the desire for approval, and negative face, representing the desire for autonomy. Brown and Levinson identify certain speech acts as face-threatening acts (FTA), which have the potential to threaten either the speaker's (S) or hearer's (H) face. Orders, requests, advice, and warnings threaten H's negative face, while criticism, complaints, and disagreement endanger H's positive face. Conversely, apologies threaten S's face. Brown and Levinson propose that the weightiness of a specific FTA is determined by an additive combination of three social factors: the degree of social distance between S and H, H's power over S, and the level of imposition associated with the FTA. They formulate the following equation:

$$Wx = D(S,H) + P(H,S) + Rx$$

where Wx represents the weightiness of the FTA, $D(S,H)$ refers to the social distance between S and H, $P(H,S)$ reflects H's power over S, and Rx denotes the level of imposition of the FTA within a particular cultural context. As the equation illustrates, an increase in distance, H's power, or the imposition of the FTA results in a corresponding increase in face-threat. Intuitively, this statement appears reasonable. For instance, it is more threatening for a subject to criticize a king (high weightiness due to high P[H,S]) than vice versa (low weightiness due to low P[H,S]).

In response to the weightiness of FTAs, competent speakers must select appropriate politeness strategies to save face in accordance with the seriousness of the FTA. Brown and Levinson outline five main types of linguistic strategies in

---

[31] They draw on Goffman's (1967, 5) concept of face, which he defines as "the positive social value a person effectively claims for himself by the line others assume he has taken during a particular contact."

ascending levels of politeness: (1) *bald on-record*, (2) *positive politeness*, (3) *negative politeness*, (4) *off-record*, and (5) *don't do the FTA*. Bald on-record is a strategy where S straightforwardly states the action without attempting to save face. For example, a command without "please" exemplifies this strategy ("Shut the door!"). In Brown and Levinson's scheme, this strategy is considered "impolite." *Positive politeness* addresses H's positive face by affirming H and indicating solidarity (e.g., "How about shutting the door *for us*?"). *Negative politeness* addresses H's negative face by showing respect for H's autonomy (e.g., "*Could* you shut the door?"). *Off-record* strategies address face concerns by keeping the meaning of the communication ambiguous. S demonstrates concern for H's face by granting H the freedom to interpret the meaning of the message and respond as desired (e.g., "It *seems* cold in here" indirectly suggests that H should shut the door). Lastly, *don't do the FTA* entails refraining from performing the act altogether. Brown and Levinson consider this the politest strategy.

Within these five strategies, Brown and Levinson (1987, 102–31) further elaborate on positive and negative politeness, delineating a number of substrategies in ascending levels of politeness, as follows.

Table 1.5. Positive and Negative Politeness

#	Strategies of Positive Politeness	#	Strategies of Negative Politeness
1.	Notice H's interests, wants, needs, and goods	1.	Be conventionally indirect
2.	Exaggerate interest, approval, and sympathy with H	2.	Question, hedge
		3.	Be pessimistic
		4.	Minimize the imposition
3.	Intensify interest to H	5.	Give deference
4.	Use in-group identity markers	6.	Apologize
5.	Seek agreement	7.	Impersonalize S and H: Avoid the pronouns "I" and "you"
6.	Avoid disagreement		
7.	Assert common ground	8.	State the FTA as a general rule
8.	Joke	9.	Nominalize
9.	Assert S's knowledge of and concern for H's wants	10.	Go on record as incurring a debt, or as not indebting H
10.	Offer, promise		
11.	Be optimistic		
12.	Include both S and H in the activity		
13.	Give reasons		
14.	Assume or assert reciprocity		
15.	Give gifts to H (goods, sympathy, understanding, cooperation)		

Since the publication of Brown and Levinson's work, their theory has undergone extensive cross-cultural testing, and its limitations have been identified.[32]

---

[32] See Goldsmith (2007, 227) for the bibliography.

The primary challenge in applying Brown and Levinson's theory to the Hebrew Bible lies in the inability to measure the level of imposition (R*x*) associated with various FTAs due to a lack of native informants. Consequently, the weightiness of FTAs cannot be determined, rendering Brown and Levinson's graded scale of politeness strategies ineffective.

Nevertheless, it is undeniable that the weightiness of an FTA is somehow connected to the social distance between S and H, H's power over S, and the level of imposition associated with the FTA. Therefore, when encountering certain politeness strategies employed in the Hebrew Bible, we can still attempt to explain them in terms of these three social factors. In fact, many of Brown and Levinson's politeness strategies can be identified in the speech between biblical characters.[33] Within these strategies, three sub-strategies appear particularly relevant to our examination of Hebrew forms of address.

First, *in-group identity markers* are utilized to remind the addressee of their connection to the speaker (Brown and Levinson 1987, 107–9). In the Hebrew Bible, kinship terms are often employed in this manner, such as when a king of northern Israel refers to the prophet Elisha as אבי *ʔɔḇi* "my father" in 2 Kgs 6:21.

Second, *give deference* involves the speaker either humbling themselves or elevating the addressee. The speaker may elevate the addressee's status by using honorific titles that directly reflect the relative social position between them, such as אדני *ʔaḏoni* "my lord" or המלך *hammɛlɛḵ* "the king." Deference is typically shown to superiors but may also be extended to inferiors as a means of mutual respect. For example, King Ahasuerus addresses Queen Esther as אסתר המלכה *ʔɛster hammalkɔ* "Queen Esther!" in Esth 5:3; 7:2.

Third, *impersonalize S and H* involves avoiding the use of personal pronouns "I" and "you." The speaker refers to the addressee in the third person to convey politeness (אל יאמר המלך כן *ʔal-yoʔmar hammɛlɛḵ kɛn* "let not *the king* say so" in 1 Kgs 22:8). This strategy is also referred to as *indirect address*, creating a sense of increased distance between the speaker and the addressee (Svennung 1958, 3).

Throughout this study, Brown and Levinson's politeness theory will be employed not only to identify politeness strategies utilized in the Hebrew Bible but also to explore the factors that influenced the speaker's selection of specific strategies. This theory provides a useful tool for comprehending diverse forms of communication and analyzing the address behavior of the characters.

---

[33] See my review of Bridge above.

2.
FREE FORMS OF ADDRESS: INTERNAL STRUCTURE

2.1. Introduction

Nominal forms of address in Biblical Hebrew and Epigraphic Hebrew can be divided into two groups based on the syntactic criterion: 'bound' and 'free' forms.[1] Bound forms are integrated into the syntax of a sentence, such as אדני *ʔᵃḏoni* "my lord" in (4):

(4) לא נכחד מאדני
    loʔ-nəḵaḥeḏ   *meʔᵃḏoni*
    not-we.will.hide   from=lord=my
    We will not hide from *my lord*. (Gen 47:18)

Free forms of address, however, stand outside the sentence structure.[2] They do not occupy a main constituent slot in the clausal syntax. Instead, they precede the sentence, follow it, or be inserted into it, as seen in the example of אברם *ʔaḇrɔm* "Abram" in (5):

---

[1] The syntactic distinction between bound and free forms has proven to be highly valuable in analyzing many European languages. (see Schubert 1984; Braun 1988; Kiełkiewicz-Janowiak 1992; Dickey 1996, 2002). It is important to note that in linguistics, the terms "bound" and "free" are typically used for *morphological* distinction: bound forms refer to forms that cannot occur in isolation, such as pronominal suffixes, whereas free forms refer to forms that can stand alone, such as independent personal pronouns. However, in address studies, these terms are used for *syntactic* distinctions: bound forms of address are forms that are integrated into the syntax of the sentence, whereas free forms of address function more like adjuncts, which do not serve as arguments of the verb.

[2] Revell (1996, 325) defines a free form of address as "a noun or noun phrase used to designate an addressee who is otherwise represented by second person pronouns." However, this definition is insufficient since it could also apply to a bound form of address. To accurately differentiate the two, the definition must emphasize the syntactic feature that distinguishes a free form from a bound form.

(5) אל תירא אברם
    ʔal-tirɔʔ   ʔaḇrɔm
    not-you.be.afraid   Abram
    Do not be afraid, *Abram*! (Gen 15:1)

Thus, a free form of address in Biblical Hebrew can be defined based on a combination of several criteria. Morphologically, it takes a form of a nominal element. Syntactically, it is separated from the sentence it may accompany and functions as an adjunct. Semantically and pragmatically, it serves to refer to the addressee, typically fulfilling the roles of calling, summoning, or identifying the addressee.[3]

This chapter aims to examine the internal structure of free forms of address in Biblical Hebrew by analyzing their constituents, word order, and distribution patterns.[4] It is noteworthy that these aspects have often been overlooked by grammarians. Through the analysis, it will become evident that biblical authors adhere to specific structural patterns in their use of free forms of address.

2.2. Previous Studies

Previous studies on addresses in both ancient and modern languages have attempted to analyze the internal structure of address forms using grammatical or semantic categories. A notable example of a grammatical analysis is found in Athanasios Kambylis's (1964, 95–199) study of Greek forms of address used in the works of Pindar. In his study, Kambylis classified address forms into two main groups: single-word addresses and multi-word addresses. Within each group, he further categorized the forms based on their grammatical structure, including proper nouns, proper nouns with attributive adjectives, and so on. Additionally, Kambylis considered the type of addressee, such as gods, goddesses, or humans, and the presence or absence of the particle ὦ ("O"). Through this comprehensive categorization, Kambylis sought to present the grammatical and syntactic regularities as well as unique characteristics exhibited by different address forms.

Dickey (1996) took a different approach by using lexical meaning as the basis for organizing free forms of address in Greek prose. Drawing from Braun's (1988, 9–11) classification for modern languages, she assigned a semantic type to each

---

[3] I agree with Revell (1996, 325) who equates a free form of address with the vocative in Biblical Hebrew. Zwicky (1974, 787), Leech (1999, 107), and Busse (2006, 29) also equate them, understanding the vocative as a form of address loosely integrated with the rest of the sentence. Curiously, Miller (2010b, 348) thinks that Leech differentiates the vocative from a free form of address. Judging from the definition and the examples of the vocative that Leech provides, however, it is certain that he identifies the vocative with a free form of address.

[4] Note that there are no examples of free forms of address in Epigraphic Hebrew.

address, such as personal names, kinship terms, titles, and so on. By examining the different semantic types and their usage, Dickey explored the ways in which these forms of address were employed within the Greek language.

In the following sections, I aim to categorize free forms of address in Biblical Hebrew based on both grammatical and semantic criteria, providing a more comprehensive understanding of their internal structure. Taking inspiration from Kambylis's methodology, I will initially divide address forms into two groups: *simple address* and *complex address*. A simple address consists of a single word, while a complex address is composed of two or more words. It is worth noting that in Biblical Hebrew, it is not uncommon for simple or complex addresses to be combined, resulting in a long string of addresses, which can be referred to as a *compound address*. Throughout my discussions, I will frequently refer to these three terms to analyze the various forms of address in Biblical Hebrew.[5]

2.3. Grammatical Categories

A free form of address in Biblical Hebrew typically consists of a nominal element, which can take the form of a noun phrase, adjective, or participle. In some cases, it may be expanded with a modifier, such as an attributive adjective, relative clause, or prepositional phrase. According to Joüon (§137g), the free form of address is pragmatically definite, as it refers to a specific participant in the speech situation. To convey this definiteness, when a nominal element is used as a free form of address, it should be marked with the appropriate categories of nominal definiteness in Biblical Hebrew. These include the use of the definite article, a pronominal suffix, construct noun(s) with a definite *nomen rectum*, or a proper noun. However, there are instances where nominals function as free forms of address without being proper nouns or bound to another definite element, yet they lack the definite article. In my organization of free forms of address based on grammatical categories, I will set aside these cases for further discussion in §2.3.3, where we will explore possible reasons for the absence of the definite article.

2.3.1. Simple Addresses

A simple address can be used alone or as part of a compound address. In our corpus, nearly all the simple addresses exhibit definiteness either intrinsically or through explicit marking.[6] This includes instances where a simple address

---

[5] In this study, the number of free forms of address reflects the sum of simple and complex addresses. Simple address(es) and/or complex address(es) within a compound address are counted individually. Thus, a compound address would not count as just one form of address (contrary to Miller 2010a, 48).
[6] For a discussion of the distribution of actual forms in the corpus, see below.

consists of a proper noun (6a), a common noun bearing a pronominal suffix (6b), or a common noun, adjective, or participle prefixed with the definite article (6c):[7]

(6a) ויאמר אלי מלאך האלהים בחלום יעקב
    wayyoʔmɛr   ʔelay   malʔak   hɔʔᵉlohim   baħᵃlom   yaʕᵃqob
    and=he.said   to=me   messenger.of   the=God   in=dream   Jacob
    Then the messenger of God said to me in the dream, "*Jacob!*" (Gen 31:11)

(6b) ויאמר המלך אל אבשלום אל בני אל נא נלך כלנו ולא נכבד עליך
    wayyoʔmɛr   hammɛlɛk   ʔɛl-ʔabšɔlom   ʔal-bəni   ʔal-nɔʔ
    and=he.said   the=king   to-Absalom   not-son=my   not-POL
    nelek   kullɔnu   wlɔʔ   nikbad   ʕɔlɛkɔ
    we.will.go   all.of=us   and=not   we.will.be.heavy   upon=you
    The king said to Absalom, "No, *my son*, let us not all go, lest we be burdensome to you." (2 Sam 13:25)

(6c) ויאמר להם שמעו נא המרים המן הסלע הזה נוציא לכם מים
    wayyoʔmɛr   lɔhɛm   šimʕu-nɔʔ   hammorim
    and=he.said   to=them   hear-POL   the=rebels
    hᵃmin-hassɛlaʕ   hazzɛ   noṣiʔ   lɔkɛm   mɔyim
    INTER=from-the-rock   the=this   we.will.bring   for=you   water
    He (i.e., Moses) said to them (i.e., the assembly), "Hear, *rebels*! Shall we bring water for you out of this rock?" (Num 20:10)

However, a few simple addresses consist of a common noun (7a), adjective (7b), or participle (7c) unmarked with the definite article:[8]

(7a) ויקרא על המזבח בדבר יהוה ויאמר מזבח מזבח
    wayyiqrɔʔ   ʕal-hammizbeaḥ   bidbar   yhwh
    and=he.called   against-the=altar   in=word.of   YHWH
    wayyoʔmɛr   mizbeaḥ   mizbeaḥ
    and=he.said   altar   altar
    He cried against the altar by the word of YHWH, saying, "O *Altar, Altar!*"[9] (1 Kgs 13:2)

---

[7] See §1.1.1 in appendix B for a list of examples of proper nouns, including common nouns functioning as proper nouns, as well as §1.1.2 for a list of examples of common nouns with a pronominal suffix, and finally, §1.1.3 for a list of examples of common nouns, adjectives, and participles that are prefixed with the definite article.

[8] See §1.2 in appendix B for a list of examples of common nouns, adjectives, and participles that do not have the definite article.

[9] For the translation with the capital letter "A" in "Altar," see §2.3.3.

(7b) ונערים קטנים יצאו מן העיר ויתקלסו בו ויאמרו לו עלה קרח עלה קרח
unəʕɔrim   qəṭannim   yɔṣəʔu   min-hɔʕir
and=boys   small   they.went.out   from-the=city
wayyitqalləsu-bo   wayyoʔməru   lo   ʕᵃle
and=they.mocked-in.him   and=they.said   to=him   go.up
qereaḥ   ʕᵃle   qereaḥ
bald   go.up   bald

Some young boys came out of the city and jeered at him, saying, "Go up, *baldy*! Go up, *baldy*!" (2 Kgs 2:23)

(7c) לכן זונה שמעי דבר יהוה
lɔken   zɔnɔ   šimʕi   dəbar-yhwh
therefore   prostitute   hear   word.of-YHWH

Therefore, *prostitute*, hear the word of YHWH! (Ezek 16:35)

Out of the 682 free forms of address found in our corpus, 473 forms are categorized as simple addresses, accounting for approximately 69 percent of the total. Among these simple addresses, a significant majority, specifically 461 forms (over 97 percent), exhibit inherent or overt markers of definiteness. The breakdown of these definiteness markers is as follows: 217 instances of proper nouns, 207 instances of common nouns with pronominal suffixes, and thirty-five instances of common nouns, one adjective, and one participle prefixed with the definite article. However, there are twelve instances (less than 3 percent) of simple addresses consisting of a common noun, adjective, or participle without the definite article.

The most frequently occurring proper nouns are יהוה *yhwh* 'YHWH' (104 times) and ישראל *yiśrɔʔel* "Israel" (15 times). Among the common nouns that bear pronominal suffixes or the definite article, אדני *ʔᵃdoni* "my lord" is the most frequent, occurring 50 times, followed by אדני *ʔᵃdonɔy* "(my) Lord" with 44 instances, and המלך *hammɛlɛk* "the king" with 28 occurrences.[10]

---

[10] There has been considerable debate over the ending *qɔmeṣ yod* of the word אדני *ʔᵃdonɔy*. Eissfeldt (1974, 70) claims that it is "a nominal afformative, which elevate(s) the basic form (*ʔɔdon*) to a *status emphaticus* and g(ives *ʔᵃdonɔy*) the meaning 'the Lord of all.'" He is followed by Waltke and O'Connor (*IBHS* §7.4.3e–f). Eissfeldt's claim is based on four Ugaritic words: *ulny*, *ṣ̌ᵃmny* (*CTU* 1.2 iv 5), *hnny*, and *ṯmny* (*CTU* 2.11:10, 14). However, his vocalization with /ā/ before {y} in these words is questionable (see Bordreuil and Pardee 2009, 161, 234; Pardee 2003, 128–29; Huehnergard 2012, 104). Moreover, if the vowel before {y} were indeed /ā/, its Hebrew reflex would have been /ō/ due to the Canaanite shift. In addition, *qɔmeṣ yod* as a nominal affirmative is not evident elsewhere in Biblical Hebrew, and thus there is no clear reason why it should only be preserved with *ʔᵃdonɔy* (Brettler 1989, 41–42). Since Dalman's monograph *Studien zur biblischen Theologie: der Gottesname Adonaj und seine Geschichte* in 1889, many Hebrew grammarians and lexicographers have held that *qɔmeṣ yod* is a first-person singular pronominal suffix

2.3.2. Complex Addresses

A complex address comprises two or more words and can be used independently or as part of a compound address. There are four possible constructions for a complex address. The first is a construct chain, which can be formed with three or more words (e.g., בן נעות המרדות [11] *bɛn-naʕᵘwaṯ hammarduṯ* "son of a perverse, rebellious woman" in 1 Sam 20:30). However, most construct chains in our corpus involve two words, where the first word (*nomen regens*) is bound to the second word (*nomen rectum*) in a genitive relationship. While the construct chain is considered definite when the *nomen rectum* is definite, as in (8a), there are instances where the common noun of the *nomen rectum* is not prefixed with the definite article, as shown in (8b):[12]

(8a) ותאמר אל אליהו מה לי ולך איש האלהים

wattoʔmɛr	*ʔɛl-ʔeliyyɔhu*	*ma-lli*	*wɔlɔḵ*
and=she.said	to-Elijah	what-to=me	and=to=you
ʔiš	*hɔʔᵉlohim*		
man.of	the=God		

Then she said to Elijah, "What have you against me, *man of God*?" (1 Kgs 17:18)

---

attached to the plural of majesty *ʔaḏonim*, denoting a personal relationship of the speaker to God (GKC §135q; Joüon §136d; Blau 2010, 272; BL §29t; BDB 11; *HALOT* 13; *DCH* 1:122, 133). The use of *qɔmeṣ* instead of *pataḥ* expected in this form might represent the pausal form, which presumably resulted from its frequent use as a free form of address in prayers (BL §29t), an attempt to distinguish the term referring to the divine Lord (*ʔᵃḏonɔy*) from that referring to human lord(s) (*ʔᵃḏoni* or *ʔᵃḏonay*; Baudissin 1929, 2:27), or both (Revell, 1996, 197 n.2). As the Greek Septuagint (LXX) consistently translates *ʔᵃḏonɔy* as (ὁ) κυριος "(the) Lord" instead of κυριος μου "my lord" or κυριοι μου "my lords," it seems probable that the significance of the suffix had disappeared by the second century BCE. As Dalman (1889, 33) states, however, "on the basis of the written material available today, one can hardly speak of a real history of the use of אדני in the time covered by the Old Testament books... least of all a transition from a conscious use of the suffix to a use of the suffix which has no significance." I adopt the view that *qɔmeṣ yod* was originally a first-person singular pronominal suffix, while acknowledging the uncertainty regarding the maintenance of its significance throughout the period depicted in the Old Testament books. To reflect this situation, I have chosen to include parentheses around 'my' in my translation of *ʔᵃḏonɔy*.

[11] On the basis of the LXX's κορασίων "of girls," a feminine construct noun נַעֲרַת *naʕᵃraṯ* "girl of" may be read instead of נַעֲוֺת *naʕᵘwaṯ* "a twisted one of" (Niphal PTCP F SG CSTR). However, as the plural in the LXX is improbable and the MT, as it stands, clearly intensifies the degree of insult, I follow the MT.

[12] See §2.1.1 in appendix B for a list of examples of definite construct phrases, as well as §2.1.2 for a list of examples of construct phrases with an anarthrous *nomen rectum*.

(8b) ויאמר אל תירא איש חמדות שלום לך
wayyoʔmɛr   ʔal-tirɔʔ   ʔiš-ħᵃmudot   šɔlom   lɔḵ
and=he.said not-you.be.afraid man.of-preciousness well-being for=you
He said, "Do not be afraid, *precious man*, it will be well for you." (Dan 10:19)

Second, a complex address can be formed by combining a definite construct phrase with a definite noun phrase, as in (9):[13]

(9) וירד אליו יואש מלך ישראל ויבך על פניו ויאמר אבי אבי רכב ישראל ופרשיו
wayyerɛd   ʔelɔyw   yoʔɔš   mɛlɛḵ-yiśrɔʔel   wayyeḇək
and=he.went.down to=him   Joash   king.of-Israel   and=he.wept
ʕal-pɔnɔyw   wayyoʔmɛr   ʔɔḇi   ʔɔḇi   rɛḵɛḇ
upon-face=his   and=he.said   father=my father=my   chariot.of
yiśrɔʔel   uṗɔrɔšɔyw
Israel   and=horsemen=its

Joash king of Israel went down to him (i.e., Elisha) and wept before him and said, "My father, my father! *Israel's chariot and its horsemen!*" (2 Kgs 13:14)

Joash's utterance to Elisha on his deathbed consists of four noun phrases: "my father," "my father," "Israel's chariot," "its horsemen." While Miller (2010b, 354) considers only the first two noun phrases as forms of address, I consider the last two noun phrases to be part of the address as well.[14] They stand in apposition to the initial two noun phrases, specifically referring to Elisha, who has been a source of power and guidance for the northern kingdom of Israel. Interestingly, the exact same form of address was used by Elisha himself when his mentor Elijah was taken up to heaven in a whirlwind, as described in 2 Kgs 2:12. As Robert Alter (2013, 737) points out, the imagery of the chariot and horsemen, perhaps triggered by the vision of the chariot of fire in verse 11, conveys the idea that "Elijah has been Israel's true power, as chariotry is the driving power of an army." This form of address, which combines a construct phrase with a noun phrase, now serves as a proverbial epithet for a leader and is applied to Elisha.

Third, a complex address can consist of a definite construct phrase followed by a definite noun phrase in apposition to the *nomen rectum* of the construct phrase, as in (10):[15]

---

[13] See §2.2 in appendix B for an example of a definite construct phrase conjoined with a noun phrase.

[14] I view the final two noun phrases as a fixed expression referring to Elisha. Thus, they constitute one form of address.

[15] See §2.3 in appendix B for a list of examples of a definite construct phrase plus a noun phrase appositional to the *nomen rectum* of the construct phrase.

(10) ויאמר דויד ברוך אתה יהוה אלהי ישראל אבינו מעולם ועד עולם
    wayyoʔmɛr   dɔwid̠   bɔruk̠   ʔattɔ   yhwh
    and=he.said   David   blessed   you   YHWH
    ʔᵉlohe   yiśrɔʔel   ʔɔb̠inu   meʕolɔm   waʕad̠-ʕolɔm
    God.of   Israel   father=our   from=eternity   and=to-eternity
    David said, "Blessed are you, YHWH, *God of Israel our father*, forever and ever." (1 Chr 29:10)

In this example, a simple address consisting of the proper noun יהוה *yhwh* "YHWH" is followed by a complex address headed by אלהי *ʔᵉlohe* "God of." It is important to note that a common noun with a pronominal suffix אבינו *ʔɔb̠inu* "our father" is in apposition to the *nomen rectum* of the preceding construct phrase ישראל *yiśrɔʔel* "Israel," rather than to אלהי *ʔᵉlohe* "God of." Thus, the phrase אלהי ישראל אבינו *ʔᵉlohe yiśrɔʔel ʔɔb̠inu* "God of Israel our father" should be regarded as a single address form comprising three words, with the same referent as יהוה *yhwh* "YHWH."

Finally, a complex address can take the form of a definite noun phrase followed by a modifier. This modifier can be an attributive adjective, relative clause headed by אשר- *ʔᵃšɛr-*, -ה *h-*, or "zero-" relative complementizer,[16] or even prepositional phrase, as in (11a):[17]

(11a) ויאמר ירמיהו אל כל העם ואל כל הנשים שמעו
    דבר יהוה כל יהודה אשר בארץ מצרים
    wayyoʔmɛr   yirmǝyɔhu   ʔɛl-kol-hɔʕɔm   wǝʔɛl   kol-hannɔšim
    and=he.said   Jeremiah   to-all-the=people   and=to   all-the=women
    šimʕu   dǝb̠ar-yhwh   kol-yǝhudɔ   ʔᵃšɛr   bɔʔɛrɛṣ   miṣrɔyim
    hear   word.of-YHWH   all-Judah   who   in=land.of   Egypt
    Jeremiah said to all the people and all the women, "Hear the word of YHWH, *all you people of Judah who are in the land of Egypt!*" (Jer 44:24)

---

[16] I align with Holmstedt (2002, 83–90; 2010, 27–31) in his argument, drawing on the works of Barr (1989) and Siloni (1995), that the ה prefix attached to a participle serves as a relative complementizer. In this construction, the participle functions as the main verb within the relative clause. For an argument supporting the idea that the definite article in Phoenician and Hebrew originally acted as a relative marker, see Gzella 2006, 11. Furthermore, in accordance with Holmstedt (2002, 60), I consider a participle without the prefix ה as the main verb within a "zero-" relative clause, wherein no overt relative complementizer is present.

[17] See §2.4.1 in appendix B for a list of examples of a definite noun phrase followed by a modifier.

However, there are several cases where a modifier follows an anarthrous common noun phrase, as in (11b):

(11b) שובו בנים שובבים נאם יהוה כי אנכי בעלתי בכם
    šubu   bonim   šobobim   nə?um-yhwh   ki   ?ɔnoki
    return   sons   faithless   utterance-YHWH for   I
    bɔʕalti   bɔkɛm
    I.am.master over=you
"Return, *faithless children*," declares YHWH; "for I am your true master." (Jer 3:14)

To sum up, there are a total of 209 complex addresses in our corpus, which make up approximately 30 percent of all free forms of address. Out of these, 110 complex addresses are grammatically definite. This includes eighty-two construct phrases with a definite *nomen rectum,* two definite construct phrases conjoined with a definite noun phrase, six definite construct phrases followed by a noun phrase appositional to the *nomen rectum* of the construct phrase, and twenty definite noun phrases followed by a modifier. However, ninety-nine complex addresses are unmarked with the definite article: ninety-five construct phrases with an anarthrous *nomen rectum* and four anarthrous noun phrases followed by a modifier.

2.3.3. Reasons for the Absence of the Definite Article in Free Forms of Address

When comparing the frequency of nominal forms of address with the definite article to those without it,[18] we find that the latter outnumber the former. For the sake of comparison, the statistics for both prose and poetry are presented in table 2.1:[19]

Table 2.1. Nominal Forms of Address and the Definite Article in Biblical Hebrew

	+ Definite Article	- Definite Article	Total
Prose	55	111	166
Poetry	74	212	286
Total	129	323	452

From a statistical point of view, it appears that both prose and poetry tend to favor the absence of definite articles in nominal forms of address. These statistical findings led Miller (2010a, 43) to assert that the definite article does not mark the

---

[18] This comparison excludes anarthrous forms of address that are definite: proper nouns, nouns with a pronominal suffix, and nouns in construct with any of these nouns.
[19] Miller (2010a, 48) has a similar table, but the numbers are slightly different as she employs a different counting method. For example, she counts multiple appositional appositives referring to the same addressee as one form of address.

vocative (i.e., free form of address) in Biblical Hebrew. Instead, nominals used as vocatives can be either definite or indefinite.

However, Miller's conclusion is misleading since she fails to consider the following significant factors underlying the statistics. First, there is a skewed distribution of nominal forms of address without the definite article in prose. In table 2.2, anarthrous nominal forms of address in prose are listed according to the books of the Hebrew Bible:

Table 2.2. Nominal Forms of Address without the Definite Article in Prose

Form	Verse	Form	Verse
פלשתים	1 Sam 4:9	זונה	Ezek 16:35
מזבח	1 Kgs 13:2 (2x)	חלל רשע	Ezek 21:30[20]
עמים	1 Kgs 22:28 = 2 Chr 18:27	עיר שפכת ...	Ezek 22:3
קרח	2 Kgs 2:23 (2x)	כרוב הסכך	Ezek 28:16
בנים שובבים	Jer 3:14	רשע	Ezek 33:8
רעים מאבדים...	Jer 23:1[21]	רעים	Ezek 34:7
אדון	Jer 34:5	חזה	Amos 7:12
בן אדם	Ezek 2:1, etc. (91x); Dan 8:17	איש חמדות	Dan 10:11, 19

Looking at the table, it is evident that out of the 111 anarthrous nominal forms of address, a staggering ninety-two belong to a single form, בן אדם *ben-ʔɔḏɔm* "son of man." Remarkably, all but one of these instances come from a single book, that is, the book of Ezekiel.[22] It is noteworthy that throughout this book, the prophet Ezekiel is consistently addressed by YHWH using this phrase, never by his personal name. This observation leads to the argument that the phrase serves as a substitute for Ezekiel's personal name and should therefore be construed as definite, like saying "*O Human!*"[23] As David J. A. Clines (1972, 287) points out, this phrase accentuates the distance between Ezekiel and the majestic God who speaks to him, highlighting "the comparative insignificance of the one who is addressed not by his proper name, but only by the name of his 'father.'"

---

[20] I view this expression as a construct phrase, following *BHS*'s repointing *ḥalal rešaʕ*. This may be supported by the fact that two adjectives in apposition are rare in Biblical Hebrew and that there is a corresponding plural construct phrase *ḥalle rəšɔʕim* in Ezek 21:34.

[21] For a defense of viewing what follows after הוי *hoy* "woe" as a form of address in Jer 23:1, see Hillers 1983, 185–88.

[22] The phrase *ben-ʔɔḏɔm* in Dan 8:17 may have been derived from that in Ezekiel. See Eichrodt 1970, 61 and Block 1997, 30.

[23] Note that the phrase בן־אדם is in form a perfectly plausible personal name, and personal names (virtually) never include the definite article. Thus, it is quite possible that the phrase was created in the form of a personal name, as a substitute for the personal name, with the second element, which is usually theophoric, being nontheophoric in this phrase.

Second, if we exclude the phrase בן אדם *bɛn-ʔɔḏɔm*, we are left with only nineteen anarthrous forms of address in prose, which accounts for about one-third of the number of forms with the definite article. Again, the distribution of these remaining forms is uneven, with twelve out of the nineteen occurrences found in prophetic books, especially Jeremiah and Ezekiel. These books consist of a combination of prose and poetry, and are well known for freely incorporating poetic features in the prose section, including the restricted use of the definite article, which Francis I. Andersen and A. Dean Forbes (1983, 165) refer to as a "prose particle."[24] Thus, the absence of the definite article in the thirteen forms of address in the prose sections of the prophetic books may be attributed to this stylistic reality.[25]

The seven anarthrous forms of address in the historical books actually belong to only four forms. Six of these instances are the result of repetition within the same verse (מזבח *mizbeaḥ* "altar" in 1 Kgs 13:2; קרח *qereaḥ* "baldy" in 2 Kgs 2:23) or in parallel passages (עמים *ʕammim* "peoples" in 1 Kgs 22:28 = 2 Chr 18:27). The absence of the definite article in these four forms of address can be explained as follows:

First, in 1 Sam 4:9, the form of address פלשתים *plištim* "O Philistines!" is a gentilic plural adjective. Unlike other gentilic plural forms that regularly take the definite article when referring to the entire group (e.g., העברים *hɔʕiḇrim* "the Hebrews"), פלשתים is almost always found without the definite article (228 out of 257 occurrences).[26] Thus, the absence of the article in this form of address should not come as a surprise.

Second, the expression מזבח מזבח *mizbeaḥ mizbeaḥ* "O altar, altar!" in 1 Kgs 13:2 is an example of a rhetorical device known as apostrophe, in which the speaker turns away from the audience to address "a dead or absent person, or an abstraction or inanimate object" (Baldick 2008, 22). This technique is used to emphasize a point, intensify grief, or express indignation, often involving

---

[24] According to Garr (1985, 89), the definite article is a relatively recent innovation in Hebrew, making its first appearance during the early first millennium BCE. Thus, its frequent omission in archaic biblical poetry, such as the song of Deborah in Judges 5, may be accounted for. The reasons for the absence of the definite article in poetry in subsequent periods may vary, including archaizing, rhythm, brevity, and stylistic elegance. For a list of biblical poems that do not use the definite article at all, see Andersen and Forbes 1983, 165. See also Freedman (1985, 49–62) for a discussion of the use of the three "prose particles," i.e., *ʔeṯ*, *ʔᵃšer*, and *ha-*, in the poetry embedded in the prose narratives of the Hebrew Bible.

[25] This also corresponds to the general tendency of the reduced use of the definite article in free forms of address in poetry shown in table 2.1.

[26] Only ten times is ה used. In nineteen cases is a preceding position (ב, ל, כ) given the pointing of the definite article.

personification. In this instance, an unnamed man of God from Judah directly addresses an altar, an inanimate object, while Jeroboam, the king of Israel, stands nearby to offer sacrifices at Bethel. The man of God employs this technique to shockingly shift attention from the royal but self-appointed priest, Jeroboam, and redirect it towards an entirely illegitimate altar and cult. The man of God completely ignores Jeroboam as if he were not even present and personifies the altar as if it were capable of hearing his prophecy. Thus, it can be argued that the common noun מזבח functions as a quasi-proper noun, akin to saying "Mr. Altar! Mr. Altar!" Hence, the use of the definite article may not be necessary.[27] The same explanation can be applied to the absence of the definite article in other common nouns for inanimate objects used as free forms of address, such as עיר שפכת דם ʕir šōpeḵet dɔm "O City that sheds blood!" (Ezek 22:3).

Third, the form of address עמים ʕammim "O peoples!" in 1 Kgs 22:28 (= 2 Chr 18:27) may not be original in the Masoretic Text (MT) but rather a scribal gloss. According to the MT, this anarthrous form of address comes from the mouth of Micaiah, the son of Imlah. After prophesying Ahab's death in a battle against Aram, Micaiah is ordered to be imprisoned by Ahab until his safe return (vv. 19–27). However, unperturbed, Micaiah boldly makes another declaration introduced by ויאמר wayyoʔmɛr "then he said": "If you return safely, YHWH has not spoken to me" (v. 28). Without any intervening response from Ahab, we encounter another ויאמר introducing Micaiah's final address: ויאמר שמעו עמים כלם wayyoʔmɛr šimʕu ʕammim kullɔm "He said, 'Hear, all you peoples!'" (v. 28). As Alter (2013, 725) points out, it is too abrupt and odd for Micaiah to say this in this narrative context. In fact, certain versions of the Greek Septuagint (LXX) exclude these four words. Considering that the exact same words שמעו עמים כלם are found at the beginning of the prophecy of the literary prophet Micah (Mic 1:2), it is probable that the four words ויאמר שמעו עמים כלם in 1 Kgs 22:28 are a scribal interpolation intended to establish a connection between Micaiah, the son of Imlah, and Micah of Moresheth. Thus, the lack of the definite article in the form of address עמים may be attributed to the fact that it was directly borrowed from the poetic section of the book of Micah.

Finally, in 2 Kgs 2:23 we see a group of young boys mocking the prophet Elisha, saying, עלה קרח עלה קרח ʕᵃle qereaḥ ʕᵃle qereaḥ "Go up, baldy! Go up, baldy!" The absence of the definite article in קרח can be explained by Miller (2010a, 54), who argues that the address form consisting of an evaluative term is

---

[27] Waltke and O'Connor's (*IBHS* §13.5.2c) explanation is similar when they state that "quite frequently the article is not used when reference is to persons not present or who are more or less imaginary."

anarthrous[28] when the speaker wishes "to highlight the *nature, characteristics*, or *attributes* of the addressee." In contrast, the definite article is employed when the speaker intends "to specify the identity of the addressee." Thus, the definite article is not used in קרח, since the young boys are sarcastically taunting and insulting Elisha by drawing attention to his physical defect with the term.[29] However, when Saul re-identifies his son Jonathan using an insulting term בן נעות המרדות *ben naʕᵃwat hammardut* "You son of a perverse, rebellious woman!" (1 Sam 20:30), the definite article is used.[30]

Based on the examination of all the anarthrous forms of address in prose, it can be concluded that the lack of the definite article in free forms of address does not necessarily indicate that the form is functionally indefinite. Typically, individuals being addressed, known as addressees, are identifiable within the context of the speech or text. Therefore, the form of address should be considered definite. The exclusion of the definite article in free forms of address can be attributed to various factors discussed above.

2.3.4. Correlation between Free Forms of Address and Speech Participants

When examining the types of address forms and the types of speech participants, a close correlation between them becomes apparent. Simple addresses are commonly found in conversations between two humans, accounting for 175 occurrences or 37 percent of the total simple addresses. On the other hand, the usage of complex addresses in such situations is significantly lower, with only 19 instances, making up 9 percent of the complex addresses. Interestingly, none of the twenty-four complex addresses, which consist of a noun phrase followed by a modifier, appears in human-to-human conversations. Instead, they are primarily employed in dialogues between God and human(s) or in a prophet's address to a group of people or inanimate object(s). In these cases, the speaker describes specific features and characteristics of the addressee(s).[31] In (11b) above, for example,

---

[28] Note that Miller uses the term "indefinite" instead of anarthrous. I view free forms of address as pragmatically definite, regardless of the presence or absence of the definite article, since they point to a specific participant in the speech situation.

[29] Perhaps other anarthrous forms of address consisting of an evaluative term for praise, such as איש־חמדות *ʔiš-ḥᵃmudot* "O precious man!" in Dan 10:11, 19, may be explained in the same way.

[30] Another possible explanation for the use of the definite article in this insulting phrase is that the phrase נעות המרדות *naʕᵃwat hammardut* specifically refers to Jonathan's mother (Ahinoam?), and therefore is definite. See also 2 Sam 16:7, in which the definite article is used as Shimei specifies the identity of David by two insulting phrases איש הדמים ואיש הבליעל *ʔiš haddᵃmim wᵉʔiš habbliyyoʕal* "You man of blood, (and) you man of worthlessness!"

[31] For God's address to human(s), see Isa 10:24; Jer 3:14; 23:1; Ezek 21:30; 22:3; 28:16; 34:2. For human's address to God, see Gen 32:10; Num 16:22; 2 Kgs 19:15; Isa 37:16; Dan 9:4,

God addresses the people of Judah בנים *bɔnim* "children," using an attributive adjective שובבים *šobɔbim* "faithless" to describe their spiritual state. In (11a), when the prophet Jeremiah addresses the people of Judah, he specifies their location (Egypt) using a relative clause. Thus, it can be concluded that complex addresses, in general, and those consisting of a noun phrase followed by a modifier, in particular, do not reflect everyday conversations between two humans in ancient Israel. Rather, they are used in specific speech contexts where the speaker finds it necessary to describe the characteristics and attributes of the addressee(s).

2.3.5. Compound Addresses

A compound address is created when simple address(es) and/or complex address(es) are combined to refer to the same entity. There are three types of compound addresses distinguished by the methods through which their constituent addresses are combined: *apposition, repetition,* and *coordination.*

2.3.5.1. Apposition

Two or three coreferential addresses can be juxtaposed asyndetically to form a compound address. In our corpus, there are 106 compound addresses made up of appositional addresses. With the exception of one, all of these compound addresses consist of two addresses. Table 2.3 presents a breakdown of the combinations and their respective frequencies in both dialogues between two humans and overall:

Table 2.3. Combinations of Two Appositional Addresses

Combination	Human-to-Human	Total
Simple + Simple	29	75
Simple + Complex	2	27
Complex + Complex	–	3

The statistics clearly demonstrate that the structure of two simple addresses in apposition is the most commonly employed, surpassing any other structure. Additionally, over one-third of these compound addresses occur in human-to-human conversations. Interestingly, our corpus does not include any examples of a complex address followed by a simple address.

When a simple address appears as the head of a compound address, it almost always (99 times) consists of a proper noun or a common noun with a pronominal suffix, as in (12a) and (12b), respectively:[32]

15; Neh 1:5. For the prophet's address to a group of people, see Jer 7:2; 17:20 (3x); 22:2; 29:20; 44:24, 26. For the prophet's address to inanimate objects, see Ezek 37:4; Zech 4:7.

[32] See §3.1.1 and §3.1.2 in appendix B for a list of compound addresses headed by a simple address.

FREE FORMS OF ADDRESS: INTERNAL STRUCTURE

(12a) ויקרא עלי את שמואל ויאמר שמואל בני
  wayyiqrɔʔ   ʕeli   ʔɛt-šəmuʔel   wayyoʔmɛr   šəmuʔel   bəni
  and=he.called Eli   ACC-Samuel   and=he.said Samuel   son=my
  Eli called Samuel and said, "*Samuel, my son!*" (1 Sam 3:16)

(12b) ויכר שאול את קול דוד ויאמר הקולך זה בני דוד ויאמר דוד קולי אדני המלך
  Wayyakker   šɔʔul   ʔɛt-qol   dɔwid   wayyoʔmɛr
  and=he.recognized Saul   ACC-voice.of   David   and=he.said
  hᵃqolə<u>k</u>ɔ   zɛ   bəni   dɔwi<u>d</u>   wayyoʔmɛr
  INTER=voice=your this   son=my   David   and=he.said
  dɔwi<u>d</u>   qoli   ʔᵃdoni   hammɛlɛ<u>k</u>
  David   voice=my   lord=my   the=king
  Saul recognized David's voice and said, "Is this your voice, *my son* David?"
  David replied, "It is my voice, *my lord* the king." (1 Sam 26:17)

When a complex address is positioned as the head component of a compound address, it is consistently followed by an appositive complex address, as in (13):[33]

(13) כי אתה יהוה צבאות אלהי ישראל גליתה את אזן עבדך
  ki-ʔatɔ   yhwh   ṣəbɔʔot   ʔᵉlohe   yiśrɔʔel   golitɔ
  for-you   YHWH.of   hosts   God.of   Israel   you.uncovered
  ʔɛt-ʔozɛn   ʕab̪dəkɔ
  ACC-ear.of   servant=your
  For you, *YHWH of hosts*,[34] *God of Israel*, have revealed to your servant. (2 Sam 7:27)

There are three instances that demonstrate this structure in our corpus, all of which appear in conversations between God and human(s), never between two humans. Thus, it appears that this structure does not represent a characteristic feature of everyday conversations in ancient Israel.

Our corpus contains only one compound address consisting of three appositional addresses:

(14) ואמר אנא יהוה אלהי השמים האל הגדול והנורא
     שמר הברית וחסד לאהביו ולשמרי מצותיו
  wɔʔomar   ʔɔnnɔʔ   yhwh   ʔᵉlohe   haššɔmayim   hɔʔel
  and=I.said   please   YHWH   God.of   the=heavens   the=God

---

[33] See §3.1.3 in appendix B for a list of compound addresses headed by a complex address.
[34] For epigraphic evidence of a proper noun in the construct state, see KAjr 18.2 and 19A.5–6 where *yhwh šmrn* "YHWH of Samaria" and *yhwh tmn* "YHWH of Teman" are attested, respectively. For a defense of this interpretation, see Emerton 1982, 2–20.

haggɔdol	wəhannorɔʔ	šomer	habbərit	wɔḥɛsɛd
the=great	and=the=awesome	keeping	the=covenant	and=mercy

ləʔohᵃbɔyw	uləšomre	miṣwotɔyw
to=loving=him	and=to=keeping	commandments=his

I said, "Please, O YHWH, God of heaven, great and awesome God, who keeps covenant and mercy with those who love him and keep his commandments!" (Neh 1:5)

A simple address consisting of the proper noun יהוה *yhwh* "YHWH" is followed by two complex addresses—אלהי השמים *ʔᵉlohe haššɔmayim* "God of heaven" and האל הגדול והנורא *hɔʔel haggɔdol wəhannorɔʔ* "great and awesome God"—both modified by a zero-relative clause. Again, this lengthy compound address occurs within the context of a prayer addressed to God. While the data is limited, it can be argued that this structure would have been rarely employed in human-to-human dialogues in ancient Israel.

2.3.5.2. Repetition

A compound address can be constructed, either partially or entirely, through the repetition of a simple address consisting of a proper or common noun. There are five examples of compound addresses in our corpus in which a simple address is repeated consecutively, such as the repetition of אברהם *ʔabrɔhɔm* "Abraham" in (15):[35]

(15) ויקרא אליו מלאך יהוה מן השמים ויאמר אברהם אברהם ויאמר הנני

wayyiqrɔʔ	ʔelɔyw	malʔak	yhwh	min-haššɔmayim
and=he.called	to=him	messenger.of	YHWH	from-the=heavens

wayyoʔmɛr	ʔabrɔhɔm	ʔabrɔhɔm	wayyoʔmɛr	hinneni
and=he.said	Abraham	Abraham	and=he.said	behold=me

The LORD's messenger called to him from heaven, "*Abraham! Abraham!*" And he answered, "Here I am!" (Gen 22:11)

Two examples of compound addresses consist of two simple addresses repeated twice or three times, as in (16):[36]

(16) והמלך לאט את פניו ויזעק המלך קול גדול בני אבשלום אבשלום בני בני

wəhammɛlɛk	lɔʔaṭ	ʔɛt-pɔnɔyw	wayyizˤaq	hammɛlɛk
and=the=king	he.covered	ACC-face=his	and=he.cried.out	the=king

---

[35] See §3.2.1 in appendix B for a list of compound addresses consisting of a simple address repeated twice in a row.

[36] See §3.2.2 in appendix B for a list of compound addresses consisting of two simple addresses repeated twice or three times.

FREE FORMS OF ADDRESS: INTERNAL STRUCTURE   43

qol	gəḏol	bəni	ʔaḇšɔlom	ʔaḇšɔlom	bəni	bəni
voice	great	son=my	Absalom	Absalom	son=my	son=my

The king covered his face and cried out loudly, "*My son, Absalom! O Absalom, my son, my son!*" (2 Sam 19:5)

There are three instances of compound addresses that consist of two addresses, with one of them repeated twice, as in (17):[37]

(17) ואלישע ראה והוא מצעק אבי אבי רכב ישראל ופרשיו

wɛʔlišoʕ	roʔɛ	wəhuʔ	məṣaʕeq	ʔɔḇi	ʔɔḇi
and=Elisha	seeing	and=he	crying	father=my	father=my

rɛḵɛḇ	yiśrɔʔel	upɔrɔšɔyw
chariot.of	Israel	and=horsemen=its

While Elisha was watching, he was crying out, "*My father, my father! Israel's chariot and its horsemen!*" (2 Kgs 2:12)

From a functional perspective, the repetition of simple addresses, along with the interjections, serves to fulfill what Roman Jakobson (1960, 354) refers to as the "emotive function" of verbal communication. This function aims to convey the speaker's emotional attitude towards the addressee and the content of their speech. For example, in (15), the repetition of the proper noun "Abraham" conveys a sense of urgency on the part of the speaker, who is a messenger of YHWH. This urgency is intended to prevent Abraham from proceeding with the act of sacrificing his son, Isaac (Hamilton 1995, 111; Hartley 2000, 209; Sarna 2001, 153). A similar sense of urgency can be detected in Exod 3:4, where YHWH calls out Moses's name twice, "*Moses, Moses!*," in an effort to keep him from approaching the burning bush.

The emotive function of repeating simple addresses becomes more apparent in example (16). When David receives the news of his son Absalom's death, he is overwhelmed with distress and sorrow, leading to outbursts of grief. The repetition of "Absalom" and the threefold repetition of "my son" intensify the depth and intensity of David's sorrow and anguish (Anderson 1989, 226; Bar-Efrat 1989, 211).

In example (17), the repetition of a simple address occurs in a similar context to that of (16): the speaker is faced with the imminent loss of his beloved addressee. When Elijah is taken up to heaven by a whirlwind, his disciple Elisha cries out in desperation. The repetition of "my father" followed by the coreferential noun phrases "Israel's chariot and its horsemen" emphasizes Elisha's mixed emotions of surprise, sorrow, and despair. Elisha's emotional state is further

---

[37] See §3.2.2 in appendix B for a list of compound addresses consisting of two simple addresses, one of which is repeated twice.

revealed as he tears his own clothes, a gesture symbolizing extreme grief, at the loss. Interestingly, the same address form is later used by Joash, the king of Israel, at Elisha's death-bed, as seen in example (9). Again, the repetition of "my father" serves to heighten Joash's profound sadness, which he expresses by weeping before him (2 Kgs 13:14).

2.3.5.3. Coordination

A compound address can be formed by combining two coreferential addresses with the coordinating conjunction ן‍ *w* "and," as in (18):[38]

(18) וכה אמר שמעי בקללו צא צא איש הדמים ואיש הבליעל

wkְo-ʔɔmar	*šimʕi*	*bəqaləlo*	*ṣe*	*ṣe*
and=so-he.said	Shimei	in=cursing=his	get.out	get.out
ʔiš	*haddɔmim*	*wəʔiš*	*habbəliyyɔʕal*	
Man.of	the=blood	and=man.of	the=worthlessness	

Shimei said as he cursed, "Get out! Get out! *You man of blood, (and) you man of worthlessness!*" (2 Sam 16:7)

In this example, during David's escape from Jerusalem in response to his son Absalom's rebellion, Shimei, a Benjamite from the house of Saul, curses David as he approaches Bahurim (2 Sam 16:5). Two complex addresses are employed, each consisting of the construct phrases, "man of blood" and "man of worthlessness." The construct form איש *ʔiš* "man of" is repeated, with two different nouns, "blood" and "worthlessness," serving as its *nomen rectum* (although in Gen 14:19, the construct form קנה *qone* "possessor" is not repeated). The two complex addresses are joined together by the coordinating conjunction ן‍ *w* "and." It is evident from the context that both complex addresses are referring to none other than David himself.

There is one compound address in our corpus that contains both a coordinating conjunction and an appositive, as in (19):

(19) ויאמר יעקב אלהי אבי אברהם ואלהי אבי יצחק יהוה האמר אלי

wayyoʔmer	*yaʕᵃqob*	*ʔlohe*	*ʔɔbi*	*ʔabrɔhɔm*
and=he.said	Jacob	God.of	my father	Abraham
weʔlohe	*ʔɔbi*	*yiṣḥɔq*	*yhwh*	*haʔomer*	*ʔelay*
and=God.of	my father	Isaac	YHWH	the=saying	to=me

Jacob said, "*O God of my father Abraham and God of my father Isaac, YHWH who said to me,* …" (Gen 32:10)

---

[38] See §3.3.1 in appendix B for a list of compound addresses consisting of two coreferential addresses linked by the conjunction *w*.

The two coreferential complex addresses, אלהי אבי אברהם *ʔlohe ʔəḇi ʔaḇrɔhɔm* "God of my father Abraham" and אלהי אבי יצחק *ʔlohe ʔəḇi yiṣḥɔq* "God of my father Isaac" are linked by the coordinating conjunction ו *wə* "and." They are in apposition to the following simple address, consisting of the proper noun יהוה *yhwh* "YHWH," which is modified by the ה- *h-* relative clause.[39]

To sum up, there are 119 compound addresses in our corpus. Almost all of these compound addresses (106 forms, constituting 89 percent of compound addresses) are formed by placing simple and complex addresses in apposition. There are a small number of compound addresses formed through the repetition of a simple address or the coordination of simple and complex addresses (13 forms, constituting 11 percent of compound addresses).

2.4. Semantic Categories

In addition to their grammatical categories, free forms of address can also be categorized based on their lexical meaning. The classification commonly used in modern languages was developed by Braun (1988, 9–11). To adapt it to the Biblical Hebrew system, I have slightly modified her categories and present the following scheme that will be employed throughout this study:

Table 2.4. Semantic Types of Free Forms of Address in Biblical Hebrew

	Category	Examples
1.	Personal Name (PN)	"David"
2.	Kinship Term (KT)[40]	"my father"
3.	Title (T)[41]	"commander"
4.	P/Matro/Andronymic[42]	"son of Ahitub"
5.	Group Address (GA)	"house of Israel"
6.	Evaluative Term (ET)[43]	"wicked one"
7.	Geographic Name (GN)	"Tyre"
8.	Gentilic	"Philistines"
9.	Other	"Altar! Altar!"

---

[39] See footnote 16.

[40] A kinship term is defined as any term that implies relationship by blood or marriage (Braun 1988, 9; Dickey 1996, 62).

[41] As Braun (1988, 10) notes, there is no consensus on the definition of 'title.' I define it as a term used when addressing a person or deity to express his/her social, political, or religious status, determined by a combination of factors such as rank, occupation, or age.

[42] P/Matro/Andronymic refers to terms that define addressees as son, daughter, or wife of someone.

[43] Evaluative terms refer to descriptive terms that express the speaker's attitudes and evaluation of the addressee (cf. Zwicky 1974, 792; Miller 2010a, 54). Revell (1996, 50) calls these terms "nonce epithets."

The following sections provide a description of the distribution patterns of these semantic categories. Each simple and complex address has been assigned a specific semantic type. Address forms can be broadly divided into two groups based on the types of addressees: those used for animate beings and those used for inanimate objects. The former group can be further subdivided into those used for human beings and those used for divine beings. In order to compare and contrast how these groups are addressed, I will discuss them in separate sections. In each section, I will examine cases where a simple or complex address is used alone, as well as cases where a compound address is used. Note that a simple or complex address consists of a single semantic type (e.g., "troublemaker of Israel" for ET), while a compound address is composed of two or more semantic types (e.g., "Hagar, servant of Sarai!" for PN + occupational T).

2.4.1 Addresses to Animate Beings

2.4.1.1. Human Beings

When addressing human being(s), the speaker may employ either a simple or complex address alone or a compound address. In our corpus, there are 330 instances in which a simple or complex address is used alone, while a compound address is used fifty-one times.

2.4.1.1.1. Simple/Complex Addresses Alone

Table 2.5 shows the frequency distribution of simple and complex addresses used alone when addressing human being(s):

Table 2.5. Simple/Complex Addresses to Human(s)[44]

	Category	Frequency
1.	PN	64
2.	KT	57
3.	T	49
4.	GA	39
5.	ET	13
6.	P/Matro/Andronymic	101
7.	GN	3
8.	Gentilic	2
9.	Other	2

The semantic category "P/Matro/Andronymic" immediately stands out in this table due to its higher frequency compared to other categories. However, this category is skewed by the dominance of one specific form, בן אדם *bɛn ʔɔdɔm* "son of man," which occurs ninety-two times in the book of Ezekiel. Although this

---

[44] See §1.1.1 in appendix C for a list of simple/complex addresses used alone for humans.

form takes the patronymic form, it should not be considered a typical patronymic that derives from the personal name of a father or paternal ancestor. As discussed earlier, it functions as a substitute for Ezekiel's personal name in the book of Ezekiel, that is, "*O Human!*" In light of this, the occurrences of this form are separated from the P/Matro/Andronymic category, leaving only nine remaining instances. Thus, P/Matro/Andronymic is placed after ET in the table.

Apart from this skewed P/Matro/Andronymic category, the two most frequent semantic types are PN and KT. This aligns with the cross-linguistic observation that PNs and KTs comprise the core lexical domain for free forms of address (Daniel and Spencer 2009, 632; Braun 1988, 9). As in example (5) above, most PNs are used to address a single person,[45] but they can also be used to address a group of people by employing the name of an eponymous ancestor.[46] It is also worthwhile to note that PN is exclusively used for equal or lower social relations, as will be discussed in §3.4.1.

About 50 percent of KTs are used literally to refer to the addressee(s) who are genetically related to the speaker, as in (6b) above.[47] The other half of KTs, however, have an "extended" meaning[48] and are used to address individuals or groups who are not biologically related to the speaker,[49] as demonstrated in (17)

---

[45] 43 times in total for 31 different names: "Abram" (Gen 15:1); "Hagar" (Gen 21:17); "Abraham" (Gen 22:1); "Jacob" (Gen 31:11); "Korah" (Num 16:6); "Samson" (Judg 16:9, 12, 14, 20); "Hannah" (1 Sam 1:8); "Samuel" (1 Sam 3:6); "Jonathan" (1 Sam 14:44); "Abner" (1 Sam 17:55; 26:14); "Ahimelech" (1 Sam 22:16); "Asahel" (2 Sam 2:20); "Mephibosheth" (2 Sam 9:6; 19:26); "David" (1 Kgs 12:16); "Elijah" (1 Kgs 19:9, 13); "Micaiah" (1 Kgs 22:15; 2 Chr 18:14); "Elisha" (2 Kgs 2:4); "Gehazi" (2 Kgs 5:25); "Jehu" (2 Kgs 9:22); "Ahaziah" (2 Kgs 9:23); "Jeremiah" (Jer 1:11; 24:3); "Pashhur" (Jer 20:6); "Hananiah" (Jer 28:15); "Baruch" (Jer 45:2); "Oholibah" (Ezek 23:22); "Gog" (Ezek 38:16); "Amos" (Amos 7:8; 8:2); "Daniel" (Dan 9:22; 10:12; 12:4, 9); "Jeroboam" (2 Chr 13:4); "Asa" (2 Chr 15:2); "Uzziah" (2 Chr 26:18).

[46] 21 times in total for 5 different names: "Israel" (Exod 32:4, 8; Deut 4:1; 5:1; 6:3, 4; 9:1; 10:12; 20:3; 27:9; Josh 7:13; 1 Kgs 12:16, 28; Ezek 13:4; 2 Chr 10:16); "Gilead" (Judg 12:4); "Moab" (2 Kgs 3:23); "Judah" (Jer 11:13; 2 Chr 20:17, 20); "David" (2 Chr 10:16).

[47] 30 times in total for 7 KTs: "my father" (Gen 22:7; 27:18, 34, 38 [2x]; Gen 48:18; Judg 11:36; Isa 8:4); "my son" (Gen 22:7, 8; 27:1, 8, 13, 18, 20, 21, 26, 37, 43; 48:19; 2 Sam 13:25; 1 Chr 22:11); "my sons" (1 Sam 2:24); "my brother" (Gen 33:9; 2 Sam 13:12); "my daughter" (Judg 11:35); "my sister" (2 Sam 13:11, 20); "my mother" (1 Kgs 2:20; Isa 8:4).

[48] I find the term *extended* coined by Dickey (2004) to be more appropriate than *fictive* by Braun (1988), Contini (1995), and Esposito (2009), as the latter has a connotation of "not genuine."

[49] "My brother" (2 Sam 20:9; 1 Kgs 9:13; 13:30); "my brothers" (Gen 19:7; 29:4; Judg 19:23; 1 Sam 30:23); "my daughter" (Ruth 2:2, 8, 22; 3:1, 10, 11, 16, 18); "my daughters" (Ruth 1:11, 12, 13); "my father" (1 Sam 24:12; 2 Kgs 5:13; 6:21); "my son" (Gen 43:29; Josh 7:19; 1 Sam 3:6; 4:16; 2 Sam 18:22); "my sons" (2 Chr 29:11).

above, where Elisha addresses Elijah as אבי *ʔɔḇi* "my father," despite not being his biological father.[50]

The category T can be further divided into two types according to its nature and function: honorific T and occupational T. Honorific T refers to conventional terms used to convey respect and deference to addressees who hold power and authority by virtue of their rank, status, or age.[51] In our corpus, there is only one term that fits this definition, that is, אדון *ʔɔḏon* "lord/master," which is typically used with a first-person common singular pronominal suffix, as in (12b).[52] Occupational T designates the addressee's profession or function. There are seven types of occupational Ts in our corpus, such as המלך *hammɛlɛḵ* "the king" in (12b).[53] In contrast to PN, T is almost always used for higher social relations (see §3.4.2).

GA is a term used to address a group of people. While other semantic types can also be used for addressing groups, GA does not fit into any of those categories. GAs used for humans can be further divided into two subcategories: ethnic terms and other descriptive terms. The former has the form of either "a noun phrase of PN/GN" (e.g., "house of Israel") or "all PN ± a relative clause" (e.g., "all Judah"),[54] while the latter consists of "a noun phrase ± a relative clause" (e.g., "my flock").[55]

ETs, which express the speaker's attitudes and evaluation of the addressee, can be divided into two categories: praise (20a) and insult (20b):

---

[50] A more detailed discussion of how KTs index the social relationship between speaker and addressee in Biblical Hebrew will be provided in §3.4.3.

[51] This definition is adapted from Pickett (2000, 843).

[52] Gen 23:6, 11, 15; 24:18; 42:10; 43:20; 44:18; Num 12:11; Judg 4:18; 1 Sam 1:15, 26 (2x); 22:12; 25:24, 26; 1 Kgs 1:17; 3:17, 26; 2 Kgs 6:5, 15; Jer 34:5 (with no pronominal suffix); Ruth 2:13.

[53] "The king(s)" (Judg 3:19; 1 Sam 17:55; 23:20; 26:22; 2 Sam 14:4; 15:34; 24:23; Jer 17:20; 19:3; 22:2; Esth 7:3; 2 Chr 25:7; 35:21); "man of God" (1 Kgs 17:18; 2 Kgs 1:9, 11, 13; 4:40); "seer" (Amos 7:12); "princes of Israel" (Ezek 45:9); "the king's son" (2 Sam 13:4); "shepherds" (Jer 23:1; Ezek 34:2, 7, 9); "the commander" (2 Kgs 9:5 [2x]).

[54] "Leaders of Shechem" (Judg 9:7); "house of Israel" (Jer 10:1; 18:6 [2x]; Ezek 11:5; 18:25, 29, 30, 31; 20:31, 39, 44; 33:11, 20; 36:22, 32; 44:6; Amos 3:1; 5:1); "inhabitants of Jerusalem" (Jer 19:3; 2 Chr 20:15, 20); "remnant of Judah" (Jer 42:15, 19); "all Judah" (2 Chr 15:2; 20:15); "all Israel" (2 Chr 13:4); "(all) Benjamin" (2 Chr 15:2); "all Judah who enter these gates to worship the LORD" (Jer 7:2); "all Judah (who enter these gates)" (Jer 17:20); "all Judah who are in the land of Egypt" (Jer 44:24); "all Judah who dwell in the land of Egypt" (Jer 44:26); "all the inhabitants of Jerusalem (who enter these gates)" (Jer 17:20).

[55] "All his company" (Num 16:6); "my people" (Ezek 37:12, 13); "my flock" (Ezek 34:17); "my people who dwell in Zion" (Isa 10:24); "all you exiles whom I sent away from Jerusalem to Babylon" (Jer 29:20).

(20a) וירא אליו מלאך יהוה ויאמר אליו יהוה עמך גבור החיל
wayyerɔʔ   ʔelɔyw   mallʔak̠   yhwh   wayyoʔmɛr
and=he.appeared to=him   messenger.of YHWH   and=he.said
ʔelɔyw   yhwh   ʕimməkɔ   gibbor   hɛḥɔyil
to=him   YHWH   with=you   mighty.of strength

YHWH's messenger appeared and said to him, "The LORD is with you, O mighty man of valor!" (Judg 6:12)[56]

(20b) ויהי כראות אחאב את אליהו ויאמר אחאב אליו האתה זה עכר ישראל
Wayhi   kirʔot   ʔaḥʔɔb̠   ʔɛt-ʔelyyɔhu   wayyoʔmɛr
and=it.was as=seeing Ahab   ACC-Elijah   and=he.said
ʔaḥʔɔb̠   ʔelɔyw   haʔattɔ   zɛ   ʕok̠er   yiśrɔʔel
Ahab   to=him   INTER=you   this   troubling Israel

When Ahab saw Elijah, he said to him, "Is it you, *troublemaker of Israel*?" (1 Kgs 18:17)[57]

Apart from the recurring phrase בן אדם *bɛn ʔɔdɔm* "O Human!" in the book of Ezekiel, there are nine address forms that fall into the P/Matro/Andronymic category. Five of them are used to refer to a group of people (e.g., "sons of Levi"),[58] while the remaining forms address either one or three individuals. These forms take the shape of patronymics (e.g., "son of Ahitub"),[59] matronymics (e.g., "sons of Zeruiah"),[60] or andronymics (e.g., "wife of Jeroboam").[61] It is noteworthy that all of the p/matro/andronymic addresses to individuals appear to convey a derogatory tone, as they occur in contexts in which the speaker rebukes the addressee(s).[62]

---

[56] ETs for praise include "blessed of Yahweh" (Gen 24:31), "mighty man of valor" (Judg 6:12), and "man greatly loved" (Dan 10:19).

[57] ETs for insult are "the rebels" (Num 20:10), "faithless children" (Jer 3:14), "rebellious house" (Ezek 12:25), "prostitute" (Ezek 16:35), "son of a perverse, rebellious woman" (1 Sam 20:30), "troublemaker of Israel" (1 Kgs 18:17), "my enemy" (1 Kgs 21:20), "baldhead" (2 Kgs 2:23 [2x]), and "wicked one" (Ezek 33:8).

[58] "Sons of Levi" (Num 16:7, 8); "sons of Israel" (Isa 31:6; 2 Chr 13:12; 30:6).

[59] 1 Sam 22:12.

[60] 2 Sam 16:10; 19:23.

[61] 1 Kgs 14:6.

[62] See Lande (1949, 35), who argues that the expression "wife of Jeroboam" carries a disparaging nuance. Kugel (2007, 599) finds a hint of condescension even in the patronymic-like expression בן־אדם *ben-ʔɔdɔm* "son of man," translating it as "little man" or "mere man." Block (1997, 30–31) shares the same view, pointing out that the expression highlights the distance between God and man.

There are three GNs and two instances of Gentilic forms, all of which are used to address an ethnic group of people.[63] The category labeled as Other consists of two noun phrases that do not seem to fit into any of the previously discussed semantic categories: הנער *hannoʕar* "lad" (1 Sam 17:58) and כרוב הסכך *kruḇ hassoḵeḵ* "guardian cherub" (Ezek 28:16).[64]

2.4.1.1.2. Compound Addresses

Compound addresses to humans can be categorized based on the semantic type that appears at the head of the address form. The frequency distribution of compound addresses to human(s) is presented in table 2.6:

Table 2.6. Compound Addresses to Human(s)[65]

Head	Structure	Frequency
T	Honorific T + Occupational T	19
	Honorific T + PN	2
	Occupational T + PN	1
PN	PN + Occupational T	6
	PN + PN	4
	PN + KT	2
	PN + ET	2
	PN + KT + KT	1
KT	KT + PN	4
	KT + KT + Other T	2
	KT + GA	1
	KT + PN + KT + KT + PN	1
	KT + PN + PN + KT + KT	1
ET	ET + ET	1
	ET + Occupational T	1
GA	GA + GA	2
	GA + Patronymic	1

As shown in table 2.6, there are 51 compound addresses headed by T, PN, KT, ET, or GA, while no examples are found with P/Matro/Andronymic, GN, or Gentilic at the head. When T comes as the head, the compound addresses are always used for social superiors. Furthermore, honorific T is never found after other semantic types but consistently precedes occupational T or PN. Thus, it can

---

[63] GNs include "Tyre" (Ezek 26:3), "Sidon" (Ezek 28:22), and "Jerusalem" (2 Chr 20:17). Gentilics are "Philistines" (1 Sam 4:9) and "Levites" (2 Chr 29:5).
[64] Whether הנער *hannoʕar* "lad" denotes an age or social position will be discussed in chapter 3.
[65] See §1.1.2 in appendix C for a list of compound addresses used for humans.

tentatively be argued that honorific T prefers the first position in compound addresses used for social superiors.⁶⁶

The majority of compound addresses with the structure honorific T + occupational T come from the term אדני המלך *ʔªḏoni hammɛlɛḵ* "my lord the king" as in (12b). It occurs eighteen times as a free form in our corpus, while its reverse form המלך אדני *hammɛlɛḵ ʔªḏoni* "O king, my lord," is never attested as a free form. The latter appears once as a bound form (2 Sam 14:15), but the former prevails as a bound form as well (39 times). Although it cannot be ruled out that המלך אדני *hammɛlɛḵ ʔªḏoni* "O king, my lord," was used as a free form in the biblical period, it is evident that the biblical writers strongly preferred אדני המלך *ʔªḏoni hammɛlɛḵ* "my lord the king." This is in stark contrast to the almost exclusive use of "O king my lord" in ancient Near Eastern writings during the second and first millennium BCE.⁶⁷

---

⁶⁶ Unfortunately, there are no examples in Biblical Hebrew or Epigraphic Hebrew for a combination of honorific T, KT, ET, and GA to make this claim stronger.

⁶⁷ For a free form, "O king my lord," see line 12 of the Egyptian Bentresh Stela, which was made to appear as a monument of Ramesses II, but which was actually written much later, either in the Persian or the Ptolemaic period. Examples of a bound form "the king my lord" abound in the Assyrian letters in the first millennium BCE as well as in the Ugaritic and Amarna letters in the second millennium BCE: RS 18.040:1; RS 18.113A:1; RS 34.148:5; RS 94.2391:1; EA 51; EA 53; EA 60; EA 63–65; EA 68; EA 70; EA 74–76; EA 78–79; EA 81; EA 83–85; EA 87–92; EA 94; EA 102–109; EA 112; EA 114; EA 116–119; EA 121–123; EA 125–126; EA 128–132; EA 135–144; EA 147–162; EA 164–166; EA 168; EA 171–172; EA 174–177; EA 179; EA 182–187; EA 189; EA 191–209; EA 211–212; EA 214–217; EA 221; EA 223–235; EA 237; EA 239–245; EA 248–262; EA 264–265; EA 267–275; EA 277; EA 279–290; EA 292–302; EA 304–305; EA 315; EA 317–321; EA 323–331; EA 335; EA 337; EA 362–366; EA 371; EA 378; SAA 1.1; SAA 1.29; SAA 1.31–39; SAA 1.41–60; SAA 1.62; SAA 1.64–67; SAA 1.70–78; SAA 1.80; SAA 1.82–85; SAA 1.87–94; SAA 1.96–102; SAA 1.104; SAA 1.106–110; SAA 1.112; SAA 1.115–119; SAA 1.121; SAA 1.124–125; SAA 1.128–139; SAA 1.143–144; SAA 1.146; SAA 1.148–150; SAA 1.152; SAA 1.155–156; SAA 1.158–161; SAA 1.163–165; SAA 1.171–177; SAA 1.179; SAA 1.181–186; SAA 1.188–190; SAA 1.192–202; SAA 1.204–208; SAA 1.210; SAA 1.212; SAA 1.216; SAA 1.219; SAA 1.222–224; SAA 1.226–227; SAA 1.229–231; SAA 1.233; SAA 1.235–243; SAA 1.245–246; SAA 1.249; SAA 1.251–252; SAA 1.256–260. Note that Abimilki, the ruler of Tyre, addresses the king of Egypt once with a free form, *be-li* LUGAL "my lord the king" (EA 150:18), but otherwise he always addresses him as LUGAL *be-li* "the king my lord" in his nine letters to him (EA 146–154). For the sake of comparison, the Hittite emperor was typically addressed by his officials as dUTU-*ši be-lí-ia* "(the) sun, my lord" (e.g., *HKM* 46:15), not as LUGAL *be-lí-ia* "the king my lord." The king of Mari was addressed simply as *be-lí-ia* "my lord" (e.g., ARM 27/1:1). There is an Aramaic letter by an Assyrian officer Bel-etir to his fellow officer, Pir-amurri, where the king of Assyria (Ashurbanipal) was referred to, not addressed, as *mry mlkʔ* "my lord the king" (VAT 8384:6).

When PN comes as the head of a compound address, it can be followed by occupational T, PN, KT, or ET. Similar to PN used alone, all compound addresses headed by PN are used for social inferiors, as in (12a).[68] KT can be followed by PN, KT, GA, or other T.[69] It may be used with a literal or extended meaning, indicating either an equal (e.g., "my brothers") or unequal (e.g., "my father"; "my son") relationship between the speaker and the addressee, as in (6b). When KT is used in an extended sense, as in (9), it also appears to highlight an intimate relationship.

2.4.1.2. Divine Beings

Similar to addresses to human(s), when addressing divine beings, the speaker can employ either a simple or complex address alone or a compound address.

2.4.1.2.1. Simple/Complex Addresses Alone

There are ninety-six simple and complex addresses used for divine beings. Almost 90 percent of them are used for the God of Israel (85 times), while the remaining addresses are for his messengers (9 times), Satan (once), and Baal (once). Table 2.7 presents the frequency distribution of simple and complex addresses to divine being(s):

Table 2.7. Simple/Complex Addresses to Divine Being(s)[70]

	Category	Frequency
1.	PN	51
2.	T	45

What stands out immediately from this table is the absence of KT. Unlike addresses to human(s), KT is never used to address divine being(s) in our corpus.[71] Furthermore, in comparison to the common images used to describe God in the Hebrew Bible, such as king and shepherd, the references to God as 'father' are

---

[68] Jer 34:4, in which Jeremiah the prophet addresses Zedekiah the king of Judah by his PN + occupational T, may not be an exception to my claim, as he functions as a spokesperson for God, the ultimate king of Israel. At this moment, Jeremiah speaks to the king as God does. The relationship between prophets and kings in ancient Israel is complex. In order to figure out the exact nature of their relationship, therefore, a variety of factors must be considered. In chapter 3, I will discuss their relationship from the perspective of address usage.
[69] The titles that do not fit into any of the honorific or occupational Ts, such as רכב ישראל ופרשיו *reḵeḇ yiśrɔʔel upɔrɔšɔyw* "Israel's chariot and its horsemen" in 2 Kgs 2:12 and 13:14 are classified as 'Other T.'
[70] See §1.2.1 in appendix C for a list of simple/complex addresses used alone for divine beings.
[71] Note that there are two poetic passages outside our corpus in which "my father" occurs as a free form of address used for God (Jer 3:4, 19).

relatively few.[72] This is quite remarkable considering that attributing fatherhood to deities was so common in the surrounding nations, where their gods were freely addressed as 'father.'[73] The limited mentions of God's fatherhood in the Hebrew Bible might be explained by polemical concerns (vanGemeren 1988, 397).

All the free forms of address directed to divine being(s) are concentrated in PN and T. With the exception of three instances, all the PNs come from addresses to God (e.g., אל *ʔel*, אלהים *ʔᵉlohim*, האלהים *hɔʔᵉlohim*, יהוה *yhwh*, יהוה צבאות *yhwh ṣᵉbɔʔot*).[74] Thus, God is addressed more often by PN than any other semantic type in our corpus. The question arises as to why the supreme being in the Israelite religion is addressed by PN, a term typically used for social equals and inferiors in human society. The practice of addressing God by PN, however, aligns with the practices in other ancient Near Eastern religions, in which deities were commonly addressed by their PNs. Addressing God by PN initially emphasized intimacy rather than social hierarchy. However, after the Israelites' return from Babylon, the use of אדני *ʔᵃdonɔy* "(my) Lord" as a surrogate began to develop to express distance between God and humans, as reflected in the use of χυριος "Lord" for יהוה *yhwh* "YHWH" in the LXX.[75]

Three PNs are used for divine beings other than God: a messenger of God, (גבריאל *gabriʔel* "Gabriel" [Dan 8:16]), Satan (השטן *haśśɔṭɔn* "Satan" [Zech 3:2]), and Baal (הבעל *habbaʕal* "Baal" [1 Kgs 18:26]). Note that השטן *haśśɔṭɔn* "Satan" and הבעל *habbaʕal* "Baal" may be taken as personal names, as the combination of definite article and common noun, through usage, can function as the equivalent of a proper name (e.g., האלהים *hɔʔᵉlohim* "God"; הנהר *hannɔhɔr* "the Euphrates").[76]

T can be either divine or honorific. Divine T refers to the appellatives for YHWH (e.g., אלהי ישראל *ʔᵉlohe yiśrɔʔel* "God of Israel" [1 Kgs 8:26]; אלהינו *ʔᵉlohenu* "our God" [Dan 9:17]; אלהי *ʔᵉlohay* "my God" [Ezra 9:6]) and thus is exclusively used for God.[77] On the other hand, honorific T is used for God (אֲדֹנָי

---

[72] Deut 32:6; 2 Sam 7:14; Isa 63:16; 64:8; Jer 3:4, 19; 31:9; Mal 1:6; 2:10; Pss 68:5; 89:26; 1 Chr 17:13; 22:10; 28:6.

[73] For Sumero-Akkadian, Hittite, Egyptian, and Ugaritic examples, see *ANET* 385–86, 397, 365, and *COS* 1.103:344, respectively.

[74] See §1.2.1.1.1 in appendix C for a list of personal names for God of Israel, which includes common nouns functioning as proper names. I classify אל *ʔel*, אלהים *ʔᵉlohim*, and האלהים *hɔʔᵉlohim* as personal names, as they are unique appellatives that function more or less as names (*IBHS* §13.4b).

[75] The appearance of אדני *ʔᵃdonɔy* "(my) Lord" instead of יהוה *yhwh* "YHWH" in the first position of compound addresses in Dan 9:4, 15 might be an indication of this development.

[76] For more examples, see *IBHS* §13.6a.

[77] See §1.2.1.2.1 in appendix C for a list of divine Ts.

ʾᵃdonɔy "[my] Lord") and his messenger(s) (אדני ʾᵃdoni "my lord"; אדני ʾᵃdonay "my lords").[78]

2.4.1.2.2. Compound Addresses

There are sixty-seven compound addresses used for divine being(s) with all but one of them used to refer to God. Table 2.8 presents the frequency distribution of compound addresses to divine being(s):

Table 2.8. Compound Addresses to Divine Being(s)[79]

Head	Structure	Frequency
PN	PN + Divine T	31
	PN + PN	7
	PN + Divine T + Divine T	1
T	Honorific T + PN	27
	Divine T + Divine T + PN	1

All the examples headed by PN come from addresses to God, with the majority of PNs being *yhwh*. However, אדני ʾᵃdonɔy "(my) Lord" in Dan 9:4, 15 and אל *ʾel* "God" in Num 16:22 are construed as PNs, as they occupy the head position of compound addresses, which is typically held by יהוה *yhwh* "YHWH." The appellative אלהים *ʾᵉlohim* "God" following יהוה *yhwh* "YHWH" functions more or less as a divine name; and hence, is classified as a PN.[80] Except for Dan 9:4, where the divine T האל *hɔʾel* follows the PN אדני ʾᵃdonɔy "(my) Lord," all the divine Ts immediately following PN are forms derived from אלהים *ʾᵉlohim* "God," as in (10).[81]

Similarly, all the examples headed by T also come from addresses to God.[82] As is the case with compound addresses to human(s), the honorific T אדני ʾᵃdonɔy "(my) Lord" always occupies the first slot in a compound address to God. All the

---

[78] See §1.2.1.2.2 and §1.2.1.2.3 in appendix C for a list of honorific Ts.
[79] See §1.2.2 in appendix C for a list of compound addresses used for divine beings.
[80] "YHWH God" (2 Sam 7:25; 1 Chr 17:16, 17; 2 Chr 1:9; 6:41 [2x], 42).
[81] See §1.2.2.1 in appendix C for a list of examples of PN + Divine T.
[82] In Judg 6:22 we see Gideon crying out, אהה אדני יהוה *ʾᵃhɔh ʾᵃdonɔy yhwh* "Alas, (my) Lord YHWH!" What is interesting is that he does so right after a messenger of YHWH who was conversing with him has vanished from his sight. Thus, it appears that Gideon is identifying the messenger with YHWH. This is confirmed by the fact that throughout this story the narrator alternates Gideon's conversation partner between the messenger (vv. 12, 20) and YHWH (vv. 14, 16, 18, 23). For a discussion of how the messenger of YHWH is identified with YHWH himself in this passage, see Cole 2013, 64–65 and Webb 2012, 232–33.

examples in the category of honorific T + PN share the same form יהוה אדני *ʾᵃdonɔy yhwh* "(my) Lord YHWH."[83]

As we have seen above, PN usually precedes divine Ts that are headed by forms derived from אלהים *ʾᵉlohim* "God" (32 times). However, there is one exceptional case where two phrases headed by the divine T אלהי *ʾᵉlohe* "God of" are followed by the PN יהוה *yhwh* "YHWH," as in (19).

2.4.2. Addresses to Inanimate Objects

In the prose sections of the Hebrew Bible, it is uncommon for inanimate objects to be addressed.[84] There are a total of eight addresses used for inanimate objects in our corpus: seven simple/complex addresses used alone and one compound address. These addresses are directed towards various inanimate objects such as a city, stones, mountain(s), bones, breath, and altar. Table 2.9 presents the address forms used for inanimate objects:

Table 2.9. Addresses to Inanimate Object(s)

Form	Verse	Form	Verse
הר הגדול	Zech 4:7	העצמות היבשות	Ezek 37:4
הרי ישראל	Ezek 36:1, 4, 8	הרוח	Ezek 37:9
עיר שפכת דם בתוכה ...	Ezek 22:3	מזבח מזבח	1 Kgs 13:2

As can be seen in table 2.9, all the address forms used for inanimate objects come from two prophetic books, Ezekiel and Zechariah, except for one compound address מזבח מזבח *mizbeaḥ mizbeaḥ* "O Altar, Altar!", which is found in a historical book. Although this compound address is recorded in a historical book, it actually comes from the mouth of an unnamed prophet from Judah, and thus, all the address forms for inanimate objects in our corpus have their origins in prophetic utterances.

As discussed earlier, these address forms exemplify a rhetorical technique known as apostrophe, where the speaker direct their words to a dead or absent individual, or even an inanimate object. Thus, the inanimate addressees are naturally personified:

---

[83] See §1.2.2.4 in appendix C for a list of honorific T + PN. Note that the MT has the vowels of אלהים *ʾᵉlohim* "God" under the *Tetragrammaton* to avoid the repetition of *ʾᵃdonɔy* after the honorific T אדני *ʾᵃdonɔy*.

[84] However, addresses for inanimate objects are often found in the poetic section of the prophetic books, as they are called on to witness YHWH's judgment and consolation towards Israel (e.g., שמים ... ארץ *šɔmayim ... ʾereṣ* "O heavens!... O earth!" [Isa 1:2]; איים *ʾiyyim* "O coastlands!" [Isa 41:1]).

Zech 4:7	YHWH addresses the great mountain as if it could hear.
Ezek 36:1, 4, 8	Ezekiel addresses the mountains of Israel as if they could hear.
Ezek 22:3	Ezekiel describes the city as if it were shedding blood.
Ezek 37:4	Ezekiel addresses the dry bones as if they could hear and move.
Ezek 37:9	Ezekiel addresses breath as if it could hear and move.
1 Kgs 13:2	A man of God addresses the altar as if it could hear.

Since common-noun address forms used for these personified objects are definite by context, it can be argued that they function as quasi-proper nouns. Thus, the absence of the definite article in מזבח מזבח *mizbeaḥ mizbeaḥ* "O Altar! Altar!" in 1 Kgs 13:2 and עיר *ʿir* "O City!" in Ezek 22:3 can be explained in this way, although it may also result from the poetic nature of prophetic utterances.

2.5. Conclusion

In this chapter, I have examined the internal structure of free forms of address in Biblical Hebrew, categorizing them as simple, complex, and compound addresses based on the number of constituents in the address form. Through the classification based on grammatical and semantic categories, several meaningful patterns have emerged. First, out of 682 free forms of address in our corpus, 69 percent of them are simple addresses. Complex addresses in general, especially those consisting of a noun phrase plus a modifier, are rare in dialogues between two humans and are mostly found in special circumstances like prayer. Thus, they do not seem to be a common feature of everyday conversation between two humans in ancient Israel. Second, both simple and complex addresses are to be construed as definite. The absence of the definite article in common noun address forms can be explained in various ways. Third, compound addresses in Biblical Hebrew may be formed through apposition, repetition, or coordination of coreferential simple address(es) and/or complex address(es). Nearly 90 percent of compound addresses are formed by placing simple and complex addresses in apposition. Fourth, when a simple or complex address is used alone, the most frequently occurring semantic types are PN and KT. This aligns with the cross-linguistic phenomenon where PNs and KTs constitute the core lexical domain for free forms of address. Fifth, honorific T always occupies the first position in a compound address. Sixth, the biblical writers show a strong preference for the word order אדני המלך *ʔᵃdoni hammɛlɛḵ* "my lord the king," which is in stark contrast to the almost exclusive use of its reverse order "O king my lord" in other ancient Near Eastern writings during the second and first millennia BCE. Seventh, unlike addresses to human(s), KT is never used to address God in our corpus, possibly for polemical reasons. Finally, apostrophe, a rhetorical technique in which inanimate objects are addressed and personified, is prevalent in prophetic literature. Common-noun address forms may function as quasi-proper nouns.

3.
FREE FORMS OF ADDRESS: SOCIAL DYNAMICS

3.1. Introduction

Free forms of address are often considered "extragrammatical" because they do not play a significant role in the basic grammatical structure of a sentence (Daniel and Spencer 2009, 633). They neither hold the main constituency slot in the clausal syntax nor serve as an argument of another element of the sentence. However, free forms of address carry important social and cultural meanings. They encode information about the speaker's perception of him-/herself, the addressee, and the relationship between them in a speech context (Parkinson 1985, 1). As widely recognized in sociolinguistic research on address terms, address usage follows rules and exhibits regular patterns, rather than occurring randomly (Kroger 1982, 810; Parkinson 1985, 3). While these rules may change over time and vary across situations, languages, and cultures, sociolinguists have found that the speaker's choice of address forms is primarily influenced by two factors: the relationship between the speaker and the addressee, and the speech context (Fasold 1990, 1; Dickey 1996, 7; Qin 2008, 409). Competent speakers evaluate their relationship with the addressee in a given situation, consider the address rules in their speech community, and choose the most appropriate form—whether correct or intentionally wrong—from the available repertoire of address forms.[1] Thus, by examining the patterns in the speaker's choice of address forms, we can gain insights into the perceived social relationship between the speaker and the addressee, as well as the address rules operating in a specific speech context.

This chapter provides a descriptive analysis of address rules governing three nominal types of free forms of address: personal names (PNs), titles (Ts), and

---

A revised version of §3.4.1 and §3.4.2 in this chapter has been published as Young Bok Kim, "Free Forms of Address and the Cases of Expressive Shift in Biblical Hebrew," *Journal for Semitics* 30.2 (2021): 1–26.

[1] In this study, therefore, I am in favor of Hymes's (1966) broader concept of "communicative competence," which refers to a speaker's capability to function appropriately in a whole communicative situation rather than the Chomskian (1965) "linguistic competence," which merely refers to the capability to produce grammatical sentences.

kinship terms (KTs). These forms are most commonly used between two human beings in Biblical Hebrew prose.[2] Drawing on Brown, Gilman, and Ford's (Brown and Gilman 1960; Brown and Ford 1961) address theory and Brown and Levinson's (1987) politeness theory, I demonstrate that address usage is guided by the social relationship of the speech participants and the speech context in which the address occurs. After describing the general rules of address usage in Biblical Hebrew, I also explore potential instances of "expressive shift" as described by Brown and Gilman (1960, 270–73), which involve the tactical and strategic violation of address rules to convey the speaker's temporary feelings and attitudes. These rule-breaking cases produce powerful discourse-pragmatic effects, holding not only social and emotive significance but also of exegetical importance. The chapter is organized into three main sections: (1) theoretical frameworks; (2) data; (3) analysis.

3.2. Theoretical Frameworks

3.2.1. Brown, Gilman, and Ford's Address Theory

In this chapter, the social dynamics of free forms of address in Biblical Hebrew are discussed primarily within the context of Brown, Gilman, and Ford's (Brown and Gilman 1960; Brown and Ford 1961) sociolinguistic theory of address. Their pioneering cross-linguistic analyses of the use of the second-person pronouns in European languages and nominal forms of address in American English remain highly influential in the field of address theory.[3] A brief review of their articles has been provided in §1.2.2.1 and §1.2.2.2. Of central interest in this chapter are the theoretical contributions that they have made to address theory, which can be summarized as follows.

3.2.1.1. T/V Distinction

In their work from 1960, Brown and Gilman introduce the symbols of T and V as abbreviations for the putative origins in Latin *tu* and *vos*. These symbols are used to refer to the so-called "familiar" and "polite" second-person pronouns in French, German, Italian, and Spanish.

---

[2] For the significance of free forms of address used for and by God, angel(s), group(s), and inanimate being(s), see chapter 2.
[3] Before Brown, Gilman, and Ford, there were many works on the address pronouns in Shakespeare's works, including Abbott (1870), Franz (1900), and Byrne (1936). However, their works were the first comprehensive and comparative effort to theorize the use of the second-person pronouns in European languages as well as English, suggesting a "universal" pattern that underlies all languages.

3.2.1.2. Power and Solidarity

Brown and Gilman argue that the choice between T and V is influenced by two social considerations: power and solidarity. The "power semantic" emphasizes social inequality and differences between the speaker and the addressee based on their personal attributes and social roles that convey power differences (e.g., physical strength, wealth, age, sex, the role in the state, the army, or within the family). In situations of social inequality, those of inferior status are expected to use V while receiving T. As a result, the pronoun usage in this power relation is asymmetrical and nonreciprocal.

Conversely, a "solidarity semantic" highlights social equality and commonalities between the speaker and the addressee based on factors such as kinship ties, membership in political, religious, and professional groups, sex, birthplace, and the frequency of their contact. In situations of social equality, interlocutors who share commonalities are expected to exchange T, while those who perceive a sense of distance exchange V. Therefore, the pronoun usage in this context is symmetrical and reciprocal.

3.2.1.3. Diachronic Development

Brown and Gilman outline roughly four stages in the development of pronominal address in European languages:

1. In the fourth century, the Latin plural *vos* was initially used when addressing the emperor and gradually extended to include other prestigious individuals.
2. In medieval Europe, the power semantic dominated. Superior used T and received V,[4] while equals from higher social classes exchanged V and equals from lower classes used T.[5]
3. In the Early Modern period, there was a shift towards the solidarity semantic, which introduced a differentiation in pronominal address among equals. T was used for inferiors or intimate equals, while V was reserved for superiors or distant equals (see figure 3.1a).
4. From the nineteenth century onwards, the solidarity semantic gained prominence across all dyadic relationships. This led to the reciprocal T for solidary

---

[4] E.g., the nobility said T to commoners and received V; the priest said T to penitents and received V; the master of a household said T to his slave and received V; parents said T to children and received V; God says T to his angels and receives V in Froissart.

[5] In the drama of seventeenth century France, for example, the nobility and bourgeoisie address one another as V, whereas servants and peasantry use T among themselves.

relationships and reciprocal *V* for nonsolidary relationships.⁶ Subsequently, there was an expansion of *T* usage (see figure 3.1b).⁷

Figure 3.1. Brown and Gilman's Power and Solidarity Semantic

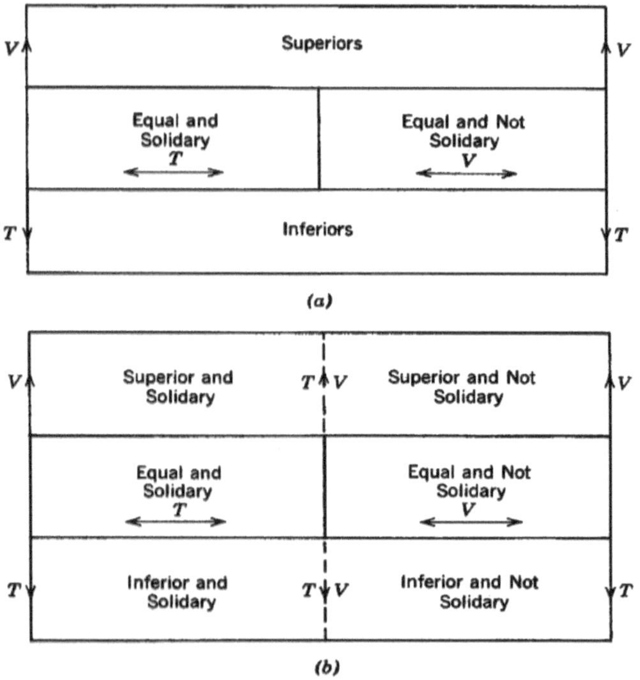

3.2.1.4. Correlation of Address, Social Structure, and Ideology

Brown and Gilman's research reveals that the usage of address forms is closely intertwined with social structure and ideological attitudes within a language community. In societies characterized by static and hierarchical structures, like the feudal society of medieval Europe, the dominant pattern is the nonreciprocal power semantic. However, in societies with social mobility and an equalitarian ideology, the reciprocal solidarity semantic emerges as a guiding principle in address usage.

3.2.1.5. Expressive Shift

Brown and Gilman argue that a switch between *T* and *V*, which violates a "group norm" of power and solidarity, may signal the speaker's "transient moods and

---

⁶ According to Brown and Gilman (1960, 264), the emergence of this reciprocal solidarity semantic was due to a change in the social structure of European societies that led to "social mobility and an equalitarian ideology."

⁷ E.g., parents and children exchange *T*; the master and his faithful servant exchange *T*.

attitudes" towards the addressee. This type of pronoun shift is frequently witnessed in Medieval and Early Modern European literature. For example, in order to express emotions such as contempt or anger, those who typically use *V* switch to *T* or an inferior addresses a superior using *T*. Likewise, irony or mockery can be conveyed when a superior uses *V* to address an inferior. Additionally, admiration or respect may be expressed through a switch to *V* by a superior towards an inferior.[8] The precise interpretation of the speaker's attitude depends not only on the violated address norm but also on the contextual information, encompassing their accompanying words, actions, and the overall setting.

3.2.1.6. Address in American English

According to Brown and Ford (1961), while American English does not have a *T/V* distinction in the second person pronominal system, the distinction can be achieved through nominal forms of address. They observe that the principal variants are first name (FN, e.g., James) and title plus last name (TLN, e.g., Professor Pardee), which exhibit three dyadic patterns: reciprocal exchange of FN between intimates, reciprocal exchange of TLN between newly introduced adults, and nonreciprocal exchange of FN and TLN, where TLN is used for individuals of higher age or occupational status and FN is used for those of lower status. Thus, power and solidarity semantics are also present in American English, albeit using different grammatical structures. Brown and Ford further discuss the use of less significant address variants, organizing them based on the level of deference: title (T, e.g., Sir, Madam, Ma'am, Miss) being most deferential, last name (LN, e.g., Jones) falling between TLN and FN, and multiple names (MN, e.g., several versions of the proper name for the same addressee) being the least deferential. As the relationship between interlocutors develops over time, there is a progression from more deferential to more intimate forms of address (mutual T → nonreciprocal T and TLN → mutual TLN → nonreciprocal TLN and LN → mutual LN → nonreciprocal LN and FN → mutual FN → nonreciprocal FN and MN → mutual MN). However, it should be noted that some steps may be skipped in actual dyads.

3.2.1.7. Linguistic Universal

Based on the patterns of nominal address in American English and the behavior of pronominal address in various European and non-European languages, Brown and Ford (1961, 380) go so far as to claim that the "linkage in personal address of intimacy and condescension, distance and deference" is a "linguistic universal." In his monograph *Social Psychology*, Brown (1965, 92) summarizes the findings

---

[8] The examples of expressive shifts are witnessed in non-European languages as well, such as in Yoruba (Oyetade 1995, 531), Mijikenda (McGivney 1993, 31), and postrevolutionary Iranian Persian (Keshavarz 1988, 570).

presented in his earlier articles and reconfirms his claim by formulating an "invariant norm of address": "the linguistic form that is used to an inferior in a dyad of unequal status [X] is, in dyads of equal status, used mutually by intimates; the form used to a superior in a dyad of unequal status [Y] is, in dyads of equal status, used mutually by strangers." This can be illustrated as shown in figure 3.2.

Figure 3.2. Brown and Ford's Linguistic Universal in Abstract Terms

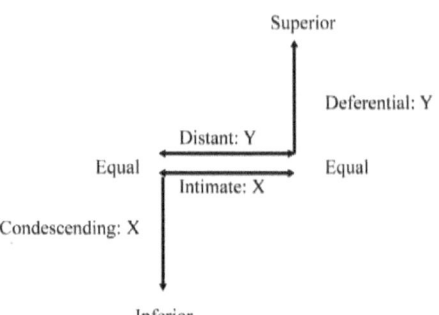

Brown, Gilman, and Ford's articles sparked a wave of studies on address forms in different languages and societies, which can be divided into two broad groups. First, many of these studies have provided findings that support their claim of a "linguistic universal." For example, Dan I. Slobin (1963) investigated the use of second person pronouns in Yiddish—the singular *du* and the plural *ir*, finding that *du* is used both towards intimates and as a downward address, while *ir* is used both as an upward address and towards nonintimates.[9] However, there are also works that highlight language, group, and individual peculiarities and differences. Parkinson (1985, 71), for instance, reports a striking phenomenon in Egyptian Arabic known as "address inversion," where a father addresses his sons and daughters with the term بابا *bābā* "daddy." According to Braun (1988, 309), the reciprocation of a senior kinship term to a junior is a normal expression of affection and authority, especially when speaking to children, and this phenomenon can be found in various languages such as Georgian, Italian, and Romanian.[10]

---

[9] For studies that confirm Brown and Ford's "linguistic universal," see Kroger, Cheng, and Leong (1979) for Chinese; Hijirida and Sohn (1983) for Japanese and Korean; Kroger, Wood, and Beam (1984) for Greek; Kroger and Wood (1992) for German; Qin (2008) for Chinese.

[10] For studies that highlight language particulars in terms of address usage, see Bates and Benigni (1975) for Italian; Kuglin (1977) for German and Turkish; Wales (1983) for Early Modern English; Oyetade (1995) for Yoruba; and Dickey (1996) for ancient Greek. Also, for a complete reanalysis of Brown and Gilman's presentation of the *T/V* system according to the concept of "indexical orders," see Silverstein 2003, 204–11.

The above observations provide the *raison d'être* for my analysis of free forms of address in Biblical Hebrew. Like modern English, Biblical Hebrew does not exhibit a T/V distinction in its second person pronominal system. However, the distinction can be achieved in nominal forms of address, especially with the alternation between PNs and Ts. Currently, there is no comprehensive study that describes these two address forms in Biblical Hebrew within the framework of Brown, Gilman, and Ford's address theory. Thus, one of the aims of this chapter is to apply their bi-dimensional power/solidarity model and examine whether the usage of nominal address in Biblical Hebrew aligns with their claim of a "linguistic universal" or if it exhibits unique rules and patterns. Additionally, I aim to identify possible instances of "expressive shift," where address rules in Biblical Hebrew are strategically violated to convey the speaker's temporary feelings and attitudes.

3.2.2. Brown and Levinson's Politeness Theory

In this chapter, particular attention is given to KTs within the framework of Brown and Levinson's pragmatic theory of politeness.[11] While Brown, Gilman, and Ford's address theory has proven to be a useful tool for describing address phenomena in languages that have a T/V pronominal distinction, its applicability to languages with more complex systems of nominal address, especially KTs, has often been questioned by some scholars (e.g., Braun 1998, 6–7). Brown and Levinson offer a fresh perspective to address research by considering addressing as a behavioral strategy aimed at preserving the interlocutor's face. The following are their notable contributions to the field of address theory.

3.2.2.1. Face

Drawing upon Erving Goffman's (1967, 5) concept of face,[12] Brown and Levinson (1987, 61) define face as the "public self-image" that individuals strive to establish in social interactions within a society. In other words, face is "one's situated identity" (Holtgraves 2001, 38). One may "lose" it when his/her identity is not validated during an interaction and "save" it when he/she successfully maintains his/her challenged identity. Thus, face requires constant attention during

---

[11] For an extensive review of Brown and Levinson's work, see §1.3.7.

[12] Goffman (1967, 5) defines the term "face" as "the positive social value a person effectively claims for himself by the line others assume he has taken during a particular contact." His concept of face is modelled on the Chinese concept of face, which was identified as a key component of Chinese culture more than a hundred years ago in the writings of two missionaries, Smith (1894, 16–18) and Macgowan (1912, 301–12). Goffman employs a dramaturgical metaphor in which he likens daily face-to-face interaction to theatrical performance; people are actors on a stage, and those who watch their performances are the audience. Face is like a mask that an actor chooses to put on in a given situation. He is emotionally attached to it, strives to maintain it by using certain strategies, and often loses it.

interpersonal communication. Inspired by Émile Durkheim's (1912, 427–555) differentiation between positive and negative rites, as well as Goffman's (1967, 62–76) distinction between presentational and avoidance rituals, Brown and Levinson (1987, 61) propose that an individual's face consists of two universal desires: the desire for approval and solidarity, referred to as "positive face," and the desire for autonomy and unimpeded freedom of action, termed "negative face."

3.2.2.2. Face Threatening Acts (FTA)

These two desires, whether belonging to the hearer or the speaker, can be jeopardized by certain inherently face-threatening acts (FTAs) that occur during social interactions. For example, acts such as apology and confession pose a threat to the positive face of the speaker as they undermine the speaker's standing, while acts like promise, acceptance of offer, excuse, and thanks pose a threat to the negative face of the speaker as they hinder the speaker's desire to avoid imposition. On the other hand, acts such as disagreement, challenges, criticism, contempt, accusations, insults, and complaint pose a threat to the positive face of the hearer as they express disapproval towards the hearer, while acts like order, request, offer, suggestion, advice, and warning pose a threat to the negative face of the hearer as they restrict the hearer's autonomy. The typology of FTAs is depicted in figure 3.3.

Figure 3.3. Typology of Face-Threatening Acts (FTAs)

Now, there exists a fundamental conflict for interlocutors. On the one hand, they need and want to perform these FTAs to each other's face. On the other hand, they also want to cooperatively maintain each other's face. It is this conflict that motivates interlocutors to engage in "face-work" or "politeness," which refers to the mitigation of face threats posed by FTAs towards one another.

3.2.2.3. Positive and Negative Politeness

According to Brown and Levinson (1987, 70), the mitigation of face threats can be achieved by employing positive and negative politeness that are oriented toward the positive and negative face of the hearer, respectively. Positive politeness is an "approach-based" strategy in which the speaker attempts to meet the hearer's desire for approval by emphasizing solidarity and intimacy. Brown and Levinson present fifteen behavioral sub-strategies of positive politeness (see table 1.5), and among them, the strategy of "use in-group identity markers" is particularly relevant to our study as KTs are frequently used as polite address terms to indicate shared membership between the speaker and the hearer (e.g., a king of northern Israel addressing the prophet Elisha as אבי *ʔɔḇi* "my father!" in 2 Kgs 6:21).

On the other hand, negative politeness is an "avoidance-based" strategy in which the speaker tries to respect the hearer's desire for autonomy by maintaining distance and being indirect. Brown and Levinson present ten sub-strategies of negative politeness (see table 1.5), and the strategy of *"give deference"* is most relevant to this chapter as honorific and occupational Ts are often used as deferential address terms to convey a status difference between the speaker and the hearer (e.g., אדני *ʔᵃdoni* "my lord!" or המלך *hammɛlek̠* "O king!"). According to Brown and Levinson, negative politeness is considered more polite than positive politeness because it avoids presuming solidarity, an assumption that may or may not be true from the hearer's point of view.[13]

3.2.2.4. Social Determinants of Politeness

Brown and Levinson (1987, 76–78) argue that the choice of a particular strategy by the speaker depends on the "weightiness" of the FTA that the speaker intends to perform, which refers to the degree of risk to the hearer's face. The higher the weightiness of the FTA, the more likely it is for the speaker to choose a more polite strategy.[14] The weightiness of the FTA is determined by the speaker's perception of three social factors: (1) the social distance between the speaker and the hearer; (2) the hearer's power over the speaker; and (3) the culturally influenced level of imposition associated with the FTA.

Increasing the weightiness of a given FTA is associated with increasing social distance between the speaker and the hearer (e.g., requesting a pen from a stranger is weightier than requesting it from a friend), increasing power of the hearer over the speaker (e.g., requesting a pen from a teacher is weightier than requesting it from a friend), and increasing level of imposition of the FTA (e.g., requesting to borrow a car is weightier than requesting to borrow a pencil). Therefore, it is more likely for the speaker to employ more polite strategies when addressing a person of higher status compared to someone of equal or lower status, when addressing

---

[13] One of the major claims made by Brown and Levinson (1987, 68) is that five super-strategies may be arranged in order of increasing levels of politeness: (1) bald on-record, (2) positive politeness, (3) negative politeness, (4) off-record, and (5) don't do the FTA. Their ordering of negative and positive politeness is consistent with that of Durkheim's (1912, 427–555) and Goffman's (1967, 62–76) ordering of negative rites/avoidance rituals as being more deferential than positive rites/presentational rituals.

[14] This must be balanced, however, against the need for efficient communication. In emergency situations, for example, concerns with politeness may be outweighed by the motive for clarity and efficiency. In this sense, therefore, all politeness can be viewed as violations of Grice's (1975) conversational maxims (quality, quantity, relevance, and manner).

a stranger instead of a friend, and when making a request for a significant favor rather than a small favor.

3.3. Data

There are forty-one PNs, eighty-one Ts, and sixty-four KTs, which account for 95 percent of the total number of the semantic categories used in address between two human beings in Biblical Hebrew prose. These address forms are used either alone or as part of a compound address. They appear in a wide variety of situations, ranging from private conversations between husband and wife (e.g., 1 Sam 1:8) to diplomatic negotiations between Israelite and Syrian kings (e.g., 1 Kgs 20:4).

Upon examination of these address forms, the resulting data include the semantic category of each form, the situational context in which each form is used, and the personal information of the speaker and the addressee, such as their age, gender, and occupation.[15] The relative power status of a speech participant is classified as "superior," "inferior," or "equal" to his/her interlocutor based on their social roles (e.g., kings, officers, servants, father, son), personal attributes (e.g., age, gender, wealth), and other contextual clues that indicate the power differential between them (e.g., posture and gesture).[16] The social distance between two interlocutors is classified as "close" or "distant" based on the degree of their like-mindedness that results from frequent contact (Brown and Gilman 1960, 258).[17]

---

[15] Such information may not always be available in the text. Especially, the ages of biblical characters are rarely provided. In many cases, however, their approximate ages can be inferred from the context.

[16] Revell (1996, 43–44) describes the status system in ancient Israel in terms of three levels: (1) the top level (kings, queens, prophets, and perhaps other religious leaders); (2) the middle level (members of the king's family, officers in the service of the king, elders, and anyone who does not belong to the top or bottom level); (3) the bottom level (servants). God and celestial beings are above this ranking system, always treated as superior to human beings. Further gradations within the same level are possible. For example, members of the king's family appear to be superior to king's officers, as can be seen in 2 Sam 14:29–32, where Absalom, a king's son, treats Joab, the commander-in-chief in Israel, as a subordinate. In this chapter, I use Revell's tripartite scheme as a starting point for attempting to determine the status of the interlocutors in our corpus. In the course of my discussion below, however, I attempt to refine his scheme from the perspective of address usage, questioning some of his assumptions and interpretations, such as his claim that kings and prophets are equal in status.

[17] The term (social) "distance" is the most often used label for the horizontal dimension of interlocutor relations in sociolinguistics. Other terms used for this dimension include solidarity, closeness, familiarity, and relational intimacy. See Spencer-Oatey (1996, 3) for a list of labels and glosses used for the variable "social distance." Following Brown and Gilman (1960, 258) and Brown and Levinson (1987, 76–77), I take social similarity/difference based on the frequency of interaction between two interlocutors as a key determinant of levels of

All this information is categorized as a separate row in the data table according to the following structure:

Table 3.1. Data Table for Address Forms

Verse	Form	Semantic	S > A	P	D	Context
2 Sam 9:6	Mephibosheth	PN	David > Mephibosheth 40s[18] > 20s Male > Male King > Friend's son	s>i	d	Doing Mephibosheth a favor for his father's sake
1 Sam 17:55	King	occupational T	Abner > Saul Younger than Saul? > 60s?[19] Male > Male Commander > King	i>s	c	Responding to Saul who asked him about David
2 Sam 13:12	My brother	KT	Tamar > Amnon Teen?[20] > 20? Female > Male half-sister > half-brother	e>e	c	Trying to keep Amnon from raping her

Note: S = speaker; A = addressee; P = power relation; D = social distance; PN = personal name; T = title; KT = kinship term; s = superior; e = equal; i = inferior; c = close; d = distant.

---

social distance. Thus, I regard the following relationships as "close": members of a nuclear family (e.g., Abraham and Isaac), friends (e.g., Jonadab and Amnon), lovers, and those who have worked together for a common purpose for a long time (e.g., Saul and Abner). Acquaintances (e.g., Absalom and Hushai) and strangers (e.g., Rebekah and Abraham's servant), however, are considered "distant." Role relationships are commonly used in the field of address studies to identify and illustrate a given degree of social distance, as we all have prototypical conceptions of the nature of the types of relationships.

[18] The text does not tell us how old David and Mephibosheth are when they first meet. However, their appropriate ages may be inferred from the context in the following way. David is thirty years old when he begins to reign at Hebron right after the death of Saul and Jonathan (2 Sam 5:4). Mephibosheth is five years old when Saul and Jonathan die (2 Sam. 4:4). Thus, David is twenty-five years older than Mephibosheth. He begins to reign in Jerusalem when he is about thirty-seven years old (2 Sam 5:5) and meets Mephibosheth in Jerusalem (2 Sam 9:13) sometime before he commits adultery with Bathsheba (2 Sam 11:1–4). According to McFall's (2010, 527) reckoning, David is about fifty years of age at the time of his adultery with Bathsheba. Therefore, David is between thirty-seven and fifty years old, and Mephibosheth is between twelve and twenty-five years old when they first meet.

[19] The determination of Saul's age at the time of David's victory over Goliath is based on the assumption that he is 30 years old when he is selected by God to be the first king of Israel. See McFall 2010, 527.

[20] It is impossible to determine the age of Tamar when she was raped by Amnon. She appears to be a couple of years younger than Absalom who was probably about seventeen years old at the time of the rape of his sister. See McFall 2010, 527.

In most cases, the power relation and social distance between the interlocutors can be assessed with a fair degree of confidence. However, there are some instances where determining these two variables with certainty is challenging due to a lack of information. For example, it is unclear whether the relationship between Jahaziel the Levite and King Jehoshaphat is close or distant when the former encourages the latter to fight against the Moabites and Ammonites (2 Chr 20:15). In such cases, a question mark is placed in the data cell to indicate uncertainty regarding the status and/or distance.

My objective is to describe general rules of address based on relatively clear cases, including a correlation between status/distance and the speaker's choice of address forms. Then, I investigate the uncertain cases, attempting to determine the most likely possibilities for status and/or distance based on the address rules observed in the clearer cases. Finally, I suggest potential instances of expressive shift that strategically violate the norms of address to communicate the speaker's momentary attitude toward the addressee.

3.4. Analysis

3.4.1. Personal Names

Personal names (PNs) are considered prototypical forms of address. Naming individuals is a practice found across various human societies, as acknowledged by most anthropologists (Murdock 1945, 124; Lévi-Strauss 1966, 161; Alford 1988, 1; Brown 1991, 181).[21] Typically, parents assign a PN to their child at birth, and unless special circumstances arise, the child usually does not seek to change it. Through naming, parents individualize, classify, and connect their child's identity to his/her community (Bramwell 2016, 279).

The ancient Israelite society portrayed in the Hebrew Bible follows this universal practice. It was typically the mother's responsibility to name the child (e.g., Gen 4:25; 19:37–38; 29:31–30:24; 35:18; 38:4–5; Judg 13:24; 1 Sam 1:20; 4:21; 1 Chr 4:9; 7:16). However, in certain cases, the father took on the task of naming (e.g., Gen 4:26; 5:3, 29; 16:15; 38:3; Exod 2:22; 1 Chr 7:23) and sometimes even altered the mother's choice (Gen 35:18).[22] There were instances where nonparental figures,

---

[21] While naming behavior is a cultural universal, the types of names and the ways in which they are bestowed and used in social interaction vary from society to society See, for example, Alford (1988, 2–4), who provides a detailed description of the naming practices of two societies, the Dogon of West Africa and the Iroquois of northeastern United States, to illustrate the cross-cultural variability in naming practices. A Dogon child receives three given names plus a surname from the eldest male in the child's paternal group three weeks after he/she is born. An Iroquois child, however, is provided with a single given name, which is selected at or even before the child's birth by the mother or sometimes the maternal grandmother.

[22] For a survey of naming practices in the ancient Near East, see Seymour 1983, 108–20.

including God, performed the naming (e.g., Gen 17:19; Exod 2:10; 2 Sam 12:25; Isa 8:3; Hos 1:4, 9; Ruth 4:17). Furthermore, birth names of individuals were occasionally changed by God and others at important junctures in their lives (e.g., Abram to Abraham [Gen 17:5]; Joseph to Zaphenath-Paneah [Gen 41:45]; Azariah to Abednego [Dan 1:7]). These acts of naming and renaming often involved prophetic declarations about the person's destiny (e.g., nations and kings will come from Jacob [Gen 35:10–12]), along with folk-etymologies or wordplays (e.g., Edom for the "red" stew exchanged for his birthright [Gen 25:30]).[23]

As widely recognized by biblical scholars, a PN in Israelite society carried more than a mere label for distinguishing individuals; it represented the essence, character, and reputation of the individual bearing it.[24] Hence, the act of naming signified an endowment of new essence, wherein the name-giver exerted power and authority over the one being named. For example, Adam demonstrated his dominion over the animals by naming them (Gen 3:19).[25] Additionally, a PN was believed to influence a person's destiny, often conveying blessings and hope (Greenstein 1992, 970).[26] Changing names could serve to determine or alter destiny. For instance, as Rachel was dying, she named her second son Ben-oni, meaning "son of my sorrow," but Jacob called him Benjamin, meaning "son of the right hand" (Gen 35:18). In doing so, Jacob sought to safeguard the child's future (Avrahami 2011, 25).[27]

---

[23] There are numerous works on the folk etymology of biblical names. See, for example, Krašovec 2010; Marks 1995; Zimmermann 1966.

[24] This can be supported by a number of etiological narratives about name giving and changing throughout the Hebrew Bible (e.g., Noah [Gen 5:29]; Abraham [Gen 17:5]). There are countless works dealing with the significance of PNs and naming giving in the Hebrew Bible, including Abba (1962, 501–8), Porten (1982, 33–51), Garsiel (1991), Greenstein (1992, 968–71), Demsky (1997, 27–37), and Avrahami (2011, 15–53).

[25] For more examples of naming that marks authority and control, see Avrahami (2011, 19–20), who conveniently classifies them into three groups according to the realms in which they occur in the Hebrew Bible: theological (e.g., YHWH's changing of Abram to Abraham in Gen 17:5), political (e.g., the king of Babylon's changing of the name Mattaniah to Zedekiah in 2 Kgs 24:17), and geographical (the Danites' changing of the name Laish to Dan in Judg 18:29).

[26] The etymology, structure, and/or meaning of PNs in Biblical Hebrew are not of primary interest in this study, and thus will not be discussed here. Hebrew onomastics has been widely studied, as can be seen in Singerman's (2001, 18–46) extensive bibliography on biblical names. To add a few recent works to that list, Hess (2015) and Golub (2017).

[27] The same belief is held in the Babylonian Talmud, which states that one of four ways to avoid something evil happening to a person is to change his/her name: וא״ר יצחק ד׳ דברים מקרעין גזר דינו של אדם אלו הן צדקה צעקה שינוי השם ושינוי מעשה...שינוי השם דכתיב (בראשית יז, טו) שרי אשתך לא תקרא את שמה שרי כי שרה שמה וכתיב וברכתי אותה וגם נתתי ממנה לך בן
wʔ"r yṣḥq d'dbrym mqrʕyn gzr dynw šl ʔdm ʔlw hn ṣdqh ṣʕqh šynwy hšm wšynwy mʕśh ...

3.4.1.1. Position and Distribution

There are four address types in which PNs are used: (1) a PN used alone (e.g., אבנר ʔaḇner "Abner!"); (2) a PN used at the beginning of a compound address (e.g., שמואל בני šəmuʔel bəni "Samuel, my son!"); (3) a PN used in the middle of a compound address (e.g., בני אבשלום אבשלום בני bəni ʔaḇšɔlom ʔaḇšɔlom bəni "My son, Absalom, Absalom, my son, my son!"); (4) a PN used at the end of a compound address (e.g., אדני אליהו ʔᵃḏoni ʔeliyyɔhu "My lord, Elijah!"). As discussed in §3.4.1.2, the first two types—address forms composed of a PN alone (henceforth, APNs) and compound addresses headed by a PN (henceforth, HPNs)—are treated together in this section as they convey the same power relationship between the speaker and the addressee in our corpus. However, the other two types convey different power relationships that depend on what comes at the beginning of the compound addresses. Those in which a T or a KT appears at the beginning will be discussed in §3.4.2 and §3.4.3.[28]

In our corpus, there are twenty-three APNs and seven HPNs, accounting for 15 percent of the total free forms of address used between two human beings. Table 3.2 shows the distribution of addresses by APN and HPN according to the books of the Hebrew Bible. Most of these examples are found in Samuel and Kings, which provide ample instances of speech by a superior to an inferior.

Table 3.2. Number of APNs and HPNs in Each Book of the Hebrew Bible

Book	# of APNs	# of HPNs
Numbers	1	
Judges	4	
1 Samuel	5	1
2 Samuel	3	1
1 Kings	1	
2 Kings	4	1
Jeremiah	2	1
Esther		2
1 Chronicles		1
2 Chronicles	3	
Total	23	7

šynwy hšm dktyb (brʔšyt yz, ṭw) śry ʔštk lʔ tqrʔ ʔt šmh śry ky śrh šmh wktyb wbrkty ʔwth wgm ntty mmnh lk bn And Rabbi Isaac said: "Four things avert the evil decree (by God) on man: charity, prayer, change of one's name, and change of one's deeds ... change of one's name, as it is written: 'As for Sarai your wife, you shall not call her name Sarai, but Sarah shall be her name' (Gen 17:15), and it is also written: 'And I will bless her, and I will also give you a son from her'" (Rosh Hash. 16b).

[28] There are only eight address forms that do not begin with a PN, a T, or a KT. They are excluded from our study.

3.4.1.2. Pattern

3.4.1.2.1. Superior to Inferior

The most noticeable pattern of APNs or HPNs is their usage in power relations, primarily by superiors towards inferiors.[29] Out of the thirty cases of APNs or HPNs, twenty-two involve superior-inferior dyads. Table 3.3 displays APNs and HPNs used by superiors towards inferiors, which can be categorized into three groups based on the factors determining the power relations between the speaker and the addressee: occupation/position within the family (##1–17), nonreciprocal address pattern (##18–20), and speech context (##21–22).

Table 3.3. APNs and HPNs Used by Superiors to Inferiors

#	Relation	Speaker	Form	Semantic	D	Context	Verse
1, 2	King > Queen	Xerxes	Queen Esther[30]	PN+T	c	Pleased with Esther and willing to grant her wish	Esth 5:3; 7:2
3	King > Commander	Saul	Abner	PN	c	Inquiring of Abner about David who killed Goliath	1 Sam 17:55
4		Jehoram	Jehu	PN	d	Greeting Jehu who was coming to kill him	2 Kgs 9:22
5	King > Friend's Son	David	Mephibosheth	PN	d	Doing Mephibosheth a favor for his father's sake	2 Sam 9:6
6		David	Mephibosheth	PN	c[31]	Questioning Mephibosheth's allegiance	2 Sam 19:26
7	Leader > Rebel	Moses	Korah	PN	c?	Rebuking Korah for rebelling against him	Num 16:6
8	Queen Mother > Commander	Jezebel	Zimri, murderer of his lord	PN+ET[32]	d	Greeting Jehu who came to kill her	2 Kgs 9:31

---

[29] Lande (1949, 28) also detects this tendency, but her list of exceptions is quite different from mine.
[30] Note that PN comes before T in Hebrew: אֶסְתֵּר הַמַּלְכָּה ʔester hammalkɔ "Queen Esther!"
[31] In contrast to case #5, where David and Mephibosheth had just met, I view their relationship as close here, as I assume that it has developed over time (2 Sam 9:11).
[32] Evaluative terms (ET) refer to descriptive terms that express the speaker's attitudes and evaluation of the addressee (cf. Zwicky 1974, 792). Revell (1996, 50) calls these terms "nonce epithets."

Table 3.3. APNs and HPNs Used by Superiors to Inferiors (cont.)

#	Relation	Speaker	Form	Semantic	D	Speech Context	Verse
9	Prophet > Disciple	Elijah	Elisha	PN	c	Asking Elisha not to follow him	2 Kgs 2:4
10		Jeremiah	Baruch	PN	c	Delivering God's word to Baruch that God will give him life	Jer 45:2
11	Prophet > Servant	Elisha	Gehazi	PN	c	Rebuking Gehazi for his greed and lies	2 Kgs 5:25
12	Priest > Servant	Eli	Samuel my son	PN+KT	c	Asking Samuel to let him know what God told him	1 Sam 3:16
13	Commander > Officer	Abner	Asahel	PN	d	Persuading Asahel not to pursue him	2 Sam 2:20
14	Husband > Wife	Elkanah	Hannah	PN	c	Comforting Hannah who had no child	1 Sam 1:8
15	Father > Son	Saul	Jonathan	PN	c	Taking an oath to put Jonathan to death	1 Sam 14:44
16		David	Absalom, my son, my son	PN+KT+KT	c	Mourning for the death of Absalom	2 Sam 19:1
17		David	Solomon my son	PN+KT	c	Commissioning Solomon to build the temple	1 Chr 28:9
18	King > Prophet	Ahab	Micaiah	PN	d	Asking Micaiah if he should go to battle against Aram	1 Kgs 22:15
19							2 Chr 18:14
20	King > Priest	Saul	Ahimelech	PN	d?	Pronouncing the death sentence upon Ahimelech who helped David	1 Sam 22:16
21	King > King	Abijah	Jeroboam	PN	d	Accusing Jeroboam and northern Israel of idolatry	2 Chr 13:4
22	Prophet > Prophet	Jeremiah	Hananiah	PN	d?	Prophesying Hananiah's death	Jer 28:15

In the first seventeen cases, it is evident that the speaker holds a superior position to the addressee based on the speaker's higher status, whether through occupation or family hierarchy.³³ The king is superior to the queen (##1–2), military commanders (##3–4),³⁴ and his friend's son (##5–6). The leader of a nation is superior to a rebel (#7). The queen mother is superior to a rebellious military commander (#8).³⁵ The prophets and priests are superior to their disciples and servants (##9–12). The military commander is superior to an officer (#13).³⁶ The husband is superior to the wife (#14).³⁷ The father is superior to his son (##15–17).

---

[33] Age might have been an important factor in determining the status of the individuals in certain situations (especially among siblings). However, there is no case above in which one can say that age is the sole factor that determines the relative status of the speaker and the addressee. Rather, the key determining factors seem to be their occupational status or position in the household. In fact, occupational status often prevails over age in determining the speaker's social status relative to the addressee (e.g., Aaron addresses Moses as "my lord" twice [Exod 32:22; Num 12:11], even though he was three years older than Moses [Exod 7:7]).

[34] In case #3, Saul and Abner are cousins (1 Sam 14:50). Their nonreciprocal address pattern (i.e., Saul addresses Abner by APN and receives T, "O king!" [1 Sam 17:55]) cannot be viewed as "normal" between cousins. Rather, it shows a formal address exchange between a king and his servant. In this case, occupation prevails over familial status.

[35] In 2 Kgs 9:30–31, the queen mother Jezebel receives the rebellious commander Jehu with regal nobility and defiance both by appearing at the palace window dressed like the queen mother she is and by mockingly addressing him as "Zimri, murderer of his lord." In doing so, Jezebel deliberately links Jehu to Zimri, a chariot commander who killed his king, Elah son of Baasha, and destroyed that dynasty (1 Kgs 16:8–16), because he was coming to her after he killed his king Jehoram (2 Kgs 9:24). There is no doubt that she intends to treat him as an inferior traitor by upbraiding and insulting him (Brueggemann 2000, 387–88).

[36] Abner is the commander of King Saul's army (1 Sam 14:50) and remains the real power behind Ish-bosheth after Saul's death (2 Sam 2:12–32). However, Asahel never achieves a military position as high as Abner's, being listed "among the thirty" in King David's army (2 Sam 23:24). In terms of military rank, Joab, Asahel's older brother, could be seen as equal to Abner as he is the commander of King David's army (2 Sam 20:23). It is interesting to note that Uriah the Hittite is also named "among the thirty" in King David's army (2 Sam 23:39) and he refers to Joab as "my lord" (2 Sam 11:11). Thus, it is probable that Asahel is considered inferior to Joab in the military hierarchy. Revell (1996, 331) views Abner and Asahel as equals without giving any explanation, but all the evidence seems to point to Abner's superiority over Asahel. It seems very unlikely that Abner views Asahel as an equal. For a useful table of PNs and Ts of functionaries in the Hebrew Bible and epigraphic records, see Fox 2000, 281–301.

[37] It has been traditionally held that Israelite wives were subordinate to their husbands. For recent discussion and bibliography, see Lemos 2015, 236–37. While she rejects the argument made by Wegner (1988) that Israelite wives were the "property" of their husbands, she argues that the dominant-subordinate pattern governed relations between husbands and wives in ancient Israel. For examples in biblical laws and narratives where husbands are stated to be dominant over wives, see Gen 3:16; Deut 22:20–21; Ezek 16, 23.

The unequal power relations can also be demonstrated through what Brown, Gilman, and Ford call nonreciprocal address exchange, where the speaker uses APN or HPN and receives a T or an ascending KT. About half of the first seventeen cases clearly exhibit this nonreciprocal pattern. King Ahasuerus addresses Esther by HPN, "Queen Esther" (##1–2), while he receives T, "the king," as a bound form of address (Esth 5:4, 8; 7:3, 4). King Saul addresses Abner by APN (#3), while he receives T, "O king!" (1 Sam 17:55). King David addresses Mephibosheth by APN (##5–6), while he receives T, "my lord the king," either as a free form (2 Sam 19:27) or a bound form (2 Sam 19:28, 29, 31),[38] or simply "the king" as a bound form (2 Sam 19:29).[39] The prophet Elijah addresses Elisha by APN (#9), while he receives an ascending KT, "my father!" (2 Kgs 2:12). King Saul addresses his son Jonathan by APN (#15), while he receives T, "the king," as a bound form (1 Sam 19:4). King David addresses Absalom by HPN, "Absalom, my son, my son" (#16), while he receives T, "the king," as a bound form (2 Sam 13:24).

In the other half of the seventeen cases, the speaker does not receive an address form. However, It seems reasonable to assume that the speaker would have received a T or an ascending KT if an address had been made by the

---

In the case of Elkanah and Hannah in 1 Sam 1:1–8, it seems clear that Elkanah acts as a superior by leading the whole family to go up to Shiloh, distributing portions to his household, and comforting Hannah who is in distress due to the lack of a child. See Lande (1949, 27), who also views Elkanah as superior to Hannah.

Curiously, Revell (1996, 332) states that "spouses typically converse as equals." However, the address patterns between husband and wife used in the Hebrew Bible seem to go against his statement. If we set aside address forms used between the king and the queen in which the latter addresses the former as "king," not as "husband" (e.g., Bathsheba addresses King David as "my lord the king!" in 1 Kgs 1:13–21), it appears that the address exchange between husband and wife is nonreciprocal. Lamech and Elkanah address their wives by APNs, "Adah and Zilla!" (Gen 4:23) and "Hannah!" (1 Sam 1:8), respectively, whereas there is no case where a wife addresses her husband by APN. Apart from the case in which Sarah refers to Abraham as "my lord" (Gen 18:12), a wife commonly refers to her husband as אישי ʔiši "my man" (Gen 29:32, 34; 30:15, 18, 20; 2 Sam 14:5, 7; 2 Kgs 4:1; Hos 2:9). Note that the two terms, איש ʔiš "man" and בעל baʕal "master," are often used to refer to husbands (e.g., Judg 13:9; 2 Sam 11:26). Of course, these referential usages do not necessarily prove that Israelite wives actually addressed their husbands with these terms. However, Hos 2:18 may reflect the Israelite practice that a wife would address her husband by either אישי "my man" or בעלי baʕli "my master," instead of APN.

[38] Strictly speaking, T is composed of honorific T + occupational T.

[39] In addition, Mephibosheth gives deference to King David by employing a deprecatory self-reference form, עבדך ʕabdekɔ "your servant" (2 Sam 9:6, 8).

addressee.[40] In other words, the nonreciprocal address pattern between the speaker and the addressee is a clear indication of the inequality of their status and can be used as a helpful tool to determine their unequal power relations, which may otherwise be uncertain.

As noted by many scholars (e.g., Dallaire 2014, 24–25), the power dynamics among kings, prophets, and priests in the Hebrew Bible cannot be definitively determined based solely on their respective occupations. However, their patterns of address exchange can provide valuable insights into their relative status. Therefore, the nonreciprocal pattern observed when King Ahab addresses the prophet Micaiah using APN (##18–19), and in return, receives the bound form of address "the king" (1 Kgs 22:15), may indicate that Ahab considers Micaiah inferior (or possibly equal) to himself, while Micaiah, on the other hand, views (or pretends to view) Ahab as superior to himself.[41] Similarly, it is evident that King Saul regards the priest Ahimelech as inferior, while Ahimelech acknowledges his inferiority. Saul addresses Ahimelech using APN (#20) and, in response, receives the free form of address "my lord" (1 Sam 22:12) and the bound form "the king" (1 Sam 22:14).

The power relations in cases ##21–22 may not be solely determined by occupation or the pattern of address exchange.[42] Instead, the speech context in which the address exchange occurs needs to be taken into consideration. At first glance, Abijah, the king of southern Judah, and Jeroboam, the king of northern Israel, may appear as equals based on their occupations (#21). However, it must be noted that Abijah addresses Jeroboam using APN in the context of waging war, where taunting insults are frequently exchanged. Thus, Abijah's use of APN toward Jeroboam may be seen as intentionally condescending, as if he is "putting him in his place" by treating him as a servant (2 Chr 13:1–22). Furthermore, Abijah's references to the divine legitimacy of both the Davidic dynasty and the Aaronic priests of southern Judah (2 Chr 13:5, 10), as well as his rebukes of Jeroboam for his rebellion and idolatry (2 Chr 13:6–9) also suggest that he views himself as superior to Jeroboam.

In case #22, Jeremiah and Hananiah may be viewed as equals since they are both prophets. However, Jeremiah's address to Hananiah by APN occurs in the context of prophesying Hananiah's death in the name of YHWH.[43] It is widely

---

[40] Of course, this assumption can be justified only in ordinary circumstances. One can hardly expect Jehu to abide by the norm of address usage when he intends to murder Jezebel in 2 Kgs 9:31.

[41] In fact, Ahab never shows respect to any prophets in his time.

[42] The speakers receive no address.

[43] Note that Jeremiah's prophecy of Hananiah's death begins with a "messenger formula" כה אמר יהוה *ko ʔɔmar yhwh* "Thus says YHWH" that confirms that the prophet's message is not his own, but a prophetic oracle from Yahweh (Jer 28:16).

recognized in biblical scholarship that when a true prophet acts on God's behalf, he stands above the human social hierarchy and is superior to any of its members (Thompson 1980, 540–41; Leithart 2006, 201).[44] Thus, it may be argued that Jeremiah, as a representative of God, speaks as a superior to Hananiah in this situation.

The sixth column in table 3.3 shows the distance dimension in the superior-inferior dyads. While the members in half of the dyads can be said to be closely related either by familial relationship (##1–3, 14–17) or by like-mindedness through frequent contact (##9–12), the members in the other half of the dyads are to be viewed as distant. For example, in cases #4, #8, and #13, the relationship between the speakers (Jehoram, Jezebel, and Abner) and the addressees (Jehu and Asahel) is not close, as the latter are trying to kill the former. In case #5, David and Mephibosheth are strangers, as they have just met with the help of Ziba. In cases ##18–19, Ahab and Micaiah can be considered distant from each other, as Ahab explicitly expresses his hatred towards Micaiah (1 Kgs 22:8). In case #21, Abijah and Jeroboam are distant as they are about to engage in battle. Considering all these cases, it appears that there is little correlation between the power and distance dimensions in the superior-inferior dyads. Therefore, Revell's (1996, 331) claim that the use of APN or HPN is "normally restricted to family members and intimate associates" may not be substantiated. As will be seen in §3.4.3.4, family members and intimate associates are normally addressed with KTs. The use of APN or HPN simply connotes the superiority of the speaker in the superior-inferior dyads.[45]

---

[44] For example, the prophet Nathan rebukes King David for his adultery (2 Sam 12:1–15).

[45] That the use of PN in address may mark the superiority of the speaker appears to be confirmed in the Hebrew letters dating to ca. 600 BCE in Judaea. Thirteen letters unearthed at Tel Arad were written from a superior to an inferior (Arad 1–8, 10–12, 14, 17), all of which begin with a simple address formula: אל *?l* + PN "to PN." This is in stark contrast to the address formula found in another Arad letter written from an inferior to a superior (Arad 18), in which an honorific T is inserted before PN: אל *?l* + honorific T + PN "to my lord PN." All the Lachish letters that contain address formulas appear to have been written from an inferior to a superior. All of them identify their recipients in the address formulas as either honorific T + PN (Lach 2, 3, 6) or simply honorific T (Lach 4, 5, 8, 9, 12, 17, 18).

Note, however, that there are two letters (Arad 21, 40) written by an inferior to a superior (presumably a son to his genetic father) in which the former greets and addresses the latter by PN, saying, "your son PN sends greetings to PN." These seem to constitute counterexamples to the address usage of PN as a marker of the superiority of the speaker. It is not easy to explain why PN was used this way. Might there have been an epistolary convention that allowed an inferior to address a superior in his family by PN? Or might not the sender and the addressee have been biologically related but close enough to address each other by PN? For a detailed analysis of the epistolary formulas in these letters, see Pardee et al. 1982, 145–64.

3.4.1.2.2. Between Close Equals

There are five cases where APNs are used in the seemingly close-equal dyads, as can be seen in table 3.4.

Table 3.4. APNs Used between Close Equals

#	Relation	Speaker	Form	Semantic	D	Context	Verse
1–4	Lover > Lover	Delilah	Samson	PN	c	Informing Samson of the Philistines' attack	Judg 16:9, 12, 14, 20
5	King > King	Jehoram	Ahaziah	PN	c	Informing Ahaziah of Jehu's revolt	2 Kgs 9:23

The close equal relationship between speech participants in these dyads can be deduced from their personal relationship and occupations. In cases ##1–4, Delilah addresses Samson by APN, informing him of the Philistines who came to seize him. While Revell (1996, 332) thinks of these two as a married couple, there is no textual evidence for it. However, it can be said that their relationship is close since they are lovers.[46] With respect to the power relation between the two lovers, Hélène Dallaire (2014, 75) describes Delilah as "lesser" than Samson without providing any evidence for her description, while Revell (1996, 332) views them as equals, saying, "spouses typically converse as equals." As Tracy M. Lemos (2015, 241) observes, the Hebrew Bible generally portrays Israelite women as subordinate to their husbands or fathers. However, Delilah does not seem to fit this general portrayal of Israelite women.[47] Rather, the story shows many signs of her socio-economic independence and strong personality: (1) Delilah is the only woman introduced by name in the Samson narrative; (2) unlike many other biblical women, she is not identified in terms of her relationships with male kin (cf. Gen 29:10); (3) she seems to have her own house and servants (Judg 16:9); (4) she deals with the Philistine lords without any male kin acting as a mediator (cf. Judg 15:1); (5) she manipulates and harasses Samson to bring him down.[48] In light of these factors, it is difficult to view Delilah as "lesser" than Samson, as Dallaire does. At the same time, it is equally difficult to think of Samson as socially inferior to Delilah, considering the general portrayal of the superiority of Israelite men

---

[46] Strictly speaking, the text states that Samson loved her (Judg 16:4) but mentions nothing about her emotional attachment to him. Exum (2000, 69) takes this as a hint that Delilah did not love Samson and would have "no qualms about betraying him."

[47] The text is silent about Delilah's ethnicity, though many assume that she is a Philistine (e.g., Block 1999, 454; Webb 2012, 399).

[48] See Fewell (1992, 73) and Exum (2000, 68–69) for these observations. For the objections to the idea of Delilah's independence, see Blyth 2014, 56–57.

over women in the Hebrew Bible. Thus, it seems logical to view Samson and Delilah as equals.[49]

Regarding address usage, Delilah's use of APN is unusual, as women rarely address men by APN or HPN in our corpus.[50] However, it seems that Delilah's use of APN is not particularly offensive to Samson but normal in this situation (she addresses him by APN four times throughout the narrative!). Samson never addresses Delilah back, but it seems likely that he would have used APN or HPN to address her, as men often use APN or HPN to address women (e.g., Gen 4:23; 1 Sam 1:8; Esth 5:3; 7:2; 8:7).[51] Thus, although it is an argument from silence, this reconstruction might be used as an example to demonstrate that Brown, Gilman, and Ford's address rule—the reciprocal exchange of PN in the equal-close dyad—works in the Hebrew Bible.[52]

In case #5, Jehoram, king of Israel, addresses Ahaziah, king of Judah, by APN, urgently informing him of Jehu's military coup and dynastic overthrow. Jehoram and Ahaziah may be viewed as equals based on their royal status, though one may argue for Jehoram's superiority over Ahaziah based on familial status (Jehoram is Ahaziah's uncle).[53] Their relationship appears to be close, as they are not only

---

[49] Note that this decision is the same as Revell's but on different grounds.

[50] Women usually use T or KT to address men (e.g., "my lord," "king," "man of God," "my father," "my brother," "my son," "my husband," "my man"). Apart from Delilah's use of APN, there is only one case in which a woman uses HPN to address a man: Jezebel addresses Jehu as "Zimri, murderer of his lord!" (2 Kgs 9:31).

[51] Samson might also have used KTs or ETs to address his lover Delilah, as can be seen in Song of Songs (e.g., אחתי *ʼăḥoṯi* "my sister" [Song 4:9]; רעיתי *raʿyoṯi* "my love" [Song 1:9]; יפתי *yop̄oṯi* "my beautiful one" [Song 2:10], etc.).

[52] Compare this to Arad 16 in which a PN is used by Hananyahu to address his brother Elyashib, which may be considered an equal-close dyad.

[53] This is based on the traditional assumption that there were two different Jehorams in the ninth century BCE: Jehoram the son of Jehoshaphat king of Judah and Jehoram the son of Ahab king of Israel (see, for example, Provan 1995, 206–7; Revell 1996, 332; Brueggemann 2000, 376). The former married Athaliah who was the daughter of Ahab (interpreting the phrase בת עמרי *baṯ-ʿomri* [lit. "daughter of Omri" in 2 Kgs 8:26 and 2 Chr 22:2] as "granddaughter of Omri") and the sister of the latter (2 Kgs 8:25, 29). Ahaziah was the son of Jehoram king of Judah and Athaliah (2 Kgs 8:25–26). Thus, Jehoram king of Israel was Ahaziah's uncle. Due to seeming discrepancies between the accounts of Kings and Chronicles, however, the genealogy of Jehoram and Ahaziah has been highly controversial. Many scholars have attempted to harmonize these discrepancies, offering alternatives to the traditional interpretation. For example, Hayes and Hooker (1988, 32–36) argue that Jehoram of Judah and Jehoram of Israel were actually the same person and Ahaziah was his son. While agreeing with Hayes and Hooker that the two Jehorams were the same person, Barrick (2001, 9–25) makes a case that Jehoram was Ahaziah's uncle. However, these alternatives are not entirely convincing, as the text in the book of Kings

relatives but also allies in a campaign against Hazael, king of Aram, at Ramoth-Gilead (2 Kgs 8:28).

According to Brown, Gilman, and Ford, the reciprocal exchange of PN is expected in this type of dyad.[54] Unfortunately, Jehoram receives no address from Ahaziah to justify the validity of such a claim. Furthermore, there is no case of address exchange between kings or between an uncle and nephew in our corpus that may shed light to the Jehoram-Ahaziah dyad. Thus, there is no way to tell how Ahaziah would have addressed Jehoram.[55]

3.4.1.2.3. Inferior to Superior? The Cases of Expressive Shift

So far, I have argued that the use of APN or HPN in addressing may indicate the superiority of the speaker or possibly the closeness between equals. However, there are three cases in which APN or HPN is used in the seemingly inferior-superior dyads, as shown in table 3.5.

---

clearly presents Jehoram of Judah and Jehoram of Israel as two different individuals. Moreover, what is ultimately important for the study of address usage in the narrative is not necessarily the historical reality of the genealogy, but the ways in which the narrator presents it within a given narrative context. Thus, I follow the traditional interpretation which seems to adhere to the narrator's presentation faithfully.

[54] According to Lande (1949, 20), addressing someone by PN was considered impolite in ancient Israel since PN was mostly used by a superior to address an inferior. She argues, however, that Jehoram's impolite use of PN when addressing Ahaziah was acceptable because it was used in an emergency situation. In response to Lande, Clines (1972, 273) states that Jehoram's address by PN is hardly impolite, but he offers no explanation as to why that is the case. If Jehoram and Ahaziah were equal and close, as I argued above, Jehoram's use of PN in that type of dyad is not necessarily impolite but is completely expected according to Brown, Gilman, and Ford's address rule.

[55] There are several cases in which a king addresses another king, but the former never receives an address back. The address forms that the speaker uses vary according to his view of the relationship between himself and the addressee. To whom he views as a superior or the one worthy of respect, he uses T (e.g., Adonijah addresses Solomon as "King Solomon" [1 Kgs 1:51]; Ahab addresses Ben-Hadad as "my lord the king" [1 Kgs 20:4]; Hiram addresses Solomon as "my lord" [2 Chr 2:14]; Jehoshaphat addresses Ahab as "the king" [1 Kgs 22:8=2 Chr 18:7]; Pharaoh Necho addresses Josiah as "king of Judah" [2 Chr 35:21]); To whom he views as an inferior, he uses PN (e.g., Abijah addresses Jeroboam as "Jeroboam" in the context of war [2 Chr 13:4]); To whom he views as an equal, he uses KT (e.g., Hiram addresses Solomon as "my brother" [1 Kgs 9:13]).

In a few instances, address forms are used between nephews and their uncle, yet no reciprocation of address occurs in any of these situations. Notably, the uncle in each of these cases is King David. In all these instances, King David and his nephews interact not as relatives, but rather as sovereign and subjects. For examples of Joab or Jonadab addressing King David, see 2 Sam 13:32, 33, 35; 14:22; 1 Chr 21:3. For examples of King David addressing Joab and Abishai, see 2 Sam 16:10 = 2 Sam 19:23.

Table 3.5. APNs and HPNs Used by Inferiors to Superiors

#	Relation	Speaker	Form	Semantic	D	Context	Verse
1	Prophet > King	Jeremiah	Zedekiah, King of Judah	PN+T	d	Prophesying Zedekiah's death	Jer 34:4
2	Prophet > King	Azariah	Asa	PN	d?	Encouraging Asa to carry out religious reforms	2 Chr 15:2
3	Outlaw > Commander	David	Abner	PN	d	Accusing Abner of neglecting Saul	1 Sam 26:14

As discussed in cases ##18–19 in §3.4.1.2.1, the power relation between prophets and kings cannot be determined by their occupations alone. Thus, other factors such as address patterns or speech context must be considered to determine the power relation between the prophet Jeremiah and King Zedekiah. Upon examining Jeremiah's address usage, it seems most likely that he views Zedekiah as superior to himself under normal circumstances. Except for case #1, there is one more case in our corpus where Jeremiah addresses Zedekiah. In this case, Jeremiah privately asks Zedekiah not to send him back to the house of Jonathan the secretary, and he addresses Zedekiah with the honorific T + occupational T, אדני המלך *ʾᵃdoni hammelɛk* "O my lord the king!" (Jer 37:20). This compound address is typically used by subjects to show deference to the king, indicating that the king holds a higher social status (e.g., Ebed-Melech, an Ethiopian eunuch, addresses Zedekiah as "my lord the king" in Jer 38:9).[56] By using the deferential address, Jeremiah acknowledges that he is a subject of Zedekiah who holds authority over him. There is no doubt that this deferential address would have been Jeremiah's usual way of addressing Zedekiah when discussing civil affairs.

However, in case #1, Jeremiah addresses Zedekiah by HPN, which may indicate the social superiority of the speaker.[57] Does this mean that Jeremiah speaks as a superior to Zedekiah in this case? I answer this question affirmatively by considering the speech context in which his address occurs. Jeremiah's use of HPN takes place while delivering Yahweh's message that King Zedekiah will die a peaceful death in Babylon (Jer 34:5). He makes it clear that his message is not his own, but it originates from Yahweh, using the so-called "messenger formula" כה אמר יהוה *ko ʾɔmar yhwh* "Thus says YHWH" (Jer 34:2) and the "proclamation

---

[56] For the usage of the compound address אדני המלך *ʾᵃdoni hammelɛk*, see my discussion below in §3.4.2.2.1.2.

[57] In this case, the HPN may not connote the closeness between equals. The relationship between Jeremiah and Zedekiah does not seem to be close, as Zedekiah puts him in prison (Jer 37:18).

formula" שמע דבר יהוה *šmaʕ dḇar-yhwh* "Hear the word of Yahweh!" at the beginning of his speech (Jer 34:4). As seen in case #22 in §3.4.1.2.1, when a prophet speaks as God's spokesperson, he stands above the human social hierarchy, even above the king. Thus, it can be said that as Jeremiah delivers Yahweh's message to Zedekiah in case #1, he positions himself as superior to Zedekiah and addresses him by HPN.[58]

I would argue that this is a good example of what Brown and Gilman (1960, 270–73) call "expressive shift," that is, a tactical violation of address rules to communicate the speaker's temporary attitudes toward the addressee. Jeremiah's usual address to Zedekiah would be an AT or an HT to show deference to his royal status (see §3.4.2.2.1). However, when he delivers Yahweh's message to Zedekiah, he momentarily shifts his address from AT/HT to HPN to signal that Yahweh, who is above all human beings, is speaking, and thus, one must pay attention to what is being said.

Case #2 can also be seen as an example of expressive shift. The prophet Azariah addresses King Asa by APN, encouraging him to carry out religious reforms. Again, it is clear from 2 Chr 15:1 that Azariah's message of encouragement is not his own, as the Chronicler states that the spirit of God (רוח אלהים *ruᵃḥ ʔlohim*) came upon Azariah. Thus, it can be argued that Azariah asserts his authority over King Asa as God's spokesperson by choosing to address him by APN. Unfortunately, there is no other address used by Azariah elsewhere that could demonstrate his usual address usage for Asa. However, it seems reasonable to assume that he used an AT or an HT, since all the other prophets who address kings in our corpus use an AT or an HT, except for Jeremiah's expressive shift in case #1 (Nathan addresses David as "the king" [1 Kgs 1:25] or "my lord the king" [1 Kgs 1:24, 27 (2x)]; 400 prophets address Ahab as "the king" [1 Kgs 22:6, 12 = 2 Chr 18:5, 11]; Micaiah addresses Ahab as "the king" [1 Kgs 22:15]; Jeremiah addresses Zedekiah as "O my lord the king!" (Jer 37:20); an unnamed man of God addresses Amaziah as "O king" [2 Chr 25:7]; Jahaziel addresses Jehoshaphat as "King Jehoshaphat" [2 Chr 20:15]).[59]

---

[58] Note that Yahweh consistently refers to Zedekiah by APN "Zedekiah" or HPN "Zedekiah king of Judah" throughout the book of Jeremiah (Jer 21:7; 24:8; 27:3; 32:4, 5; 44:30) but never by T + PN "King Zedekiah," which the narrator often uses to refer to him (Jer 37:3, 17, 18; 38:5, 14, 16). Thus, the way in which Jeremiah addresses Zedekiah in case #1 corresponds to the way in which Yahweh refers to him.

[59] There is a possible case of expressive shift outside of our corpus. In 2 Chr 26:18, the priest Azariah and eighty other priests address King Uzziah by APN in the context of rebuking him for burning incense to Yahweh, which is for the priests to do. According to the Chronicler, Azariah and the other priests' rebuke is an expression of Yahweh's righteous anger upon Uzziah, who sinned against Yahweh out of his pride by entering his temple. Thus, it can be said that they are acting as superiors to King Uzziah on behalf of Yahweh

Finally, David's address of Abner by APN in case #3 could be another example of expressive shift. After taking King Saul's spear and water jug from near his head, David calls Abner by APN from the top of a hill, saying, "Will you not answer, Abner?" In terms of occupation and family connections, Abner is Saul's commander-in-chief (1 Sam 14:50; 17:55) and his cousin (1 Sam 14:50), while David is a leader of outlaws (1 Sam 22:1–2; 23:13) and Saul's son-in-law (1 Sam 18:27). The last military position that David held before leaving Saul's army was commander of a thousand (1 Sam 18:13). All of these seem to indicate that Abner is superior to David. Thus, David's use of APN to address Abner is surprising given its usual function, which is to mark the superiority of the speaker.[60]

Unfortunately, there is no evidence to show how David addressed Abner before he fled from Saul. Considering their respective military ranks, however, it seems reasonable to assume that he would have addressed Abner with either an AT, an HT, or an ascending AKT,[61] similar to how Uriah the Hittite officer refers to Joab the commander of the army as אדני יואב *Pᵃdoni yoʔọb* "my lord Joab" (2 Sam 11:11).[62] Therefore, David's shift in address from AT/HT to APN in this encounter may be seen as his deliberate attempt to express his feelings of contempt or anger toward Abner.[63] This interpretation is supported by the immediately following context in which David rebukes Abner for failing to guard his master Saul while he slept (1 Sam 26:15–16).

From a narrative point of view, David's use of APN to address Abner seems to carry more than temporary expressive significance. I would argue that it serves as a pivotal moment in their power dynamic within the narrative. The Book of Samuel documents three encounters between David and Abner. Their first meeting occurs after David's triumph over Goliath (1 Sam 17:57). At that time, Abner

---

by choosing APN to address him. Unfortunately, no address is made by Azariah and the other priests to King Uzziah elsewhere that might show their normal address usage for him. However, all the other priests who address kings in our corpus use an AT or an HT (e.g., Ahimelech addresses Saul as "my lord" [1 Sam 22:12] or "the king" [1 Sam 22:14, 15]; Abiathar addresses Adonijah as "King Adonijah" [1 Kgs 1:25]). In light of these cases, though inconclusive, it seems probable that the priests address kings by AT or HT under normal circumstances.

[60] The APN may not mark the closeness of the equals in this dyad, since David and Abner are hostile to each other.

[61] See §3.4.2.2.1 and §3.4.3.4.2.1 for the function of AT, HT, and ascending AKT and HKT to mark the superiority of the addressee.

[62] Biblical characters other than military officers also address military commanders by either AT or ascending AKT: Jael addresses Sisera as אדני *Pᵃdoni* "my lord" (Judg 4:18); a young prophet addresses Jehu as השר *haśśor* "commander" (2 Kgs 9:5); and the servants address Naaman as "my father" (2 Kgs 5:13).

[63] See Lande (1949, 20) and Revell (1996, 333), who also view David's use of APN as a sign of disrespect or insult.

had no knowledge of David's lineage (1 Sam 17:55); David was seen as an insignificant figure. Subsequently, Abner appears to maintain superiority over David as the commander of the army. However, in their second recorded encounter (case #3), David asserts his superiority over Abner as the chosen king by addressing him with APN. It is noteworthy that prior to this, only one other person, King Saul, addressed Abner by APN (1 Sam 17:55). Following this encounter, David and Abner meet again to make a peace covenant after a war between the house of Saul and the house of David. During this meeting, Abner himself acknowledges David's superiority by addressing him as "my lord the king" (2 Sam 3:21). Hence, we witness a progressive shift in the power relationship between David and Abner, where David's use of APN to address Abner functions as a turning point that dramatically alters the power dynamic.

3.4.1.3. Conclusion

Cross-linguistically, PNs are recognized for their relatively "specific and direct referentiality" compared to Ts or KTs, which highlight positional or relational status (Fleming and Slotta 2015, 172). A PN like "David" directly refers to a specific individual, while a T like "King" or a KT like "my brother" may have multiple potential referents. According to Brown and Levinson's politeness theory, indirectness is often associated with politeness. Thus, PNs are generally considered less polite than Ts or KTs. Consequently, the avoidance or restriction of PNs when addressing superiors is observed in many languages and cultures, including Biblical Hebrew.[64]

As shown in figure 3.4, APNs and HPNs are almost exclusively used in a "downward" manner, specifically in superior-inferior dyads, with a couple of exceptions where APNs are used between close equals.[65] The use of APNs and

---

[64] For example, see the appendix in Fleming and Slotta (2015, 179) for the result of a cross-cultural survey of the proper name-kin term alternation. Among the thirty-five speech communities surveyed, the avoidance of PNs in address in younger-older dyads is witnessed in thirty-two speech communities.

[65] The tendency to avoid PNs when addressing or even referring to superiors is also found in the Babylonian Talmud, which reflects social practices during the Amoraic period (200–500 CE): רב נחמן אמר זה הקורא רבו בשמו דאמר רבי יוחנן מפני מה נענש גיחזי מפני שקרא לרבו בשמו שנאמר (מלכים ב ח, ה) ויאמר גחזי אדני המלך זאת האשה וזה בנה אשר החיה אלישע *rb nḥmn ʔmr zh hqwrʔ rbw bšmw dʔmr rby ywḥnn mpny mh nʕnš gyḥzy mpny šqrʔ lrbw bšmw šnʔmr (mlkym b ḥ, h) wyʔmr gḥzy ʔdny hmlk zʔt hʔšh wzh bnh ʔšr ḥḥyh ʔlyšʕ* Rav Naḥman says, "One who calls his teacher by his name (is an epikoros), as Rabbi Yoḥanan says, 'Why was Gehazi punished? It is because he called his teacher by his name, as it is stated in 2 Kgs 8:5, "Gehazi said, 'My lord the king, this is the woman, and this is her son, whom Elisha revived'"'" (Sanh. 100a).

HPNs in Biblical Hebrew appears to be primarily determined by the power relation between the speaker and the addressee. Serving to indicate the speaker's superiority, APNs and HPNs in Biblical Hebrew seem to function similarly to the *T* in Brown, Gilman, and Ford's *T/V* system, thus supporting Brown and Ford's "linguistic universal." It is worth noting that compound addresses, where a PN is placed in the middle or at the end, may convey a different power relationship compared to APNs and HPNs. In other words, the first constituent in an address, whether simple or compound, can serve as an indicator of the power relation between the speaker and the addressee. The use of APNs or HPNs in seemingly inferior-superior dyads may be regarded as "expressive shifts," wherein the speaker (or narrator) strategically violates the address rules mentioned earlier to assert authority over the addressee.

Figure 3.4. The Use of APNs and HPNs in the Hebrew Bible

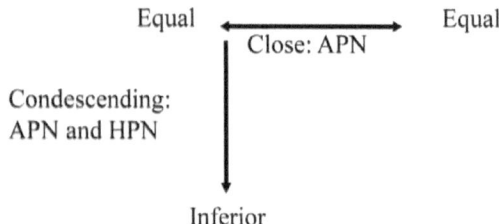

3.4.2. Titles

Ts express a nonkinship-related status or position achieved by or ascribed to an individual (Fitch 1998, 39). In Biblical Hebrew, when Ts are used in address, they can be categorized into two types based on their nature and function: honorific Ts and occupational Ts (see §2.4.1.1.1 in chapter 2). Honorific Ts are conventional terms used to show deference to the addressee who holds power over the speaker by virtue of rank, status, or age (e.g., אדני *ʔᵃḏōnî* "my lord!"). On the other hand, occupational Ts indicate the addressee's profession or function (e.g., המלך *hammɛlɛḵ* "O king!"). As we will see below, both honorific Ts and occupational

---

In his answer to the question, "What is an epikoros (i.e., one who denies the rabbinic tradition)?," Rav Naḥman points out that addressing a social superior, such as a teacher (רב *rb*), by PN alone is considered irreverent, implying that a title of respect (e.g., רבי *rby* "Rabbi") is to be used with or without PN, instead. Rabbi Yoḥanan's explanation of the reason for Gehazi's punishment is not to be taken seriously, as he was cursed by Elisha because of his greed and lies on another occasion (2 Kgs 5). However, it clearly reflects an Amoraic assumption about a sociolinguistic rule in northern Israel around the ninth century BCE: reference to a social superior by PN in his absence was disrespectful.

FREE FORMS OF ADDRESS: SOCIAL DYNAMICS   85

Ts almost invariably convey a sense of respect towards the addressee and/or formality in the relationship.

3.4.2.1. Position and Distribution

There are three types of address forms in which Ts are used: (1) a T used alone (e.g., השר *haśśor* "Commander!"); (2) a T used at the beginning of a compound address (e.g., אדני משה *ʔᵃdoni moše* "My lord Moses!"); (3) a T used at the end of a compound address (e.g., אסתר המלכה *ʔester hammalkɔ* "Queen Esther!"). In the following discussion, we will consider the first two types—the address forms composed of a T alone (henceforth, ATs) and compound addresses headed by a T (henceforth, HTs)—together since they convey the same power relationship between the speaker and the addressee in our corpus. The third type consists of only three examples (Jer 34:4; Esth 5:3; 7:2), where a T is always preceded by a PN. These cases have already been addressed in §3.4.1.2.1 and §3.4.1.2.3.

In our corpus, there are thirty-five cases of ATs and twenty-two cases of HTs. These instances account for about 29 percent of the total free forms of address used between two human beings. Therefore, ATs and HTs occur twice as frequently as APNs and HPNs. Table 3.6 presents the distribution of ATs and HTs across the books of the Hebrew Bible. As shown in the table, most of these occurrences are concentrated in Samuel and Kings, where there is a higher frequency of interactions between the speakers and high-ranking officials such as kings, prophets, priests, and military commanders. In Genesis through Numbers, where dialogues involving these officials are relatively few, only the honorific T אדני *ʔᵃdoni* "my lord" is found.

Table 3.6. ATs and HTs in Each Book of the Hebrew Bible

Book	# of AKTs	# of HKTs	Book	# of AKTs	# of HKTs
Genesis	4		Jeremiah		2
Numbers	1	1	Amos	1	
Judges	2		Ruth	1	
1 Samuel	8	2	Esther	1	
2 Samuel	4	5	1 Chronicles		1
1 Kings	4	6	2 Chronicles	2	1
2 Kings	7	4			
			Total	35	22

3.4.2.2. Pattern

3.4.2.2.1. Inferior to Superior

Similar to PNs, the use of ATs and HTs also exhibits a prominent pattern related to power relations, albeit in the opposite direction: the absolute majority of these address forms are used by inferiors when addressing superiors.[66] Out of the fifty-seven cases of ATs and HTs, fifty-five of them are found in inferior-superior dyads.

3.4.2.2.1.1. ATs

Table 3.7 shows ATs used by inferiors to superiors.

Table 3.7. ATs Used by Inferiors to Superiors

#	Form	Speaker	Addressee	Verse
1–2	My lord	Ephron	Abraham	Gen 23:11, 15
3		Rebekah	Abraham's servant	Gen 24:18
4		Judah	Joseph	Gen 44:18
5		Aaron	Moses	Num 12:11
6–8		Hannah	Eli	1 Sam 1:15, 26 (2x)
9		Jael	Sisera	Judg 4:18
10		Ahimelech	Saul	1 Sam 22:12
11–12		Abigail	David	1 Sam 25:24, 26
13		Bathsheba	David	1 Kgs 1:17
14		Prostitute	Solomon	1 Kgs 3:17
15		Prostitute	Solomon	1 Kgs 3:26
16		Prophet	Elisha	2 Kgs 6:5
17		Servant	Elisha	2 Kgs 6:15
18		Ruth	Boaz	Ruth 2:13
19	King	Ehud	Eglon	Judg 3:19
20		Abner	Saul	1 Sam 17:55
21		David	Saul	1 Sam 26:22
22		Tekoaite Woman	David	2 Sam 14:4
23		Araunah	David	2 Sam 24:23
24		Hushai	Absalom	2 Sam 15:34
25		Esther	Xerxes	Esth 7:3
26		Prophet	Amaziah	2 Chr 25:7
27–28	Commander	Prophet-in-training	Jehu	2 Kgs 9:5 (2x)
29–31	Man of God	Captain	Elijah	2 Kgs 1:9, 11, 13
32		Widow	Elijah	1 Kgs 17:18
33	King's son	Jonadab	Amnon	2 Sam 13:4

The most frequently used AT in our corpus is the honorific T, אדני *ʔᵃdoni* "my lord!"[67] While it can be used by a servant to address his/her master, as in case #17, it is much more commonly attested in interactions between social inferiors

---

[66] Revell (1996, 326) also detects this tendency.

[67] גבירה *gḇirɔ* "lady, queen, queen-mother," the female counterpart of אדון *ʔɔḏon* "lord, master," is never attested as an address form in our corpus, though it is occasionally used in reference (e.g., 2 Kgs 5:3).

and superiors who do not have a literal servant-master relationship.[68] Thus, אדני is used by: (a) a local landowner to a prominent foreigner (##1–2);[69] (b) a young girl to an elderly wealthy stranger (##3, 18);[70] (c) a Hebrew man to the vizier of Egypt (#4);[71] (d) the high priest to a national leader (#5);[72] (e) a woman to a priest (##6–8); (f) a woman to the commander of the army (#9); (g) a woman to a leader of outlaws (##11–12); (h) a disciple to his teacher (#16);[73] (i) a servant to a prophet (#17); (j) various individuals (priest [#10], king's wife [#13], prostitute [##14–15]) to their kings. In most of these cases, the speaker explicitly requests a favor from the addressee (##1–2, 4–5, 9, 11–13, 15), while the remaining cases occur in the context of offering a drink (#3), informing (##7–8), responding (#10), claiming (#14), reporting (##16–17), and thanking (#18). In all of these instances,

---

[68] Lande (1949, 29) suggests that אדני was used first in the servant-master dyads, but through metaphorical extension, it came to be used as an expression of courtesy by the speaker to whomever he/she wanted to show deference. She finds a similar development in the French *Monsieur*, which literally means "my lord." It was originally used for the eldest brother of the king in the French royal court but has now become a courtesy title, equivalent to *Mr.* or *Sir* in English.

Like KTs, אדון *ʔəḏon* "lord/master" is essentially a term of relation, designating the superior in a master-servant relationship. Thus, like KTs used in address (see below), אדון is always used in address with the first-person possessive pronoun, ־י *-i* "my." As Revell (1996, 326) argues, the speaker's use of אדני might imply that he/she wishes to appeal to his/her personal relationship with the addressee in order to receive a favor. In some cases, however, אדני seems to function merely as a term of politeness (e.g., Rebekah's use of אדני for Abraham's servant, who is a total stranger in Gen 24:18).

[69] The Hittites refer to Abraham as נשיא אלהים *nəśi(ʔ) ʔəlohim* "a prince of God" in Gen 23:6. While the precise connotation of this phrase is debatable, it is certain that they view Abraham as an individual of some importance despite his identification of himself as גר ותושב *ger wəṯošaḇ* "resident alien" (Gen 23:4). As Hamilton (1995, 129) points out, Abraham's interactions with Pharaoh (Gen 12) and Abimelech (Gen 20) might have led the Hittites to consider him as royal. For the interpretation of אלהים as conveying a superlative sense, see Davidson 1942, 49 and Thomas 1953, 219.

[70] Rebekah's use of honorific T might have been caused by the fact that Abraham's servant is described as significantly older (זקן *zaqen* "old" in Gen 24:2) or that he looks wealthy, as he has ten camels and all sorts of luxuries (Gen 24:10). Similarly, Ruth's use of honorific T might have been caused by Boaz's age or wealth.

[71] Apparently, Judah does not know that the vizier is his brother Joseph.

[72] Aaron the high priest is the elder brother of Moses. His use of honorific T to address Moses may be explained as what Brown and Levinson call a negative politeness strategy in which he desires to appease Moses's anger by humbling himself and exalting Moses. However, it may also indicate that occupational status prevailed over age or family hierarchy in the determination of deference at that time.

[73] The disciple is referred to as one of בני הנביאים *bəne hannəḇiʔim* "the sons of the prophets" (2 Kgs 6:1, 3). See below for the meaning of "the sons of the prophets."

it is evident that the speaker intends to acknowledge the superior social status of the addressee.

Similar to the honorific T אדני, occupational Ts also seem to indicate the superior status of the addressee.[74] המלך *hammelek* "O king!" is normally used by subjects (queen [#25], prophet [#26], military commander [#20], outlaw/king's son-in-law [#21], and civilians [##22–23]), almost always in the context of requesting (##21–23, 25–26).[75] It is also used by Israelites to address a foreign king (#19) and a usurper (#24). In both cases, המלך occurs when the speakers (Ehud and Hushai) begin to reveal their secret plans to deceive these kings. While the speakers' use of this particular address form might simply reflect the conventional address usage before kings during that time, it could also be seen as a deliberate strategy to convince the kings that they were faithful subjects under their authority.[76]

השר *haśśor* "O commander!" is used by an unnamed man sent by Elisha to address Jehu as he requests a private meeting to anoint him as king over Israel (##27–28). In terms of occupation, Jehu is a military commander,[77] presumably in charge of Jehoram's army (Miller and Hayes 2006, 323), while the unnamed

---

[74] Unlike the honorific T אדון *ʾɔdon* "lord/master" (or KTs), which is a term of relation, occupational T is normally incompatible with the first-person possessive pronoun, -י *-i* "my," when used in address between two human beings. Thus, for example, מלכי *malki* "my king" is never used in address in the Hebrew Bible, except when it is used to address God in two poetic passages (Ps 5:2; 84:3).

[75] The king as the head of a nation is superior to all the citizens of it. Thus, the nonreciprocal pattern of address exchange between the king and his subjects is consistently attested in our corpus: the king typically receives Ts (honorific T אדני, occupational T המלך, or a combination of both אדני המלך) from his subjects, while he addresses them by PN. There is no case in our corpus in which the king's subjects address him by PN, except when the prophet or the priest delivers the message of God to him (see §3.4.1.2.3).

[76] Strictly speaking, the address form המלך in #25 does not come directly from Hushai but from David, who dictates to him the exact script he is to use when he comes before Absalom. This seems to further support the possibility that the use of המלך was part of a deliberate strategy to deceive Absalom. When Hushai encounters Absalom later, he indeed addresses Absalom as המלך, but as a bound form of address (יחי המלך *yhi hammelek* "Long live *the king*!" [2 Sam 16:16]), not as a free form of address.

[77] Jehu is said to be one of שרי החיל *śore haḥayil* "the army commanders" in 2 Kgs 9:5. While the term שר may be used to refer to any of the civil, religious, and military leadership positions (BDB, 978–79; *HALOT*, 1350–3), the modifier החיל makes it clear that Jehu's leadership role lay in the military context. For a detailed discussion of the etymology and semantics of the term שר, see Fox (2000, 158–63), who argues that the term *śr* branched out in three directions: (1) in Mesopotamia, it was restricted to refer exclusively to a king (e.g., *šarru* in Akkadian); (2) in Egypt, it broadened to refer to "prince," "noble," "royal official," "military official and magistrate"; (3) in Israel, it covered the same meanings as in Egypt but was frequently followed by a qualifying substantive denoting particular duties.

man is referred to as אחד מבני הנביאים *ʔaḥad mibbəne hannəḇiʔim* "one of the sons of the prophets" (2 Kgs 9:1). The term בני הנביאים has traditionally been understood to refer to members of an organized guild of prophetic disciples under the leadership of great prophets such as Elijah and Elisha.⁷⁸ If this interpretation is correct, the unnamed man would have been a prophet in training under Elisha.⁷⁹

The unnamed man is also called הנער *hannaʕar* (2 Kgs 9:4).⁸⁰ While BDB (2003, 654–55) primarily defines נער as "boy, lad, youth," it is used to cover a wide range of age groups in Israelite society: from an unborn child (Judg 13:5, 7, 8, 12), to an infant (Exod 2:6), a child recently weaned (1 Sam 1:24), a seventeen-year-old youth (Gen 37:2), a thirty-year-old adult (Gen 41:12). Additionally, it is applied to Ziba, who must have been a mature man with fifteen sons and twenty servants (2 Sam 9:9–10; 16:1; 19:18). Furthermore, Carolyn Leeb's (2000, 66–67) contextual study demonstrates that נער is not primarily an age term but rather a term for social status, mostly used for individuals who are independent of their family but attached to the house of their master to perform various services. In the narrative, they are depicted as secondary characters, with their names or genealogies rarely mentioned, and their primary responsibilities are to serve and build up

---

⁷⁸ The earliest attestation of this view is found in the works of Josephus, who uses the word μαθητής "disciple" to refer to both Elisha, who was left behind by Elijah (*A.J.* 9.28), and the unnamed man sent by Elisha to anoint Jehu (*A.J.* 9.106). For modern scholars who hold this view, see, for example, Gray 1963, 384; Williams 1966, 345; Verhoef 1997, 4:1070; Brueggemann 2000, 250. Note that the phrase בני הנביאים occurs eleven times in the Hebrew Bible (1 Kgs 20:35; 2 Kgs 2:3, 5, 7, 15; 4:1, 38 [2x]; 5:22; 6:1; 9:1), all of which describe northern prophets, and all but the first occur in connection with the prophet Elisha. Thus, it has been argued that בני הנביאים during the time of Elijah and Elisha are to be distinguished from the earlier groups of prophets during the time of Samuel and Saul who are called חבל נביאים *ḥeḇel nḇiʔim* "a band of prophets" (1 Sam 10:5, 10) and להקת הנביאים *lah⁽e⁾qat hannəḇiʔim* "the company of the prophets" (1 Sam 19:20). For this argument, see Verhoef 1997, 4:1070 and Witherington 1999, 102.

⁷⁹ See Hobbs (1985, 24–27), however, who argues that בני הנביאים were "lay supporters" of Elisha rather than a guild of prophetic disciples under his leadership.

⁸⁰ In the Masoretic Text, the unnamed man is referred to as הנער הנביא *hannaʕar hannaʕar hannəḇiʔ* lit. "the lad, the lad, the prophet." The repetition of הנער is awkward. The second הנער may be the result of dittography (note that some manuscripts of the Septuagint and the Peshitta have only one הנער, reading הנער הנביא as two nouns in apposition, "the lad [that is] the prophet"), or it may be the construct noun with the definite article mistakenly added due to the preceding הנער (note that the Vulgate removed the definite article of the second הנער, reading "the lad, the prophet's lad"). While the first option cannot be ruled out, I prefer the second one, as it seems to correspond better to the traditional understanding of the meaning of בני הנביאים.

the house of their masters, rather than themselves or their own fathers.[81] Thus, the unnamed man in ##27–28 may be described as Elisha's "aide" who carries out tasks assigned by his master, such as anointing Jehu.

Considering their occupations and social statuses, it is highly likely that Jehu is socially superior to the unnamed man. Thus, the unnamed man's use of the occupational T שׂר to address Jehu can be viewed as a polite address, demonstrating deference to a social superior.[82] This interpretation is further supported by the fact that the unnamed man no longer uses the occupational T in his anointing speech to Jehu but consistently addresses him using the second-person pronoun (מקחתיך məšaḥtikɔ "I anoint you" [2 Kgs 9:6]; והכיתה wəhikkitɔ "you shall strike down"; אדניך ʔdoneḵɔ "your master" [2 Kgs 9:7]). I would argue that the unnamed man deliberately avoids using the occupational T in his speech to indicate that he anoints Jehu as the representative of God, thereby establishing himself as superior to Jehu.[83]

The address form איש האלהים ʔiš hɔʔlohim "man of God" is used to address the prophet Elijah in the northern kingdom of Israel.[84] In one instance, a captain of fifty men addresses him as איש האלהים when delivering the king's message to come down from a hilltop (##29–31). Similarly, the widow of Zarephath addresses him using the same T when expressing her complaint about her son's death (#32). As Revell (1996, 326) correctly suggests, there is no doubt about Elijah's superior status compared to a captain of fifty men or the widow of Zarephath.[85]

בן המלך ben hammeleḵ "son of the king, prince" is used by Jonadab to address Amnon, who was deeply infatuated with his half-sister Tamar to the point of making himself ill (#33 in table 3.7). Amnon was the eldest son of King David (2 Sam 3:2) and the presumptive heir to the throne. Thus, בן המלך, an occupational T derived

---

[81] For other principal works on the term נער, see MacDonald (1976, 169), who defines נער as "squire" or "young knight"; Stähli (1978), who proposes two sematic domains for נער: "servant" and "unmarried dependent"; Stager (1985, 25), who connects נער to a young, unmarried male who takes a career path in the military, government, or priesthood until he marries and becomes the head of a household, like the aristocratic youth of twelfth-century France.

[82] Note that שׂר is also used as a bound form to address a superior in Meṣad Ḥashavyahu (lines 1 and 12). The superiority of the addressee is clear as שׂר is preceded by אדני in line 1. The addressee might have been either the local commander or the district governor located elsewhere (Pardee et al. 1982, 21).

[83] Note that the unnamed man begins his speech with the so-called prophetic messenger formula, כה אמר יהוה ko ʔɔmar yhwh "Thus says YHWH," which signals that his message is not his own but Yahweh's (2 Kgs 9:6). See my discussion of #1 in §3.4.1.2.3.

[84] Note that Elisha is addressed as "man of God" in 2 Kgs 4:40 as well. However, it was excluded from our corpus since it is addressed by more than one person.

[85] Ahaziah, the king of Israel, dispatches to Elijah three captains at different times, each of whom is referred to as שׂר. Their inferior status compared to Elijah is clearly demonstrated when the third one falls on his knees as he entreats him to come down from a hilltop.

from genealogy and reserved for members of the royal family, is fitting for Amnon.[86] Jonadab, on the other hand, was the son of Shimeah (2 Sam 13:3), David's elder brother (1 Chr 2:13), making him a cousin to Amnon. No specific information is given about Jonadab's occupation, except that he is referred to as Amnon's "friend" (רע *reaʕ*) and a "very wise man" (איש חכם מאד *ʔiš ḥɔkɔm məʔod* [2 Sam 13:3]). While רע in this instance may simply denote a friend (Anderson 1989, 174), it is also possible that it denotes a court title for a royal counselor, such as רעה המלך *reʕɛ hammɛlɛk* lit. "king's friend," who played an official role as the king's counselor (e.g., Hushai, David's counselor [1 Chr 27:33; cf. 2 Sam 15:37; 16:16] and Zabud, Solomon's counselor [1 Kgs 4:5]).[87] The narrator's description of Jonadab as a "wise man" further strengthens the likelihood of רע being a title for a counselor (Alter 2013, 495). Considering the personal relationship and occupations of Amnon and Jonadab, it is evident that Amnon holds a higher status than Jonadab.[88] Thus,

---

[86] In the Hebrew Bible, the term בן־המלך is attested in reference to nine men. Often it is used explicitly for known sons of a king: Amnon son of David (2 Sam 13:4); Absalom son of David (2 Sam 18:12, 20); Solomon son of David (Ps 72:1); Joash son of Ahaziah (2 Kgs 11:4 = 2 Chr 23:3, 11); Jotham son of Azariah (2 Kgs 15:5). In four instances, however, the term is used for those whose genealogy is uncertain: Joash (1 Kgs 22:26 = 2 Chr 18:25); Jerahmeel (Jer 36:26); Malchiah (Jer 38:6); Maaseiah (2 Chr 28:7).

Ever since Clermont-Ganneau (1888, 33–36) first suggested that the term בן־המלך can refer to minor administrative officials not of royal blood, the proposal was embraced by subsequent scholars without serious critique (e.g., Diringer 1934, 232–33; De Vaux 1965, 119–20; Yeivin 1965, 160; Brin 1969, 433–65). However, this long-standing consensus was challenged by Rainey (1975, 427–32), who showed both from Hebrew sources and Hittite practices as reflected in cuneiform texts from el-Amarna and Boghazköy that the bearers of the title בן־המלך in ancient Israel were sons of the monarch only. Rainey's view has been adopted and expanded by Avigad (1978; 55; 1986, 28), Lemaire (1979, 59–65), Barkay (1993, 110–12), Avishur and Heltzer (2000, 62–74), and Fox (2000, 43–53). Avishur and Heltzer, for example, argue that the term בן־המלך designates the position/status of a person who could not only be an actual son of the reigning king but also any member of royal genealogy, such as the king's nephews and their descendants. I find their argument to be most convincing, as there is no Israelite material that contains an example of a בן־המלך whose origin is clearly nonroyal.

[87] Van Selms (1957, 119) is the first who suggested that רע in this instance functions as an official title. For detailed studies of the meaning and use of רעה המלך, see Donner 1961, 260–77; Mettinger 1971, 63–69; and Fox 2000, 121.

[88] Even if we take the term רע to denote a "friend," it does not automatically guarantee that Amnon and Jonadab are socially equal. A close relation could develop between two men in ancient Israel who are not of equal status. For example, the relationship between Jonathan and David has traditionally been interpreted as a platonic friendship (e.g., see Guttmacher 1903, 5:520–21). In their dialogue, however, David consistently refers to himself as עבדך *ʕabdekɔ* "your servant" (e.g., 1 Sam 20:7, 8 [2x]), while Jonathan addresses

Jonadab's use of the occupational T בן המלך to address Amnon can be seen as a polite address, showing deference to a social superior.

3.4.2.2.1.2. HTs

Similar to ATs, HTs can also mark the superior status of the addressee. Table 3.8 demonstrates two types of HTs found in our corpus: those headed by the honorific T אדני (##1–21) and those headed by the occupational T המלך (#22).

Table 3.8. HTs Used by Inferiors to Superiors

#	Form	Speaker	Addressee	Verse
1–2	My lord the king	David	Saul	1 Sam 24:9; 26:17
3–5		Bathsheba	David	1 Kgs 1:13, 18, 20
6		Nathan	David	1 Kgs 1:24
7–8		Joab	David	2 Sam 14:22; 1 Chr 21:3
9–10		Tekoaite Woman	David	2 Sam 14:9, 19
11		Mephibosheth	David	2 Sam 19:27
12		Ziba	David	2 Sam 16:4
13		Ahab	Ben-Hadad	1 Kgs 20:4
14		Servant	King of Aram	2 Kgs 6:12
15		Woman	King of Israel	2 Kgs 6:26
16		Gehazi	King of Israel	2 Kgs 8:5
17		Jeremiah	Zedekiah	Jer 37:20
18		Ebed-Melech	Zedekiah	Jer 38:9
19	My lord man of God	Woman	Elisha	2 Kgs 4:16
20	My lord Moses	Joshua	Moses	Num 11:28
21	My lord Elijah	Obadiah	Elijah	1 Kgs 18:7
22	King Jehoshaphat	Jahaziel	Jehoshaphat	2 Chr 20:15

When the honorific T אדני comes at the head of a HT, it is most commonly followed by the occupational T המלך *hammɛlɛk* "the king" (##1–18).[89] Similar to cases where המלך is used alone, אדני המלך is typically used by subjects to address kings (outlaw [##1–2]; king's wife [##3–5]; prophet [##6, 17]; commander [##7–8]; woman [##9–10, 15]; son of king's friend [#11]; servant [##12, 14, 16]; eunuch [#18]) in a variety of contexts (calling [#1]; responding [#2]; requesting [##3–5, 9, 12, 15, 17]; informing [##6, 10–11, 14, 16, 18]; thanking [#7];

David by APN (1 Sam 20:12, 15). The nonreciprocal exchange of self-referential and address terms between these two clearly demonstrates that they remained close friends despite being socially unequal in status. For the deferential use of the self-referential terms in the book of Samuel, see Kim 2015, 588–605.

[89] Lande (1949, 32) counts seventeen cases of אדני המלך, but I count eighteen of them.

opposing [#8]).[90] However, there is one exception in which Ahab, king of Israel, addresses Ben-Hadad, king of Aram, as אדני המלך (#13), as Ahab acknowledges Ben-Hadad's sovereignty over him (1 Kgs 20:4).[91]

In sociolinguistics, it is commonly assumed that the level of deference shown by the speaker to the addressee increases as the number of appositional honorific titles used by the speaker increases (Aliakbari and Toni 2008, 9). Thus, it can be said that when the occupational T המלך is used together with the honorific T אדני, the degree of deference given to the king increases. The speaker not only acknowledges the superior position of the king through the use of the occupational T המלך but also expresses respect for the king through the use of the honorific T אדני.[92]

The honorific T אדני can also be followed by the occupational T איש האלהים *ʔiš hɔʔelohim* "man of God" (#19), which is exclusively used as an address form for Elijah and Elisha in the Hebrew Bible (see §3.4.2.2.1.3 below). After the prophet Elisha informs the Shunammite woman that she will have a son in return for her kindness to him, she addresses him as אדני איש האלהים *ʔᵃdoni ʔiš hɔʔelohim* "my lord man of God," asking him not to give her false expectations (2 Kgs 4:16). By using this compound address composed of the honorific T and the occupational T, she elevates the level of deference towards Elisha compared to when either T is used individually. Through this address, she not only acknowledges Elisha's superior status as the prophet of Yahweh but also expresses her deference towards him.

There are two cases in which the honorific T אדני is followed by a PN (##20–21). In both instances, the superior status of the addressee over the speaker is clear. Joshua, who addresses Moses as אדני משה *ʔᵃdoni mošɛ* "my lord Moses!", is his assistant (משרת משה *mašɔreṯ mošɛ* "the assistant of Moses" [Num 11:28]). Obadiah, a high administrative official in Ahab's court (אשר על הבית *ʔᵃšɛr ʕal-habbɔyiṯ* "a minister over the royal house" [1 Kgs 18:3]), the honorific T אדני

---

[90] As Lande (1949, 32) perceptively observes, המלך as an address form is particularly prevalent in older texts (1x in Judges; 2x in 1 Samuel; 3x in 2 Samuel; 1x in Esther; 1x in 2 Chronicles), while אדני המלך frequently occurs in later texts (2x in 1 Samuel; 5x in 2 Samuel; 5x in 1 Kings; 3x in 2 Kings; 2x in Jeremiah; 1x in 1 Chronicles). Compare, for example, the Tekoaite woman's cry for help to King David, הושעה המלך, *hošiʕɔ hammɛlɛḵ* "Save, O king!" (2 Sam 14:4) with a woman's cry for help to the unnamed king of Israel הושיעה אדני המלך *hošiʕɔ ʔᵃdoni hammɛlɛḵ* "Save, my lord the king!" (2 Kgs 6:26).
[91] Note that after Israel's victory at the battle of Samaria and Aphek, Ahab refers to Ben-Hadad as his "brother," treating him as an equal (1 Kgs 20:32). This is one of the rare examples that demonstrate that the speaker may choose different forms of address as the situation changes over time, as seen in §3.2 (f).
[92] Examples equivalent to compound addresses composed of honorific T + occupational T include "Mr. President" in English and *Monsieur le Président* in French.

when addressing Elijah.[93] The narrator's description of Obadiah as a fearer of Yahweh (1 Kgs 18:3) clearly indicates that he fully recognizes Elijah's spiritual authority as the prophet of Yahweh.

In §3.4.1.2, I have demonstrated that APNs and HPNs are used to indicate the superiority of the speaker. Hence, one might question whether it is appropriate for the superior addressee to receive a compound address in which a PN comes in the second position, as seen in the cases mentioned above. In response, I would argue that the placement of the honorific T אדני at the beginning prevents the addressee from possibly perceiving the speaker's use of the PN as presumptuous. This word order may explain why there is no indication in the text that Moses was offended by Joshua's address, nor Elijah by Obadiah's address.

There is one case in which the occupational T המלך is followed by a PN in an address (#22). Jahaziel addresses Jehoshaphat as המלך יהושפט *hammɛlɛk yəhošɔpɔṭ* "King Jehoshaphat!," as he encourages him to go out to battle against Moab and Ammon (2 Chr 20:15–17). Nothing is known about Jahaziel except that he was a Levite from the family of Asaph (2 Chr 20:14), who served as the chief temple musician during David's time (1 Chr 16:5). Therefore, it can be reasonably assumed that Jahaziel was among the Levitical musicians in Jehoshaphat's court, indicating Jehoshaphat's superiority over Jahaziel. Consequently, similar to cases where the occupational T המלך is used alone, Jahaziel's use of compound address headed by the occupational T המלך can be interpreted as an expression of respect towards King Jehoshaphat.

3.4.2.2.1.3. Excursus: נביא VS. איש האלהים

Revell (1996, 164) argues that נביא *nɔḇiʔ* "speaker, spokesman, prophet" and איש האלהים *ʔiš hɔʔlohim* "man of God" are free variants. However, this argument stems from a failure to recognize the distinction between their referential and address usages.[94] As Arnold Zwicky (1974, 790) points out, there are words that can be used as references but not as addresses, such as 'physician,' 'assistant professor,' or 'person' in English (compared to 'doctor,' 'professor,' or 'man,' respectively, which can be used as addresses).[95] A similar phenomenon can be observed in the use of נביא, which is the most common term for prophets in the Hebrew Bible (317 times).[96] Generally, it functions as a professional designation

---

[93] For a full discussion of the rank, functions, and jurisdiction of the bearers of the title אשר על הבית, see Fox 2000, 81–96.

[94] A term of reference is a linguistic expression by which speaker A *refers to* or *talks about* B in communication with C, whereas a term of address is a linguistic item by which speaker A *addresses* B in a one-on-one interaction.

[95] Conversely, some terms are used in address but never in reference, such as "Sir!"

[96] For the etymology and semantics of נביא, see Müller 1974, 9:130–35; Jeremias 1997, 2:697; Verhoef 1997, 4:1065.

used not only for the prophets of Yahweh (e.g., Samuel [1 Sam 3:20]) but also for false prophets (e.g., Hananiah [Jer 28:1]) and pagan prophets (e.g., the prophets of Baal and Asherah [1 Kgs 18:19]).[97] It is widely used as a referential term throughout the Hebrew Bible but is never used as an address.[98]

In contrast, איש האלהים, the second most common term for prophets, specifically denotes someone who acts under Yahweh's power and authority. It is used both as a referential term (71 times) and as an address term (5 times).[99] Table 3.9 shows the distribution of נביא and איש האלהים in the Hebrew Bible.[100]

Table 3.9. The Distribution of נביא and איש האלהים in the Hebrew Bible

	Reference	Address
נביא	X	–
איש האלהים	X	X

When איש האלהים is used as an address term, it exclusively applies to Elijah and Elisha (#30–33 in table 3.7 and #19 in table 3.8). To gain more a clearer understanding of how נביא and איש האלהים are used in reference and address within the Elijah-Elisha narrative, it is necessary to focus on the narrative spanning from 1 Kgs 17–2 Kgs 13. In this narrative, איש האלהים is exclusively employed for

---

[97] See Jeremias (1997, 2:700) who views נביא as a professional designation.
[98] The distribution of the word נביא is uneven. It occurs most often in prophetic books (especially in Jeremiah [95x]) and the older historical books (especially in Kings [84x]), while less often in the Pentateuch (14x) and poetic books (3x).
[99] Twelve individuals are referred to or addressed as איש האלהים in the Hebrew Bible (with or without the article before אלהים): Moses (Deut 33:1; Josh 14:6; Ps 90:1; Ezra 3:2; 1 Chr 23:14; 2 Chr 30:16); the messenger of Yahweh who appeared to Manoah's wife (Judg 13:6; 8); the man who delivered Yahweh's judgment message to Eli (1 Sam 2:27); Samuel (1 Sam 9:6, 7, 8, 10); Shemaiah (1 Kgs 12:22; 2 Chr 11:2); the man from Judah who proclaimed a message of judgment against the altar in Bethel (1 Kgs 13:1, 4, 5, 6 [2x], 7, 8, 11, 12, 14 [2x], 21, 26, 29, 31; 2 Kgs 23:16, 17); Elijah (1 Kgs 17:18, 24; 2 Kgs 1:9, 10, 11, 12, 13); the man who delivered Yahweh's message to Ahab that Israel would defeat the Arameans (1 Kgs 20:28); Elisha (2 Kgs 4:7, 9, 16, 21, 22, 25 [2x], 27 [2x], 40, 42, 5:8, 14, 15, 20; 6:6, 9, 10, 15; 7:2, 17, 18, 19; 8:2, 4, 7, 8, 11, 13:19); Hanan the son of Igdaliah (Jer 35:4); David (Neh 12:24, 36; 2 Chr 8:14); the man who advised King Amaziah of Judah to refrain from taking the army of Israel to war (2 Chr 25:7, 9 [2x]).
[100] ראה *roʔɛ* "seer" and חזה *ḥozɛ* "seer" are also used for the prophets who "saw" God's message by dreams or visions. While these two terms are synonymous and occasionally alternate with each other (2 Chr 16:7; 19:2), it seems that they were used in different time periods. According to 1 Sam 9:9, ראה was the older equivalent of נביא, a common term for prophets in the narrator's day. The term חזה is an Aramaic loanword and mostly used in the later books of the Hebrew Bible (e.g., 1 Chr 25:5). For a discussion of the meaning and the usage of these terms, see Naudé 1997, 2:56–61; 3:1004–12.

addressing Elijah and Elisha, and it is also exclusively used for referring to them. No other character in the narrative is referred to as איש האלהים. However, נביא, which consistently serves as a referential term, applies not only to the prophets of Yahweh, including Elijah and Elisha (e.g., 1 Kgs 18:36; 2 Kgs 6:12), but also to false prophets of Israel (e.g., 1 Kgs 22:6) and the prophets of Baal and Asherah (e.g., 1 Kgs 18:19). Table 3.10 provides an overview of the distribution of נביא and איש האלהים in the Elijah-Elisha narrative.

Table 3.10. The Distribution of נביא and איש האלהים in the Elijah-Elisha Narrative

	Reference	Address
נביא	Any Prophets	–
איש האלהים	Exclusively Elijah & Elisha	Exclusively Elijah & Elisha

This distribution pattern indicates that the narrator's portrayal of Elijah and Elisha differs from that of other prophets within the narrative. For the narrator, Elijah and Elisha are primarily איש האלהים as well as נביא, while other prophets are simply נביא. Therefore, Revell's claim that נביא and איש האלהים are free variants cannot be supported by the Elijah-Elisha narrative.

The narrator's intention to distinguish Elijah and Elisha from other prophets becomes more evident when נביא is not used in address. Could it be possible that the speaker (ultimately, the narrator) deliberately avoided using נביא as a term of address for Elijah and Elisha (and perhaps other prophets as well)? If so, why? While no definitive explanation can be drawn due to the limited data, I propose the following as a potential possibility. As discussed earlier, נביא serves as a *neutral* professional title and is often used for false prophets and pagan prophets in the Elijah-Elisha narrative. To avoid any negative connotations associated with נביא, the narrator may have chosen to have the characters address Elijah and Elisha as איש האלהים. By exclusively using this *theologically-oriented* title for Elijah and Elisha, the narrator successfully sets them apart from other (false) prophets.[101]

3.4.2.2.2. Superior to Inferior? The Cases of Expressive Shift

So far, I have argued that the use of ATs or HTs in addressing someone may indicate the superiority of the addressee. However, there are two cases in which an AT is used in seemingly superior-inferior dyads, as shown in table 3.11.

---

[101] A reviewer of this manuscript kindly reminded me that the distinction between true and false prophets was indeed apparent in certain ancient translations of the Hebrew Bible. One notable example can be observed in the LXX translation of Jeremiah, where the translators employed the prefix 'pseudo-' to denote false prophets (Jer 6:13; 35:1).

Table 3.11. ATs Used by Superiors to Inferiors

#	Form	Speaker	Addressee	Relation	Context	Verse
1	King of Judah	Necho	Josiah	king of Egypt > king of Judah	Asking Josiah to leave the way open at Megiddo	2 Chr 35:21
2	Seer	Amaziah	Amos	Priest > Prophet	Trying to stop Amos from prophesying	Amos 7:12

In case #1, it seems clear that Pharaoh Necho II was superior to Josiah, king of Judah. James M. Miller and John H. Hayes (2006, 450–53) present several pieces of historical evidence suggesting that Judah was under Egyptian dominance throughout Josiah's reign (641–609 BCE). For example, the Babylonian Chronicle records the Egyptian campaigns against Nabopolassar's forces in Gablini in 616 BCE and in Harran in 610 BCE (Grayson 1975, 91). These military expeditions would not have been possible without control over trade routes throughout the Syro-Palestinian states, including the Via Maris, which ran through the western edge of Judean territory and the Jezreel valley near Megiddo.[102]

Therefore, it can reasonably be assumed that under normal circumstances, Necho would have addressed Josiah, who was militarily inferior, as either APN or HPN (see §3.4.1.2.1).[103] Furthermore, Necho's speech takes place in the context of a military confrontation. The Egyptian pharaoh was leading his army to Carchemish to assist his Assyrian ally against the Babylonian army, but Josiah and his army intercepted him at the plain of Megiddo to attack his forces (2 Chr 35:20).[104] In such situations, the condescending use of an APN or HPN (or derogatory terms) is to be expected (see case #21 in §3.4.1.2.1).[105] However, at the

---

[102] See also Schipper (2010, 200–26) who argues that Egypt filled the power vacuum created by the departure of the Assyrians in the southern Levant at the end of the seventh century BCE. Based on archaeological, epigraphic and Egyptian source, he claims that Pharaoh Psammetichus I, with the help of his Greek mercenaries, established an Egyptian-controlled system of vassal-states with a fortress at Meṣad Ḥashavyahu sometime after 616 BCE.

[103] See also EA 162:1, 367:1, 369:1, and 370:1, in which an Egyptian pharaoh addresses his vassal by PN + T.

[104] Josiah's rationale for blocking and attacking the Egyptians at Megiddo is unknown. It may have been his fear of Assyrian dominance over Judah once again, the result of a coalition with Babylon (Falk 1996, 181), or his own desire to reunite Israel and Judah (Frost, 1968, 371; Hamilton 2002, 90).

[105] For the condescending referential use of PN in the context of war, see the speech of the Assyrian Rab-shakeh to Hezekiah's officials in 2 Kings 18. He consistently refers to King Hezekiah by APN (vv. 19, 22, 29–32), while he refers to his master Sennacherib by honorific T or occupational T (e.g., אשור מלך הגדול מלך *melek haggaḏol melek ʔaššur* "the great king, the king of Assyria" [vv. 19, 28]).

beginning of his speech, Necho addresses Josiah by the occupational T מלך יהודה *mɛlɛk yəhudɔ* "King of Judah!" (2 Chr 35:21).

Considering the context in which Necho speaks, I view his use of the occupational T as a case of expressive shift. Immediately after addressing Josiah by the occupational T, Necho states that he has no quarrel with Josiah and that it is God (אלהים *ʔlohim*) who commanded him to hurry (2 Chr 35:21).[106] Undoubtedly, the ultimate goal of his statement is to secure a right of way without unnecessary delays and casualties at Megiddo. Thus, it can be argued that in order to dissuade Josiah from fighting him, the powerful Egyptian pharaoh deliberately avoids the expected APN or HPN, which might convey a sense of condescension and potentially provoke Josiah. Instead, he chooses to show respect to Josiah by using the occupational T.

In case #2, Amaziah addresses Amos using the occupational T חזה *ḥozɛ* "seer," as he forbids Amos from prophesying in Bethel, the chief northern sanctuary and a rival of Jerusalem. In terms of occupation, Amaziah is referred to as כהן בית אל *kohen beṯ-ʔel* "the priest of Bethel" in Amos 7:10.[107] This title probably indicates that he was the head priest at the shrine (Petersen 1981, 428; Andersen and Freedman 1989, 766; Noble 1998, 428; Garrett 2008, 217), which may be supported by the authoritative tone in which he deals with Amos (vv. 12–13).

Amaziah also plays a political role by informing King Jeroboam II of Amos's prophecy.[108] It is noteworthy that Amaziah presents Amos's message purely in political terms, completely removing its theological dimension. He portrays Amos as a conspirator rather than a prophet (קשר *qɔšar* "he conspired" [v. 10]). He parodies the so-called prophetic messenger formula, כה אמר יהוה *ko ʔɔmar yhwh*

---

[106] There has been a debate over whether Pharaoh Necho indeed referred to the god of Israel. For example, Rudolph (1955, 332) argues that while the Egyptian pharaoh spoke in the name of one of his own gods, the Chronicler turned it into the word of the god of Israel. Based on Tractate Sof. 4:9, however, Kimḥi (2007, 277) asserts that Necho indeed spoke of the god of Israel. One can never be sure about the historical reality. It seems certain, though, that the Chronicler viewed Necho's speech as the word of the god of Israel, as can be seen in his comment on Josiah's military action: "[Josiah] did not listen to the words of Necho *from the mouth of God* [אלהים]" (2 Chr 35:22; italics mine).

[107] The title כהן בית אל occurs only here in the Hebrew Bible. While the titles of priests with divine names are relatively common (e.g., כהן יהוה, [*kohen yhwh* "the priest of Yahweh" in 1 Sam 14:3; 22:17, 21; Isa 61:6; 2 Chr 13:9]; כהן הבעל [*kohen habbaʕal* "the priest of Baal" in 2 Kgs 11:18 = 2 Chr 23:17]; כהני דגן [*koh^ene ḏɔḡon* "the priests of Dagon" in 1 Sam 5:5]), those containing the place of office are rarely attested (e.g., כהן מדין [*kohen miḏyɔn* "the priest of Midian" in Exod 3:1]; כהן אן [*kohen ʔon* "the priest of On" in Gen. 41:45]). For a discussion on a title written on an eighth-century BCE Hebrew seal, כהן דאר *khn dʔr* "the priest of Dor," see Avigad 1975, 101–5.

[108] The fact that Amaziah had a direct access to King Jeroboam might indicate that he was a high-ranking officer.

"Thus says Yahweh" by saying, כה אמר עמוס *kō ʔɔmar ʕɔmos* "Thus says *Amos*" (v. 11). He omits the beginning part of the final clause of Amos's prophecy in verse 9, "I (the Lord) will rise against," turning the rest of it into an explicit prediction of the violent death of the king, saying, "Jeroboam shall die by the sword" (v. 11). In short, Amaziah was a high-ranking official in northern Israel who held significant influence in the religious and political realms.

As for Amos's occupation, there can be no question that he functioned as a prophet of Yahweh. In verse 15, he himself states that he received a personal call from Yahweh to prophesy against the northern kingdom of Israel (cf. 3:8). However, in verse 14, Amos seems to deny being a prophet:

(21) לא נביא אנכי ולא בן נביא אנכי כי בוקר אנכי ובולס שקמים
    lɔʔ-nɔbiʔ   *ʔɔnoki*   *wəlɔʔ*   *ben-nɔbiʔ*   *ʔɔnoki*
    not-prohet   I   and=not   son.of-prophet   I
    ki-boqer   *ʔɔnoki*   *uboles*   *šiqmim*
    but-herdsman   I   and=dresser.of   sycamore figs
    I am no prophet, nor a prophet's son, but I am a herdsman and a dresser of sycamore figs. (Amos 7:14)

Most scholars are divided into two groups regarding this seeming contradiction.[109] Some (e.g., Wolff 1977, 312; Hayes, 1988, 236; Witherington 1999, 109) see no contradiction between verse 14 and verse 15, asserting that Amos's statement in verse 14 should be understood as a direct response to Amaziah's prohibition of Amos's prophetic ministry at Bethel in verses 12–13. According to them, Amos is not denying his prophetic activities (note that he testifies that Yahweh said to him, הנבא *hinnɔbeʔ* "Prophesy!" in v. 15) but repudiating Amaziah's insinuation that he is a hireling, that is, a professional prophet who earns his living from his prophetic activities (see v. 12 in which Amaziah demands Amos, אכל שם לחם ושם תנבא *ʔᵉkɔl-šɔm leḥem wəšɔm tinnɔbeʔ* "eat bread and prophesy there [Judah]!"). Stating that he is involved in various agricultural enterprises in verse 14 (בוקר *boqer* "herdman"; בולס שקמים *boles šiqmim* "a dresser of sycamore figs"),[110] Amos asserts that he has no need to prophesy for money. Thus, he is taking pains to distinguish between one called by Yahweh to prophesy and a professional prophet (נביא), between one commissioned by Yahweh and a prophet's

---

[109] For a survey of different attempts to resolve the problem of a contradiction between v. 14 and v. 15, see Paul 1991, 244–47.

[110] For a discussion on the meaning and significance of בוקר and בולס, see Andersen and Freedman 1989, 778–79 and Steiner 2003. Note also that the narrator identifies Amos's profession as a shepherd in 1:1: בנקדים *bannoqdim* "[he was] among the shepherds."

disciple (בן־נביא),[111] and between a financially independent man sanctioned by Yahweh and a salaried cult official. This interpretation, however, is not without criticism. For example, Shalom M. Paul (1991, 246) questions the validity of interpreting נביא as a prophet by profession.

Others (e.g., Paul 1991, 246; Noble 1998, 430) view all the nominal clauses in verse 14 as dependent on the subsequent perfective narrative clause in verse 15 (ויקחני יהוה *wayyiqqɔḥeni yhwh* "Then Yahweh took me") and translate them in the past tense: "I was not a prophet, nor a prophet's son; on the contrary, I was a herdsman and a dresser of sycamore figs."[112] According to them, Amos is emphasizing the divine initiative, declaring that he was not a prophet but became one when Yahweh charged him to prophesy. This interpretation, however, fails to explain adequately the meaning of the second nominal clause in verse 14: ולא בן נביא אנכי. If Amos is indeed saying that he was not a prophet (נביא) before but now he is, he must also be saying that he was not a prophet's disciple (בן נביא) before but now he is, which can hardly be the case.

While scholars are divided over Amos's occupation at the time of his confrontation with Amaziah, there is a broad consensus that Amaziah held a socially superior position in relation to Amos (e.g., Andersen and Freedman 1989, 766). It seems certain that Amaziah's religious and political power as the head priest of Bethel outweighed that of Amos, who came from another nation (Judah) without an official position, institutional background, or external certification (Andersen and Freedman 1989, 772). Thus, under normal circumstances, Amaziah's address to Amos, who was socially inferior, would have been an APN or HPN (see §3.4.1.2.1). It is worth noting that Amaziah refers to Amos by PN when he sends Jeroboam II a report of his preaching in verse 10, indicating that Amos's name was known to Amaziah. However, when addressing Amos directly, he uses the occupational T חזה, which is normally used to express the speaker's respect toward a superior addressee.

I would argue that Amaziah's use of the occupational T חזה is an example of expressive shift. Unlike case #1, however, in which the speaker (Necho II) conveys respect toward the inferior addressee (Josiah) by using an occupational T, Amaziah's address seems to reveal his derogatory attitude toward Amos. As Brown and Gilman (1960, 275) rightly point out, the interpretation of the speaker's attitude does not solely depend on the literal meaning of an address term but on the context in which it is used. While the occupational T חזה itself may be

---

[111] It is most likely that the term בן denotes a member of a group in this context, not a biological son.
[112] Note that the LXX translates these verbless clauses in the past tense (ἤμην "I was").

honorable in Israel,[113] it is sandwiched between Amaziah's outright rejecting Amos's message (vv. 10–11) and prohibiting Amos's prophetic activities at Bethel (vv. 12–13).[114] Thus, it can hardly be said that Amaziah's address intended to express admiration or respect for Amos, as some (e.g., Wolff 1977, 311) argue. Rather, it is more reasonable to conclude that Amaziah's intention was to mock Amos ironically with a seemingly respectful address, implying his denial of Amos's prophetic authority.

Amaziah's address of the occupational T חזה not only carries momentary expressive significance but also serves as a phraseological link between a series of Amos's vision reports (7:1–3, 4–6, 7–9; 8:1–3; 9:1–6) and the prose narrative of Amaziah's confrontation with Amos embedded within them (7:10–17). It is important to note that each of these visions begins with the verb ראה *rʔh* "to see" (7:1, 4, 7; 8:1; 9:1), which is synonymous with חזה *ḥzh* "to see" (cf. 1:1). The use of the noun חזה instead of its semantic equivalent ראה might have been inevitable as the latter became obsolete by the time of Amos (see 1 Sam 9:9; footnote 100). It is possible that Amaziah used חזה simply because he had heard Amos reporting visions he had seen (Mays 1969, 126; Garrett 2008, 220). However, it is also possible that the narrator placed it in Amaziah's mouth when inserting the dialogue between Amaziah and Amos amidst the vision reports (Paul 1991, 240). In any case, the encounter between Amaziah and Amos should not be considered an isolated incident but rather closely connected to the surrounding vision reports through Amaziah's use of the address term חזה. Readers are compelled to view this encounter in the context of Amos's visions, especially the third (7:7–9) and fourth ones (8:1–3), where the messages of doom upon political and religious institutions are declared.[115]

---

[113] The title חזה, denoting the one who receives divine revelation by seeing, is mainly applied to royal officials, such as court prophets (Gad [2 Sam 24:11; 1 Chr 21:9; 29:29; 2 Chr 29:25]), scribes (Iddo [2 Chr 9:29; 12:15]; Jehu [2 Chr 19:2; cf. 2 Chr 20:34]), and worship leaders (Heman [1 Chr 25:5; 2 Chr 35:15]; Asaph [2 Chr 29:30; 35:15]; Jeduthun [2 Chr 35:15]). While those who are called חזה are sometimes condemned by Yahweh for their sinful actions (Isa 29:10; Mic 3:7), the title itself is never viewed in a negative light (contra Cohen [1961, 177] and Crenshaw [1971, 67] who assume that חזה is a derogatory title). See Petersen (1981, 56–57), who views חזה as a technical term for a Judahite prophet. Note that the term חזה was rarely used in the preexilic books.

[114] Because of the presence of the "ethical dative" in v. 12 (ברח לך *bəraḥ-ləkā* "Flee away!"), some commentators (e.g., Wolff 1977, 306, 311; Hayes 1988, 234) view Amaziah's directives in vv. 12–13 as an expression of personal goodwill to save Amos before King Jeroboam could act. This view, however, fails to explain why Amaziah sent Jeroboam a report of Amos's activities (vv. 10–11) if he wanted to save Amos in the first place.

[115] For an extensive discussion on the interrelationship between Amos's vision reports and the account of Amaziah's confrontation with Amos, see Landy 1987.

3.4.2.3. Conclusion

In contrast to APNs and HPNs, ATs and HTs in our corpus are normally used "upward," that is, in the inferior-superior dyads, as can be seen in figure 3.5. Their address usage, therefore, seems to be influenced by the power dynamic between the speaker and the addressee. Marking the superiority of the addressee, ATs and HTs seem to function similarly to the *V* form in Brown, Gilman, and Ford's *T/V* system and partially confirm Brown and Ford's "linguistic universal" (Note that there are no instances in our corpus where distant equals exchange address forms). In Brown and Levinson's framework, both ATs and HTs serve as deferential terms. They are strategically chosen by the speaker to acknowledge the greater power of the addressee. By doing so, the speaker seeks to decrease the degree of potential threats to the addressee's desire for autonomy (Brown and Levinson call it a negative politeness strategy). The use of ATs in the seemingly superior-inferior dyads can be considered as "expressive shifts" where the speaker (or narrator) strategically violates the rules of address above to convey feelings of respect or contempt. These shifts produce powerful pragmatic and literary effects that the readers should consider for a proper understanding of the text.

Figure 3.5. The Use of ATs and HTs in the Hebrew Bible

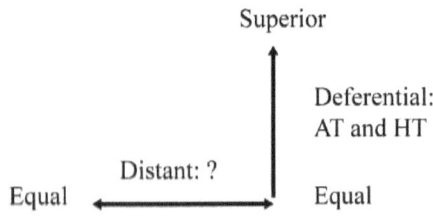

3.4.3. Kinship Terms

3.4.3.1. Taxonomy

Kinship is a system of family relations. In anthropology, two types of kinship are commonly recognized: consanguineal and affinal kinship.[116] Consanguineal kinship refers to family relations established through blood ties, that is, biological procreation (from Latin *con* "with" and *sanguis* "blood"), while affinal kinship is derived from marriage (from Latin *affinis* "relation by marriage"). Thus, kingship terms (KTs) can be defined as words that refer to consanguineal or affinal kinship.

---

[116] These are by no means the only criteria by which kin relations can be established. In some societies, kinship can be established through adoption, a godparent relationship, and suckling (El Guindi 2012, 551–53).

For English speakers, consanguineal KTs include father, mother, son, daughter, brother, sister, nephew, niece, and cousin, while husband, wife, and terms marked with the "-in-law" suffix (e.g., mother-in-law) belong to the affinal KTs. Some KTs, such as uncle and aunt, can be both consanguineal (Ego's parent's siblings) and affinal (Ego's parent's sibling's spouse).[117]

KTs can be categorized based on the degree of closeness between Ego and his/her kin: primary, secondary, and tertiary KTs. Primary KTs are words that refer to kin who are directly related to Ego (e.g., father, mother, brother, sister, son, daughter, husband, wife). Secondary KTs refer to the primary kin of Ego's primary kin (e.g., grandparents, uncle, aunts, in-laws, etc.). Tertiary KTs refer to the primary kin of Ego's secondary kin or the secondary kin of Ego's primary kin (e.g., great-grandparents, first cousins, etc.).

KTs can also be grouped according to the generation affiliation of Ego and his/her kin: ascending, descending, and horizontal KTs. Ascending KTs are terms that refer to kin belonging to a generation above Ego (by one step or more), such as father, mother, grandfather, grandmother, uncle, aunt, et cetera. Descending KTs are terms that refer to kin belonging to a generation below Ego (by one step or more), including son, daughter, nephew, niece, grandson, granddaughter, et cetera. Horizontal KTs are terms that refer to kin belonging to the same generation as Ego, such as brother, sister, cousin, et cetera.

It is important to note that all these KTs are terms of reference, meaning they are used by Ego to *refer to* his/her kin when communicating with others. As we will see below, these KTs, when used as terms of reference and not as terms of address, express the actual kin relationships between Ego and his/her kin. Table 3.12 provides a list of KTs used as terms of reference in the Hebrew Bible.[118] For brevity and clarity, I will employ George P. Murdock's (1947, 56) kin-type notation, which uses two-letter abbreviations for primary kins (Fa[ther], Mo[ther], Br[other], Si[ster], So[n], Da[ughter], Hu[sband], Wi[fe]) and their combinations to indicate possessive relations (e.g., FaMo for "father's mother").

---

[117] The term *Ego* is commonly used in anthropology to designate a given individual who forms the starting point in kinship reckoning.

[118] Note that דוד *doḏ*, דדה *doḏɔ*, יבם *yɔḇɔm*, and יבמת *yɔḇemeṯ* are excluded from this table, as it is difficult to determine the precise kin relationships that these terms denote. For a discussion of the semantic range of each term, see McClenney-Sadler 2007, 50–52.

Table 3.12. KTs Used in Reference in the Hebrew Bible[119]

			Consanguineal		Affinal	
		Generation	Terms	Notation	Terms	Notation
Primary	Ascending		אב ʔɔḇ	Fa		
			אם ʔem	Mo		
	Horizontal		אח ʔɔḥ	Br	בעל baʕal / איש ʔiš	Hu
			אחות ʔɔḥot	Si	אשה ʔiššɔ	Wi
	Descending		בן ben	So		
			בת baṯ	Da		
Secondary	Ascending		אבי אם ʔᵃḇi ʔem[120]	MoFa	חם ḥɔm[121]	HuFa
			אחי אב ʔᵃḥi-ʔɔḇ[122]	FaBr	חמות ḥɔmot[123]	HuMo
			אחות אב ʔɔḥot-ʔɔḇ[124]	FaSi	חתן ḥoten[125]	WiFa
			אחי אם ʔᵃḥi-ʔem[126]	MoBr	חתנת ḥotenet[127]	WiMo
			אחות אם ʔɔḥot-ʔem[128]	MoSi		
	Horizontal		בת אב baṯ-ʔɔḇ[129]	FaDa	אשת אח ʔešeṯ ʔɔḥ[130]	BrWi
			בת אם[131] baṯ-ʔem	MoDa		
	Descending		בן אח[132] ben-ʔɔḥ	BrSo	חתן ḥɔtɔn[133]	DaHu
			בן בן[134] ben-ben	SoSo	כלה kallɔ[135]	SoWi
			בת בן[136] baṯ-ben	SoDa		
			בת בת[137] baṯ-baṯ	DaDa		

[119] Andersen (1969, 38) and McClenney-Sadler (2007, 41–43) provide similar tables of KTs, but they contain either KTs unattested in the Hebrew Bible (Andersen) or numerous errors in verse lists (McClenney-Sadler).
[120] Gen 28:2; Judg 9:1.
[121] Gen 38:13, 25; 1 Sam 4:19, 21.
[122] Gen 29:12; Lev 18:14.
[123] Ruth 1:14; 2:11, 18, 19 (2x), 23; 3:1, 6, 16, 17.
[124] Lev 18:12; 20:19.
[125] Exod 3:1; 4:18; 18:1–2, 5–8, 12 (2x),14–15, 17, 24, 27; Num 10:29; Judg 1:16; 4:11, 19:4, 7, 9.
[126] Gen 28:2; 29:10 (3x).
[127] Deut 27:23.
[128] Lev 18:13; 20:19.
[129] It refers to a half-sister of Ego. See Gen 20:12; Lev 18:9; 20:17; Deut 27:22; Ezek 22:11.
[130] Gen 38:8, 9; Lev 18:16; 20:21.
[131] It refers to a half-sister of Ego, not a full sister. See Gen 20:12; Lev 18:9; Deut 27:22.
[132] Gen 12:5; 14:12.
[133] Gen 19:12, 14 (2x); Judg 15:6; 19:5; 1 Sam 18:18; 22:14; 2 Kgs 8:27; Neh 6:18; 13:28.
[134] Gen 11:31; Exod 10:2; Deut 6:2; Judg 8:22; Jer 27:7.
[135] Gen 11:31; 38:11; 38:16; 38:24; Lev 18:15; 20:12; 1 Sam 4:19; Ezek 22:11; Mic 7:6; Ruth 1:6, 7, 8, 22; 2:20, 22; 4:15; 1 Chr 2:4.
[136] Lev 18:10, 17.
[137] Lev 18:10, 17.

3.4.3.2. Referential and Address Usages

KTs are a semantic category that often exhibits a considerable difference between their referential and address usages (Zwicky, 1974, 791; Dickey 1996, 61–62). Although the specific manifestations of this difference may vary across languages, two key aspects are particularly relevant to our study.[138]

First, certain KTs are exclusively used as terms of reference and are never employed as terms of address. For instance, the English KT "brother-in-law" may be used in reference ("My *brother-in-law* gave me this car"), but is virtually unusable as a term of address ("I wonder, *brother-in-law, if you can give me your car"). In our corpus, there are several possible examples of this phenomenon, the most illustrious one of which comes from the book of Ruth. Ruth is the wife of Mahlon, Naomi's son (4:10), and thus, she is Naomi's daughter-in-law. The KT that expresses Ruth's identity in relation to Naomi is כלה *kallɔ* "daughter-in-law," which appears seven times in the book and is consistently used as a term of reference in narration. For example, Ruth 1:22 states, "So Naomi returned, accompanied by her Moabite *daughter-in-law* (כלה) Ruth, who came back with her from the region of Moab" (see also 1:6–8; 2:20, 22; 4:15). However, when Naomi addresses Ruth, she does not use the secondary affinal KT כלה, but instead the primary consanguineal KT בת *bat* "*daughter*": "Ruth the Moabite said to Naomi, 'Let me go to the field so that I can gather grain behind anyone in whose eyes I may find favor.' Naomi replied, 'Go, my *daughter* (בת)'" (2:2). Naomi addresses Ruth five times throughout the book, and she does so consistently with בת (Ruth 2:2, 22; 3:1, 16, 18). Thus, it is reasonable to assume that כלה was exclusively used in reference but never employed as an address term during the composition of Ruth.[139]

Second, when KTs are used as terms of address, they take on an "extended" sense. This means that the speaker addresses his/her collocutor using a KT whose referential meaning does not accurately describe the actual kin relationship

---

[138] While not attested in the Hebrew Bible, KTs used in address are often used in ways radically different from their referential (= literal) meanings in other languages. In Egyptian Arabic, for instance, عم *ʕam*, which means "(paternal) uncle" when used in reference, is used only to those who are *not* the speaker's uncle when used in address (Parkinson 1982, 98). See also the so-called "address inversion" phenomenon found in various languages mentioned above.

[139] It is equally possible that Naomi's address usage may not represent the typical address usage between a mother-in-law and a daughter-in-law at that time (Lande 1949, 23). However, the fact that the KT כלה occurs thirty-four times in the Hebrew Bible but is never used as a term of address with the meaning of "daughter-in-law" (note that כלה is used as a term of address six times in Song of Songs [4:8–12; 5:1], but it denotes a "bride," not a "daughter-in-law") seems to support my claim.

between them.[140] For instance, pastors often address church attendees as "brothers and sisters," even though there is no actual familial relationship between them. Similarly, in our corpus, KTs are often used in address with an extended meaning. For example, Elisha addresses Elijah as אבי *ʔəḇi* "my father!", although Elijah is by no means the biological father of Elisha (2 Kgs 2:12). As we will see later, the use of extended KTs in address can be viewed as a politeness strategy to express the speaker's affection and/or respect for the addressee.

3.4.3.3. Position and Distribution

In our corpus, only six KTs are used in address: אבי *ʔəḇi* "my father"; אמי *ʔimmi* "my mother"; אחי *ʔəḥi* "my brother"; אחתי *ʔaḥoti* "my sister"; בני *bəni* "my son"; בתי *bitti* "my daughter." These are the primary consanguineal KTs, primarily referring to members of a nuclear family. There are three ways in which these KTs are used in address: (1) a KT used alone (e.g., בני *bəni* "My son!"); (2) a KT used at the beginning of a compound address (e.g., בני דוד *bəni dəwiḏ* "My son David!"); (3) a KT used at the end of a compound address (e.g., שלמה בני *šəlomo-bəni* "Solomon my son!"). The first two types—address forms composed of a KT alone (henceforth, AKTs) and compound addresses headed by a KT (henceforth, HKTs)—are treated together in this section as they convey the same power relationship between the speaker and the addressee in our corpus. The third type has only three examples (1 Sam 3:16; 2 Sam 19:1; 1 Chr 28:9), in which a descending KT is preceded by a PN. These cases have already been discussed in §3.4.1.2.1 and §3.4.1.2.3.

There are forty-six instances of AKTs and eight cases of HKTs in our corpus. These cases account for about 28 percent of the total free forms of address used between two human beings. Therefore, AKTs and HKTs are attested almost as frequently as ATs and HTs, and twice as frequently as APNs and HPNs. Table 3.13 displays the distribution of AKTs and HKTs across the books of the Hebrew Bible. As shown in the table, more than 60 percent of AKTs come from Genesis and Ruth, which contain a significant number of cases of family dialogue.

Table 3.13. AKTs and HKTs in Each Book of the Hebrew Bible

Book	# of AKTs	# of HKTs	Book	# of AKTs	# of HKTs
Genesis	20		1 Kings	2	
Joshua	1		2 Kings	1	2
Judges	2		Isaiah	2	
1 Samuel	3	4	Ruth	8	
2 Samuel	6	2	1 Chronicles	1	
			Total	46	8

---

[140] I find the term *extended* coined by Dickey (2004) to be more appropriate than *fictive* by Braun (1988), Contini (1995), and Esposito (2009), as the latter has a connotation of "not genuine."

3.4.3.4. Pattern

3.4.3.4.1. Literal Use of KTs

More than half of the AKTs and HKTs in our corpus are used in a literal sense, that is, the referential meaning of a KT constituent within an address form accurately describes the actual kin relation between the speaker and the addressee. These KT constituents exclusively belong to the primary consanguineal KTs, and the AKTs and HKTs used literally are employed to address members of a nuclear family. Table 3.14 shows these address forms.

Table 3.14. AKTs and HKTs Used Literally

#	Form	Semantic	Relation	S>A	Verse
1	My father	KT	So > Fa	Isaac>Abraham	Gen 22:7
2				Jacob>Isaac	Gen 27:18
3–5				Esau>Isaac	Gen 27:34, 38 (2x)
6				Joseph>Jacob	Gen 48:18
7				Boy>Isaiah	Isa 8:4
8			Da > Fa	Daughter>Jephthah	Judg 11:36
9	My mother	KT	So > Mo	Boy>Isaiah's wife	Isa 8:4
10				Solomon>Bathsheba	1 Kgs 2:20
11	My brother	KT	Br > Br	Esau>Jacob	Gen 33:9
12			FaDa > FaSo	Tamar>Amnon	2 Sam 13:12
13	My sister	KT	Br > Si	Absalom>Tamar	2 Sam 13:20
14			FaSo > FaDa	Amnon>Tamar	2 Sam 13:11
15	My son	KT	Fa > So	Abraham>Isaac	Gen 22:7, 8
16					
17				Isaac>Esau	Gen 27:1, 37
18					
19–22				Isaac>Jacob	Gen 27:18, 20, 21, 26
23				Jacob>Joseph	Gen 48:19
24				David>Absalom	2 Sam 13:25
25				David>Solomon	1 Chr 22:11
26	My son, Absalom, my son, my son, Absalom	KT+PN+KT+KT+PN		David>Absalom	2 Sam 19:1
27	My son, Absalom, Absalom, my son, my son	KT+PN+PN+KT+KT		David>Absalom	2 Sam 19:5
28–30	My son	KT	Mo > So	Rebekah>Jacob	Gen 27:8, 13, 43
31	My daughter	KT	Fa > Da	Jephthah>daughter	Judg 11:35

Children address their fathers and mothers using ascending AKTs, אבי *ʔɔbi* "my father" or אמי *ʔimmi* "my mother" (##1–10). Siblings address each other with horizontal AKTs, אחי *ʔɔḥi* "my brother" or אחתי *ʔaḥoti* "my sister" (##11–14).[141] Parents address their sons and daughters with descending AKTs, בני *bəni* "my son" or בתי *bitti* "my daughter," or descending HKTs, such as בני אבשלום *bəni ʔabšɔlom* "my son, Absalom" (##15–31).

It is noteworthy that there is a nonreciprocal address pattern between parents and children. In cases #26 and #27, a father addresses his son by a PN following a KT: בני אבשלום *bəni ʔabšɔlom* "my son, Absalom!" We have also observed three cases in table 3.3 (#15–17), where a father addresses his son using a PN or PN followed by a KT. However, children never address their parents using address forms containing a PN in our corpus. This nonreciprocal address pattern suggests that children in ancient Israel avoided using PNs when addressing their parents.

3.4.3.4.2. Extended Use of KTs

The remaining AKTs and HKTs are used in an extended sense for those outside the nuclear family. As Esposito (2009, 129) points out, the extended use of primary consanguineal KTs in address can be seen as the result of "metaphorical mappings" between the nuclear family and society at large. In other words, the nuclear family serves as a conceptual model for secondary usages of KTs, where features of family relations within the nuclear family are mapped onto society. For example, the ascending KT "father" or "mother" may be used to address teachers who share a similar educating role, akin to as parents.

Pragmatically, however, this extended use can also be seen as a politeness strategy. KTs inherently convey a sense relationship, implying solidarity and emotional closeness between Ego and the referent. At the same time, different power relations can be expressed through the use of ascending, horizontal, and descending KTs. Moreover, compared to PNs, which make specific and direct references to particular individuals, KTs can be considered relatively nonspecific and indirect in terms of referential indexicality (Fleming and Slotta 2015, 172). These semantic and referential properties of KTs allow them to function as "in-group identity markers," as described by Brown and Levinson (1987, 107), which can be used in address to convey "positive" politeness by establishing common ground between speakers and addressees across various types of social relations.

---

[141] In cases #12 and #14, Amnon and Tamar are half-siblings who have the same father, David, but have different mothers, Ahinoam and Maacah, respectively. Thus, they may be classified as secondary consanguineal kin. However, they address each other with primary consanguineal KTs, אחי *ʔɔḥi* "my brother" or אחתי *ʔᵃḥoti* "my sister." Since primary consanguineal KTs are often used to refer to half-siblings in our corpus (e.g., 2 Sam 13:8, 10), I view these two cases as literal usages. See also Esposito (2009, 133) for this view.

In the following sections, the extended usages of KTs are presented based on different power relations.

3.4.3.4.2.1. Inferior to Superior

Just as children address their parents, social inferiors may also address social superiors using ascending AKTs or HKTs. These address forms not only imply a sense of solidarity but also convey a sense of deference when used in an extended sense. Thus, the use of ascending AKTs and HKTs in an extended sense can serve as both a negative politeness strategy (by acknowledging the superior status of the addressee) and a positive politeness strategy (by claiming solidarity between the speaker and the addressee), in order to mitigate potential face-threatening acts (FTAs). Table 3.15 shows ascending AKTs and HKTs used by social inferiors towards social superiors.

Table 3.15. Ascending AKTs and HKTs Used by Inferiors to Superiors

#	Form	Semantic	Relation	S > A	Context	Verse
1	My father	KT	Outlaw > King	David > Saul	Persuading Saul to stop pursuing him	1 Sam 24:12
2		KT	King > Prophet	Jehoram > Elisha	Asking Elisha if he should strike down the Aramean army	2 Kgs 6:21
3	My father, my father, the chariot of Israel and its horsemen	KT+KT+T	Disciple > Teacher	Elisha > Elijah	Seeing Elijah going up by a whirlwind into heaven	2 Kgs 2:12
4		KT+KT+T	King > Prophet	Jehoash > Elisha	Seeing Elisha fallen sick with the illness of which he was to die	2 Kgs 13:14

In all these cases, the superiority of the addressees over the speakers is out of question: a king is superior to an outlaw (#1); [142] a teacher is superior to his disciple (#3);[143] while kings may be considered superior to prophets in the political realm, the power of the former is often overshadowed by the religious and moral authority of the latter (#2, 4). Thus, the use of ascending AKTs or HKTs in these cases is deemed appropriate.

However, it is worth noting that two of these address forms are used in the context of requesting. In case #1, David addresses King Saul using the ascending

---

[142] It seems unlikely that David addresses Saul as "my father" in the meaning of "my father-in-law," as Saul would probably have given Michal to Palti before this event (1 Sam 25:44).
[143] The ascending KT, "my father," obviously corresponds to "the *sons* of the prophets," a designation for the members of an organized guild of prophetic disciples under the leadership of great prophets, such as Elijah and Elisha (Moore, 2007, 162).

AKT, אבי *ʔəḇi* "my father," as he attempts to persuade Saul to stop pursuing him. In case #2, the king of Israel addresses Elisha as אבי *ʔəḇi* "my father," as he seeks advice from Elisha on whether to strike down the Aramean army. In such situations, the speakers are likely to employ politeness strategies to get what they want. Thus, it can be argued that the use of the ascending AKT, אבי *ʔəḇi* "my father," in these two cases should be understood as a politeness strategy. In order to mitigate the potential face-threats posed by their requests, David and the king of Israel use ascending AKTs, by which they claim solidarity with Saul and Elisha while fully acknowledging their higher power and authority.

3.4.3.4.2.2. Between Equals

Just as siblings address each other, social equals may use horizontal AKTs (or HKTs) to address each other, conveying a sense of solidarity and equal status in extended use. Thus, the extended use of horizontal AKTs can serve as a positive politeness strategy, as it claims solidarity between the speaker and the addressee to mitigate potential FTAs. Table 3.16 shows horizontal AKTs used between social equals.[144]

Table 3.16. AKTs Used between Equals

#	Form	Semantic	Relation	S > A	Context	Verse
1	My brother	KT	King > King	Hiram > Solomon	Complaining about the cities Solomon gave him	1 Kgs 9:13
2	My brother	KT	Commander > Commander	Joab > Amasa	Greeting Amasa before striking him down	2 Sam 20:9

In case #1, Hiram, the king of Tyre, addresses Solomon as אחי *ʔəḥi* "my brother."[145] There is no doubt that Hiram considers Solomon to be equal and close

---

[144] There are several cases outside our corpus in which the horizontal AKT, "my brother" or "my brothers," is used: David addresses Jonathan as "my brother" (2 Sam 1:26); people address a dead man of God as "my brother (1 Kgs 13:30); Lot addresses the inhabitants of Sodom as "my brothers" (Gen 19:7); Jacob addresses some strangers as "my brothers" (Gen 29:4); an old man in Gibeah addresses his fellow villagers as "my brothers" (Judg 19:23); David addresses his officials and his people as "my brothers" (1 Sam 30:23; 1 Chr 28:2). In all these cases, it can be argued that the speakers consider or claim the addressees to be equal and close in their relationship.

[145] KTs in general are commonly used in diplomatic relations in the ancient Near East. See Schloen 2001, 46.

in their relationship, making his use of the horizontal AKT appropriate.[146] However, it should be noted that Hiram's address occurs in the context of his complaint about the cities he received from Solomon. Thus, it can also be said that Hiram aims to claim solidarity with Solomon by deliberately using the horizontal AKT to soften the potential face threat posed by the complaint.

In case #2, Joab addresses Amasa as אחי *ʔɔḥi* "my brother." This address may come as a surprise from Amasa's point of view for several reasons. Joab and Amasa may be considered equals in power, as they are both commanders of David's army (2 Sam 19:13) and they are cousins (2 Sam 17:25). However, they are not close in their relationship since they have just finished fighting a bloody war against each other (2 Sam 17:24–18:33). Furthermore, Joab likely harbored jealousy towards Amasa, whom he saw a traitor, as he had been promised by David to take over Joab's position (2 Sam 19:13). Amasa would have been aware of these negative feelings that Joab had towards him. Nonetheless, Joab approaches Amasa in a friendly manner, addressing him as "my brother," in an apparent attempt to claim solidarity. This gesture must have been surprising to Amasa, perhaps leading him to believe it was a sign of reconciliation between them. Consequently, Amasa lets his guard down and trusts Joab, which ultimately leads to his death. It can be argued that Joab employs the horizontal AKT, "my brother," as a positive politeness strategy to deceitfully gain Amasa's trust and carry out his murder.[147]

3.4.3.4.2.3. Superior to Inferior

Just as parents address their children, social superiors may address social inferiors using descending AKTs or HKTs. These address forms not only imply a sense of solidarity but also convey a sense of inequality in extended use. Thus, the use of descending AKTs and HKTs can be seen as a positive politeness strategy, allowing the speaker to claim solidarity with the addressee and mitigate potential FTAs. Table 3.17 shows descending AKTs and HKTs used by social superiors to address social inferiors.

---

[146] In Chronicles, however, Hiram addresses Solomon as "my lord" in a bound form (2 Chr 2:14). There is no doubt that the Chroniclers updated this event to present Solomon as the Great King (Esposito 2009, 134–35).

[147] While Revell (1996, 331), Miller (2003, 270), and Esposito (2009, 133–34) also view Joab's address as a deceitful tactic, they do not explain it according to the framework of Brown and Levinson's politeness theory.

Table 3.17. AKTs and HKTs Used by Superiors to Inferiors

#	Form	Semantic	Relation	S > A	Context	Verse
1	My son	KT	Vizier > Foreigner	Joseph > Benjamin	Greeting Benjamin	Gen 43:29
2	My son	KT	Priest > Boy	Eli > Samuel	Telling Samuel that he did not call him	1 Sam 3:6
3	My son	KT	Priest > Soldier	Eli > Battle Survivor	Inquiring the man about the battle with the Philistines	1 Sam 4:16
4	My son	KT	Leader > Man	Joshua > Achan	Urging Achan to confess his sins	Josh 7:19
5	My son	KT	Commander > Priest's Son	Joab > Ahimaaz	Asking Ahimaaz not to run after the Cushite	2 Sam 18:22
6–9	My son, David	KT+PN	King > Outlaw	Saul > David	Regretting the evil he did to David	1 Sam 24:17; 26:17, 21, 25
10	My daughter	KT	Mother-in-Law > Daughter-in-Law	Naomi > Ruth	Permitting Ruth to go to the field	Ruth 2:2
11					Instructing Ruth to listen to Boaz	Ruth 2:22
12					Arranging a marriage for Ruth	Ruth 3:1
13					Inquiring Ruth about the meeting with Boaz	Ruth 3:16
14					Instructing Ruth to wait until Boaz has settled the matter	Ruth 3:18
15	My daughter	KT	Old Man > Young Woman	Boaz > Ruth	Requesting Ruth to glean in his field	Ruth 2:8
16–17	My daughter	KT	Old Man > Young Woman	Boaz > Ruth	Promising Ruth to do all that she asked	Ruth 3:10, 11

In all these cases, there is no question about the speaker's superiority over the addressee based on higher social standing or older age: an Egyptian vizier is superior to a foreigner (#1); a priest is superior to a temple servant and a soldier (##2, 3); a national leader is superior to a law-breaker (#4); a military commander is superior to a priest's son (#5); a king is superior to an outlaw (##6–9); a mother-in-law is superior to her daughter-in-law (##10–14); an old man is superior to a young woman (##16–17).

In some of these cases, the use of descending AKTs seems to reflect the social conventions of the time (#1)[148] or merely expresses kindly feelings of a senior

---

[148] See, for example, a letter from an Egyptian general to Rib-Hadda (EA 96), in which the former addresses the latter as "my son."

towards a junior (##2–3, 10–14). It is noteworthy, however, that address forms in the remaining cases appear in the context of requesting or promising. In case #4, Joshua addresses Achan as בני *bəni* "my son," urging him to confess his sins before God.[149] In case #5, Joab addresses Ahimaaz as בני *bəni* "my son," persuading him not to run after the Cushite. In case ##6–9, Saul addresses David as בני דוד *bəni dɔwid* "my son David," repenting of his wrongdoing and asking him to return. In case #15, Boaz addresses Ruth as בתי *bitti* "my daughter," requesting her to glean in his field. In case #16, Boaz addresses Ruth again as בתי *bitti* "my daughter," promising to do fulfill all her requests. In these situations, the speakers are likely to employ politeness strategies to get what they want. Thus, it can be argued that the use of descending AKTs and HKTs in these cases is a positive politeness strategy. By using these address forms, the superior speakers show their affection and sympathy towards the inferior addressees, aiming to soften the potential face-threats posed by their requests and promises.

3.5. Conclusion

In this chapter, we have studied the three most frequently appearing address terms in our corpus: PNs, Ts, and KTs. These terms can be used alone (as a simple address) or as a constituent of a compound address when used between two human beings. I have shown that the first constituent in an address, whether in a simple or compound address, serves as an indicator of the power relation between the speaker and the addressee.

When PNs are used as the first constituent, they typically mark the superiority of the speaker. Thus, APNs and HPNs are always used in "downward" relationships, that is, in the superior-inferior dyads, except for a couple of cases where APNs are used between close equals. On the other hand, when Ts are used as the first constituent, they seem to mark the superiority of the addressee. Thus, ATs and HTs are normally used in "upward" relationships, that is, in the inferior-superior dyads. Therefore, APNs and HPNs can be seen as fulfilling the role of the *T* in Brown, Gilman, and Ford's *T/V* system, whereas ATs and HTs function as the *V*. In terms of PNs and Ts, they partially confirm Brown and Ford's "linguistic universal."

However, when KTs are used as the first constituent, they can convey all types of power relations. Ascending AKTs and HKTs are used in "upward" relationships, horizontal AKTs and HKTs are used "horizontally," that is, in relationships of equal status, and descending AKTs and HKTs are used in "downward" relationships. When KTs are used in an extended sense, the majority, if not

---

[149] While Esposito (2009, 130) views Joshua's address as a deceptive strategy to elicit Achan's confession, it seems more likely that Joshua genuinely shows a paternal and sympathetic attitude to Achan by using that address.

all, can be interpreted as politeness strategies. Therefore, the address usages of KTs in Biblical Hebrew does not support Brown and Ford's "linguistic universal." Figure 3.6 shows the use of these three address terms.

Figure 3.6. The Use of Address Terms in Biblical Hebrew

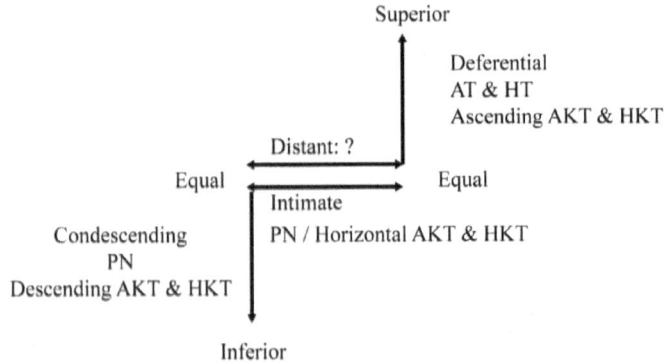

4.
FREE FORMS OF ADDRESS: POSITION AND FUNCTION

4.1. Introduction

Free forms of address in Biblical Hebrew prose can occur in a variety of syntactic positions within a sentence. They may appear at the beginning, as shown in example (22):

(22) **אבי** פציתה את פיך אל יהוה
    ʔɔbi   *pɔṣitɔ*   *ʔɛt-pikɔ*   *ʔɛl-yhwh*
    father=my you.opened ACC-mouth=your to-YHWH
    My father, you have opened your mouth to YHWH. (Judg 11:36)

They may also appear at the end, as in example (23):

(23) אמצא חן בעיניך **אדני המלך**
    ʔɛmṣɔ-ḥen   *bəʕenɛkɔ*   *ʔᵃdoni*   *hammɛlɛk*
    I.will.find-favor in=eyes.of=your lord=my the=king
    Let me find favor in your sight, *my lord the king*. (2 Sam 16:4)

They may stand in the middle, as in (24):

(24) לא תעשו כן **אחי** את אשר נתן יהוה לנו
    loʔ-taʕᵃśu   *ken*   *ʔɛḥɔy*   *ʔet*   *ʔᵃšɛr-nɔtan*
    not-you.will.do so brothers=my with what-he.gave
    yhwh   *lɔnu*
    YHWH to=us
    You shall not do so, *my brothers*, with what the LORD has given us. (1 Sam 30:23)

They may even be used alone as a complete utterance, as in (25):

(25) ויהי אחר הדברים האלה והאלהים נסה את אברהם ויאמר אליו **אברהם**
wayhi   ʔaḥar   haddəḇɔrim   hɔʔellɛ   who?ʔlohim   nissɔ
and=it.was after   the=things   the=these and=the=God   he.tested
ʔɛt-ʔaḇrɔhɔm   wayyoʔmɛr   ʔelɔyw   ʔaḇrɔhɔm
ACC-Abraham   and=he.said   to=him   Abraham

Sometime after these things God tested Abraham. He said to him, "*Abraham!*" (Gen 22:1)

As we carefully examine each of these addresses, we notice that their pragmatic functions differ significantly. For instance, the stand-alone address in (25) serves the purpose of calling or summoning the addressee (i.e., Abraham), as it occurs at the beginning of the conversation. However, in the case of (24), where David is already engaged in a conversation with the addressees, the purpose of his address, which appears at the end of a sentence, must be different.

The purpose of this chapter is to describe the correlation between the position and function of free forms of address in our corpus. Linguists have long recognized, based on their research on the use of free forms of address in various modern languages, that there is a strong correlation between the position and function of such forms. However, there is a limited amount of literature that discusses the external syntax and pragmatic function of free forms of address in Biblical Hebrew. In the following sections, I will first examine previous studies in general linguistics and Biblical Hebrew that address this issue, drawing insights from their analytical methods and research findings. Then, I will present my own methodology and analyze the data from Biblical Hebrew.

4.2. Previous Studies

4.2.1. General Linguistics

4.2.1.1. The Functions of Free Forms of Address in Initial and Final Position

Since the 1970s, linguists have made efforts to describe the correlation between the position and function of free forms of address in different languages. Zwicky (1974, 787) was the first to identify two pragmatic functions of free forms of address in English—calls and addresses, as illustrated by (i) and (ii), respectively:[1]

(i) Hey *lady*, you dropped your piano.
(ii) I'm afraid, *sir*, that my coyote is nibbling on your leg.

According to Zwicky (1974, 787, 797), calls are used to "catch the addressee's attention" and are "essentially restricted to discourse-initial position."

---

[1] Zwicky (1974, 799) notes that the distinction between calls and addresses was inspired by Schegloff (1968, 1080–81), who distinguished between *summonses* and *terms of address*.

Addresses, however, are used to "maintain or emphasize contact between the speaker and the addressee" and may occur in a variety of positions—after introductory expressions (e.g., look, look here, listen, say, well, why, please, come on, tell me, you know), after greetings (hi, hello, good morning), after exclamations (wow, atta girl, dammit, oh boy), and in positions open to parenthetical adjuncts. Zwicky (1974, 787, 798) also points out that free forms of address never occur in embedded clauses (e.g., *Melinda maintained that, dumbass, the bite was negligible) and they are set off from their host sentences by special intonation.

While many subsequent linguists have followed Zwicky's call/address dichotomy (e.g., Levinson 1983, 71; Quirk et al. 1985, 773; Dickey 1996, 6; Portner 2004, 8; Anderson 2004, 442; Huang 2014, 181; Haddad 2020, 19), some have proposed additional functions of free forms of address and have attempted to correlate them with their positions in the sentence. Geoffrey Leech (1999, 116), who conducted a corpus-based study of free forms of address in British and American English conversation, attributes three distinct functions to free forms of address:

(i)   Getting someone's attention (e.g., "*Mum!*")
(ii) Identifying someone as an addressee (e.g., "Hey *Ben*, do you remember a hole puncher coming in I ordered?")
(iii) Maintaining and reinforcing social relationships (e.g., "Oh yeah *dude* totally.")

He argues that free forms of address in initial position seem to combine function (i) with function (ii), while those in final position are more likely to combine function (ii) with function (iii).

Leech also observes a noticeable difference in the lengths of "C-units"[2] associated with the two positions: initial free forms of address tend to be associated with longer sentences (mostly six words or more), whereas final free forms of address are associated with shorter sentences (mostly three words or less). According to Leech (1999, 117), this tendency can be explained by the fact that initial free forms of address, which can serve as attention-getters, also have the function of "clearing space for a lengthy turn," while final free forms of address often occur "after a short remark, where attracting attention is not a problem."

---

[2] Leech (1999, 108) coins the term "C-unit" (where 'C' stands for 'communicative') and uses it as the unit of analysis. He defines the term as "a unit with optimal syntactic independence, in that it is not part of a larger syntactic unit, except by means of coordination." As a unit of spoken English grammar, therefore, a C-unit is "essentially the spoken analogue of a written sentence." A C-unit can be either a clausal (e.g., "So this was your mother's?") or nonclausal unit (e.g., "No!"). The former consists of an independent clause within which any dependent clauses may be embedded, while the latter has no finite verb in it. In terms of a compound sentence consisting of two or more coordinated independent clauses, each clause is treated as a separate C-unit.

On the basis of two corpora—the 5-million-word Cambridge and Nottingham Corpus of Discourse in English (CANCODE) and a 55,000-word corpus of radio phone-in calls that comes from the Irish radio program *Liveline*, Michael J. McCarthy and Anne O'Keeffe (2003, 153) expand Leech's classification of the functions of free forms of address to include the following types:

(i) relational: establishing and/or maintaining social relations.
    e.g., [group of female young friends discussing eating and weight problems]
        A. You're not fat, *Jane*.
        B. I will be if I'm not careful.

(ii) topic management: launching, expanding, shifting, changing or closing the topic.
    e.g., [speakers are discussing a well-known family of traditional Irish musicians]
        A. We were in Cork, weren't we, *Jean* and we heard his brother. Which brother was it we heard?
        B. Sean, I think.

(iii) badinage: humor, irony and general banter among participants.
    e.g., [group of female students who share a house are talking]
        A. Got a light anyone?
        B. Only my eyes, *Gillian*.
        A. You always say that [laughs].

(iv) mitigators: softening a potential threat to positive or negative face.
    e.g., [A is making a request for action that could potentially be heard as an imposition]
        A. Will you put on the fish, *Nancy*, so that it'll heat, the fish now.
        B. Oh yeah.

(v) turn management: selecting next speaker or disambiguating possible recipients in multi-party talk.
    e.g., A. I should have some change.
        B. I owe you too, don't I, *Jodie*.
        C. Yes, you do.

(vi) call management: dealing with the exigencies of the channel, bringing callers in, controlling their talk, and dismissing them when their contribution is deemed to be sufficient.
    e.g., [Introducing a caller whose son narrowly escaped death from meningitis]
        A. Now to a couple that had a very, very difficult Christmas this year, however, all's well that ends well. Ah, *Austin*, good afternoon to you.
        B. Good afternoon, *Marian*.
        A. Your little boy went back to playschool yesterday?
        B. Yesterday, that's right.

(vii) summons: calling the recipient.
    e.g., A. *Sue*! Your cup of tea is poured.

McCarthy and O'Keeffe (2003, 167–180), observe that summonses are typically utterance-initial whereas final and medial free forms of address tend to be associated with relational, call management, topic management, and mitigators.

Melita Stavrou (2014, 327) identifies three functions of free forms of address in Modern Greek:

(i) calls (e.g., *Maria*, trekse! "*Maria*, run!")
(ii) maintaining contact with the addressee and expressing a whole array of feelings (e.g., To kakao su *Dimitraki*! "Your cocoa, *Dimitraki*!")
(iii) conveying an additional emphasis on sociolinguistic import of the lexical choice (e.g., O jatros, *pedja*, me simvulepse taksidi "The doctor, *kids*, advised me to travel.")

Stavrou (2014, 325–29) notes that calls are most commonly utterance-initial, whereas utterance-final address forms are employed as a means of maintaining contact with the addressee. Additionally, free forms of address in medial position, situated at the juncture of major constituents like parentheticals, can fulfill function (iii), but they should not intrude into a lexical constituent such as a noun phrase or adverbial phrase.

Maja Glušac and Ana M. Čolič (2017, 449–69) classify the linguistic functions of free forms of address in the Croatian language according to the six parts of the communicative process:

(i) Conative (e.g., *Ivane*, reci što se dogodilo. "*Ivan*, say what happened.")
(ii) Emotive (e.g., Ustani, *ljubljena moja, ljepotice moja*! "Rise, *my beloved one, my beauty*!")
(iii) Phatic (e.g., *Vi, domine Pisarovič*. "*You, dominus Pisarovič*.")[3]
(iv) Poetic (e.g., Ah, znate, *gospodin profesor*.... Jeste li ikada mislili da se vrtimo u krugu apsurda, *gospodin profesor*. "Ah, you know, *Mr. Professor*.... Have you ever thought that we are spinning in a circle of absurd, *Mr. Professor*.")[4]

---

[3] Glušac and Čolić (2017, 468) define the phatic function as establishing and maintaining communication.

[4] According to Glušac and Čolić (2017, 452), the use of nominative forms instead of the expected vocative ones can have a poetic function, i.e., can serve as a stylistic instrument contributing to the linguistic characterization of a protagonist. The example above comes from the novel *Kiklop* (*Cyclops*), which features this practice as a means of emphasizing the German nationality of Kurt, the innkeeper.

(v) Referential (e.g., Štije knjigu *starče Radoslave*, knjigu štije, a suze proliva "A book readeth *old man Radoslav*, a book he readeth, spilling tears")[5]
(vi) Metalinguistic (e.g., A: *Ivane!* "*Ivan!*" // B: *Ivane?* Ne zove se on Ivan nego Marko! "*Ivan?* His name is not Ivan, it's Marko!")[6]

They argue that free forms of address in initial position have a more pronounced conative function, while those in medial and final positions tend to fulfil the emotive, poetic and/or phatic functions.

These linguists commonly recognize the pragmatic functions that initial and final free forms of address may perform, that is, drawing the addressee's attention and maintaining contact with the addressee, respectively. However, none of them seems to offer an adequate explanation as to how free forms of address in medial position function. Leech does not discuss the function of medial free forms of address at all, while the functions suggested by others are so broad that they are not unique to address forms in medial position. Furthermore, free forms of address in medial position may be divided according to the different positions they occupy within the host sentences. Thus, the question arises whether all medially positioned address forms may be said to fulfil the same pragmatic function regardless of their precise medial position within the host sentences.

4.2.1.2. The Functions of Free Forms of Address in Medial Position

There have been a few attempts to answer this question from an information structure perspective. Viewing free forms of address as a type of parenthetical expression that may be inserted freely within a sentence, Josef Taglicht (1984, 12–31) argues that they may participate in information structuring. In his analysis of different sentence types in English based on Michael Halliday's (1967–1968) Theme-Rheme structure,[7] he demonstrates that free forms of address may

---

[5] Glušac and Čolić (2017, 447) argue that the referential function of free forms of address, i.e., referring to the subject matter of the message, is confined to the subject and predicative role in the language of folk poetry.

[6] According to Glušac and Čolić (2017, 469), free forms of address with explicit "orientation to the code" in view may fulfill a metalinguistic function. In the example above, speaker A calls his/her collocutor (not speaker B) by name, and speaker B reacts to speaker A's call.

[7] Halliday (1967, 205; 2004, 64; 2014, 83) believes that in all languages a clause has the character of a "message," or "quantum of information": it takes on some form of structure by which it contributes to the flow of discourse. The structure presents the distribution of information within the clause. In English, information is allocated in two parts of the clause—"Theme" and "Rheme." The Theme is the element that serves as "the point of departure of the message" or "that which locates and orients the clause within its context." Thus, it is naturally the first constituent of the clause. The Rheme is the remainder of the clause in which the Theme is developed.

function as "partitions" between a marked Theme/Rheme and the rest of the sentence. In (i) below, for example, the address form "my dear" is placed between the marked Theme "That shed" and the Operator "will" (Note that 'MTh,' 'Op,' and 'Rh' stand for 'marked Theme,' 'Operator,' and 'Rheme'):

(i) That shed,   my dear,   will   have to be painted
    MTh   partition   Op   Rh

For Taglicht (1984, 16), the division of a declarative sentence into Theme and Rheme is strictly based on "sequential ordering" of syntactic constituents: the first constituent of the sentence, typically the subject, is Theme and the remainder of the sentence is Rheme (often preceded by an auxiliary verb labelled Operator, as in (i)). The sequence of constituents that results from purely syntactic constraints with no special pragmatic motivation is called "unmarked sequence." Marked sequence, on the other hand, is characterized by the "breaking" of one or more of the links in the corresponding unmarked sequence and the "detachment" of one or more of the constituents from other constituent(s) with which it is contiguous in the unmarked sequence (Taglicht 1984,20). The breaking of the link(s) may be realized either by fronting one or more of the constituents (e.g., "That shed, John painted yesterday") or by inserting parenthetical expressions, such as "my dear" in (i). The detached constituent(s) may be initial or final in the marked sentence. If it is initial, like "That shed" in (i), it is a marked Theme; if it is final, like "a warm weather" in (ii) below, it is a marked Rheme.

According to Taglicht (1984, 25), marked sequences formed by the intrusion of parenthetical expressions tend to involve an element of "delay." In sentences with marked Theme, as in (i) above, the hearer is kept waiting for the predicate, while in sentences with marked Rheme, as in (ii), the hearer is kept waiting for the final part of the predicate:

(ii) They   prefer,   I think,[8]   a warm weather
     Th   Rh   Partition   MRh

Thus, this element of delay does not have the same effect in (i) and (ii). The delayed item in (i) "will have to be painted" is textually unmarked, whereas the delayed item in (ii) "a warm weather" is the marked item.

Taglicht (1984, 25–28) also notes that every marked item contains intonation focus and is assessed by the hearer as conveying "new information." Thus, it can be said that both intonation structure and information structure serve to distribute "emphasis" and to establish "cohesion" in the text. To sum up, what the marked

---

[8] Taglicht (1984, 31) notes that free forms of address before marked Rheme seem to be very rare in English and does not provide any examples.

items have in common are: detachment, terminal (i.e., initial or final) position, and intonation and information focus. All these features of the marked items may be brought by the insertion of free forms of address.

Like Taglicht, Michi Shiina (2007, 17–32; 2008, 29–48) argues that free forms of address in medial position can serve the function of "information management." In her study of selected English gentry comedies from the seventeenth and eighteenth centuries, Shiina adopts Leech's (1999, 108) concept of the C-unit, which she divides into three parts: preface(s), body, and tag(s).[9] Prefaces and tags refer to expressions that are loosely attached to the core of the clause (the body) either at the beginning (e.g., *Well*, I don't like it) or at the end (e.g., It makes you wonder, you know, *all this unemployment*). Free forms of address often follow the prefaces, contributing to the function of information management, as shown in (iii):

(iii) Pray, *good dear my lord*, let me beg you do now: I'll come immediately, and tell you all, will you my Lord?

In this example, as Lady Touchwood implores her husband to allow her to go, she uses the preface "pray" to capture his attention and direct it towards her or the following utterance. Shiina (2008, 34–35) argues that the address form "good dear my lord" collaborates with the preface "pray" to draw attention to the following utterance and reinforce its illocutionary force, such as a suggestion or directive.

Free forms of address can also appear after fronted constituents, which Shiina (2008, 30) categorizes as a type of preface. In these instances, the information management function becomes more evident, as illustrated in (iv):

(iv) In the Name of Politeness, *my Lord Marquis*, don't mention your Letters again.

Shiina considers fronting as a means of information management, where the fronted element gains thematic prominence in the immediate context. Thus, the adverbial phrase "in the Name of Politeness" is highlighted primarily by being fronted and further emphasized by being followed by the address form "my Lord Marquis." After the address form, a pause allows the speaker to attract the addressee's attention to what follows.

Free forms of address can also occur within the body of a sentence, as in (v):

(v) I shall send to you, *Mr. Serjeant*, as soon as Sir Geoffry comes to Town.

---

[9] Shiina borrows the terms preface(s), body, and tag(s) from Biber et al. (2007, 1072).

In this example, the address form "Mr. Serjeant" is inserted between the main and subordinate clauses of a complex sentence. The main clause conveys a conclusive remark, while the subordinate clause provides additional information with a temporal condition. Shiina (2008, 37) argues that the address form inserted between the two clauses serves to adjust the flow of information by reinforcing the illocutionary force of the declarative statement in the main clause and maintaining the addressee's attention to the subsidiary information in the subordinate clause.

Lillian Parrott shares a similar viewpoint and provides a summary of the function of medial free forms of address in Russian as follows:

> Medial direct address forms typically have a focusing function: they orient the addressee's attention to important information at the junction where they occur …, such as a preceding theme or a following rheme, or to the link between the preceding and following information. Medial direct address forms thus function like other parentheticals in that they can be interpolated at strategic points in the host utterance, like linguistic flags marking important landmarks, in order to correctly orient and maintain the addressee's attention. (2010, 220)

Building on Taglicht's work, Poppy Slocum (2016, 106) argues that free forms of address in medial position have semantic significance as they mark "the edge of the focus domain." According to Slocum, the content preceding the address functions as "background information" or "a contrastive topic," while the content following it provides "new information" or "focus." To illustrate her point, Slocum provides the following example.

(vi) *Jessica*: "I want to go home."
    Paul: (*a*) "I, *Jessica*, want to go to a movie."
          (*b*) "I want to go, *Jessica*, to a movie."

In response to Jessica expressing her desire to go home, Paul can reply in two ways. In (*a*), Paul places the address form immediately after the self-referential pronoun "I." By doing so, Paul is contrasting himself with Jessica, making "I" function as a contrastive topic, while "want to go to a movie" provides new information. On the other hand, in (*b*), Paul addresses Jessica between "to go" and "to a movie." Here, Paul is not contrasting himself with Jessica, but rather his desire to go with her desire to go. Thus, "I want to go" functions as a contrastive topic and "to a movie" provides new information.[10]

---

[10] Note that Slocum's terminology is different from Taglicht's. For Taglicht (1984, 28), every marked item contains new information, and thus, he would regard the marked Theme "I" in (10a) as new information. For Slocum, however, the following Rheme "want to go to a movie" contains new information.

In summary, the linguists studying the function of medial free forms of address commonly acknowledge their role in information structuring. These addresses create a division within a sentence, separating the preface and the body or the first and second part of the body, thereby marking the boundary between them. They serve a focusing function by directing the addressee's attention to important information. Determining which information is considered "important," Taglicht's criterion of "detachment" appears to be the most convincing. In other words, the constituent(s) detached from other constituent(s) with which it is contiguous in the unmarked sequence receives information focus.

4.2.2. Hebrew Studies

To the best of my knowledge, two works have discussed the correlation between the position and function of free forms of address in Biblical Hebrew: one by Revell (1996) and another by Miller (2010b). In his study, which focuses on the prose sections of Judges, Samuel, and Kings, Revell identifies five syntactic positions within the host sentence where free forms of address can appear.

These positions are as follows:

(i) An utterance that consists only of a vocative.
(ii) Before the clause, including the address forms following אהה $?^{e}hɔh$ "Alas" or עתה $ʕattɔ$ "now."
(iii) After the first word or constituent (e.g., an imperative verb, אל $?al$, an interrogative particle, an asseverative expression, the subject of the clause, an extraposed pronoun, a prepositional phrase) in a clause of two or more constituents.
(iv) After the clause.
(v) After the subject and the head of the predicate, but followed by one or more constituents.

According to Revell (1996, 337), approximately 87 percent of the address forms in positions (ii) or (iii) are used to address superiors, while only 38 percent of the address forms in position (iv) designate superior addressees. Based on this observation, Revell (1996, 338) concludes that the use of free forms of address in positions (ii) or (iii) marks the superiority of the addressee, whereas the use of such forms in position (iv) indicates the inferiority of the addressee.

While the statistics indicate a tendency for free forms of address used for superior addressees to occur towards the beginning of the clause, it is difficult to accept Revell's conclusion that the syntactic position of address forms marks the relative power/status of the addressee over the speaker. There are a considerable number of counterexamples to this tendency, such as Elijah's address for his disciple Elisha by name in 2 Kgs 2:4, which occurs at the beginning of the sentence. Furthermore, the correlation between the position of free forms of address and the relative power/status of the addressees over the speaker is not attested cross-linguistically. Finally, as I have demonstrated in chapter 3, the relative power/status of the addressee over the speaker is clearly marked by the semantic types of free forms of address, that is, personal names or descending kinship terms are used for inferior addressees, while titles or ascending kinship terms are used for superior addressees. These reasons lead us to explore another explanation for the correlation between the position and function of address forms.

In her article titled "Vocative Syntax in Biblical Hebrew Prose and Poetry: A Preliminary Analysis," Miller (2010b, 347–64) aims to describe the specific locations within the host clause that serve as a niche for free forms of address. Her prose corpus includes Genesis, Joshua, Judges, Samuel, and Kings, while Psalms and the inset poems from the prose corpus constitute her poetic corpus. When discussing free forms of address used in prose, Miller excludes those standing alone or occurring at the very beginning or end of an utterance. Instead, she focuses on those that occur within the utterance. She categorizes these address forms based on the positions in which they occur in the host clause: (i) clause-initial position; (ii) clause-final position; (iii) clause-medial position. The clause-initial addresses include those that come after interjections (e.g., אהה *ʔªhɔh* "Alas!"), oath formula (e.g., חי נפשך *ḥe napšəkɔ* "As you live"), interrogatives (e.g., למה *lɔmɔ* "Why?"), sentential adverbs (e.g., ועתה *wəʕattɔ* "Now therefore"), presentative particles (e.g., הנה *hinne* "Look"), and negatives (e.g., לא *loʔ* "No"). Free forms of address in clause-final position include those that occur between the matrix clause and the dependent clause, as well as between the matrix clause and the noun phrase that is coreferential with the subject of the matrix clause (1 Sam 22:16). The clause-medial addresses appear in one of the following constructions: (a) between the independent second-person pronoun and a verb; (b) between the predicate and the subject of a verbless clause or vice versa; (c) between a verb and its object; (d) between the core of the clause and a prepositional phrase.

In terms of the function of free forms of address in clause-medial position, Miller (2010b, 358) argues that those occurring in (a) or (b) seem to "highlight the informational status of the initial constituent as contrastive focus," while those occurring in (d) seem to "draw rhetorical attention" to the following prepositional phrase.

Miller's description of the external syntax of free forms of address, in terms of the positions that they occupy in the host clause, is more refined and elaborate compared to Revell's. Her argument about the information-managing function of the clause-medial addresses is quite convincing. However, she does not discuss the function of free forms of address occurring in many other positions within the sentence. For example, no comment is offered on how the address forms occurring in (c) function. Moreover, Miller's classification categories of "clause-initial" or "clause-final" can be misleading as they may include addresses occurring at the very beginning or end of an utterance, which she actually excludes from her discussion. From a functional perspective, her "clause-initial" or "clause-final" addresses may not serve the same pragmatic function as those occurring at the very beginning or end of an utterance. Thus, a new classification scheme is needed to distinguish address forms in different syntactic positions that might perform different functions. I attempt to do this in the following.

4.3. Method

In order to describe the position and function of free forms of address in Biblical Hebrew prose, it is essential to establish a unit of analysis and identify the unmarked order of its constituents.[11]

4.3.1. C-unit

In the following sections, I employ Leech's (1999, 108) concept of the "C-unit" as the unit of analysis.[12] As discussed above, the C-unit refers to a syntactically independent or self-standing unit of speech, which has no structural connection with what precedes or follows in the conversation, except by means of coordination. The C-unit may be a clausal unit (e.g., פציתה את פיך אל יהוה *pəṣiṯɔ ʔɛṯ-pikɔ ʔɛl-yhwh* "You have opened your mouth to YHWH" [Judg 11:36]) or a nonclausal unit (e.g., לא *loʔ* "No!" [Gen 42:12]). A clausal C-unit may consist of a "complex sentence," comprising an independent clause with one or more dependent clauses (e.g., זאת בריתי אשר תשמרו ביני וביניכם ובין זרעך אחריך *zoʔṯ bəriṯi ʔᵃšɛr tišməru beni uḇeneḵɛm uḇen zarʕᵃḵɔ ʔaḥᵃreḵɔ* "This is my covenant, which you shall keep, between me and you and your offspring after you" [Gen 17:10]). However, a "compound sentence," which involves two or more independent clauses connected by coordinating conjunctions, such as ו *wə* "and" or כי *ki* "but, for," is separated into independent clauses, each of which is treated as a separate C-unit.[13]

Drawing from the work of Biber et al. (2007, 1072) and Shiina (2008, 29), I divide a C-unit into three parts: preface(s), body, and tag(s). Prefaces and tags are common conversational features that allow speakers to handle planning pressure

---

[11] Miller (2010b, 349) follows McCawley (1998), who uses the "host sentence" as the unit of analysis for English vocatives, but she never defines the meaning of the host sentence in Biblical Hebrew.

[12] See Biber et al. (2007, 1069–72) in which Leech further elaborates the concept of the C-unit. See also Chafe (1994), who uses the term "intonation unit" for a similar notion.

[13] Breaking down a compound sentence into independent clauses to treat them as separate units of analysis has been commonly practiced in the study of Biblical Hebrew syntax. See, for example, Moshavi (2010, 49), who examines the word order in the Biblical Hebrew finite clause. She argues that the quest for the sentence in Biblical Hebrew is a futile exercise because almost every clause in narrative begins with the coordinating conjunction ו *wə* "and."

and convey complex messages.[14] Instead of including all information within the body of the C-unit, the speaker strategically distributes crucial pieces of information across prefaces and tags.

4.3.1.1. Prefaces

Prefaces are "extra-clausal constituents" that are loosely attached to the initial edge of the body (e.g., הנה נא ידעתי כי אשה יפת מראה את *hinne-nɔʔ yɔḏaʕti ki ʔiššɔ yəp̄aṯ-marʔɛ ʔɔtt* "Look, I know that you are a beautiful woman" [Gen 12:11]).[15] In our corpus, prefaces can take the form of a clausal adverb (e.g., ועתה *wəʕattɔ* "now therefore," לכן *lɔḵen* "therefore," אמנם *ʔɔmnɔm* "truly"),[16] a "left-dislocated" constituent,[17] a preverbal adjunct clause (e.g., a conditional clause introduced by אם *ʔim* "if"), an authenticating element in oath formulas (e.g., חי נפשך *he nap̄šəḵɔ* "by the life of your inner being"), or the presentative הנה *hinne* "Look!"[18]

Adina Moshavi (2010, 64–89) examines the basic order of some of these preface elements in the prose sections of Genesis through Kings. According to her

---

[14] According to Biber et al. (2007, 957), prefaces and tags are almost exclusively conversational features in British English. Based on a sample of 200,000 words from the Longman Spoken and Written English Corpus: 25 texts of 2,000 words each from conversation (British English only), fiction, news, and academic prose, they note that prefaces and tags occur over 200 times per million words in conversation and occasionally in fictional dialogue, but very rarely in written prose. In Biblical Hebrew as well, prefaces and tags are typically used in conversation.

[15] The term *extra-clausal constituents* (ECCs) was coined by Dik (1997, 380), who developed the theory of functional grammar. According to him (1997, 383), four types of ECCs can be identified according to the place they occupy in relation to the clause: (1) Absolute or free-standing ECCs; (2) Preclausal ECCs; (3) Clause-internal or parenthetical ECCs; (4) Postclausal ECCs. He calls preclausal ECCs, which Biber et al. (1997, 389) call prefaces, *themes*, and a postclausal ECCs, which Biber et al. (1997, 401) call tags, *tails*. Dik argues that ECCs cannot be described in terms of *clausal-internal* rules but can only be understood in terms of *pragmatic* rules.

[16] See Moshavi (2010, 68–75) for a list of clausal adverbs in Biblical Hebrew prose.

[17] Left dislocation is traditionally known by Hebraists as *casus pendens*. It refers to a linguistic phenomenon in which a constituent stands outside the left-hand border of a clause. The left dislocated constituent is resumed by a coreferential pronoun within the clause (e.g., האשה אשר נתתה עמדי הוא נתנה לי מן העץ *hɔʔiššɔ ʔăšer nɔṯattɔ ʕimmɔḏi hiwʔ nɔṯənɔ-lli min-hɔʕeṣ* "The woman whom you gave to be with me, *she* gave to me from the tree" [Gen 3:12]). Note that "left" refers to the beginning of a clause and "right" to the end of a clause in linguistic terminology. While the term "left" may cause confusion to readers of Semitic languages that are written from right to left, it is commonly used among those who seek to apply modern linguistic theory to the study of Biblical Hebrew today (e.g., Moshavi 2010, 81; *BHRG*[2] §48).

[18] For a thorough treatment of oath formulas in Biblical Hebrew, see Conklin 2011.

analysis, the clausal adverb is more detached from the body than the preverbal adjunct clause or the left-dislocated constituent, and therefore it precedes them. Based on my computerized search results, the clausal adverb also comes before the authenticating element (e.g., ואולם חי־יהוה וחי נפשך כי כפשע ביני ובין המות *wəʔulɔm ḥay-yhwh wəḥe napšekɔ ki kəpeśaʕ beni uḇen hammɔweṯ* "But truly, by the life of YHWH and by the life of your soul, there is about one step between me and death" [1 Sam 20:3]), while the presentative הנה *hinne* "look!" almost always follows the preverbal adjunct clause or the left-dislocated constituent.[19] Although the exact degrees of detachedness for the preverbal adjunct clause, left-dislocated constituent, and authenticating element cannot be determined due to insufficient data, it can be assumed that they have the same degree of detachedness. Therefore, the order of the preface elements in the C-unit can be determined as shown in figure 4.1.

Figure 4.1. Word Order of the Preface Elements in the C-unit
First --->**Last**

Clausal Adverb	Preverbal Adjunct Clause Authenticating Element Left-dislocated Constituent	Presentative הנה

According to Simon C. Dik (1997, 386–401), prefaces can serve a variety of pragmatic functions, such as opening up a new conversation, introducing or shifting a topic of conversation, setting the scene with respect to time, space, and condition, or drawing the hearer's attention to the main information in the body. Biber et al. (2007, 1073) add another function to these, noting that prefaces can

---

[19] There are numerous cases, in which the presentative הנה *hinne* "look!" follows the preverbal adjunct clause or the left-dislocated constituent. Consider, for example, the following: אני הנה בריתי אתך *ʔəni hinne ḇriṯi ʔittɔḵ* "I—look, my covenant is with you" (Gen 17:4), in which the left-dislocated constituent אני precedes the presentative הנה. Also, Exod 7:27 reads ואם מאן אתה לשלח הנה אנכי נגף את כל גבולך בצפרדעים *wəʔim-mɔʔen ʔattɔ lšalleaḥ hinne ʔɔnoḵi nogep ʔeṯ-kɔl-gḇulkɔ baṣpardśim* "If you refuse to let them go, look, I will plague all your territory with frogs." Here we see the conditional clause led by אם *ʔim* "if" precede the presentative הנה *hinne* "look!" There are only two exceptions to this pattern in Biblical Hebrew prose, in which the presentative הנה precedes the conditional clause introduced by אם (Judg 21:21) or the left-dislocated constituent (1 Sam 12:2). Curiously, Moshavi (2010, 77) cites one of these exceptional cases (Judg 21:21) to claim that the presentative הנה should be classified as a clausal adverb, which normally precedes the preverbal adjunct clause or the left-dislocated constituent. Holmstedt (2014, 121) is right to point out that the presentative הנה normally follows left-dislocated constituents and precedes fronted constituents.

4.3.1.2. Tags

Tags are extra-clausal constituents that are loosely attached to the final edge of the body (e.g., ובאת אל התבה אתה ובניך ואשתך ונשי בניך אתך *ubɔʔtɔ ʔɛl-hattebɔ ʔattɔ ubɔnɛkɔ wəʔištəkɔ unəše-bɔnɛkɔ ʔittɔk* "you shall come into the ark—*you, your sons, your wife, and your sons' wives with you*" [Gen 6:18]).[20] In our corpus, tags typically take the form of a noun phrase that is coreferentially linked to a pronoun in the body.

The precise discourse-pragmatic functions of tags can be challenging to determine, but they often serve to clarify or modify the reference of a coreferent pronoun in the body that might otherwise be unknown or unclear (Biber et al. 2007, 1080). This clarifying function is clearly demonstrated in the example from Gen 6:18 above. Initially God commands Noah to enter the ark, but he soon realizes that the reference of the second person pronoun embedded in the verb ובאת *ubɔʔtɔ* "you shall come in" may be unclear. To remove any doubt, God clarifies and specifies who should enter the ark along with Noah by adding the tag: אתה ובניך ואשתך ונשי בניך אתך *ʔattɔ ubɔnɛkɔ wəʔištəkɔ unəše-bɔnɛkɔ ʔittɔk* "(not only) *you*, (but also) *your sons, your wife, and your sons' wives with you*."

While dependent clauses that come after the matrix clause may not strictly fit in to the definition of tags provided above, they occupy the same position as tags, that is, the final edge of the body (e.g., ואירא כי־עירם אנכי *waʔirɔʔ ki-ʕerom ʔɔnoki* "I was afraid, *because I was naked*" [Gen 3:10]). Thus, they can be classified as tags based on syntactic criteria. In terms of information structure, dependent clauses serve the purpose of providing background information for the matrix clause (Dehé and Kavalova 2007, 12). In Gen 3:10 above, Adam provides the rationale for his fear by offering an explanation in the dependent clause introduced by כי *ki* "because"—his state of being naked. This function bears resemblance to the clarifying function of tags. Therefore, the classification of dependent clauses as tags can be justified from both syntactic and functional perspectives.

4.3.1.3. Body

The body of a C-unit can be divided into two parts: the initial edge and the core. The core consists of an independent clause, which can be verbal, verbless, or participial. As is widely recognized in Biblical Hebrew scholarship,[21] the unmarked

---

[20] In general linguistics, tags are commonly described as involving "right dislocation" (Biber et al. 2007, 139), while they are called "tails" in functional grammar (Dik 1997, 401).

[21] For a history of research on word order in Biblical Hebrew since Malbim (1809–1879) and a defense for the verb-subject-object order in verbal clauses and the subject-predicate order in verbless or participial clauses, see Moshavi 2010, 7–17.

word order in a verbal clause is verb-subject-direct object-indirect object-adverb or prepositional phrase (VSOX),[22] while in a verbless or participial clause, it is subject-predicate (SP).[23]

Certain grammatical elements are typically found at the initial edge of the core, always or nearly always preceding the verb in verbal clauses.[24] These include the interrogative ה, interrogative pro-forms (e.g., מה *mɔ* "what?", למה *lɔmmɔ* "why?"), certain time adverbs (e.g., עתה *ʕattɔ* "now"), the demonstrative adverb כה *ko* "thus," and negative particles (e.g., לא *loʔ* "not," אל *ʔal* "not").[25] Thus, the preverbal position is considered the unmarked position for these forms. However, one or more nonverbal constituents that follow the verb in the unmarked clause (e.g., the subject or object) may be placed in front of the verb for a variety of pragmatic reasons, such as focusing or topicalization (Moshavi 2010, 104–20). This phenomenon, commonly referred to as "fronting" (*BHRG²* §46.1.2(2)) or "preposing" (Moshavi 2010, 1), creates a marked construction. Unlike the left-dislocated constituent, which is resumed by a coreferential pronoun within the core, the fronted constituent has no resumption within it (e.g., אתי שלח יהוה למשחך למלך *ʔoti šɔlaḥ yhwh limšoḥ°kɔ ləmɛlɛk* "*Me* has YHWH sent to anoint you as king" [1 Sam 15:1]).[26]

Regarding the word order of these unmarked elements and fronted constituents at the initial core edge, the fact that all the unmarked elements, except the interrogative ה and negative particles, do not ordinarily cooccur with fronted constituents leads us to conclude that they occupy the same position as fronted constituents (Moshavi 2010, 78–80). As for the interrogative ה, it can occur with a fronted constituent, and, in such cases, the former precedes the latter (e.g.,

---

[22] Note that some of these constituents may not always be present, and there may be additional adjuncts following adverb/prepositional phrase. However, for the purpose of this chapter, it is sufficient to enumerate the five constituents mentioned above. *BHRG²* §46.1.3.2 provides a theoretical template reconstructed from the postverbal patterns in clauses with a variety of verbal lexemes: verb-subject-indirect object-prepositional object-other complement/adjunct-complement/adjunct (place)-adjunct (time).

[23] The predicate can be a noun phrase, adjective phrase, participle, or prepositional phrase.

[24] The majority of free forms of address in my corpus occur in verbal clauses. Therefore, I will not discuss word order in verbless or participial clauses here. I will comment further when these clauses appear in the next section.

[25] See Moshavi (2010, 76–80) for a list of these forms occurring in Biblical Hebrew prose.

[26] For a comparison and contrast between left-dislocation and fronting with ample examples, see Moshavi 2010, 81–83. Note also that all these unmarked and marked elements come after prefaces. For example, consider the following: ולבנתי מה אעשה לאלה היום או לבניהן אשר ילדו *wəlibnotay mɔ-ʔɛʕśɛ lɔʔellɛ hayyom ʔo libnehɛn ʔášɛr yɔlɔdu* "To my daughters, *what* can I do to these today or to their children whom they have borne?" (Gen 31:43). The interrogative particle מה *mɔ* "what" occurs after the left-dislocated constituent לבנתי *libnotay* "to my daughters."

השפט כל הארץ לא יעשה משפט *hᵃšopeṭ kɔl-hɔʔɔreṣ loʔ yaſᵃśɛ mišpɔṭ* "Shall not *the judge of all the earth* deal justly?" [Gen 18:25]). Negative particles, however, are so closely bound to the verb that they typically follow fronted constituents (e.g., ותבן לא ינתן *wɐṯɛḇɛn loʔ-yinnɔṯɛn* "Straw will *not* be given" [Exod 5:18]).

Thus, the order of the body elements in the C-unit can be determined as shown in figure 4.2.

Figure 4.2. Word Order of the Body Elements in the C-unit
First ---> **Last**

	Initial Edge		Core
	Interrogative pro-forms	Negative	VSOX
	Time Adverb		
	Demonstrative Adverb כה		
Interrogative ה [27]	Fronted Constituent		

With a unit of analysis established and the unmarked (and marked) order of C-unit elements determined, we are now ready to explore the position and function of free forms of address in our corpus. In the following sections, I will organize the address forms based on their position relative to the C-unit elements. I will then provide one or two representative examples from each group to illustrate the pragmatic function that they serve. I adopt Taglicht's notion that the markedness of an element is determined by syntactic (detachment) and/or prosodic (intonation) criteria, and that every marked element carries information focus. Since we lack prosodic data in Biblical Hebrew, we must rely solely on the syntactic criterion to identify marked elements. I will argue that the insertion of free forms of address into the C-unit makes the preceding or following element as marked, reinforcing its pragmatic function.

4.4. Analysis

In our corpus, free forms of address can be found in one of the following positions relative to the C-unit: stand-alone, initial, medial, and final.

---

[27] I would place the negative interrogative הלא *hᵃloʔ* "Is it not?" here, as there are a number of cases in Biblical Hebrew prose in which it follows a left-dislocated constituent (e.g., Gen 34:23; 1 Kgs 11:41; 14:29, etc.) and precedes a fronted constituent (e.g., Gen 20:5; Judg 4:14; 11:17; 2 Sam 11:21, etc.). However, הלא may also occur before the presentative particle הנה *hinne* "look!" (2 Chr 25:26), a conditional clause led by אם *ʔim* "if" (Gen 4:7; 1 Sam 15:17; 2 Kgs 20:19), or a left-dislocated constituent (Judg 11:24). Thus, Moshavi (2010, 70) classifies it as a clausal adverb. All that can be said at this stage is that הלא precedes fronted constituents. The precise unmarked location of הלא cannot be ascertained.

4.4.1. Stand-Alone

A C-unit can be nonclausal, consisting solely of one or more free forms of address. There are eighteen cases of such stand-alone addresses in our corpus, which make up approximately 3 percent of the total occurrences of free forms of address.[28] These stand-alone addresses are predominantly used as "calls" or "summonses" to attract the attention of the addressee at the beginning of the conversation. Consider the following:

(26) ויאמר יצחק אל אברהם **אביו** ויאמר אבי ויאמר הנני בני
wayyoʔmɛr	yiṣḥɔq	ʔɛl-ʔaḇrɔhɔm	ʔɔḇiw	wayyoʔmɛr
and=he.said	Isaac	to-Abraham	father=his	and=he.said

ʔɔḇi	wayyoʔmɛr	hinnɛnni	bəni	
father=my	and=he.said	look=me	son=my	

Isaac said to his father Abraham, "*My father!*" "Here I am, my son," he replied. (Gen 22:7)

Isaac's address takes place as he and his father Abraham approach one of the mountains in Moriah, where Abraham is tasked with offering Isaac as a burnt offering to God. The pragmatic function of Isaac's address as a call to catch Abraham's attention becomes evident through Abraham's immediate response: הנני בני *hinnɛnni bəni* "Here I am, my son."[29] In all other instances of stand-alone addresses in our corpus, the addressee provides a verbal or nonverbal reply, except in cases where the addressee is dead (2 Sam 19:5) or has departed from the scene (2 Kgs 2:12), or when the conversation is not fully recorded (Isa 8:4). Some of these stand-alone addresses involve the repetition of an address or the combination of multiple addresses, as seen in (27):

(27) ויבא יהוה ויתיצב ויקרא כפעם בפעם **שמואל שמואל**
wayyɔḇoʔ	yhwh	wayyityaṣṣaḇ	wayyiqrɔʔ
and=he.came	YWHH	and=he.stood	and=he.called

kəpaʕam-bəpaʕam	šəmuʔel	šəmuʔel
like=time-in=time	Samuel	Samuel

Then YHWH came and stood, calling as at other times, "*Samuel! Samuel!*" (1 Sam 3:10)

---

[28] Gen 22:1, 7, 11; 27:1, 18; 31:11; 46:2; Exod 3:4; 1 Sam 3:6, 10, 16; 24:9; 2 Sam 9:6; 19:5; 2 Kgs 2:12; 13:14; Isa 8:4 (2x).

[29] See Schegloff (1968, 1075–95) for a study of summons-answer sequences in telephone conversations.

This type of stand-alone address can serve additional pragmatic function, such as expressing the speaker's emotions or conveying a sense of urgency, as discussed in §2.3.5.2. Nevertheless, there is no doubt that their primary function remains as a call to capture the addressee's attention.

In our corpus, we find thirty-six instances of free forms of address, which make up approximately 5 percent of the total cases, immediately following interjections, such as אהה *ʔᵃhɔh* "Alas!",[30] אנא *ʔɔnnɔʔ* "Oh!",[31] אנה *ʔɔnnɔ* "Oh!",[32] בי *bi* "Oh!",[33] and הוי *hoy* "Woe!"[34] Syntactically, these interjections are independent of the subsequent C-unit: they neither form a part of it nor modify it. Thus, an interjection followed by a free form of address can constitute a nonclausal C-unit, as in (28):

(28) ויקראו אל יהוה ויאמרו **אנה יהוה** אל נא נאבדה בנפש האיש הזה

wayyiqrəʔu	ʔɛl-yhwh	wayyoʔməru	ʔɔnnɔ	yhwh
and=they.called	to-YHWH	and=they.said	oh	YHWH
ʔal-nɔʔ	noʔbədɔ	bənɛp̄ɛš	hɔʔiš	hazzɛ
not-POL	we.will.die	in=life.of	the=man	the=this

They called out to YHWH, "**Oh**, *YHWH*! Don't let us die on account of this man!" (Jonah 1:14)

In this verse, the address form יהוה occurs immediately after the interjection אנה, as the sailors cry out to the God of Israel for help. Undoubtedly, the primary function of the interjection is to catch the attention of the addressee, יהוה, conveying the sense of urgency for the subsequent request. The address form that follows the interjection appears to reinforce the attention-getting function of the interjection by specifying the identity of the addressee in this prayer. Thus, the address form following the interjection seems to serve the same function as stand-alone addresses. Based on their functional role, free forms of address that follow an interjection may be classified as stand-alone addresses.

4.4.2. C-unit Initial

The majority of the C-units in our corpus are clausal units, which can be verbal, verbless, or participial clauses. As discussed earlier, a C-unit can be divided into three parts: preface, body (initial and core), and tag. We observe that 145 free

---

[30] See Josh 7:7; Judg 6:22; 11:35; 2 Kgs 6:5, 15; Jer 1:6; 4:10; 14:13; 32:17; Ezek 4:14; 9:8; 11:3; 21:5.
[31] See Dan 9:4; Neh 1:5, 11.
[32] See 2 Kgs 20:3; Isa 38:3; Jonah 1:14; 4:2.
[33] See Gen 43:20; 44:18; Exod 4:10, 13; Num 12:11; Josh 7:8; Judg 6:13, 15; 13:8; 1 Sam 1:26; 1 Kgs 3:17, 26.
[34] See 1 Kgs 13:30; Jer 23:1; 34:5; Ezek 34:2.

forms of address, comprising approximately 21 percent of all the addresses in our corpus, appear at the beginning of a C-unit, that is, before any preface elements. These addresses occur either at the beginning of a conversation,[35] at the beginning of a turn,[36] or at the beginning of a C-unit within a turn.[37] We can see examples of these scenarios in (29), (30), and (31), respectively:

(29) וימצאה מלאך יהוה על עין המים במדבר על העין בדרך שור
ויאמר **הגר שפחת שרי** אי מזה באת

wayyimṣɔʔɔh	malʔak̠	yhwh	ʕal-ʕen	hammayim
and=he.found=her	messenger.of	YHWH	on-spring.of	the=water
bammid̠bɔr	ʕal-hɔʕayin		bəd̠erek̠	šur
in=the=wilderness	on-the=spring.of		in=way.of	Shur
wayyoʔmar	hɔg̠ɔr	šip̠ḥat̠	śɔray	ʔe-mizze	bɔʔt̠
and=he.said	Hagar	servant.of	Sarai	where-from=this	you.came

The messenger of YHWH found her (i.e., Hagar) near a spring of water in the wilderness—the spring on the way to Shur. He said, "Hagar, servant of Sarai, where have you come from?" (Gen 16:7–8a)

(30) ותקד בת שבע ותשתחו למלך ויאמר המלך מה לך
ותאמר לו **אדני** אתה נשבעת ביהוה אלהיך לאמתך כי שלמה בנך ימלך אחרי

wattiqqod̠	bat̠-šeb̠aʕ	wattištaḥu	lammelek̠	wayyoʔmer
and=she.bowed	Bathsheba	and=she.bowed	to=the=king	and=he.said
hammelek̠	ma-llɔk̠	wattoʔmer	lo	ʔᵃd̠oni	ʔattɔ
the=king	what-to=you	and=she.said	to=him	lord=my	you
nišbaʕt̠ɔ	bayhwh	ʔlohek̠ɔ	laʔᵃmɔt̠ek̠ɔ	ki-šəlomo
you.swore	by=YHWH	God=your	to=servant=your	that-Solomon

---

[35] For examples in which free forms of address occur at the beginning of a conversation, see Gen 16:8; 18:3; 20:4; 24:12, 42; 29:4; 32:10; Exod 5:22; Num 11:28; 12:13; Deut 3:24; 9:26; Josh 7:19; Judg 16:28; 1 Sam 1:8, 11; 23:10; 2 Sam 19:1; 1 Kgs 1:24; 8:23; 13:2; 17:20; 18:26, 36; 22:15; 2 Kgs 1:9, 11, 13; 2:4; 5:13; 6:17, 20; 8:5; 19:15; Isa 37:16; Jer 38:9; 51:62; Ezek 2:1; 3:17; 6:2; 8:5; 11:2; 11:15; 12:2, 9, 18, 22, 27; 13:2; 14:3; 13; 15:2; 16:2; 17:2; 20:3; 21:2, 7, 14; 22:3, 18, 24; 23:2, 36; 24:2, 16; 25:2; 26:2; 28:2, 12, 21; 29:2, 18; 30:2, 21; 31:2; 32:2, 18; 33:2, 8, 24; 34:2; 35:2; 36:1, 17; 37:3, 4; 38:2; 40:4; 43:7; 44:5; Amos 7:2, 5, 12; Zech 1:12; Ruth 3:1; Dan 8:16; 9:22; 10:11, 16; Ezra 9:6; 2 Chr 6:14; 14:10; 18:14; 20:6; 25:7; 30:6.

[36] For examples in which free forms of address occur at the beginning of a turn, see Gen 15:2, 8; 23:15; Num 16:22; Judg 11:36; 1 Sam 20:30; 2 Sam 19:27; 1 Kgs 1:17; 17:21; Ezek 2:3; 3:1, 3, 4, 10; 4:16; 8:6, 8; 37:3, 11; 43:18; Dan 12:8.

[37] For examples in which free forms of address occur at the beginning of a C-unit within a turn, see 1 Sam 23:11; 24:12; Dan 9:8, 16, 19 (3x); Ezra 9:15; 1 Chr 17:19, 20; 21:17; 29:16, 18; 2 Chr 6:42; 13:12; 14:10; 20:12; 29:11.

bənekֿ	yimlokֿ	ʔaḥᵃrɔy
son=your	he.will.rule	after=me

Bathsheba bowed and paid homage to the king. The king said, "What do you want?" She replied to him, "*My lord*, you swore to your servant by YHWH your God, 'Solomon your son will be king after me.'" (1 Kgs 1:16–17a)

(31) עתה עם לבבי לכרות ברית ליהוה אלהי ישראל וישב ממנו חרון אפו
בני עתה אל תשלו

ʕattɔ	ʕim-ləbɔbi̱	likֿroṯ	bəri̱ṯ	layhwh	ʔᵉlohe
now	with-heart=my	to=cut	covenant	to=YHWH	God.of
yiśrɔʔel	wəyɔšoḇ		mimmɛnnu	ḥᵃron	ʔappo
Israel	and=he.will.return		from=us	burning.of	nose=his
bɔnay	ʕattɔ	ʔal-tiššɔlu			
sons=my	now	not-you.will.be.at.ease			

"Now it is in my heart to make a covenant with YHWH, the God of Israel, so that his fierce anger may turn away from us. *My sons*, do not be negligent now." (2 Chr 29:10–11a)

In (29), the messenger of YHWH suddenly appears and approaches Hagar who has fled from her mistress Sarai due to mistreatment. He initiates the conversation by addressing her using her name and title. It is evident that the messenger's intention in addressing her at the beginning of the conversation is to attract Hagar's attention before inquiring about her whereabouts.

In (30), we see King David initiating the conversation. After Bathsheba bows to him, he asks her what she desires. Then, Bathsheba begins her turn by addressing David as אדני *ʔᵃdoni* "my lord." At this point, Bathsheba does not need to attract David's attention since he is already attentive to her (which is why he inquired about her desires). Instead, her address serves to mark the beginning of her turn and to establish David's position in relation to her before she presents her request for her son Solomon to be made king over Israel. By using the deferential address form אדני at the beginning of her turn, Bathsheba verbally (not just gesturally) acknowledges that David is her master who can grant her request, while also preparing herself to present her case before him.

Example (31) is taken from King Hezekiah's speech to the Levites before the cleansing of the temple. He begins his speech by addressing the Levites in 2 Chr 29:5, saying, שמעוני הלוים *šəmɔʕuni halwiyyim* "Hear me, Levites!" He then proceeds to argue that the wrath of YHWH has befallen Judah and Jerusalem due to the sins committed by their ancestors. Just before delivering his final charge, "Do not be negligent now," Hezekiah addresses them as "my sons." I would argue that Hezekiah's address here serves as a rhetorical device to grab the attention of the Levites just before giving his final command once again. By doing so, Hezekiah highlights the significance of his charge.

The functions of all other addresses in the initial position of a C-unit in our corpus can be explained as means of attracting the attention of the addressee, signaling the beginning of a turn, and/or identifying the addressee. This finding aligns with Leech's (1999, 116) identification of the functions of initial address forms in British and American English.

4.4.3. C-unit Final

212 free forms of address, which constitute approximately 31 percent of all addresses in our corpus, are positioned at the end of a C-unit. They can occur either at the end of a conversation,[38] at the end of a turn,[39] or at the end of a C-unit within a turn,[40] as in (32) and (33):

(32) ויאמר יצחק אל אברהם אביו ויאמר אבי ויאמר הנני **בני**
ויאמר הנה האש והעצים ואיה השה לעלה
ויאמר אברהם אלהים יראה לו השה לעלה **בני**

wayyoʔmɛr	yiṣḥɔq	ʔɛl-ʔaḇrɔhɔm	ʔɔḇiw	wayyoʔmɛr
and=he.said	Isaac	to-Abraham	father=his	and=he.said

ʔɔḇi	wayyoʔmɛr	hinnɛnni	bəni	wayyoʔmɛr
father=my	and=he.said	look=me	son=my	and=he.said

hinne	hɔʔeš	wəhɔʕeṣim	wəʔayye	haśśɛ
look	the=fire	and=the=trees	and=where	the=lamb

ləʕolɔ	wayyoʔmɛr	ʔaḇrɔhɔm	ʔᵉlohim	yirʔɛ-llo
for=burnt.offering	and=he.said	Abraham	God	he.will.see-for=him

---

[38] For examples in which free forms of address occur at the end of a conversation, see Gen 22:8; 43:29; Num 16:7; Deut 26:10; Judg 16:9, 12, 14, 20; 2 Sam 15:31; 16:4; 19:1; 20:9; 1 Kgs 8:53; 9:13; 22:28; 2 Kgs 3:23; 9:5, 23; Ezek 11:4; 20:44; 33:20; Ruth 2:2; 2 Chr 18:27.

[39] For examples in which free forms of address occur at the end of a turn, see Gen 22:7; 24:18; 27:18, 20, 26, 34, 37, 38; Judg 3:19; 6:12; 1 Sam 4:16; 14:44; 17:55, 58; 22:12 (2x); 24:17; 26:14, 17 (2x); 2 Sam 2:20; 13:11; 14:4; 19:26; 1 Kgs 12:16; 18:7, 17; 19:9, 13; 21:20; 2 Kgs 2:23; 4:40; 5:25; 6:21, 26; 9:5, 22, 31; Jer 1:11; 11:5; 24:3; Ezek 47:6; Amos 7:8; 8:2; Zech 1:9; 4:4; 6:4; Ruth 3:16; 2 Chr 10:16.

[40] For examples in which free forms of address occur at the end of a C-unit within a turn, see Gen 15:1; 21:17; 23:6; 24:31; 27:13, 38; 33:9; 48:19; Num 10:35; 14:14; 16:6 (2x), 8; 20:10; Deut 6:3, 4; 9:1; 20:3; 21:8; 27:9; Josh 7:13; Judg 4:18; 9:7; 16:28; 1 Sam 3:6, 9; 26:21, 22, 25; 2 Sam 7:18, 19 (2x), 20, 22; 13:34; 16:7, 10; 18:22; 1 Kgs 2:20; 12:16; 14:6; 17:18; 18:37; 2 Kgs 2:23; Isa 10:24; 31:6; Jer 3:14; 7:2; 10:1; 11:13; 17:20 (3x); 18:6; 19:3; 28:15; 29:20; 32:25; 34:4; 37:20; 42:15, 19; 44:24, 26; 45:2; Ezek 8:15, 17; 11:5; 18:25, 29, 30, 31; 20:4, 27, 31; 26:3; 28:22; 33:11; 36:22, 32; 37:9 (2x), 12, 13; 38:3, 14, 16; 39:1; 44:6; 45:9; Amos 5:1; Zech 3:2; 4:7; Ruth 1:11, 12; 2:8, 13; 3:10; Esth 5:3; 7:2; Dan 9:19; 10:12, 19; 12:9; Neh 3:36; 13:22; 1 Chr 17:16, 17 (2x); 28:2; 2 Chr 10:16; 13:4 (2x); 14:10; 15:2 (3x); 20:15 (3x), 17 (2x), 20 (2x); 29:5; 35:21.

haśśɛ	ləʕolɔ	bəni
the=lamb	for=burnt.offering	son=my

Isaac said to his father Abraham, "My father!" He replied, "Here I am, *my son*." He said, "Here is the fire and the wood, but where is the lamb for a burnt offering?" Abraham said, "God will provide for himself the lamb for a burnt offering, *my son*." (Gen 22:7–8a)

(33) אחר הדברים האלה היה דבר יהוה אל אברם במחזה לאמר

אל תירא **אברם** אנכי מגן לך שכרך הרבה מאד

ʔaḥar	haddəbɔrim	hɔʔellɛ	hɔyɔ	dəbar-yhwh	ʔɛl-ʔabrɔm
after	the=things	the=these	he.was	word.of-YHWH	to-Abram

bammaḥⁿzɛ	leʔmor	ʔal-tirɔʔ	ʔabrɔm	ʔɔnoki	mɔgen	lɔk
in=vision	to=say	not-you.will.fear	Abram	I	shield	to=you

śəkɔrəkɔ	harbe	məʔod
reward=your	much	very

After these things the word of YHWH came to Abram in a vision: "Fear not, *Abram*! I am your shield; your reward shall be very great." (Gen 15:1)

Example (32) shows the ongoing conversation between Abraham and Isaac, which began in (26). In response to Isaac's call using the stand-alone address, אבי *ʔɔbi* "my father," Abraham replies with הנני בני *hinnɛnni bəni* "Here I am, my son." It is evident that Abraham's address בני in the final position of his turn does not serve as a call to catch Isaac's attention. Rather, his address functions to both identify the addressee and signal the end of his turn, allowing Isaac to take his turn and ask about the burnt offering. In reply to Isaac's question, Abraham states, אלהים יראה לו השה לעלה בני *ʔᵉlohim yirʔɛ-llo haśśɛ ləʕolɔ bəni* "God will provide for himself the lamb for a burnt offering, my son." This time, Abraham's address בני occurs at the end of their conversation. Thus, it can be said that his address is used to signal the end of their dialogue as well as to reaffirm the addressee's identity once again.

In (33), YHWH appears to Abram in a vision and says, אל תירא אברם *ʔal-tirɔʔ ʔabrɔm* "Fear not, Abram!" YHWH's address אברם occurs at the end of a C-unit within his turn. Again, it does not seem to function as a call but rather as a means of identifying Abram as the addressee and maintaining contact with him before YHWH continues with his statement.

Included in this group of free forms of address in a C-unit final position are those that immediately follow elliptical negatives, such as לא *loʔ* "no,"[41] לא כן *loʔ-ken* "not so,"[42] אל *ʔal* "no,"[43] אל נא *ʔal-nɔʔ* "please no."[44] Consider the following:

---

[41] Gen 23:11; 42:10; 1 Sam 1:15; 2 Kgs 6:12; Zech 4:5, 13.
[42] Gen 48:18.
[43] Judg 19:23; 1 Sam 2:24; 2 Sam 13:12, 25; 2 Kgs 4:16; Ruth 1:13.
[44] Gen 19:18.

(34) ויען המלאך הדבר בי ויאמר אלי הלוא ידעת מה המה אלה ואמר **לא אדני**
wayyaʕan   hammalʔɔ<u>k</u>   haddo<u>b</u>er   bi
and=he.answered   the=messenger   the=speaking   with=me
wayyoʔmɛr   ʔelay   hᵃloʔ   yɔdaʕtɔ   mɔ-hemmɔ   ʔellɛ
and=he.said   to=me   INTER=not   you.knew   what-they   these
wɔʔomar   loʔ   ʔᵃḏoni
and=I.said   not   lord=my

Then the messenger who talked with me answered and said to me, "Do you not know what these are?" I responded, "**No**, *my lord.*" (Zech 4:5)

After showing Zechariah a vision of a golden lampstand and two olive trees, the messenger inquires if Zechariah understands their significance. Zechariah responds with the negative particle לא *loʔ* "no," followed by the address אדני *ʔᵃḏoni* "my lord." Here the word לא expresses a denial of everything said by the messenger, serving as an elliptical expression for a complete sentence, "No, I don't know what these are."[45] Thus, Zechariah's address following the elliptical לא may be regarded as occurring in a C-unit final position (i.e., "No, I don't know what these are, my lord"), signaling the end of his turn and giving the floor back to the messenger.

The functions of all the other addresses in a C-unit final position in our corpus can be explained as identifying the addressee, signaling the end of the conversation, marking the end of a turn to give the floor to the addressee, and/or maintaining contact with the addressee. This finding aligns with Leech's (1999, 116) identification of the functions of final address forms in British and American English.

Thus far, we have examined the functions performed by stand-alone, initial, or final addresses in our corpus. These functions include attracting the attention of the addressee, identifying the addressee, signaling the beginning or end of a turn/conversation, giving the floor to the addressee, and/or maintaining contact with the addressee. Since all these functions are directly linked to managing the flow of the conversation, we could potentially classify them under the overarching function of "conversation management."[46]

4.4.4. C-unit Medial

Approximately 20 percent of the total addresses in our corpus (139 forms) are located within a C-unit and can appear in one of the following positions: (i) between the preface and the body, (ii) within the body, or (iii) between the body and

---

[45] For the use of elliptical negatives, see Zevit 1979, 505–9.
[46] The term *conversation management* is partly borrowed from Shiina (2007, 26), who uses the term to encompass all these functions of initial and final free forms of address in Early Modern English.

the tag. I will argue that in each of these cases, free forms of address serve a dual function. First, they act as a partition marker, indicating the boundary between the two parts of a C-unit. Second, they serve as a focusing device, orienting the addressee's attention to a "marked" element, which can be determined by the criterion of the "detachment."

4.4.4.1. *Between Preface and Body*

There are forty-eight instances of free forms of address that immediately follow one of the preface elements in our corpus. These preface elements include clausal adverbs (ועתה *wəʕattɔ* "now therefore," לכן *lɔken* "therefore," אמנם *ʔomnɔm* "truly"),[47] preverbal adjunct clauses (a conditional clause led by אם *ʔim* "if"),[48] authenticating elements (חי נפשך *ḥe napšəkɔ* "by the life of your inner being"),[49] left-dislocated constituents (ואתה *wəʔattɔ* "as for you [M.SG.]," ואתם *wəʔattɛm* "as for you [M.PL.]," ואתנה *wəʔattenɔ* "as for you [F.PL.]"),[50] or presentative particles (הנה *hinne* or הנה נא *hinne nnɔʔ* "look").[51] Nearly two-thirds of these address forms are directly followed by the first element of the core of the body as in (35), while one-third are followed by an initial element of the body as in (36). There are only three cases in which the address occurs between two preface elements, as in (37).

(35) אמנם יהוה החריבו מלכי אשור את הגוים ואת ארצם

| *ʔomnɔm* | *yhwh* | *heḥˤriḇu* | *malke* | *ʔaššur* |
| Truly | YHWH | they.destroyed | kings.of | Assyria |

ʔɛt-haggoyim   *wəʔɛt-ʔarṣɔm*
ACC-the=nations   and=ACC-land=their

Truly, O YHWH, the kings of Assyria have destroyed the nations and their lands. (2 Kgs 19:17)

---

[47] For free forms of address occurring after ועתה, see Gen 27:8, 43; Deut 4:1; 10:12; 1 Sam 25:26; 2 Sam 7:25, 28; 13:20; 24:10; 1 Kgs 1:18; 3:7; 8:25, 26; 2 Kgs 19:19; Isa 37:20; Jonah 4:3; Ruth 3:11; Dan 9:15; 1 Chr 17:23, 26; 29:13; 2 Chr 6:16, 17. For free forms of address occurring after לכן, see Ezek 16:35; 23:22; 34:7, 9; 36:4. For free forms of address occurring after אמנם, see 2 Kgs 19:17; Isa 37:18.
[48] For free forms of address occurring after a conditional clause led by אם, see: Exod 34:9; Esth 7:3.
[49] For free forms of address occurring after חי נפשך, see 1 Sam 1:26; 17:55; 2 Sam 14:19.
[50] For free forms of address occurring after ואתה, see 1 Kgs 1:20; Ezek 3:25; 7:2; 21:30; 22:2; 24:25; 33:7, 30; 39:17. For free forms of address occurring after ואתם, see Ezek 20:39. For free forms of address occurring after ואתנה, see Ezek 34:17.
[51] For free forms of address occurring after הנה, see Judg 20:7. For free forms of address occurring after הנה נא, see Gen 19:2.

(36) **לכן אהליבה** כה אמר אדני יהוה
הנני מעיר את מאהביך עליך את אשר נקעה נפשך מהם

lɔken	ʔohŏlibɔ	ko-ʔɔmar	ʔᵃdonɔy	yhwh
therefore	Oholibah	thus-he.said	Lord	YHWH
hinni	meʕir	ʔɛt-məʔahᵃbayik	ʕɔlayik	ʔɛt
look=me	string.up	ACC-lovers=your	against=you	ACC
ʔᵃšer-nɔqəʕɔ		napšek	mehɛm	
whom-she.was.disgusted		life=your	from=them	

Therefore, *Oholibah*, thus says the Lord YHWH: "Look, I am about to stir up against you your lovers with whom you were disgusted. (Ezek 23:22)

(37) **ועתה אדני** חי יהוה וחי נפשך
אשר מנעך יהוה מבוא בדמים והושע ידך לך ועתה יהיו כנבל איביך

wəʕattɔ	ʔᵃdoni	ḥay-yhwh	wəhey-napšəkɔ	ʔšer
and=now	lord=my	life.of-YHWH	and=life.of-life=your	that
mənɔʕᵃkɔ	yhwh	mibboʔ	bədɔmim	wəhošeᵃʕ
he.restrained=you	YHWH	from=to.enter	in=blood	and=saving
yɔdəkɔ	lɔk	wəʕattɔ	yihyu	kənɔbɔl	ʔoybɛkɔ
hand=your	for=you	and=now	they.will.be	like=Nabal	enemies=your

Now therefore, *my lord*, by the life of YHWH and by your own life, (I swear that) since YHWH prevented you from entering into bloodshed and taking matters into your own hand, now then, may your enemies be like Nabal. (1 Sam 25:26)[52]

Example (35) is part of Hezekiah's prayer to YHWH after receiving a threatening letter from Sennacherib, king of Assyria. Hezekiah's address יהוה *yhwh* "O YHWH!" occurs between the clausal adverb אמנם *ʔɔmnɔm* "truly" and the verb החריבו *hehŕibu* "they destroyed." In (36), the prophet Ezekiel delivers a message from YHWH against Oholibah (symbolizing Jerusalem), who continues her "whoring" with the Babylonians. His address, אהליבה *ʔohŏlibɔ* "Oholibah," comes between the clausal adverb לכן *lɔken* "therefore" and the demonstrative adverb כה *ko* "thus." In (37), Abigail takes an oath against David's enemies who seek to harm him, wishing that they will be cursed like Nabal. Her address אדני *ʔᵃdoni* "my lord" falls between the clausal adverb ועתה *wəʕattɔ* "now therefore"[53] and the authenticating element חי יהוה וחי נפשך *ḥay-yhwh wəhey-napšəkɔ* "by the life of YHWH and by your own life."

---

[52] For the examples that omit the expected כי or אם לא to mark the positive oath, see Conklin 2011, 64–65.

[53] In the Hebrew Bible, ועתה (= the conjunction ו + the time adverb עתה) is predominantly used as a clausal adverb functioning as a discourse marker. For the distribution and function of ועתה as a discourse marker, see *BHRG²* §40.39.

The insertion of these addresses breaks the unmarked sequence of the C-unit, partitioning it into a preface element and the rest of the C-unit. The preface element that precedes the address can be considered "marked" since it is "further detached"[54] from the following constituent(s) that would typically be adjacent in an unmarked sequence. I argue that the marked preface element contains information focus and that its discourse-pragmatic function is reinforced. In (35) above, the discourse-pragmatic function of the clausal adverb אמנם is to draw the attention of the addressee to and confirm the veracity of the following proposition (i.e., the destruction of the nations by the Assyrians).[55] In (36), the clausal adverb לכן is used as a discourse marker which orients the addressee(s) both backward to the grounds of the following prophetic announcements (i.e., Oholibah's "whoring" with the Babylonians) and forward to the consequences of said grounds (i.e., the Babylonian conquest of Jerusalem).[56] The clausal adverb ועתה in (37) also functions as a discourse marker which orients the addressee both backward to the speaker's explanation of the background situation (i.e., Nabal's stupidity) and forward to the implications of said background (i.e., the destiny of David's enemy like Nabal). All these functions of the preface elements seem to be further highlighted by the intrusion of the addresses, which not only detach them from but also "delay" the rest of the C-unit. The addressees are directed to the preceding and/or following parts of the preface elements according to their discourse-pragmatic functions, as they are kept waiting for the rest of the C-unit. All the other addresses that immediately follow a preface element seem to reinforce its discourse-pragmatic function(s).

4.4.4.2. Within the Body

Free forms of address that occur within the body of the C-unit can be divided into two groups: those that occur between the initial edge and the core of the body, and those that occur within the core of the body.

4.4.4.2.1. Between the Initial Edge and the Core

There are forty-nine free forms of address in our corpus that occur immediately after an initial-edge constituent. Eight of them occur after an "unmarked" initial-edge constituent, such as the negative interrogative הלא *hᵃlo?* "is it not?" as in (38),[57] the interrogative pro-form למה *lɔmɔ* "why?" as in (39),[58] the time

---

[54] As discussed above, the preface elements are considered already syntactically detached from the body.
[55] Note that the clausal adverb אמנם occurs only in reported speech. For a discussion of the distribution and use of אמנם, see *BHRG²* §40.13.
[56] For a detailed analysis of the clausal adverb לכן, see van der Merwe 2014.
[57] 1 Chr 21:3.
[58] Exod 32:11; Judg 21:3.

adverb עתה ʕattɔ "now" as in (40),[59] and the negative אל נא ʔal-nɔʔ "please not" as in (41):[60]

(38) **הלא אדני המלך** כלם לאדני לעבדים
h*a*loʔ   ʔ*a*doni   hammɛlɛḵ   kullɔm   laʔdoni   laʕ*a*ḇoḏim
INTER=not   lord=my   the=king   all=their   to=lord=my   to=servants
Are not, *my lord the king*, all of them my lord's servants? (1 Chr 21:3)

(39) **למה יהוה** יחרה אפך בעמך אשר הוצאת מארץ מצרים בכח גדול וביד חזקה
lɔmɔ   yhwh   yeḥ*e*rɛ   ʔappəḵɔ   bəʕammɛḵɔ   ʔ*a*šɛr
why   YHWH   he.will.burn nose=your   in=people=your REL
hoṣeʔtɔ   meʔɛrɛṣ   miṣrayim   bəḵoᵃḥ   gɔḏol
you.brought.out   from=land.of Egypt   with=power   great
uḇəyɔḏ   ḥ*a*zɔqɔ
and=with=hand   strong
Why, *O YHWH*, does your anger burn against your people, whom you have brought out from the land of Egypt with great power and with a mighty hand? (Exod 32:11)

(40) **עתה יהוה** קח נפשי
ʕattɔ   yhwh   qaḥ   nap̄ši
now   YHWH   take   life=my
Now, *O YHWH*, take my life! (1 Kgs 19:4)

(41) **אל נא אחי** תרעו
ʔal-nɔʔ   ʔaḥay   tɔreʕu
not-POL   brothers=my   you.will.act.wickedly
Do not please, *my brothers*, act wickedly! (Gen 19:7)

In (38), we see Joab counseling King David as he attempts to order a census of the people of Israel. His deferential address אדני המלך ʔ*a*doni hammɛlɛḵ "my lord the king" comes between the negative interrogative הלא h*a*loʔ "are not" and the subject of the verbless clause כלם kullɔm "all of them." In (39), Moses is attempting to appease and entreat YHWH as he is about to consume the people of Israel who have made a golden calf for themselves and have worshiped it. His address יהוה yhwh "YHWH" occurs between the interrogative pro-form למה lɔmɔ "why?" and the verb יחרה yeḥ*e*rɛ "it burns." In (40), we see Elijah asking God to take his life as he is so afraid of and depressed with Jezebel's threat. His address occurs between the time adverb עתה ʕttɔ "now" and the imperative verb קח qaḥ "take!" In (41), Lot is attempting to prevent the men of Sodom from violating the

---

[59] 1 Kgs 19:4; 1 Chr 22:11; 2 Chr 1:9; 6:40.
[60] Gen 19:7.

two guests who have come to his house. His address occurs between the negative אל נא *ʔal-nɔʔ* "please not" and the verb תרעו *tɔreʕu* "you act wickedly."

The intrusion of these addresses, as in the addresses that occur between the preface and the body, also breaks the unmarked sequence of the C-unit, partitioning it into an unmarked initial-edge constituent and the rest of the C-unit. The unmarked initial-edge constituent that precedes the address can now be considered "marked" as it is "detached" from the following constituent(s) with which it is typically connected in the unmarked sequence. I would argue that the marked initial-edge constituent carries information focus. In (38), therefore, the negative interrogative הלא, which introduces a negative rhetorical question, is highlighted to maximize the illocutionary force of a positive assertion, that is, all of the Israelites are David's servants. It can be said that הלא, in this case, is functionally and semantically equivalent to the clausal adverb "surely" or "indeed."[61] The interrogative pro-form למה in (39) introduces a critical rhetorical question, expressing Moses's criticism of YHWH's anger mentioned in verse 10.[62] It receives special focus through detachment, intensifying the degree of criticism conveyed by the rhetorical question. In doing so, Moses increases the persuasive force of his rhetorical question in order to convince YHWH that his anger towards his chosen people is improper.[63] The time adverb עתה in (40) refers to "a point in time concurrent with the speech time of an utterance, that is, 'now'" (*BHRG*² §40.39). As it expresses information focus, it emphasizes a sense of immediacy: Elijah desires to die "immediately" due to his extreme exhaustion and despair. In (41), the negative particle followed by the particle of entreaty אל נא is highlighted, possibly conveying a sense of urgency in Lot's negative request.[64]

---

[61] Cf. the LXX πάντες τῷ κυρίῳ μου παῖδες "all are the servants of my lord." It has long been recognized that הֲלֹא warrants an asseverative meaning in certain contexts. See GKC §150e; Steiner 1979, 149; Brongers 1981, 177–89; Moshavi 2011, 91–105; McAffee 2015, 130.

[62] For the implications and communicative functions of rhetorical "WH" questions in Biblical Hebrew prose, see Moshavi 2014, 93–108.

[63] Note that YHWH spoke of "your people, whom you brought up out of the land of Egypt" in v. 7, and Moses counters with "your people, whom you brought out of the land of Egypt" in v. 11.

[64] It is also possible to take אל נא as elliptically standing for an entire sentence denying what was said by his or her collocutor rather than negating the following verb תרעו: "No, please (don't violate my guests), my brothers! You are acting wickedly." For this possibility, see my discussion in (19) above. Note that example (26) is the only case in which an address breaks a negative particle and a verb in Biblical Hebrew prose. Compare with Judg 19:23; 2 Sam 13:12, 25; and 2 Kgs 4:16, in which an address is both preceded and followed by the negative particle אל.

Forty-one free forms of address occur after a "marked" initial-edge constituent, such as a fronted subject or prepositional phrase in a verbal clause as in (42),[65] and a fronted predicate in a verbless clause as in (43):[66]

(42) כי **אתה אדני יהוה** דברת

ki-ʔattɔ	ʔᵃdonɔy	yhwh	dibbartɔ
for-you	Lord	YHWH	you.spoke

For **you**, *O Lord YHWH*, have spoken. (2 Sam 7:29)

(43) **עלי אדני המלך** העון ועל בית אבי והמלך וכסאו נקי

ʕɔlay	ʔᵃdoni	hammɛlɛk	hɛʕɔwon	wəʕal-bet
on=me	lord=my	the=king	the=guilt	and=on-house.of
ʔɔbi	wəhammɛlɛk	wəkisʔo	nɔqi	
father=my	and=the=king	and=throne=his	innocent	

On me, *my lord the king*, be the guilt, and on my father's house; let the king and his throne be innocent! (2 Sam 14:9)

In (42), we see David's prayer to YHWH following the promise of an everlasting kingdom. Here the second-person masculine singular subject pronoun אתה ʔattɔ "you" is fronted before the verb דברת dibbartɔ "you have spoken" and hence, is marked for information focus.[67] I agree with Miller (2010b, 357) who argues that the fronted pronoun is in "contrastive focus"—it is specifically YHWH and no one else who has spoken to David about the everlasting kingdom. Now the address אדני יהוה ʔᵃdonɔy yhwh "O Lord YHWH!" is inserted between the fronted pronoun and the verb, detaching the former from the latter. Thus, the pronoun is "doubly" marked for information focus. I would argue that the inserted address serves to reinforce the pragmatic function of the fronted pronoun, that is, contrastive focus.

In (43) we see the woman of Tekoa speaking to King David about her son who killed his brother and is facing the threat of being put to death by the entire clan. It is evident from the context that the fronted predicate עלי ʕɔlay "on me" is in contrastive focus—the woman of Tekoa asks that the guilt be on her instead of David. The address אדני המלך ʔᵃdonɔy hammɛlɛk "my lord the king" is inserted between the fronted predicate עלי ʕɔlay "on me" and the subject העון hɛʕɔwon "the guilt." Hence, it can be said that the predicate עלי is "doubly" marked for

---

[65] For the fronted subjects, see 2 Sam 7:24, 27, 29; 1Kgs 1:13; Jer 20:6; Ezek 2:6, 8; 4:1; 5:1; 12:3; 13:4, 17; 21:11, 24, 33; 27:2; 33:10, 12; 36:1, 8; 37:16; 39:1; 43:10; Jonah 1:14; Dan 12:4; Ezra 9:13; 1 Chr 17:22, 27; 28:9; 2 Chr 6:41; 20:7. For the fronted prepositional phrases, see 1 Sam 23:20; Ezek 12:25.

[66] For the fronted predicates, see 1 Sam 25:24; 2 Sam 14:9; 1 Kgs 20:4; Ruth 2:22; Dan 9:7; 1 Chr 29:11 [2x]; 2 Chr 26:18.

[67] For a discussion of the semantic-pragmatic functions of fronting, see *BHRG²* §47.2.1.

information focus. Similar to (42), I would argue that the inserted address serves to reinforce the contrastive focus function of the fronted predicate.[68]

In summary, in all the other cases in which an address comes after an unmarked or marked initial-edge constituent, the address seems to highlight or reinforce the semantic-pragmatic function of the initial-edge constituent, which receives information focus through the insertion of the address.

4.4.4.2.2. Within the Core

There are twenty-three free forms of address that occur between two constituents within the core of the body. Fifteen of them occur immediately before a clause-final prepositional phrase, as in (44),[69] while eight of them come between a verb and its object, as in (45):[70]

(44) ויאמר לו מדוע אתה ככה דל **בן המלך בבקר בבקר**
wayyoʔmɛr lo   madduaʕ   ʔattɔ   kɔkɔ   dal
and=he.said to=him   why   you   thus   poorly
bɛn-hammɛlɛk   babboqɛr   babboqɛr
son.of-the=king   in=the=morning   in=the=morning

He said to him, "Why do you look so poorly, *O son of the king*, **morning after morning**? (2 Sam 13:4)

(45) הטה יהוה אזנך ושמע פקח יהוה עיניך וראה
haṭṭe   yhwh   ʔoznəkɔ   ušᵃmaʕ   pəqaḥ   yhwh
Incline   YHWH   ear=your   and=hear   open   YHWH
ʕenɛkɔ   urəʔe
eyes=your   and=see

Incline, *YHWH*, **your ear** and hear. **Open**, *YHWH*, **your eyes** and see! (2 Kgs 19:16)

---

[68] There are three cases in which an address intervenes between the subject and the predicate in a verbless clause: Num 14:14; 1 Kgs 18:37; 2 Kgs 19:19. Miller (2010b, 357) argues that the subject in each of these cases seems to be in contrastive focus but does not explain how it obtains that function. I would argue that the subject gains the function of contrastive focus as the insertion of the address breaks the unmarked sequence SP and marks the subject for information focus. Thus, while all these addresses occur within a dependent clause, they may be treated here due to the similar function that the constituent in the initial position performs, whether it is the subject or the predicate.

[69] Judg 12:4; 1 Sam 30:23; 2 Sam 13:4; 24:23; Ezek 28:16; Amos 3:1; Dan 9:17; Ezra 9:10; Neh 5:19; 6:14; 13:14, 29, 31; 1 Chr 29:10; 2 Chr 6:41.

[70] Num 10:36 (adverbial accusative); Deut 5:1; 2 Kgs 19:16 (2x); Isa 37:17 (2x); Dan 9:18; Ezra 9:6.

In (44), Jonadab, David's nephew, is speaking to Amnon, David's eldest son, who is lovesick for Tamar, his half-sister. The address בן המלך *bɛn-hammɛlɛk* "O son of the king!" is placed between the adjective דַּל *dal* "poorly" and two consecutive prepositional phrases בבקר בבקר *babboqer babboqer* "morning after morning." Thus, the address breaks the unmarked sequence of the verbless clause, detaching the prepositional phrases from the core of the clause with which they are contiguous in the unmarked sequence. The detached prepositional phrases become a marked constituent, which receives information focus. It can be argued, therefore, that the address is inserted in this particular position to draw the addressee's (i.e., Amnon's) attention to the prepositional phrases, highlighting the iterative nature of Amnon's lovesickness that they describe.[71]

Example (45) is part of Hezekiah's prayer to YHWH, which immediately precedes example (35) that we have discussed above. In this prayer, we have two instances of the address יהוה *yhwh* "YHWH," both occurring between the imperative verb and its direct object. Thus, each address breaks the unmarked sequence of the imperative clause, detaching the direct object from the imperative verb with which it is contiguous in the unmarked sequence. The detached direct objects become marked constituents that receive information focus. It can be argued, therefore, that each address functions to draw the addressee's (i.e., YHWH's) attention to the respective direct object, highlighting the body parts ("ear" and "eyes") that YHWH needs to incline and open to hear Hezekiah's prayer and see his current situation.[72]

In all the other cases where an address occurs within the core of the body, the constituent(s) immediately following the address can be considered marked for information focus. It can be said, then, that the address serves to draw the addressee's attention to the following marked constituent(s), highlighting or reinforcing their semantic-pragmatic function.

4.4.4.3. Between Body and Tag

There are sixteen instances of free forms of address in our corpus that occur between the body and the tag of the C-unit. Fourteen of them occur between the

---

[71] The construction in which an address occurs immediately before a clause-final prepositional phrase is common in poetry (e.g., Pss 7:7, 9; 21:14, etc.). See Miller 2010b, 360.

[72] All of the eight addresses that come between a verb and its object in our corpus occur within a prayer except one in Deut 5:1 in which Moses addresses the whole Israel. It is interesting to note that this construction is very frequently attested in poetry (e.g., Pss 24:7, 9; 25:22; 27:7; 48:10; 64:2; 66:8; 86:1 [note that the wording is exactly the same as the first part in 2 Kgs 19:16 above], etc.). The absence of this construction in dialogues between two human beings in Biblical Hebrew prose may indicate that it was not commonly used in everyday conversation in ancient Israel.

matrix clause and the dependent clause, as in (46),[73] while two of them intervene between the matrix clause and noun phrases coreferentially linked to a pronoun in the matrix clause, as in (47):[74]

(46) ותאמר שבי בתי עד אשר תדעין איך יפל דבר

wattoʔɛr	šəḇi	bitti	ʕaḏ	ʔᵃšɛr
and=she.said	sit	daughter=my	until	REL
teḏəʕin	ʔek	yippol	dɔḇɔr	
you.will.know	how	he.will.fall	matter	

She said, "**Stay put**, *my daughter*, **until you know how the matter turns out**." (Ruth 3:18)

(47) ויאמר המלך מות תמות אחימלך אתה וכל בית אביך

wayyoʔmɛr	hammɛlɛk	mot	tɔmut	ʔᵃḥimɛlɛk
and=he.said	the=king	dying	you.will.die	Ahimelech
ʔattɔ	wəkɔl-beṯ	ʔɔḇiḵɔ		
you	and=all-house.of	father=your		

The king said, "**You** shall surely die, *Ahimelech*, **you and all your father's house**." (1 Sam 22:16)

In (46), Naomi is speaking to Ruth after hearing that Boaz had given Ruth six measures of barley. Naomi's address בתי *bitti* "my daughter" further detaches the dependent clause introduced with עד אשר *ʕaḏ ʔᵃšɛr* "until" (i.e., tag) from the matrix clause (i.e., body), marking the former for information focus. Thus, it can be said that the address draws the addressee's (Ruth's) attention to the following dependent clause, highlighting its discourse-pragmatic function—qualifying the matrix clause by providing the temporal limit of Naomi's command.

In (47), King Saul is pronouncing a death sentence upon Ahimelech the priest and all his father's house immediately after Ahimelech begs Saul not to attribute guilt to him or his father's household. Saul's address אחימלך *ʔᵃḥimɛlɛk* "Ahimelech" further detaches the right-dislocated noun phrase אתה וכל בית אביך *ʔattɔ wəkɔl-beṯ ʔɔḇiḵɔ* "you and all your father's house" (i.e., tag) from the matrix clause (i.e., body), marking the former for information focus. Thus, it can be argued that the address draws the addressee's (Saul's) attention to the following

---

[73] For examples in which the address occurs before a dependent clause introduced with פן *pen* "lest," see 1 Sam 4:9; with כי *ki* "that, because," see 2 Sam 19:23; Dan 8:17; 1 Chr 29:17; with ה *ha* "whether," see Gen 27:21; with אשר *ʔᵃšɛr* "which, that," see Exod 32:4, 8; 2 Sam 14:22; 1 Kgs 12:28; Ezek 8:12; with עד אשר *ʕaḏ ʔᵃšɛr* "until," see Ruth 3:18. For examples in which the address occurs before a dependent infinitival clause, see 2 Sam 23:17; 1 Kgs 8:28; 2 Chr 6:19.

[74] For examples in which the address occurs before the right-dislocated noun phrase, see 1 Sam 22:16; Jer 22:2.

noun-phrase, highlighting its discourse-pragmatic function—clarifying the reference of the coreferent subject pronoun of the matrix clause תמות *tɔmuṯ* "**you** shall surely die."

In all the other cases where an address intervenes between the body and the tag, the tag can be considered marked for information focus. Therefore, it can be said that the address draws the addressee's attention to the tag, highlighting or reinforcing its discourse-pragmatic function.

4.5. Conclusion

In this chapter, I have sought to describe the correlation between the position and function of free forms of address in Biblical Hebrew prose. Nearly three quarters of the addresses occur either at the beginning (including the stand-alone addresses) or at the end of the C-unit. It appears that their primary functions have to do with conversation management, such as attracting the attention of the addressee, identifying the addressee, signaling the beginning or end of a turn/conversation, giving the floor to the addressee, and/or maintaining contact with the addressee. The rest of the addresses occur within the C-unit, occupying one of the following positions: (i) between the preface and the body, (ii) between an initial-edge element and the core, (iii) within the core, and (iv) between the body and the tag. I have argued that these addresses typically have a partitioning and focusing function. They draw the addressee's attention to significant information at the specific junction where they occur. Thus, the addresses placed in position (i) or (ii) mark for information focus the element *preceding* them by detaching it from the rest of the C-unit, highlighting or reinforcing its discourse-pragmatic function. The addresses placed in position (iii) or (iv), however, mark for information focus the element *following* them by detaching it from what precedes them, highlighting or reinforcing its discourse-pragmatic function.

5.
BOUND FORMS OF ADDRESS

5.1. Introduction

In the preceding chapters, the focus has been on addresses that are syntactically "free" forms, that is, forms "outside" the sentence structure. These forms can occur before, after, or within a sentence, or sometimes even without any immediate linguistic context. In this chapter, the attention shifts to addresses that are syntactically "bound" forms, that is, forms integrated into the syntax of a sentence.[1]

According to Braun (1988, 7–11), pronouns, nominals, and verb forms that function as syntactic constituents (or parts of constituents) within a sentence, can refer to the addressee. This can be observed in examples in (i) through (iii):

(i) Would *you* like something to drink?
(ii) May I ask *your majesty* to consider our petition?
(iii) Mihin *menet*? "Where do *you* go?"

In languages where subject pronouns are optional, such as Finnish, verbs alone can bear the reference to the addressee. Thus, in example (iii), the verb *mene-t* serves as a form of address since the inflectional suffix *-t* (indicating second person singular) is the only element expressing reference to the addressee.

By adopting Braun's definition of bound forms of address, it follows that second-person pronouns and pronominal suffixes in Biblical Hebrew and Epigraphic Hebrew can be considered as bound forms of address, as demonstrated in (48):

(48) עתה ארור **אתה** מן האדמה אשר פצתה את פיה לקחת את דמי אחיך מידך
  waʕattɔ   ʔɔrur   ʔottɔ   min-hɔʔⁿdɔmɔ   ʔᵃšer   pɔṣɔtɔ
  and=now   cursed   you   from-the=ground   REL   she.opened
  ʔɛt-pihɔ   lɔqaḥat   ʔɛt-dəme   ʔɔḥikɔ   miyyɔdɛkɔ
  ACC-mouth=her to=take ACC-blood.of brother=your from=hand=your

---

[1] It is Braun (1988, 11) who coins the term "free" and "bound" forms of address according to the syntactic criterion.

Now therefore, *you* are cursed from the ground, which has opened its mouth to receive *your* brother's blood from *your* hand. (Gen 4:11)

Verbs in the second person that contain inflectional morphemes indicating the subject "you" can serve as bound forms of address, as illustrated in example (49):

(49) ויקם שמואל וילך אל עלי ויאמר הנני כי **קראת לי**

wayyɔqɔm	šəmuʔel	wsayyelɛk	ʔɛl-ʕeli	wayyoʔmɛr
and=he.arose	Samuel	and=he.went	to-Eli	and=he.said
hinni	ki	qɔrɔʔtɔ	li	
look	for	you.called	to=me	

Samuel arose and went to Eli and said, "Here I am, for *you* called me." (1 Sam 3:6)

Nominal forms may be employed as bound forms of address, as seen in example (50):

(50) ועתה **ישמע נא אדני המלך** את דברי עבדו

wəʕattɔ	yišmaʕ-nɔʔ	ʔᵃdoni	hammɛlɛk	ʔɛt
and=now	he.will.hear-POL	lord=my	the=king	ACC
dibre	ʕabdo			
words.of	servant=his			

Now therefore let *my lord the king* hear the words of his servant. (1 Sam 26:19)

Josef Svennung (1958, 451) categorizes the first two types of bound forms of address in (48) and (49) as "direct" address, whereas he refers to the third type of the bound forms of address in (50) as "indirect" address.[2] In Biblical Hebrew and Epigraphic Hebrew, direct addresses can be used towards any addressee regardless of their social status. they can be used by an inferior towards a superior, as exemplified in (51):

(51) ואבי ראה גם ראה את כנף מעילך בידי כי בכרתי את כנף מעילך ולא הרגתיך דע וראה כי אין בידי רעה ופשע ולא חטאתי לך **ואתה** צדה את נפשי לקחתה

waʔɔbi	rəʔe	gam	rəʔe	ʔɛt-kənap̄	məʕiləkɔ
and=father=my	see	also	see	ACC-corner.of	robe=your
bəyɔdi	ki	bəkɔrti		ʔɛt-kənap̄	məʕiləkɔ
in=hand=my	that	in=cutting=my		ACC-corner.of	robe=your

---

[2] Note that Revell (1996, 267) uses the term *third person address* instead of indirect address.

BOUND FORMS OF ADDRESS 151

wəloʔ	hᵃragtikɔ	daʕ	uraʔe	ki	ʔen
and=not	I.killed=you	know	and=see	that	there.is.not
bəyɔḏi	rɔʕɔ	wɔp̄ɛšaʕ	wəloʔ-ḥɔṭɔʔti		lɔḵ
in=hand=my	evil	and=treason	and=not-I.sinned		to=you
wəʔattɔ	ṣoḏɛ	ʔɛṯ-nap̄ši	lɔqaḥtɔh		
and=you	lying.in.wait	ACC-life=my	to=take=her		

Look, my father, see the corner of *your* (i.e., Saul) robe in my (i.e., David) hand! When I cut off the corner of *your* robe, I did not kill *you*. So realize and understand that there is no evil or treason in my hands. I have not sinned against *you*, though *you* are waiting in ambush to my life. (1 Sam 24:12)

They can be used by a superior to an inferior, as in (52):

(52) ויאמר אל דוד צדיק **אתה** ממני כי **אתה** גמלתני הטובה ואני גמלתיך הרעה

wayyoʔmɛr	ʔɛl-dɔwiḏ	ṣaddiq	ʔattɔ	gəmaltan
and=he.said	to-David	righteous	you	you.treated=me
haṭṭoḇɔ	waʔᵃni	gəmaltikɔ	hɔrɔʕɔ	
the=good	and=I	I.treated=you	the=evil	

He (i.e., Saul) said to David, "*You* are more righteous than I, for *you* have treated me well, even though I have treated *you* poorly." (1 Sam 24:18)

They can be used among equals, as in (53) and (54):

(53) ויאמר הפלשתי אל דוד הכלב אנכי כי **אתה** בא אלי במקלות

wayyoʔmɛr	happəlišti	ʔɛl-dɔwiḏ	hᵃḵɛlɛḇ	ʔɔnoḵi	ki-ʔattɔ
and=he.said	the=Philistine	to-David	the=dog	I	that-you
ḇɔʔ-ʔelay	bammaqloṯ				
coming-to=me	in=sticks				

The Philistine said to David, "Am I a dog, that *you* are coming to me with sticks?" (1 Sam 17:43)

(54) ויאמר דוד אל הפלשתי **אתה** בא אלי בחרב ובחנית ובכידון ואנכי בא אליך בשם יהוה צבאות

wayyoʔmɛr	dɔwiḏ	ʔɛl-happəlišti	ʔattɔ	bɔʔ	ʔelay
and=he.said	David	to-the=Philistine	you	coming	to=me
baḥɛrɛḇ	uḇaḥᵃniṯ	uḇəkiḏon			wəʔɔnoḵi
with=sword	and=with=spear	and=with=javelin			and=I
ḇɔʔ-ʔelɛḵɔ	bəšem	yhwh	ṣəḇɔʔoṯ		
coming-to=you	in=name.of	YHWH.of	hosts		

Then David said to the Philistine, "*You* are coming to me with sword and spear and javelin, but I am coming to *you* in the name of Yahweh of hosts." (1 Sam 17:45)

Thus, it can be argued that direct addresses in Biblical Hebrew and Epigraphic Hebrew do not inherently convey social information, except for their relatively "direct" referentiality to the addressee(s).[3] The primary focus of this chapter, therefore, will be on the third type of bound forms of address, that is, indirect address. Furthermore, the scope of my discussion will be limited to indirect addresses used to humans (241 forms), as the usage of indirect addresses for nonhuman entities is relatively limited (39 forms). This chapter is structured into three main parts. First, I examine the internal structure of indirect forms of address in Biblical Hebrew and Epigraphic Hebrew, comparing it with that of free forms of address. Second, I discuss the external syntax of indirect forms of address. Finally, I attempt to describe their social dynamics by exploring the underlying motivations and effects of their usage, and identifying possible cases of "expressive shift," wherein address rules are strategically violated to convey the speaker's temporary feelings and attitudes.

5.2. Internal Structure of Indirect Forms of Address

A total of 280 indirect forms of address can be found in the prose sections of the Hebrew Bible and Epigraphic Hebrew letters. These forms account for less than half of the total number of free forms of address, which amount to 682 forms.[4] Among the indirect forms of address, approximately 86 percent (241 forms) are used for addressing human addressees, while the remaining forms are employed when addressing divine beings. It is worth noting that unlike free forms of address, there are no instances of indirect addresses used for inanimate entities within our corpus. In a similar manner to chapter 2, semantic types have been assigned to each indirect address. Table 5.1 provides the frequency distribution and examples of indirect addresses used for addressing humans:

---

[3] Revell (1996, 309) argues that the second-person pronoun may function as a marker of "immediacy" in contexts in which deferential reference to the addressee would be appropriate.

[4] Seventeen address forms used in address formulas in the Arad letters (1:1; 2:1; 3:1; 4:1; 5:1; 6:1; 7:1; 8:1; 10:1; 11:1; 12:1; 14:1; 17:1; 18:1–2; 24:1–2) and the Lachish letters (2:1; 6:1) are excluded from our discussion in this chapter because, even though they may be considered syntactically "bound" forms following the preposition אל *ʔl* "to," they are functionally direct addresses.

Table 5.1. Indirect Addresses to Humans[5]

Structure		#	Examples
Honorific T		84	אדני ʔᵃḏoni "my lord"
	+Occupational T	41	אדני המלך ʔᵃḏoni hammɛlɛḵ "my lord the king"
	+Occupational T + PN	2	אדני המלך דוד ʔᵃḏoni hammɛlɛḵ dɔwiḏ "my lord the king David"
	+PN	2	אדני יאוש ʔdny yʔwš "my lord Yaush"
Occupational T		78	המלך hammɛlɛḵ "the king"
	+Honorific T	1	המלך אדני hammɛlɛḵ ʔᵃḏoni "the king my lord"
	+PN	3	המלך שלמה hammɛlɛḵ šəlomo "King Solomon"
Other T		15	פרעה parʕo "Pharaoh";[6] משיח יהוה məšiᵃḥ yhwh "anointed of Yahweh"
PN		13	ירבעם yɔrɔḇʕɔm "Jeroboam"
	+Patronymic	1	גדליהו [בן] אליאר gdlyhw [bn] ʔlyʔr "Gedalyahu [son of] Elyair"
KT		1	אבי ʔɔḇi "my father"

One striking observation from this table is that the absolute majority of indirect addresses to humans are composed of T ± the following element(s) (94 percent). In contrast, there is a significantly smaller number of indirect addresses consisting of PN ± the following element(s) or KT. This unequal distribution sharply contrasts with the distribution of free forms of address to humans, where those composed of PN ± the following element(s) or KT ± the following element(s)

---

[5] See appendix D for a full list of indirect addresses used for humans.

[6] The term פרעה parʕo "Pharaoh" is a loanword from Egyptian Pr- ʕ, which literally means "Great House" (Lambdin 1953, 153). It was used as a designation of the royal palace in the early third millennium BCE. However, during the Eighteenth Dynasty, sometime prior to the reign of Thutmose III (1479–1425 BCE), the term "Great House" began to be applied to the reigning king by metonymy and was widely used as a polite circumlocution for him by the end of the Twentieth Dynasty (1077 BCE; see Redford 1992, 288–89). While the term occurred alone without juxtaposed personal name until the tenth century BCE, the name of the king was generally added on in subsequent periods. As Hoffmeier (1996, 87) points out, this Egyptian practice seems to conform to the practice found in the Hebrew Bible: while the term פרעה parʕo "Pharaoh" occurs alone in the period covered from Abraham to Solomon, after Shishak (ca. 925 BCE), it appears together with a name (e.g., Pharaoh Necho [2 Kgs 23:33]). According to Revell (1996, 149), its use in combination with a name makes it unlikely that "Pharaoh" was regarded as a name (contra Higginbotham [2009, 483], who views "Pharaoh" as a name due to the fact that it never takes the definite article in Biblical Hebrew). Following Revell, therefore, I take "Pharaoh" as a title.

occur as frequently as those composed of T ± the following element(s) (79, 66, and 71 forms, respectively).

All the combinations of semantic types presented in table 5.1 are also found as free forms of address, except for honorific T + occupational T + PN, occupational T + honorific T,[7] and PN + patronymic. These exceptional combinations are quite rare, accounting for only four cases. On the other hand, not all the semantic types used for free forms of address are utilized in indirect addresses. For instance, group addresses, geographical names, or gentilics are never employed as indirect addresses.

Almost all the examples provided in table 5.1 are also used as free forms of address. However, there are two notable exceptions: פרעה *parʿo* "Pharaoh" and משיח יהוה *məšiaḥ yhwh* "anointed of Yahweh." The term פרעה occurs thirteen times as an indirect address (Gen 41:10, 16, 25 [2x], 28 [2x], 32, 33, 34, 35; Exod 8:25 [2x]; 11:5), while it is never used as a free form of address. The title משיח יהוה is used twice as an indirect address—once for Saul (1 Sam 26:23) and the other for David (2 Sam 19:22)—but it never occurs as a free form of address.

5.3. External Syntax of Indirect Forms of Address

Indirect addresses refer to nominal forms used as bound forms of address. They are integrated into the syntax of a sentence and function as constituents (or parts of constituents) within the sentence. In our corpus, indirect addresses appear in six different syntactic positions.[8] These positions are presented below in descending order of frequency for each position.

5.3.1. Syntactic Positions of Indirect Forms of Address

First, an indirect address may be used as the object of a preposition, as in (55):[9]

---

[7] The only example consisting of occupational T + honorific T is המלך אדני *hammeleḵ ᵃḏoni* "the king my lord" (2 Sam 14:15), which is never attested as a free form of address in our corpus. Its reverse form, אדני המלך *ᵃḏoni hammeleḵ* "my lord the king," however, occurs thirty-nine times as an indirect address and eighteen times as a free form of address. Thus, it is clear that the biblical writers had a strong preference for אדני המלך. This is in stark contrast to the almost exclusive use of "O king my lord!" in ancient Near Eastern writings during the second and first millennium BCE. See my discussion in §2.4.1.1.2.

[8] Note that there are seven cases in which the syntactic positions of indirect addresses cannot be determined: Arad 26:4; Lach 6:8; 8:7; 12:1, 6; 17:2, 3.

[9] There are eighty-three cases in which an indirect address is used as the object of a preposition: Gen 32:6, 19; 33:14; 41:25, 28, 32, 35; 44:9, 16 (2x), 20, 22, 33; 47:18 (3x); Exod 8:25 (2x); 1 Sam 20:12; 25:26, 27, 28, 30, 31 (2x); 26:23; 29:8; 2 Sam 1:10; 3:21; 4:8; 14:12, 15; 17:16; 18:28; 19:28, 29 (2x), 35, 36, 37, 38; 24:23; 1 Kgs 1:2 (3x), 27, 37; 14:10, 11; 16:3; 18:13; 21:21, 24; 2 Kgs 4:28; Esth 1:16, 19 (3x); 2:2; 3:8, 9; 5:4, 8; 7:3, 9; 8:5 (2x); 9:13; Neh 2:5, 7, 8; 1 Chr 21:3; Arad 16:2; 21:1–2, 4; 26:2; 40:3, 6, 10; Lach 3:2, 21; 5:7; KAjr 19A.9–10.

(55) ... תאמר האשה התקועית אל המלך
ועתה אשר באתי לדבר אל **המלך אדני** את הדבר הזה

wattoʔmɛr	hɔʔiššɔ	hatəqoʕit	ʔɛl-hammɛlɛk...
and=she.said	the=woman	the=Tekoite	to-the=king

wəʕattɔ	ʔªšɛr	bɔʔti	lədabber	ʔɛl-hammɛlɛk	ʔªdoni
and=now	REL	I.came	to=speak	to-the=king	lord=my

ʔɛt-haddɔbɔr	hazzɛ
ACC-the=matter	the=this

The Tekoite woman said to the king (i.e., David),..."Now I have come to say this to *the king my lord*." (2 Sam 14:9–15)

Second, an indirect address may be used as the subject of a finite verb, as in (56):[10]

(56) וידבר יהונתן בדוד טוב אל שאול אביו ויאמר אליו
אל יחטא **המלך** בעבדו בדוד כי לוא חטא לך

waydabber	yəhonɔtɔn	bədowid	ṭob	ʔɛl-šɔʔul
and=he.spoke	Jonathan	in=David	good	to-Saul

ʔɔbiw	wayyoʔmɛr	ʔelɔyw	ʔal-yɛhᵉṭɔʔ
father=his	and=he.said	To=him	not-he.will.sin

hammɛlɛk	baʕabdo	bədowid	ki	loʔ	hɔṭɔʔ	lɔk
the=king	in=servant=his	in=David	for	not	he.sinned	to=you

Jonathan spoke well of David to Saul his father and said to him, "Let not *the king* sin against his servant David, because he has not sinned against you." (1 Sam 19:4)

Third, an indirect address may be used as the *nomen rectum* in a construct chain, as in (57):[11]

---

[10] There are seventy-six cases in which an indirect address is used as the subject of a finite verb: Gen 27:31; 33:13, 14; 41:10, 33, 34; 44:7, 19; Num 32:25, 27; 36:2; 1 Sam 10:24; 16:16; 19:4; 22:15; 24:15; 25:25, 28; 26:18, 19, 20; 2 Sam 6:20; 9:11; 13:24, 32, 33; 14:9, 11, 17, 18, 19, 20, 22; 15:15, 21; 16:16 (2x); 18:31; 19:20 (2x), 28, 31, 37; 24:3, 21, 22; 1 Kgs 1:31; 2:38; 22:8; 2 Kgs 2:19; 8:12; 11:12; Esth 2:3; 5:4, 8; 6:7, 8 (2x), 9; Neh 2:3; 1 Chr 21:3, 23; 2 Chr 2:14; 18:7; 23:11; MHsh 1; Arad 21:3; Lach 2:4; 3:6, 8; 4:2, 4–5, 12; 6:3; 18:2; Mous 2.2.

[11] There are fifty-five cases in which an indirect address is used as the *nomen rectum* in a construct chain: Gen 31:35; 33:8, 15; 41:16, 25; 44:18, 24; 47:25; Exod 11:5; 32:22; 1 Sam 20:15; 22:14; 23:20; 25:25, 27, 29, 41; 2 Sam 11:11, 24; 13:30, 32, 33, 35; 15:21; 16:2; 18:29, 32, 42; 24:3; 1 Kgs 1:19, 20, 25, 27, 36, 37; 14:10 (2x); 16:4; 22:6, 12, 15; Esth 1:16, 18, 20; 2:3, 4; 3:8, 9; 5:8 (2x); 6:9; 7:4; 8:5; 2 Chr 18:5, 11.

(57) ויען יוסף את פרעה לאמר בלעדי אלהים יענה את שלום **פרעה**

wayyaʕan	yosep̄	ʔɛt-parʕo	leʔmor	bilʕɔday
and=he.answered	Joseph	ACC-Pharaoh	to=say	without=me
ʔᵉlohim	yaʕᵃnɛ	ʔɛt-šəlom		parʕo
God	he.will.answer	ACC-welfare.of		Pharaoh

Joseph answered Pharaoh, "It is not in me; God will give *Pharaoh* a favorable answer" (lit. God will answer the welfare of *Pharaoh*"). (Gen 41:16)

Fourth, an indirect address may be used as the object of a finite verb, as in (58):[12]

(58) ויגד לשלמה לאמר הנה אדניהו ירא את **המלך שלמה**
והנה אחז בקרנות המזבח לאמר ישבע לי כיום המלך שלמה אם ימית את עבדו בחרב

wayyuggaḏ	lišlomo	leʔmor	hinne	ʔᵃdoniyyɔhu
and=it.was.told	to=Solomon	to=say	look	Adonijah
yɔreʔ	ʔɛt-hammɛlɛḵ	šəlomo		wəhinne
he.fears	ACC-the=king	Solomon		and=look
ʔɔḥaz	bəqarnoṯ	hammizbeᵃḥ		leʔmor
he.seized	in=horns.of	the=altar		to=say
yiššɔḇaʕ-li	kayyom	hammɛlɛḵ		šəlomo
he.will.swear-to=me	like=the=day	the=king		Solomon
ʔim-yɔmiṯ	ʔɛt-ʕaḇdo	bəḥɔrɛḇ		
if-he.will.put.to.death	ACC-servant=his	with=the=sword		

Then it was told Solomon, "Look, Adonijah fears *King Solomon*, for look, he has taken hold of the horns of the altar, saying, 'May King Solomon solemnly promise me first that he will not put his servant to death with the sword.'" (1 Kgs 1:51)

Fifth, an indirect address may be used as the subject of the infinitive, as in (59):[13]

(59) ... ותפל על רגליו ותאמר
ולא תהיה זאת לך לפוקה ולמכשול לב לאדני ולשפך דם חנם ולהושיע **אדני** לו

wayyippol	ʕal-raḡlɔyw	wattoʔmɛr...	wəloʔ	tihyɛ
and=she.fell	on-feet.his	and=she.said	and=not	she.will.be
zoʔṯ	ləḵɔ	ləp̄uqɔ	uləmiḵšol	leḇ	laʔḏoni
this	to=you	to=staggering	and=to=stumbling.of	heart	to=lord=my

---

[12] There are fourteen cases in which an indirect address is used as the object of a finite verb: Gen 41:28; Num 36:2; 2 Sam 16:9; 19:22, 42; 1 Kgs 1:51; Lach 2:2, 5–6; 3:3; 4:1; 5:1; 6:2; 8:1; 9:1–2.

[13] There are five cases in which an indirect address is used as the subject of the infinitive: 1 Sam 25:31; 2 Sam 14:13 (2x); 19:20; 1 Kgs 1:21.

(55) ... תאמר האשה התקועית אל המלך
ועתה אשר באתי לדבר אל **המלך אדני** את הדבר הזה

wattoʔmɛr	hɔʔiššɔ	hatəqoʕit	ʔɛl-hammɛlɛk...
and=she.said	the=woman	the=Tekoite	to-the=king

wəʕattɔ	ʔᵃšer	bɔʔti	lədabber	ʔɛl-hammɛlɛk	ʔᵃdoni
and=now	REL	I.came	to=speak	to-the=king	lord=my

ʔɛt-haddɔbɔr	hazzɛ
ACC-the=matter	the=this

The Tekoite woman said to the king (i.e., David),... "Now I have come to say this to *the king my lord*." (2 Sam 14:9–15)

Second, an indirect address may be used as the subject of a finite verb, as in (56):[10]

(56) וידבר יהונתן בדוד טוב אל שאול אביו ויאמר אליו
אל יחטא **המלך** בעבדו בדוד כי לוא חטא לך

waydabber	yəhonɔtɔn	bədɔwid	tob	ʔɛl-šɔʔul
and=he.spoke	Jonathan	in=David	good	to-Saul

ʔɔbiw	wayyoʔmɛr	ʔelɔyw	ʔal-yɛhᵉtɔʔ
father=his	and=he.said	To=him	not-he.will.sin

hammɛlɛk	bəʕabdo	bədɔwid	ki	loʔ	hɔtɔʔ	lɔk
the=king	in=servant=his	in=David	for	not	he.sinned	to=you

Jonathan spoke well of David to Saul his father and said to him, "Let not *the king* sin against his servant David, because he has not sinned against you." (1 Sam 19:4)

Third, an indirect address may be used as the *nomen rectum* in a construct chain, as in (57):[11]

---

[10] There are seventy-six cases in which an indirect address is used as the subject of a finite verb: Gen 27:31; 33:13, 14; 41:10, 33, 34; 44:7, 19; Num 32:25, 27; 36:2; 1 Sam 10:24; 16:16; 19:4; 22:15; 24:15; 25:25, 28; 26:18, 19, 20; 2 Sam 6:20; 9:11; 13:24, 32, 33; 14:9, 11, 17, 18, 19, 20, 22; 15:15, 21; 16:16 (2x); 18:31; 19:20 (2x), 28, 31, 37; 24:3, 21, 22; 1 Kgs 1:31; 2:38; 22:8; 2 Kgs 2:19; 8:12; 11:12; Esth 2:3; 5:4, 8; 6:7, 8 (2x), 9; Neh 2:3; 1 Chr 21:3, 23; 2 Chr 2:14; 18:7; 23:11; MHsh 1; Arad 21:3; Lach 2:4; 3:6, 8; 4:2, 4–5, 12; 6:3; 18:2; Mous 2.2.

[11] There are fifty-five cases in which an indirect address is used as the *nomen rectum* in a construct chain: Gen 31:35; 33:8, 15; 41:16, 25; 44:18, 24; 47:25; Exod 11:5; 32:22; 1 Sam 20:15; 22:14; 23:20; 25:25, 27, 29, 41; 2 Sam 11:11, 24; 13:30, 32, 33, 35; 15:21; 16:2; 18:29, 32, 42; 24:3; 1 Kgs 1:19, 20, 25, 27, 36, 37; 14:10 (2x); 16:4; 22:6, 12, 15; Esth 1:16, 18, 20; 2:3, 4; 3:8, 9; 5:8 (2x); 6:9; 7:4; 8:5; 2 Chr 18:5, 11.

(57) ויען יוסף את פרעה לאמר בלעדי אלהים יענה את שלום **פרעה**

wayyaʕan	yosep̄	ʔɛt-parʕo	leʔmor	bilʕɔḏɔy
and=he.answered	Joseph	ACC-Pharaoh	to=say	without=me
ʔᵉlohim	yaʕⁿɛ	ʔɛt-šəlom	parʕo	
God	he.will.answer	ACC-welfare.of	Pharaoh	

Joseph answered Pharaoh, "It is not in me; God will give *Pharaoh* a favorable answer" (lit. God will answer the welfare of *Pharaoh*"). (Gen 41:16)

Fourth, an indirect address may be used as the object of a finite verb, as in (58):[12]

(58) ויגד לשלמה לאמר הנה אדניהו ירא את **המלך שלמה**
והנה אחז בקרנות המזבח לאמר ישבע לי כיום המלך שלמה אם ימית את עבדו בחרב

wayyuggaḏ	lišlomo	leʔmor	hinne	ʔᵃḏoniyyɔhu
and=it.was.told	to=Solomon	to=say	look	Adonijah
yɔreʔ	ʔɛt-hammɛlɛḵ	šəlomo	wəhinne	
he.fears	ACC-the=king	Solomon	and=look	
ʔɔḥaz	bəqarnoṯ	hammizbeᵃḥ	leʔmor	
he.seized	in=horns.of	the=altar	to=say	
yiššɔḇaʕ-li	kayyom	hammɛlɛḵ	šəlomo	
he.will.swear-to=me	like=the=day	the=king	Solomon	
ʔim-yɔmiṯ	ʔɛt-ʕaḇdo	beḥɔrɛḇ		
if-he.will.put.to.death	ACC-servant=his	with=the=sword		

Then it was told Solomon, "Look, Adonijah fears *King Solomon*, for look, he has taken hold of the horns of the altar, saying, 'May King Solomon solemnly promise me first that he will not put his servant to death with the sword.'" (1 Kgs 1:51)

Fifth, an indirect address may be used as the subject of the infinitive, as in (59):[13]

(59) ...ותפל על רגליו ותאמר
ולא תהיה זאת לך לפוקה ולמכשול לב לאדני ולשפך דם חנם ולהושיע **אדני** לו

wayyittippol	ʕal-raḡlɔyw	wattoʔmɛr...	wəloʔ	tihyɛ
and=she.fell	on-feet.his	and=she.said	and=not	she.will.be
zoʔṯ	ləḵɔ	ləp̄uqɔ	uləmiḵšol	lēḇ	laʔḏoni
this	to=you	to=staggering	and=to=stumbling.of	heart	to=lord=my

---

[12] There are fourteen cases in which an indirect address is used as the object of a finite verb: Gen 41:28; Num 36:2; 2 Sam 16:9; 19:22, 42; 1 Kgs 1:51; Lach 2:2, 5–6; 3:3; 4:1; 5:1; 6:2; 8:1; 9:1–2.

[13] There are five cases in which an indirect address is used as the subject of the infinitive: 1 Sam 25:31; 2 Sam 14:13 (2x); 19:20; 1 Kgs 1:21.

wəlišpok-dɔm   hinnɔm   uləhošiaʕ   ʔadoni   lo
and=to=pour.out-blood   for.nothing   and=to=save   lord=my   for=him

She (i.e., Abigail) fell at his (i.e., David) feet and said,... "My lord shall have no cause of grief or pangs of conscience for having shed blood without cause or for *my lord* having avenged himself." (1 Sam 25:24–31)

Finally, an indirect address may be used as the object of the infinitive, as in (60):[14]

(60) ... ויאמר אל המלך
והנה באתי היום ראשון לכל בית יוסף לרדת לקראת **אדני המלך**
wayyoʔmɛr   ʔɛl-hammɛlɛk...   wəhinne   bɔʔti   hayyom   riʔšon
and=he.said to-the=king   and=look   I.came   the=day   first
ləkɔl-bet   yosep   lɔrɛdɛt   liqraʔt   ʔadoni   hammɛlɛk
to=all-house.of   Joseph   to=come.down   to=meet   lord=my   the=king

He (i.e., Shimei the son of Gera) said to the king (i.e., David),... "Look, I have come today as the first of all the house of Joseph to come down to meet *my lord the king.*" (2 Sam 19:20–21)

5.3.2. *Rule of Concord*

In general, an indirect address is treated as third person within the clause in which it appears, while the pronoun(s) coreferential with the indirect address can be in the second[15] or third person[16] outside that clause. Thus, in example (56) above, the indirect address המלך *hammɛlɛk* "the king" serves as the subject of the main clause, which is preceded by the third-person singular verb יחטא *yeḥtɔʔ* "let him sin" and followed by the anaphoric third-person possessive pronoun "his" in בעבדו *baʕabdo* "against his servant." However, in the subsequent dependent clause introduced by the conjunction כי *ki* "because," the pronoun coreferential with the preceding indirect address is in the second person (לך *lɔk* "against you").

This rule of concord is not without exceptions. Consider the following example.

(61) ותאמר יזכר נא **המלך** את יהוה אלהיך
wattoʔmɛr   yizkɔr-nɔʔ   hammɛlɛk   ʔɛt-yhwh   ʔɛlohɛkɔ
and=she.said   he.will.remember-POL   the=king   ACC-YHWH   God=your

---

[14] There is only one case in which an indirect address is used as the object of the infinitive.
[15] See Gen 31:35; 32:6; 33:14; 41:10; 44:18, 19; Exod 8:25; 11:5; 32:22; 1 Sam 20:12; 22:15; 24:15; 25:25; 25:28, 31; 26:18, 19; 2 Sam 3:21; 9:11; 11:24; 13:35; 14:9, 13, 17, 19, 22; 18:31; 19:20, 28, 29, 38, 42; 24:23; 1 Kgs 1:19, 20, 21, 27; 2:38; 16:3; Esth 2:3; Neh 2:5; 1 Chr 21:23; Lach 2:2–3.
[16] See 1 Kgs 16:4; Esth 1:19; 8:5 (cf. Neh 2:5).

She (i.e., the Tekoite woman) said (to David), "Please let *the king* invoke Yahweh *your* God." (2 Sam 14:11)

While engaging in conversation with Kind David, the Tekoite woman refers to him twice, once by the indirect address המלך *hammɛlɛḵ* "the king" and once by the pronoun ך *ḵɔ* "your." Interestingly, even though both indirect address and the pronoun coreferential with it appear within the same clause, the pronoun is in the second person instead of the expected third person.[17] No definitive explanation for this seeming mismatch in grammatical person can be offered. However, it is worth noting that there is another instance in our corpus where the phrase "your God" occurs alongside the indirect address "the king" in the same clause (1 Sam 25:29). Additionally, the fact that the third-person possessive pronoun in the phrase "his God" consistently refers to its antecedent, not the addressee (which occurs fifty-seven times in the Hebrew Bible), suggests the possibility that the second-person possessive pronoun "your" was consistently used with the word "God" to refer to the addressee.[18]

In the following example, however, there seems to be a clear reason for the use of the second-person possessive pronoun in the clause containing an indirect form of address.

(62) ויבא אבשלום אל המלך ויאמר ... ילך נא **המלך** ועבדיו עם עבד**ך**

wayyɔḇoʔ	*ʔaḇšɔlom*	*ʔɛl-hammɛlɛḵ*	*wayyoʔmɛr ...*
and=he.came	Absalom	to-the=king	and=he.said
yelɛḵ-nɔʔ	*hammɛlɛḵ*	*waʕᵃḇɔḏɔyw*	*ʕim-ʕaḇdɛḵɔ*
he.will.go-POL	the=king	and=servants=his	with-servant=your

Absalom came to the king (i.e., David) and said,... "Please let *the king* and *his* servants go with *your* servant." (2 Sam 13:24)

In his invitation for David to accompany him to a sheep shearing festival, Absalom addresses him three times. He does so first by the indirect address המלך *hammɛlɛḵ* "the king" and then by using the third-person possessive pronoun in עבדיו *ʕᵃḇɔḏɔyw* "his servants" to agree with the grammatical person of its antecedent המלך. However, when Absalom addresses David for the third time within the same clause, he uses the second-person possessive pronoun ך *ḵɔ* "your," rather than the third-person possessive pronoun ו *o* "his." The use of the second-person possessive pronoun seems to be an effort to avoid any potential ambiguity, as the phrase with the third-person possessive pronoun "his servant" could potentially

---

[17] See also 1 Sam 16:16; 25:29; 2 Sam 18:32; Arad 16:2; 21:1–2; Lach 3:6; Mous 2:2.
[18] Note that the LXX reads θεὸν αὐτοῦ "his God" in 2 Sam 14:11 and reads τῷ θεῷ "God" without any possessive pronouns in 1 Sam 25:29, both of which seem to reflect the attempt to ensure grammatical person agreement with the preceding indirect address.

refer to someone other than the speaker, that is, Absalom. It is worth noting that the deferential phrase "your servant" is almost exclusively used to refer to the speaker in conversations in our corpus.[19]

5.4. Social Dynamics of Indirect Forms of Address

The analysis of the internal structure and external syntax of indirect addresses in Biblical Hebrew and Epigraphic Hebrew yields an important insight into their particular function, namely as a means to convey two social variables: power and distance.

5.4.1. Two Social Variables: Power and Distance

On the one hand, similar to free forms of address discussed in chapter 3, the relative power dynamics between a speaker and an addressee can be conveyed through the semantic type of the first element in indirect addresses. As we will see in §5.4.5, almost without exception in our corpus, indirect addresses that begin with a T or an ascending KT are used for social superiors, while those beginning with a PN are used for social inferiors.

On the other hand, when a speaker refers to an addressee in the third person using an indirect address, it may indicate a greater social distance between them compared to a second-person form of address. The expression of social distancing through third-person addresses is a well-known but seldom researched phenomenon in many languages (Head 1978, 167). As Paul Listen (1999, 62–68) demonstrates, the functional differences between second and third person addresses are conceptually rooted in the metaphorical mapping of physical proximity and distance onto the domain of social relations.[20] In other words, the physical proximity or distance in personal interactions can metaphorically correspond to the social intimacy or aloofness between speech participants. Thus, an intimate friendship may be described as "close," while aloofness may be expressed as "distant." This metaphorical analogy between physical and social relations can be symbolically represented through grammatical person marking: second-person addresses may signify intimacy, directness, and/or informality, whereas third-person addresses may signify aloofness, indirectness, and/or formality (Head 1978, 194–95; Listen 1999, 39).

5.4.2. Motivations behind Indirect Forms of Address

As discussed in chapter 3, Brown and Levinson (1987, 178) propose that a speaker's use of nominal address forms beginning with a T or an ascending KT

---

[19] For a linguistic description of the use of the "addressee-based" deferential form, "your servant," see Miller 2003, 271–81.
[20] For studies that seek to describe conceptual background behind forms of address in terms of metaphorical mappings, see Keown (2004) and Domonkosi (2018, 129–41).

can be seen as a (negative) politeness strategy to show deference to an addressee of higher power. Furthermore, when a speaker employs a third-person address, it can be interpreted as an effort to create distance between himself and the addressee by avoiding direct address through second-person pronouns or verbs. Once again, according to Brown and Levinson (1987, 203), the avoidance of the direct address "you" can be considered a (negative) politeness strategy by which the speaker attempts to avoid an undue closeness and ensure the addressee's freedom of action. Thus, third-person addresses beginning with a T or an ascending KT can serve as a unique linguistic tool for a speaker to express politeness towards the addressee, acknowledging the addressee's power over himself while simultaneously creating a sense of distance.

5.4.3. Effects of Indirect Forms of Address

As observed in table 5.1, the absolute majority of indirect addresses to humans in our corpus begin with a T or an ascending KT (94 percent). Furthermore, as we will see in §5.4.5, almost all of them are used for social superiors. Therefore, the primary effect of indirect addresses in Biblical Hebrew and Epigraphic Hebrew appears to convey deference towards social superiors.

As Listen (1999, 66–68) points out, however, indirect addresses do not necessarily entail deference alone. Manipulating the power and/or distance variables can lead to a range of pragmatic effects beyond showing deference to social superiors. In our corpus, there are a few instances in which indirect forms of address begin with a PN. In such cases, deference can hardly be expected, as the use of PN as the initial element of an address form almost exclusively marks the inferiority of the addressee (see chapter 3 and §5.4.6). If these addresses are used by a superior, they may signify an attempt to create distance from an inferior addressee, potentially conveying emotions such as anger, contempt, rejection, and/or formality. Conversely, if these addresses are used by an inferior, they may evoke a sense of insult and/or formality. Nevertheless, the precise effect of each of these addresses should ultimately be determined by the contextual factors surrounding their usage. In §5.4.6, I classify all addresses that manipulate the power and/or distance variables as instances of what Brown and Gilman (1960, 270–73) call "expressive shift," that is, strategic violation of address rules to convey the speaker's temporary feelings and attitudes.

5.4.4. Previous Studies on Social Dynamics of Indirect Addresses

Revell (1996) and Miller (2003) deal with indirect addresses in Biblical Hebrew and Epigraphic Hebrew in some detail. However, both of them approach the topic under the heading of "deferential language," which encompasses not only deferential free and bound forms of address but also deferential-self references, such as עבדך ʕaḇdək̠ɔ "your servant," אמתך ʔᵃmɔṯek̠ɔ "your maidservant," or שפחתך

šip̲ḥɔt̲ɔk̲ɔ "your maidservant." Since their primary focus is on the use of these deferential terms, other socio-pragmatic effects that indirect addresses may produce are either largely ignored (Miller) or only partially treated in different sections throughout the book (Revell). The analysis presented in the following sections aims to bridge this gap and provide a more comprehensive understanding of indirect addresses.

5.4.5. Giving Deference

Table 5.1 above reveals that approximately 94 percent of indirect addresses used for humans in our corpus begin with a T or an ascending KT, while only 6 percent of them commence with a PN. As discussed in chapter 3, the initial element of a free form of address, whether simple or compound, serves as an indicator of the power dynamic between the speaker and the addressee. Consequently, when a T or an ascending KT is employed as the first element, it signifies the superiority of the addressee. On the other hand, when a PN or a descending KT is used as the initial element, it denotes the inferiority or equality of the addressee. This rule of address for free forms of address also extends to indirect addresses. Except for one case ("Pharaoh" in Exod 11:5), all indirect forms of address beginning with a T or an ascending KT come from the inferior-superior dyads (i>s), as shown in table 5.2.[21]

Table 5.2. Indirect Forms of Address Beginning with T or Ascending KT

Form (Frequency)	Power	Form (Frequency)	Power
My lord (83x)	i>s	King Ahasuerus (2x)	i>s
Our lord (1x)	i>s	King Solomon (1x)	i>s
My lord the king (39x)	i>s	King my lord (1x)	i>s
My lord the king David (2x)	i>s	King of Israel (3x)	i>s
My lord the official (2x)	i>s	Pharaoh (13x)	i>s; s>i
My lord Esau (1x)	i>s	The anointed of Yahweh (2x)	i>s
My lord Yaush (1x)	i>s	My father (1x)	i>s
The king (75x)	i>s[22]		

---

[21] See §3.3 for my discussion on the method by which the power relation between the speaker and the addressee can be determined.

[22] This includes two cases in which Jehoshaphat King of Judah addresses Ahab King of Israel by the indirect address המלך *hammelek̲* "the king" in 1 Kgs 22:8 (= 2 Chr 18:7): אל יאמר המלך כן *ʔal-yoʔmar hammelek̲ ken* "Let not *the king* say so." Here Jehoshaphat is making a negative request of Ahab to abandon what he just said: "I hate him (i.e., Micaiah)." Jehoshaphat and Ahab may be considered equal as both of them are kings. Thus, Jehoshaphat's use of the deferential title "the king" may simply be viewed as expressing politeness towards his equal partner. However, the problem is that if they were truly equal, mutual respect is to be expected. But Ahab never employs a deferential term to address Jehoshaphat throughout their conversation, nor uses any identifiable politeness strategy for Jehoshaphat.

Indirect addresses beginning with a T or an ascending KT are most frequently used for kings (139x), while other types of social superiors, such as high officials, military officers, prophets, and fathers, also receive them. More than half of these addresses are used in the context of requesting favors, while the rest occur in other contexts such as informing and responding. It can be concluded, then, that indirect addresses in Biblical Hebrew and Epigraphic Hebrew primarily function as a (negative) politeness strategy by which an inferior gives deference to a superior and maintains distance between them, especially when there is a significant power differential between them.

The only case in which an inferior receives an indirect form of address beginning with a T occurs in Exod 11:5, where God, who is considered superior to all human beings in the Hebrew Bible, addresses a king of Egypt with the title פרעה *parʕo* "Pharaoh." This exceptional case can be classified as a case of expressive shift. A possible reason for the use of the title in this superior-inferior dyad will be provided in §5.4.6.1.

5.4.6. Expressive Shift

All of the indirect addresses beginning with a PN in our corpus can be conveniently classified as cases of "expressive shift," that is, strategic violation of address rules to communicate the speaker's temporary feelings and attitudes. Also, there are a few other cases, including the exceptional one mentioned earlier, in which the use of indirect addresses beginning with a T appears inadequate. In the following sections, I will demonstrate that these rule-breaking indirect addresses are a result of manipulating the power and/or distance variables. These addresses produce special effects other than giving deference to social superiors. These effects are not only socially and emotionally significant but also have exegetical importance. The following sections are organized based on the discourse-pragmatic effects caused by these expressive shifts.

Note that when the title "the king" is used as indirect address elsewhere, it is always used by the king's subjects. In other words, the use of the indirect address "the king" is a common technique for the subjects to give deference to their king. Perhaps Jehoshaphat's use of this deferential form might be a little piece of evidence for northern Israel's political supremacy over southern Judah around the eighth century BCE (see Miller and Hayes [2006, 304] who view southern Judah as a vassal state subservient to the Omrides around eighth century BCE). Note also that Jehoshaphat uses a variety of politeness strategies when he speaks with Ahab. In v. 4, he offers a promise to Ahab to go to war with him against Ramoth Gilead. In v. 5, he uses the so-called particle of entreaty, נא *naʔ* "please." All these might imply the unequal power existing between Ahab and Jehoshaphat.

5.4.6.1. Rejection

There are instances in which the speaker's rejection of the addressee appears to be conveyed through the use of indirect address. First, God uses indirect addresses composed of PNs when announcing the punishment of three kings of Israel: Jeroboam (1 Kgs 14:10–11), Baasha (1 Kgs 16:3–4), and Ahab (1 Kgs 21:21–24). These are the only occasions in our corpus in which God uses a PN as an indirect address. Consider the following passage.

(63) לכן הנני מביא רעה אל בית **ירבעם** והכרתי **לירבעם** משתין בקיר עצור ועזוב בישראל
ובערתי אחרי בית **ירבעם** כאשר יבער הגלל עד תמו המת **לירבעם** בעיר יאכלו הכלבים

ləken	hinni	mebiʔ	rəʕə	ʔel-bet	yərobʕəm
therefore	look=I	bringing	evil	to-house.of	Jeroboam

wəhikratti	ləyərobʕəm	maštin	baqir	ʕəṣur	wəʕəzub
and=I.will.cut.off	to=Jeroboam	urinating	in=wall	bound	and=free

bəyiśrəʔel	ubiʕarti	ʔaḥ^are	bet-yərobʕəm	kaʔ^ašer
in=Israel	and=I.will.burn	after	house.of-Jeroboam	as=REL

yəbaʕer	haggələl	ʕad-tummo	hammet
he.will.burn	the=dung	until-be.complete=his	the=dying

ləyərobʕəm	bəʕir	yoʔkəlu	hakkəlobim
to=Jeroboam	in=the=city	they.will.eat	the=dogs

Therefore, I will bring harm upon the house of *Jeroboam* and will cut off from *Jeroboam* every male,[23] both bond and free in Israel, and will burn up the house of *Jeroboam*, as one burns up dung until it is completely consumed. Dogs will eat anyone belonging to *Jeroboam* who dies in the city. (1 Kgs 14:10–11a)

The announcement of God's punishment against King Jeroboam is introduced with the clausal adverb לכן *ləken* "therefore." Throughout this dire message, God addresses Jeroboam by PN four times. God's use of PN itself does not pose any problem, considering that he is superior to all human beings. However, God's choice to address Jeroboam in the third person is "expressive," as Jeroboam is inferior to him. This use of third person address may indicate God's deliberate "distancing" from Jeroboam, conveying his message of rejecting Jeroboam as king of Israel.

The passage in (63) is immediately preceded by the passage in (64) in which God explains the reasons for his punishment against Jeroboam.

---

[23] Lit. he who urinates against a wall (see also 1 Sam 25:22, 34; 1 Kgs 16:11; 21:21; 2 Kgs 9:8).

(64) כה אמר יהוה אלהי ישראל יען אשר הרימתיך מתוך העם ואתנך נגיד על עמי ישראל
ואקרע את הממלכה מבית דוד ואתנה לך ולא היית כעבדי דוד אשר שמר מצותי
ואשר הלך אחרי בכל לבבו לעשות רק הישר בעיני ותרע לעשות מכל אשר היו
לפניך ותלך ותעשה לך אלהים אחרים ומסכות להכעיסני ואתי השלכת אחרי גוך

ko-ʔɔmar	yhwh	ʔlohe yiśrɔʔel	yaʕan ʔᵃšer hᵃrimotiḵɔ
thus-he.said	YHWH	God.of Israel	because REL I.exalted=you
mittoḵ	hɔʕɔm	wɔʔettenɔḵɔ	nɔḡid ʕal
from=midst.of	the=people	and=I.made.you	ruler over
ʕammi	yiśrɔʔel	wɔʔeqraʕ ʔet-hammamlɔḵɔ	mibbet
people=my	Israel	and=I.tore ACC-the=kingdom	from=house.of
dɔwid	wɔʔettɔnɛhɔ	lɔḵ	wɔloʔ-hɔyitɔ kɔʕabdi
David	and=I.gave=it	to=you	and=not=you.were like=servant=my
dɔwid	ʔᵃšer šɔmar miṣwotay		waʔᵃšer-hɔlaḵ ʔaḥᵃray
David	REL he.kept commandments=my		and=REL-he.walked after
bɔḵɔl-lɔḇɔḇo	laʕᵃśot raq	hayyɔšɔr	bɔʕenɔy
with=all-heart=his	to=do only	the=upright	in=eyes=my
wattɔraʕ	laʕᵃśot mikkol	ʔᵃšer-hɔyu	lɔpɔnɛḵɔ
and=you.did.evil	to=do from=all	REL-they.were	before=you
wattelɛḵ	wattaʕᵃśɛ-llɔḵɔ	ʔᵉlohim	ʔᵃḥerim
and=you.went	and=you.made-for=you	gods	other
umassɛḵot	lɔhaḵʕiseni wɔʔoti	hišlaḵtɔ	ʔaḥᵃre
and=metal.images	to=vex=me and=ACC=me	you.cast	after
gawwɛḵɔ			
back=your			

"Thus says Yahweh, God of Israel: "Given the fact that I exalted *you* from among the people and made *you* ruler over my people Israel and tore the kingdom away from the house of David and gave it to *you*, and yet *you* have not been like my servant David, who kept my commandments and followed me with all his heart, doing only what was right in my eyes, but *you* have done evil more than all who came before *you* and (*you*) have gone and (*you*) made for *yourself* other gods and metal images, provoking me to anger, and (*you*) have cast me behind *your* back." (1 Kgs 14:7–9)

What is striking in this passage is that God consistently addresses Jeroboam in the second person (11x). This is in stark contrast to the subsequent announcement of punishment, where he addresses Jeroboam in the third person. The shift from second person to third person serves as a literary device to separate God's punishment from his accusation, signaling that these two aspects are qualitatively different. While Jeroboam is treated directly and perhaps personally in the accusation section, he is now placed outside the speech event in the punishment section

(Domonkosi 2018, 131). Thus, in contrast to the accusation section, God's rejection of Jeroboam is further highlighted in the punishment section.

The other two passages containing the message of God's punishment against Baasha and Ahab (1 Kgs 16:3–4; 21:21–24) are almost identical to the passages we have seen above. The use of third person addresses in these passages appears to serve the same purpose: to convey God's rejection of Baasha and Ahab.[24]

Second, Michal addresses her husband, King David, using the indirect address composed of T, מלך ישראל *mɛlɛḵ yiśrɔʔel* "the king of Israel," as he comes to bless his household:

(65) ותאמר מה נכבד היום **מלך ישראל**
אשר נגלה היום לעיני אמהות עבדיו כהגלות נגלות אחד הרקים

wattoʔmɛr	ma-nniḵbad		hayyom	mɛlɛḵ	yiśrɔʔel
and=she.said	how-he.distinguished.himself		the=day	king.of	Israel
ʔăšɛr	niḡlɔ		hayyom	ləʕene	ʔamhot
REL	he.exposed.himself		the=day	to=eyes.of	slave.girls.of
ʕăḇɔḏɔyw	kəhiggɔlot	niḡlot	ʔaḥad	hɔreqim	
servants=his	as=uncover	uncovering	one.of	the=worthless.ones	

She (i.e., Michal) said, "How *the king of Israel* has distinguished himself today! He exposed himself today before his servants' slave girls as one of the vulgar fellows would!" (2 Sam 6:20)

Miller comments on the significance of Michal's use of the indirect address, stating:

> David's wife mocks him by addressing him as 'the king of Israel,' his political position. Throughout the quotation, third-person pronouns are used to refer to the addressee. In this way, the speaker rebukes her husband by distancing herself

---

[24] As in the cases of Jeroboam, Baasha, and Ahab, the only case in which an inferior receives an indirect form of address beginning with T (§5.4.5) occurs in the context of God's punishment. In Exod 11:5, God addresses a king of Egypt by the title פרעה *parʕo* "Pharaoh": "Every firstborn in the land of Egypt shall die, from the firstborn of *Pharaoh* who sits on his throne, to the firstborn of the slave girl who is behind the hand mill, and all the firstborn of the cattle." God's use of the title "Pharaoh" does not seem to convey deference in this context, as in the other cases in which the title is used by pharaoh's subjects (Gen 41:10, 16, 25 [2x], 28 [2x], 32, 33, 34, 35; Exod 8:25 [2x]). Thus, God's indirect address by the title could be viewed as a case of expressive shift, conveying his rejection of Pharaoh by distancing from him. Jacob (1992, 289), however, suggests that the choice of the expression "the firstborn of Pharoah" rather than "*your* firstborn," which seems to be expected in this superior-inferior dyad, results from the narrator's attempt to indicate that God's punishment affects everyone in Egypt by the repetition of the expression "the firstborn of X."

from the person she addresses (and his behavior). Michal's subversion of the deferential language of the court to ridicule her husband is particularly stinging. (2003, 274)

According to Miller, Michal's use of David's political title, "the king of Israel," and her use of third-person pronouns create the effects of mocking and rebuking. However, it is worth noting that the use of political titles by kings' wives to address their husbands appears to be a common practice, as evidenced by examples such as 1 Kgs 1:20–21 and Esth 5:4. Additionally, kings' wives address their husbands using third-person pronouns in these passages, without intending to mock or rebuke them. Therefore, it cannot be concluded that the use of political titles or third-person pronouns inherently implies mocking and rebuking. Thus, Miller's explanation seems inadequate.

Revell offers an interesting perspective on Michal's use of the indirect address, stating:

> Where a subject addresses or refers to King David or either of the other kings of the divided monarchy, using the title alone as a designation, the form is 'the king' (המלך).... The title in the form 'king of Israel' (מלך ישראל) is used for these kings in speech, but it is typically used by foreigners. (1996, 17)

In essence, Michal's disdainful attitude towards David can be observed through her choice of the "wrong" form of address for her situation. In her view, David's behavior of dancing before the ark (2 Sam 6:14) is unworthy of a king ("she despised him in her heart" [2 Sam 6:16]). Consequently, by utilizing the title commonly used by foreigners when referring to the kings of Israel (1 Sam 29:3; 1 Kgs 15:19 [=2 Chr 16:3]; 20:31; 22:31–32; 2 Kgs 5:5; 6:11–12; 7:6; 16:7; 2 Chr 18:30–31), she distances herself from David and presents herself as someone for whom David is not the king. Effectively, she rejects him as her king. Thus, Michal's employment of the indirect address serves as a notable example of "expressive shift," where distancing is achieved by manipulating the form of address itself, rather than solely relying on third-person reference.

There are two additional instances in which the title "the king of Israel" is used by a subject to address their king. Both occurrences take place during David's confrontation with King Saul (1 Sam 24:15; 26:20), where David criticizes Saul for seeking his life. Similar to Michal's case, David's use of the title "the king of Israel" can be interpreted as instances of expressive shift, wherein David distances himself from Saul and rejects him as his king.

5.4.6.2. Insult

There is one case in our corpus in which the speaker seems to express insult towards his addressee through the use of indirect address. Consider the following.

(66) והנה כל איש ישראל באים אל המלך ויאמרו אל המלך מדוע גנבוך אחינו איש יהודה
ויעברו את המלך ואת ביתו את הירדן וכל אנשי דוד עמו

wəhine	kɔl-ʔiš	yiśrɔʔel	bɔʔim	ʔɛl-hammɛlɛk	wayyoʔməru
and=look	all-men.of	Israel	coming	to-the=king	and=they.said

ʔɛl-hammɛlɛk	madduaʕ	gənɔbukɔ	ʔaḥenu	ʔiš
to-the=king	why	they.stole=you	brothers=our	men.of

yəhudɔ	wayyaʕbiru	ʔɛt-hammɛlɛk	wəʔɛt-beto
Judah	and=they.brought.over	ACC-the=king	and=ACC-house=his

ʔɛt-hayyarden	wəkɔl-ʔanše	dɔwid	ʕimmo
ACC-the=Jordan	and=all-men.of	David	with=him

Then all the men of Israel came to the king (i.e., David) and said to the king, "Why have our brothers the men of Judah stolen *you* away and brought *the king* and his household over the Jordan, and all *David*'s men with him?" (2 Sam 19:42)

This conversation takes place as King David returns to Jerusalem from across the Jordan river, and tension arises as the northern tribes feel excluded in welcoming him. They bring their case before David, accusing the men of Judah of claiming exclusive rights to honor him. In presenting their case, they refer to David using various forms of indirect address, including second-person pronoun "you", the title "the king," and his name "David." While the first two forms may be considered acceptable for addressing King David, the use of his PN appears improper, as inferiors typically do not address superiors by their PNs. Therefore, the use of David's PN by the men of Israel can be seen as "expressive," signaling their insults towards David, who has granted the men of Judah permission to escort him. The shift in address forms in the speech of the men of Israel starkly contrasts with the consistent use of the title "the king" in the speech of the men of Judah (2 Sam 19:43 [2x]). This implies a difference in attitude towards David between the northern and southern tribes.

5.4.6.3. *Formality*

There are several instances where the use of indirect address appears to convey a sense of formality. First, when Jonathan takes an oath with David, he addresses David using his PN.

(67) ויאמר יהונתן אל דוד יהוה אלהי ישראל כי אחקר את אבי
כעת מחר השלשית והנה טוב אל דוד ולא אז אשלח אליך וגליתי את אזנך ...
ולא תכרת את חסדך מעם ביתי עד עולם ולא בהכרת יהוה
את איבי דוד איש מעל פני האדמה

wayyoʔmɛr	yəhonɔtɔn	ʔɛl-dɔwid	yhwh	ʔᵉlohe	yiśrɔʔel
and=he.said	Jonathan	to-David	YHWH	God.of	Israel

ki-ʔehqor	ʔεt-ʔɔḇi	kɔʕεt	mɔhɔr	haššəlišiṯ
that-I.will.check	ACC-father=my	about=time	tomorrow	the=third
wəhine-ṭoḇ	ʔεl-dɔwiḏ	wəloʔ-ʔɔz	ʔεšlaḥ	ʔelεḵɔ
and=look-good	to-David	and=not-then	I.will.send	to=you
wəgɔliṯi	ʔεt-ʔɔznεḵɔ		wəloʔ-ṯaḵriṯ	
and=I.will.disclose	ACC-ear=your		and=not-you.will.cut	
ʔεt-ḥasdəḵɔ	mεʕim	bεṯi	ʕaḏ-ʕolɔm	wəloʔ
ACC-loyalty=your	from=with	house=my	unto-eternity	and=not
bəhaḵriṯ	yhwh	ʔεt-ʔoyḇe	ḏɔwiḏ	ʔiš
in=cut	YHWH	ACC-enemies.of	David	every
mεʕal	pəne	hɔʔᵃḏɔmɔ		
from=upon	face.of	the=ground		

Jonathan said to David, "(By) Yahweh, God of Israel, (I swear)[25] that I will check with my father about this time tomorrow or the third day. If he is favorably inclined toward *David*, will I not then send word to you and let you know?... Do not cut off your loyalty from my house forever, when Yahweh has cut off every one of the enemies of *David* from the face of the earth." (1 Sam 20:12, 15)

It is certain that Jonathan is superior to David at this stage, as David refers to himself as Jonathan's servant (1 Sam 20:7–8). Thus, Jonathan's use of David's PN is expected. However, his addressing of David in the third person rather than the second person is "expressive," as David is inferior to him. The indirect form of address occurs in a friendly environment, so it cannot be interpreted as a sign of Jonathan's rejection or insult towards David, as in the cases of Jeroboam, Baasha, and Ahab. Instead, as noted by Revell (1996, 356), the sense of formality seems to be induced by the use of David's name. The taste of formality can also be detected in Jonathan's use of his own name in 1 Sam 20:13. In his oath, Jonathan pledges to stand with David against Saul, his father and king. Jonathan's use of PN as an indirect address and self-reference appears to be intended to lend credibility to this extraordinary undertaking. While the oath is taken in a friendly environment, it carries a solemn and serious tone.

Second, in three Hebrew letters, the sender refers to the recipient by an indirect address beginning with a PN.

(68) אחכ·חנניהו·שלח לשל
מ·**אלישב**·ולשלמ ביתכ בר
כתכ ליהוה
ʔḥk ·ḥnnyhw ·šlḥ lšl

---

[25] For a thorough treatment of oath formulas in Biblical Hebrew, see Conklin 2011.

m ʔlyšb wlšlm bytk br
ktk lyhwh
Your brother Hananyahu (hereby) sends greetings
to *Elyashib* and to your household. I bless
you to Yahweh. (Arad 16:1–3)

(69) בנכ·יהוכל·שלח·לשלמ·**גדליהו** [בנ]
אליאר·ולשלמ·ביתכ·ברכתכ ל[יהו]
ה
bnk yhwkl šlḥ lšlm gdlyhw [bn]
ʔlyʔr wlšlm bytk brktk l[yhw]
h
Your son Yehukal (hereby) sends greetings to *Gedalyahu [son of]
Elyair* and to your household. I bless you to [Yahwe]h. (Arad 21:1–3)

(70) בנכמ·גמר[יהו] ונח
מיהו·שלח[ו לשלמ]
מלכיהו ברכת]כ ליהו[ה
bnkm gmr[yhw] wnḥ
myhw šlḥ[w lšlm]
mlkyhw brkt[k lyhw]h
Your son Gemar[yahu], as well as Nehemyahu,
(hereby) sen[d greetings to]
Malkiyahu. I bless [you to Yahwe]h. (Arad 40:1–3)

In (68), the sender and the recipient appear to be equal in status, as indicated by the use of the horizontal KT "your brother" for the sender's self-reference. Thus, the use of the PN "Elyashib" for the recipient may not pose a problem. However, in (69) and (70), both senders appear to be inferior to their recipients, as evident from each sender's self-reference using the descending KT "your son." Consequently, the use of PNs for the recipients seems to be problematic.

According to Pardee et al. (1982, 49–50), only these three letters among all the Northwest Semitic letters contain the same form of the *praescriptio*, which consists of the conflate address/greeting formula *PN šlḥ lšlm PN* and the greeting formula *brk l*. They interpret this *praescriptio* as "a caritative address/greeting + greeting formula used between family members," considering all the KTs used in these letters as literal designations of kinship. If this interpretation is correct, the use of PNs is purely formulaic and/or formal, and thus, the use of PNs for social superiors can be justified.

5.5. Conclusion

In this chapter, I have examined the internal structure, external syntax, and social dynamics of indirect addresses used for humans in Biblical Hebrew and

Epigraphic Hebrew. The analysis of their internal structure and external syntax informs us that they can serve as a means of expressing the power and distance variables. Indirect addresses in Biblical Hebrew and Epigraphic Hebrew primarily function as a politeness strategy through which an inferior gives deference to a superior while maintaining a certain distance, particularly in the cases of significant power differentials. However, the manipulation of the power and/or distance variables can result in a variety of pragmatic effects beyond deference, including expressions of rejection, insult, or formality.

6.
CONCLUSIONS

This book undertook a comprehensive examination of the forms of address employed in the prose sections of the Hebrew Bible and the epigraphic Hebrew letters. By applying the theories and methodologies of contemporary sociolinguistics, particularly the address theory proposed by Brown and Gilman (1960) and subsequently refined by Brown and Ford (1961), as well as the politeness theory presented by Brown and Levinson (1987), the study explored the distribution and usage patterns of address forms in both Biblical Hebrew and Epigraphic Hebrew. The primary objective of this analysis was to identify the underlying rules that govern the use of address and to detect instances where these rules are violated. Through this interdisciplinary approach, merging sociolinguistics with Hebrew studies, the research contributes to our understanding in two ways: first, by shedding light on the social structure of ancient Hebrew society and highlighting the exegetical significance of address variations, and second, by providing sociolinguists with an opportunity to empirically test specific assumptions and conclusions derived from their analyses of modern languages.

Previous attempts at describing the use of address forms in Biblical Hebrew and Epigraphic Hebrew are limited in number and provide only partial treatment of the subject. Furthermore, the definition and categorization of address forms developed in sociolinguistic studies have not been sufficiently applied to Biblical Hebrew and Epigraphic Hebrew. This book aimed to address and rectify these issues.

Dividing Hebrew forms of address into *free* forms (i.e., forms occurring "outside" the sentence structure, such as preceding, following, or inserted into a sentence, or occurring without any immediate linguistic context) and *bound* forms (i.e., forms integrated into the syntax of a sentence) based on the syntactic criterion, chapters 2 to 5 focused on examining their internal structure, social dynamics, and external syntax. chapter 2 conducted an extensive analysis of the internal structure of free forms of address in Biblical Hebrew. These forms were classified into three distinct categories: *simple addresses* (consisting of a single word), *complex addresses* (composed of two or more words), and *compound addresses* (combining simple and/or complex addresses). This classification was primarily based on the number of constituents present in each address form. Furthermore, grammatical and semantic types were assigned to each constituent within the address form, facilitating the identification of the following meaningful patterns:

1. Out of 682 free forms of address in the corpus, approximately 69 percent of them are simple addresses. Complex addresses are rare in dialogues between two humans, and are primarily found in special contexts, such as prayer.
2. Both simple and complex addresses are to be understood as definite. The occasional absence of the definite article in common noun address forms can be attributed to various factors, such as poetic features or potential scribal interpolation.
3. Compound addresses in Biblical Hebrew can be formed through apposition, repetition, or coordination of coreferential simple and/or complex addresses. Notably, nearly 90 percent of compound addresses are formed by placing simple and complex addresses in apposition.
4. When a simple or complex address is used alone, the two most commonly occurring semantic types are personal names and kinship terms. This aligns with the cross-linguistic phenomenon that personal names and kinship terms form the core lexical domain for free forms of address.
5. The honorific title always occupies the initial position in a compound address.
6. The biblical writers show a strong preference for the word order אֲדֹנִי הַמֶּלֶךְ *ʔᵃdoni hammɛlek* "my lord the king," which is in stark contrast to the almost exclusive use of its reverse order, "O king my lord," in other ancient Near Eastern writings during the second and first millennia BCE.
7. Unlike addresses directed at human(s), kinship terms are never employed to address God in our corpus, perhaps due to polemical reasons.
8. Apostrophe, a literary device in which inanimate objects are addressed and thus personified, is commonly employed in prophetic literature. Common-noun address forms can function as quasi-proper nouns.

In chapter 3, the social dynamics of free forms of address in Biblical Hebrew were examined, primarily within the context of Brown, Gilman, and Ford's sociolinguistic theory of address. The focus was on the three most frequently appearing address terms in the corpus: personal names, titles, and kinship terms. When these semantic types are used between two human beings, they can be used either alone as a simple address (referred to as "APN," "AT," and "AKT," respectively) or as the head constituent of a compound address (referred to as "HPN," "HT," and "HKT," respectively). It was demonstrated that the head constituent in an address, whether in a simple or a compound address, serves as an indicator of the power relation between the speaker and the addressee.

When personal names are used as the head constituent, they seem to mark the superiority of the speaker. Thus, APNs and HPNs are almost exclusively used in "downward" relationships, that is, in superior-inferior dyads, although there are a couple of instances in which APNs are used among close equals. In contrast, when titles are used as the head constituent, they seem to mark the superiority of the addressee. Thus, ATs and HTs are typically used in "upward" relationships, that is, in inferior-superior dyads, with no cases of ATs or HTs used between equals. Therefore, APNs and HPNs seem to function as the T in Brown, Gilman, and Ford's T/V system, while ATs and HTs seem to serve as the V. As far as personal names and titles are concerned, they partially confirm Brown and Ford's "linguistic universal," which associates personal address with intimacy and condescension, as well as distance and deference. However, when kinship terms are used as the head constituent, they can convey all types of power relations. Ascending AKTs and HKTs are used in "upward" relationships, horizontal AKTs and HKTs are used in "horizontal" relationships, and descending AKTs and HKTs are used in "downward" relationships. When kinship terms are used in an extended sense, most, if not all, can be interpreted as politeness strategies. Therefore, the address usage of kinship terms in Biblical Hebrew does not support Brown and Ford's "linguistic universal" (see figure 6.1 below). The use of APNs or HPNs in seemingly inferior-superior dyads can be viewed as what Brown and Gilman refer to as "expressive shifts," in which the speaker (or narrator) strategically violates the rules of address to assert authority over the addressee (e.g., 1 Sam 26:14; Jer 34:4; 2 Chr 15:2). Similarly, the use of ATs in seemingly superior-inferior dyads can be also interpreted as "expressive shifts," to convey feelings of respect (e.g., 2 Chr 35:21) or contempt (e.g., Amos 7:12). These shifts create powerful pragmatic and literary effects that the readers should consider in order to properly understand the text.

Figure 6.1. The Social Dynamics of Free Forms of Address

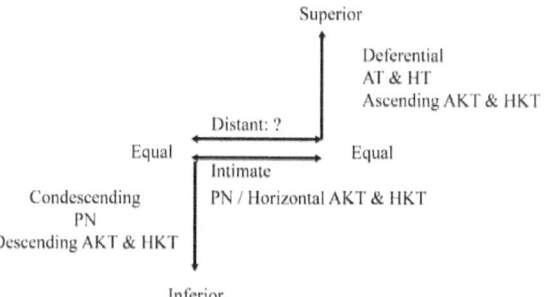

Chapter 4 delved into the external syntax of free forms of address in Biblical Hebrew, examining the correlation between their syntactic position and function through the utilization of the methods proposed by Taglicht and Leech. The analysis revealed that a significant portion, approximately 60 percent, of the addresses occur either at the beginning or at the end of the communicative unit, including stand-alone addresses. These addresses primarily serve conversation management purposes, such as attracting the addressee's attention, identifying the addressee, signaling the initiation or conclusion of a turn or conversation, giving the floor to the addressee, and maintaining contact with the addressee. The remaining addresses are found within the communicative unit and occupy one of the following positions: (i) between the preface and the body; (ii) between an initial-edge element and the core; (iii) within the core; (iv) between the body and the tag. Addresses in these positions generally assume a partitioning and focusing function, directing the addressee's attention to significant information at the respective juncture. Consequently, addresses in positions (i) or (ii) mark the *preceding* element for information focus by separating it from the rest of the communicative unit and highlighting or reinforcing its discourse-pragmatic function. On the other hand, addresses in positions (iii) or (iv) mark the *following* element for information focus by separating it from what precedes it and emphasizing or reinforcing its discourse-pragmatic function.

Chapter 5 undertook an examination of the internal structure, external syntax, and social dynamics of indirect addresses to humans in Biblical Hebrew and Epigraphic Hebrew. Regarding the internal structure, the absolute majority of indirect addresses to humans are composed of a title with or without additional element(s) (94 percent). In contrast, there are only a few indirect addresses consisting of a personal name with or without accompanying element(s), or consisting of a kinship term. With respect to the external syntax, an indirect address is treated as third person within the clause in which it occurs, while the pronoun(s) coreferential with the indirect address may appear in the second or third person outside that clause. The analysis of the internal structure and external syntax of indirect addresses informs us that they can convey power dynamics and interpersonal distance. In both Biblical Hebrew and Epigraphic Hebrew, indirect addresses primarily function as a manifestation of what Brown and Levinson term a negative politeness strategy. This strategy involves individuals of lower social status demonstrating deference towards their superiors while also maintaining a certain level of social distance. This tendency is particularly pronounced in situations where there is a significant power differential between the interlocutors. However, it is important to note that manipulating the variables of power and distance can produce a diverse range of pragmatic effects beyond the expression of deference. These effects may include instances of rejection (2 Sam 6:20), insult (2 Sam, 19:42), or formality (1 Sam 20:12, 15; Arad 16:1–3; 21:1–3; 40:1–3). Thus, the analysis of indirect addresses contributes to a nuanced understanding of the intricate dynamics of power and social interaction within their respective contexts.

This book serves as a foundational stepping stone for future research, aiming to expand the scope of address studies beyond the prose sections of the Hebrew Bible and the epigraphic Hebrew letters. The first proposed step involves conducting a comprehensive analysis of address systems in letters written in other Semitic languages, such as Ugaritic, Aramaic, and Akkadian. Previous attempts to elucidate address systems in these Semitic languages are incomplete and simplistic. A comparative analysis can be undertaken to examine how forms of address are employed in each language and how they differ from Hebrew forms of address.

Furthermore, a sociolinguistic analysis of forms of address in the poetic sections of the Hebrew Bible and Ugaritic narrative poetry warrants exploration. Comparisons and contrasts can be drawn between address usage in Hebrew poetry and that in the prose sections of the Hebrew Bible and letters written in other Semitic languages. To the best of my knowledge, there are only two works on address terms in Hebrew poetry: Rosenbaum (1997) and Miller (2010). However, these works primarily focus on the syntax of address terms rather than their sociolinguistic significance. Moreover, their corpora are limited, with Rosenbaum focusing on Isa 40–55 and Miller on the Book of Psalms. A more comprehensive examination of the sociolinguistic significance of address terms in poetry remains to be undertaken.

The book, alongside the proposed studies, paves the way for further analysis of terms of reference in the Hebrew Bible. Reference terms can be categorized into two groups: self-reference pointing to the speaker and reference pointing to a third person in dialogue. Understanding the speaker's self-reference is crucial as it not only reflects their self-view but also their perception of the addressee. The presence or absence of a third person may significantly impact how the speaker refers to them. Additionally, certain words are used exclusively as reference terms rather than address terms, analogous to the English term "physician." In the prose sections of the Hebrew Bible, for instance, כלה *kallɔ* "daughter-in-law, bride" exclusively appears as a reference term, while בת *baṯ* "daughter" serves as the corresponding address term (Ruth 1:8, 11). A comparative analysis of address and reference terms would be a captivating area of study that could shed light on the speaker's self-view, their perception of the addressee, and the presence or absence of a third person during the recorded conversation.

APPENDIX A:
TEXT AND TRANSLATION (1 KINGS 22:1–28)

V	Text	Translation
1	וישבו שלש שנים אין מלחמה בין ארם ובין ישראל	There was no war between Aram and Israel for three years.
2	ויהי בשנה השלישית וירד יהושפט מלך יהודה אל מלך ישראל	In the third year Jehoshaphat the king of Judah came down to the king of Israel.
3	ויאמר מלך ישראל אל עבדיו הידעתם כי לנו רמת גלעד ואנחנו מחשים מקחת אתה מיד מלך ארם	The king of Israel said to his servants, "Do you know that Ramoth Gilead is ours, and we keep quiet and do not take it out of the hand of the king of Aram?"
4	ויאמר אל יהושפט התלך אתי למלחמה רמת גלעד ויאמר יהושפט אל מלך ישראל כמוני כמוך כעמי כעמך כסוסי כסוסיך	Then he said to Jehoshaphat, "Will you go with me to battle at Ramoth Gilead?" Jehoshaphat replied to the king of Israel, "I am as you are, my people as your people, my horses as your horses."
5	ויאמר יהושפט אל מלך ישראל דרש נא כיום את דבר יהוה	Jehoshaphat said to the king of Israel, "Please seek first the word of Yahweh."
6	ויקבץ מלך ישראל את הנביאים כארבע מאות איש ויאמר אלהם האלך על רמת גלעד למלחמה אם אחדל ויאמרו עלה ויתן אדני ביד המלך	So the king of Israel assembled the prophets, about four hundred men, and said to them, "Shall I go to battle against Ramoth Gilead, or shall I refrain?" They said, "Go up so that the Lord may give (it) into the hand of the king."
7	ויאמר יהושפט האין פה נביא ליהוה עוד ונדרשה מאותו	But Jehoshaphat said, "Is there not here still a prophet of Yahweh of whom we may ask?"

V	Text	Translation
8	ויאמר מלך ישראל אל יהושפט עוד איש אחד לדרש את יהוה מאתו ואני שנאתיו כי לא יתנבא עלי טוב כי אם רע מיכיהו בן ימלה ויאמר יהושפט אל יאמר המלך כן	The king of Israel said to Jehoshaphat, "There is yet one man by whom we may inquire of Yahweh. But I hate him because he does not prophesy good concerning me, but evil. His name is Micaiah the son of Imlah." Jehoshaphat said, "Let not the king say so."
9	ויקרא מלך ישראל אל סריס אחד ויאמר מהרה מיכיהו בן ימלה	Then the king of Israel summoned an officer and said, "Bring quickly Micaiah the son of Imlah."
10	ומלך ישראל ויהושפט מלך יהודה ישבים איש על כסאו מלבשים בגדים בגרן פתח שער שמרון וכל הנביאים מתנבאים לפניהם	Now the king of Israel and Jehoshaphat the king of Judah were sitting on their thrones, dressed in their robes, at the threshing floor at the entrance of the gate of Samaria. All the prophets were prophesying before them.
11	ויעש לו צדקיה בן כנענה קרני ברזל ויאמר כה אמר יהוה באלה תנגח את ארם עד כלתם	Zedekiah the son of Kenaanah made for himself iron horns and said, "Thus Yahweh says, 'With these you shall push Aram until they are destroyed.'"
12	וכל הנבאים נבאים כן לאמר עלה רמת גלעד והצלח ונתן יהוה ביד המלך	All the prophets were prophesying the same, saying, "Go up to Ramoth Gilead and triumph; Yahweh will give it into the hand of the king."
13	והמלאך אשר הלך לקרא מיכיהו דבר אליו לאמר הנה נא דברי הנביאים פה אחד טוב אל המלך יהי נא דבריך כדבר אחד מהם ודברת טוב	Now the messenger who went to summon Micaiah said to him, "Look, the words of the prophets are unanimously good for the king. Let your word, please, be like the word of one of them, and speak favorably."
14	ויאמר מיכיהו חי יהוה כי את אשר יאמר יהוה אלי אתו אדבר	But Micaiah said, "By the life of Yahweh, I will say what Yahweh says to me."
15	ויבוא אל המלך ויאמר המלך אליו מיכיהו הנלך אל רמת גלעד למלחמה אם נחדל ויאמר אליו עלה והצלח ונתן יהוה ביד המלך	When he came to the king, the king said to him, "Micaiah, shall we go up to Ramoth Gilead to battle or shall we refrain?" He answered him, "Go up and triumph; Yahweh will give (it) into the hand of the king."

Text and Translation (1 Kings 22:1–28)

V	Text	Translation
16	ויאמר אליו המלך עד כמה פעמים אני משבעך אשר לא תדבר אלי רק אמת בשם יהוה	The king said to him, "How many times shall I make you swear that you speak to me nothing but the truth in the name of Yahweh?"
17	ויאמר ראיתי את כל ישראל נפצים אל ההרים כצאן אשר אין להם רעה ויאמר יהוה לא אדנים לאלה ישובו איש לביתו בשלום	He said, "I saw all Israel scattered on the mountains like sheep that have no shepherd. Then Yahweh said, 'These have no master; let each return to his home in peace.'"
18	ויאמר מלך ישראל אל יהושפט הלוא אמרתי אליך לוא יתנבא עלי טוב כי אם רע	The king of Israel said to Jehoshaphat, "Didn't I tell you that he would not prophesy good concerning me, but evil?"
19	יאמר לכן שמע דבר יהוה ראיתי את יהוה ישב על כסאו וכל צבא השמים עמד עליו מימינו ומשמאלו	Micaiah said, "Therefore hear the word of Yahweh: I saw Yahweh sitting on his throne, and all the host of heaven standing beside him on his right and on his left.
20	ויאמר יהוה מי יפתה את אחאב ויעל ויפל ברמת גלעד ויאמר זה בכה וזה אמר בכה	Yahweh said, 'Who will deceive Ahab so that he may go up and fall at Ramoth Gilead?' One said one thing, and another said another.
21	ויצא הרוח ויעמד לפני יהוה ויאמר אני אפתנו ויאמר יהוה אליו במה	Then a spirit came forward and stood before Yahweh. He said, 'I will deceive him.' Yahweh said to him, 'How?'
22	ויאמר אצא והייתי רוח שקר בפי כל נביאיו ויאמר תפתה וגם תוכל צא ועשה כן	He said, 'I will go out, and will be a lying spirit in the mouth of all his prophets.' He said, 'You will deceive, and you will succeed; go out and do so.'
23	ועתה הנה נתן יהוה רוח שקר בפי כל נביאיך אלה ויהוה דבר עליך רעה	So now, look, Yahweh has put a lying spirit in the mouth of all these your prophets; but Yahweh has declared disaster for you."
24	ויגש צדקיהו בן כנענה ויכה את מיכיהו על הלחי ויאמר אי זה עבר רוח יהוה מאתי לדבר אותך	Then Zedekiah the son of Kenaanah approached and hit Micaiah on the cheek and said, "Which way did the Yahweh's spirit go from me to speak to you?"

V	Text	Translation
25	ויאמר מיכיהו הנך ראה ביום ההוא אשר תבא חדר בחדר להחבה	Micaiah said, "Look, you will see on that day when you go into an inner chamber to hide yourself."
26	יאמר מלך ישראל קח את מיכיהו והשיבהו אל אמן שר העיר ואל יואש בן המלך	The king of Israel said, "Seize Micaiah, and take him back to Amon the city official and to Joash the king's son,
27	ואמרת כה אמר המלך שימו את זה בית הכלא והאכילהו לחם לחץ ומים לחץ עד באי בשלום	and say, 'Thus says the king, "Put this man in prison and give him only a little bread and water until I safely return."'"
28	ויאמר מיכיהו אם שוב תשוב בשלום לא דבר יהוה בי ויאמר שמעו עמים כלם	Micaiah said, "If you safely return, Yahweh has not spoken through me." Then he added, "Hear, all you peoples!"

APPENDIX B:
FREE FORMS OF ADDRESS: GRAMMATICAL CLASSIFICATION

1. Simple Addresses
1.1. Definite
1.1.1. Proper Nouns[1]

Address	Verses
אבנר	1 Sam 17:55; 26:14
אברהם	Gen 22:1, 11 (2x)
אברם	Gen 15:1
אבשלום	2 Sam 19:1 (3x), 5 (2x)
אדני	Dan 9:4, 15
אהליבה	Ezek 23:22
אחזיה	2 Kgs 9:23
אחימלך	1 Sam 22:16
אל	Num 12:13; 16:22
אלהים	2 Sam 7:25; 1 Chr 17:16, 17 (2x); 2 Chr 1:9; 6:41 (2x), 42
האלהים	Judg 16:28
אליהו	1 Kgs 18:7; 19:9, 13
אלישע	2 Kgs 2:4
אסא	2 Chr 15:2
אסתר	Esth 5:3; 7:2
הבעל	1 Kgs 18:26
ברוך	Jer 45:2
גבריאל	Dan 8:16
גוג	Ezek 38:3, 16; 39:1
גֵּחֲזִי	2 Kgs 5:25
גִּלְעָד	Judg 12:4
דוד	1 Sam 24:17; 26:17, 21, 25; 1 Kgs 12:16; 2 Chr 10:16
דניאל	Dan 9:22; 10:11, 12; 12:4, 9
הגר	Gen 16:8; 21:17
חנניה	Jer 28:15
יהוא	2 Kgs 9:22

---

[1] This includes common nouns functioning as proper nouns.

יהודה	Jer 11:13; 2 Chr 20:17; 2 Chr 20:20
יהוה	Gen 15:2, 8; 24:12, 42; Exod 32:11; Num 10:35, 36; 14:14 (2x); Deut 3:24; 9:26; 21:8; 26:10; Josh 7:7; Judg 6:22; 16:28; 21:3; 1 Sam 3:9; 23:10, 11; 2 Sam 7:18, 19 (2x), 20, 22, 24, 25, 28, 29; 15:31; 23:17; 24:10; 1 Kgs 3:7; 8:23, 25, 28, 53; 17:20, 21; 18:36, 37 (2x), 19:4; 2 Kgs 6:17, 20; 19:15, 16 (2x), 17, 19 (2x); 20:3; Isa 37:17 (2x), 18, 20; 38:3; Jer 1:6; 4:10; 11:5; 14:13; 32:17, 25; 51:62; Ezek 4:14; 9:8; 11:13; 21:5; 37:3; Amos 7:2, 5; Jonah 1:14 (2x); 4:2, 3; Dan 9:8; Ezra 9:15; Neh 1:5; 1 Chr 17:16, 17, 19, 20, 22, 23, 26, 27; 21:17; 29:10, 11 (2x), 16, 18; 2 Chr 1:9; 6:14, 16, 17, 19, 41 (2x), 42; 14:10 (3x); 20:6
יהושפט	2 Chr 20:15
יונתן	1 Sam 14:44
יעקב	Gen 31:11; Gen 46:2 (2x)
ירבעם	2 Chr 13:4
ירושלם	2 Chr 20:17
ירמיהו	Jer 1:11; 24:3
ישראל	Exod 32:4, 8; Deut 4:1; 5:1; 6:3, 4; 9:1; 10:12; 20:3; 27:9; Josh 7:13; 1 Kgs 12:16, 28; Ezek 13:4; 2 Chr 10:16
מואב	2 Kgs 3:23
מיכה	2 Chr 18:14
מיכיהו	1 Kgs 22:15
מפיבשת	2 Sam 9:6; 19:26
משה	Exod 3:4 (2x); Num 11:28
עזיהו	2 Chr 26:18
עמוס	Amos 7:8; 8:2
עשהאל	2 Sam 2:20
פשחור	Jer 20:6
צדקיהו	Jer 34:4
צידון	Ezek 28:22
צר	Ezek 26:3
קרח	Num 16:6
השטן	Zech 3:2
שלמה	1 Chr 28:9
שמואל	1 Sam 3:6, 10 (2x), 16
שמשון	Judg 16:9, 12, 14, 20

1.1.2. *Common Nouns with a Pronominal Suffix*

אבי	Gen 22:7; 27:18, 34, 38 (2x); 48:18; Judg 11:36; 1 Sam 24:12; 2 Kgs 2:12 (2x); 5:13; 6:21; 13:14 (2x); Isa 8:4
אדני	Gen 23:6, 11, 15; 24:18; 42:10, 20; 44:18; Num 11:28; 12:11; Judg 4:18; 6:13; 1 Sam 1:15, 26 (2x); 22:12; 24:9; 25:24, 26; 26:17; 2 Sam 14:9, 19, 22; 16:4; 19:27; 1 Kgs 1:13, 17, 18, 20, 24; 3:17, 26; 18:7; 20:4; 2 Kgs 4:16; 6:5, 12, 15, 26; 8:5; Jer 37:20; 38:9; Zech 1:9; 4:4, 5, 13; 6:4; Ruth 2:13; Dan 10:16; 12:8; 1 Chr 21:3
אדני	Gen 19:2, 18

FREE FORMS OF ADDRESS: GRAMMATICAL CLASSIFICATION 183

אדני	Gen 15:2, 8; 18:3; 20:4; Exod 4:10, 13; 5:22; 34:9; Deut 3:24; 9:26; Josh 7:7, 8; Judg 6:15, 22; 13:8; 16:28; 2 Sam 7:18, 19 (2x), 20, 22, 28, 29; 1 Kgs 8:53; Jer 1:6; 4:10; 14:13; 32:17, 25; Ezek 4:14; 9:8; 11:13; 21:5; 37:3; Amos 7:2, 5; Dan 9:7, 16, 19 (3x); Neh 1:11
אחותי	2 Sam 13:11, 20
אחי	Gen 33:9; 2 Sam 13:12; 20:9; 1 Kgs 9:13; 13:30
אחי	Gen 19:7; 29:4; Judg 19:23; 1 Sam 30:23; 1 Chr 28:2
איבי	1 Kgs 21:20
אלהי	1 Kgs 3:7; 8:28; 17:20, 21; Dan 9:18, 19; Ezra 9:6 (2x); Neh 5:19; 6:14; 13:14, 22, 29, 31; 1 Chr 21:17; 29:17; 2 Chr 6:19, 40
אלהינו	2 Kgs 19:19; Isa 37:20; Dan 9:17; Ezra 9:10, 13; Neh 3:36; 1 Chr 29:13, 16; 2 Chr 14:10; 20:7, 12
אמי	1 Kgs 2:20; Isa 8:4
בני	Gen 22:7, 8; 27:1, 8, 13, 18, 20, 21, 26, 37, 43; 43:29; 48:19; Josh 7:19; 1 Sam 3:6, 16; 4:16; 24:17; 26:17, 21, 25; 2 Sam 13:25; 18:22; 19:1 (5x); 2 Sam 19:5 (3x); 1 Chr 22:11; 28:9
בני	1 Sam 2:24; 2 Chr 29:11
בנתי	Ruth 1:11, 12, 13
בתי	Judg 11:35; Ruth 2:2, 8, 22; 3:1, 10, 11, 16, 18
כלכם	Judg 20:7
כלם	1 Kgs 22:28; 2 Chr 18:27
עמי	Ezek 37:12, 13; 1 Chr 28:2
צאני	Ezek 34:17

1.1.3. Common Nouns/Adjectives/Participles with the Definite Article

המלך	Judg 3:19; 1 Sam 17:55, 58; 23:20; 24:9; 26:17, 22; 2 Sam 14:4, 9, 19, 22; 15:34; 16:4; 19:27; 24:23; 1 Kgs 1:13, 18, 20, 24; 20:4; 2 Kgs 6:12, 26; 8:5; Jer 37:20; 38:9; Esth 7:3; 1 Chr 21:3; 2 Chr 20:15; 25:7
המלכה	Esth 5:3; 7:2
המרים	Num 20:10
הלוים	2 Chr 29:5
הרוח	Ezek 37:9
הרעים	Ezek 34:9
השר	2 Kgs 9:5 (2x)

1.2. Common Nouns/Adjectives/Participles without the Definite Article

אדון	Jer 34:5
זונה	Ezek 16:35
חזה	Amos 7:12
מזבח	1 Kgs 13:2 (2x)
עמים	1 Kgs 22:28; 2 Chr 18:27
פלשתים	1 Sam 4:9
קרח	2 Kgs 2:23 (2x)
רעים	Ezek 34:7
רשע	Ezek 33:8

2. Complex Addresses

2.1. Construct Phrases

2.1.1. Definite Construct Phrases

2.1.1.1. Common Noun + Proper Noun

אלהי ישראל	Judg 21:3; 1 Sam 23:10, 11; 2 Sam 7:27; 1 Kgs 8:23, 25, 26; Ezra 9:15; 2 Chr 6:14, 16, 17
אשת ירבעם	1 Kgs 14:6
בית ישראל	Jer 10:1; 18:6 (2x); Ezek 11:5; 18:25, 29, 30, 31; 20:31, 39, 44; 33:11, 20; 36:22, 32; 44:6; Amos 3:1; 5:1
בן אחיטוב	1 Sam 22:12
בני ישראל	Judg 20:7; Isa 31:6; 2 Chr 13:12; 30:6
בני לוי	Num 16:7, 8
בני צרויה	2 Sam 16:10; 19:23
בעלי שכם	Judg 9:7
הרי ישראל	Ezek 36:1, 4, 8
כל יהודה	2 Chr 20:15
כל יהודה ובנימן	2 Chr 15:2 (2x)[2]
כל ישראל	2 Chr 13:4
מלך יהודה	Jer 34:4; 2 Chr 35:21
מלכי יהודה	Jer 19:3
נשיאי ישראל	Ezek 45:9
שארית יהודה	Jer 42:15, 19
שפחת שרי	Gen 16:8

2.1.1.2. Common Noun + Common Noun with a Pronominal Suffix

כל עדתו	Num 16:6
אלהי אבתינו	2 Chr 20:6

2.1.1.3. Common Noun + Common Noun with the Definite Article

איש האלהים	1 Kgs 17:18; 2 Kgs 1:9, 11, 13; 4:16, 40
איש הבליעל	2 Sam 16:7
איש הדמים	2 Sam 16:7
אלהי השמים	Neh 1:5
בית המרי	Ezek 12:25
בן המלך	2 Sam 13:4

---

[2] Note that a construct chain *kɔl-yəhuḏɔ uḇinyɔmin* "all Judah and (all) Benjamin" in 2 Chr 15:2 is counted as two addresses, as Judah and Benjamin are two different addressees. The construct noun *kɔl* "all" governs two conjoined nouns, *yəhuḏɔ uḇinyɔmin* "Judah and Benjamin" (*IBHS* §9.3b; *BHRG*² §25.3.1b).

2.1.1.4. *Adjective + Common Noun with the Definite Article*

גבור החיל   Judg 6:12

2.1.1.5. *Participle + Proper Noun*

ברוך יהוה   Gen 24:31
עכר ישראל   1 Kgs 18:17
ישבי ירושלם   Jer 19:3; 2 Chr 20:15, 20

2.1.1.6. *Participle + Common Noun with a Pronominal Suffix*

הרג אדניו   2 Kgs 9:31

2.1.1.7. *Proper Noun + Common Noun*

יהוה צבאות   1 Sam 1:11; 2 Sam 7:27; Isa 37:16; Zech 1:12

2.1.1.8. *Common Noun + Participle + Common Noun with the Definite Article*

בן נעות המרדות   1 Sam 20:30

2.1.1.9. *Common Noun + Proper Noun + Proper Noun + waw + Proper Noun*

אלהי אברהם יצחק וישראל   1 Kgs 18:36

2.1.1.10. *Common Noun + Common Noun + Proper Noun + waw + Proper Noun*

נשיא ראש משך ותבל   Ezek 38:3; 39:1[3]

2.1.2. *Construct Phrases with an Anarthrous Nomen Rectum*

איש חמדות   Dan 10:11, 19
חלל רשע   Ezek 21:30[4]
בן אדם   Ezek 2:1, 3, 6, 8; 3:1, 3, 4, 10, 17, 25; 4:1, 16; 5:1; 6:2; 7:2; 8:5, 6, 8, 12, 15, 17; 11:2, 4, 15; 12:2, 3, 9, 18, 22, 27; 13:2, 17; 14:3, 13; 15:2; 16:2; 17:2; 20:3, 4, 27; 21:2, 7, 11, 14, 24, 33; 22:2, 18, 24; 23:2, 36; 24:2, 16, 25; 25:2; 26:2; 27:2; 28:2, 12, 21; 29:2, 18; 30:2, 21; 31:2; 32:2, 18; 33:2, 7, 10, 12, 24, 30; 34:2; 35:2; 36:1, 17; 37:3, 9, 11, 16; 38:2, 14; 39:1, 17; 40:4; 43:7, 10, 18; 44:5; 47:6; Dan 8:17

---

[3] Note that אלהי אברהם יצחק וישראל *ʔlohe ʔaḇrɔhɔm yiṣḥɔq wyiśrɔʔel* "God of Abraham, Isaac, and Israel" in 1 Kgs 18:36 has three coordinated absolute forms, while נשיא ראש משך ותבל *nśiʔ roʔš mešeḵ wṯuḇɔl* "chief prince of Meshech and Tubal" in Ezek 38:3 (=39:1) has two.

[4] I view this expression as a construct phrase, following *BHS*'s repointing *ḥalal rešaʕ*. This may be supported by the fact that two adjectives in apposition are rare in Biblical Hebrew and that there is a corresponding plural construct phrase *ḥalle ršɔʕim* in Ezek 21:34.

2.2. Definite Construct Phrase + waw + Definite Noun Phrase

רכב ישראל ופרשיו   2 Kgs 2:12; 13:14

2.3. Definite Construct Phrase + Definite Noun Phrase Appositional to the Nomen Rectum

אלהי אבי אברהם	Gen 32:10
אלהי אבי יצחק	Gen 32:10
אלהי אברהם יצחק וישראל אבתינו	1 Chr 29:18
אלהי אדני אברהם	Gen 24:12, 42
אלהי ישראל אבינו	1 Chr 29:10

2.4. Noun Phrase + Modifier

2.4.1. Definite Noun Phrase + Modifier

2.4.1.1. Construct Phrase + Relative Clause

כל הגולה אשר שלחתי מירושלם בבלה	Jer 29:20
כל יהודה אשר בארץ מצרים	Jer 44:24
נשיא ישראל אשר בא יומו בעת עון קץ	Ezek 21:30
רעי ישראל אשר היו רעים אותם	Ezek 34:2
כל יהודה הבאים בשערים האלה להשתחות ליהוה	Jer 7:2
מלכי יהודה (הבאים בשערים האלה)	Jer 17:20[5]
כל יהודה (הבאים בשערים האלה)	Jer 17:20
כל ישבי ירושלם הבאים בשערים האלה	Jer 17:20
מלך יהודה הישב על כסא דוד	Jer 22:2
כל יהודה הישבים בארץ מצרים	Jer 44:26
אלהי ישראל ישב הכרבים	2 Kgs 19:15; Isa 37:16

2.4.1.2. Construct Phrase + Prepositional Phrase

אלהי הרוחת לכל בשר	Num 16:22

2.4.1.3. Common Noun + Relative Clause

אלהינו אשר הוצאת את עמך מארץ מצרים ביד חזקה ותעש לך שם כיום הזה	Dan 9:15
עמי ישב ציון	Isa 10:24
האל הגדול והנורא שמר הברית והחסד לאהביו ולשמרי מצותיו	Dan 9:4; Neh 1:5

---

[5] Note that Jer 17:20 contains three conjoined address forms referring to three different addressees. The first two address forms are modified by a ה-relative clause which comes after the third address form. Thus, the ה-relative clause that modifies the first two address forms is put in parenthesis.

2.4.1.4. Common Noun + Adjective

הר הגדול	Zech 4:7[6]
העצמות היבשות	Ezek 37:4

2.4.1.5. Proper Noun + Relative Clause

יהוה האמר אלי שוב לארצך ולמולדתך ואיטיבה עמך	Gen 32:10

2.4.2. Anarthrous Noun Phrase + Modifier

2.4.2.1. Common Noun + Relative Clause

כרוב הסכך	Ezek 28:16
עיר שפכת דם בתוכה לבוא עתה ועשתה גלולים עליה לטמאה	Ezek 22:3
רעים מאבדים ומפצים את צאן מרעיתי	Jer 23:1[7]

2.4.2.2. Common Noun + Adjective

בנים שובבים	Jer 3:14

3. Compound Addresses

3.1. Apposition

3.1.1. Simple + Simple[8]

אסתר המלכה	Esth 5:3; 7:2
יהוה אלהי	1 Kgs 3:7; 8:28; 17:20, 21; 1 Chr 21:17; 2 Chr 6:19
יהוה אלהים	2 Sam 7:25; 1 Chr 17:16, 17; 2 Chr 1:9; 6:41 (2x), 42
יהוה אלהינו	2 Kgs 19:19; Isa 37:20; 1 Chr 29:16; 2 Chr 14:10
שלמה בני	1 Chr 28:9
שמואל בני	1 Sam 3:16
אדני אליהו	1 Kgs 18:7
אדני המלך	1 Sam 24:9; 26:17; 2 Sam 14:9, 19, 22; 16:4; 19:27; 1 Kgs 1:13, 18, 20, 24; 20:4; 2 Kgs 6:12, 26; 8:5; Jer 37:20; 38:9; 1 Chr 21:3
אדני יהוה	Gen 15:2, 8
אדני יהוה	Deut 3:24; 9:26; Josh 7:7; Judg 6:22; 16:28; 2 Sam 7:18, 19 (2x), 20, 22, 28, 29; 1 Kgs 8:53; Jer 1:6; 4:10; 14:13; 32:17, 25; Ezek 4:14; 9:8; 11:13; 21:5; 37:3; Amos 7:2, 5
אדני משה	Num 11:28
בני דוד	1 Sam 24:17; 26:17, 21, 25

---

[6] I follow *BHS* and repoint *ʔattɔ hɔhɔr-haggɔḏol* to fix the problem of mismatch in definiteness between *hɔr* and *haggɔḏol*.

[7] For a defense of viewing what follows after הוי *hoy* "woe" as a form of address in Jer 23:1, see Hillers 1983, 185–88.

[8] Arranged according to what comes as the head: proper noun, common noun with a pronominal suffix, and common noun.

המלך יהושפט	2 Chr 20:15
עמים כלם	1 Kgs 22:28; 2 Chr 18:27

3.1.2. Simple + Complex[9]

אל אלהי הרוחת לכל בשר	Num 16:22
גוג נשיא ראש משך ותבל	Ezek 38:3; 39:1
דניאל איש חמדות	Dan 10:11
הגר שפחת שרי	Gen 16:8
יהוה אלהי אברהם יצחק וישראל	1 Kgs 18:36
יהוה אלהי אברהם יצחק וישראל אבתינו	1 Chr 29:18
יהוה אלהי אבתינו	2 Chr 20:6
יהוה אלהי אדני אברהם	Gen 24:12, 42
יהוה אלהי ישראל	Judg 21:3; 1 Sam 23:10,11; 1 Kgs 8:23, 25; Ezra 9:15; 2 Chr 6:14, 16, 17
יהוה אלהי ישראל אבינו	1 Chr 29:10
יהוה אלהי ישראל ישב הכרבים	2 Kgs 19:15
זמרי הרג אדניו	2 Kgs 9:31
צדקיהו מלך יהודה	Jer 34:4
אדני איש האלהים	2 Kgs 4:16
אדני אלהינו אשר הוצאת את עמך מארץ מצרים ביד חזקה ותעש לך שם כיום הזה	Dan 9:15
אדני האל הגדול והנורא שמר הברית והחסד לאהביו ולשמרי מצותיו	Dan 9:4
כלכם בני ישראל	Judg 20:7

3.1.3. Complex + Complex[10]

יהוה צבאות אלהי ישראל	2 Sam 7:27
הוה צבאות אלהי ישראל ישב הכרבים	Isa 37:16
חלל רשע נשיא ישראל אשר בא יומו בעת עון קץ	Ezek 21:30

3.1.4. Simple + Complex + Complex

יהוה אלהי השמים האל הגדול והנורא שמר הברית וחסד לאהביו ולשמרי מצותיו	Neh 1:5

3.2. Repetition

3.2.1. Simple + Simple[11]

אברהם אברהם	Gen 22:11
יעקב יעקב	Gen 46:2
משה משה	Exod 3:4

---

[9] Arranged according to what comes as the head: proper noun and common noun with a pronominal suffix.
[10] Arranged according to what comes as the head: proper noun, common noun, and adjective.
[11] Arranged according to what comes as the head: proper noun and common noun.

שמואל שמואל	1 Sam 3:10
מזבח מזבח	1 Kgs 13:2

3.2.2. *Simple + Simple + Simple + Simple + Simple*

בני אבשלום אבשלום בני בני	2 Sam 19:5
בני אבשלום בני בני אבשלום	2 Sam 19:1

3.2.3. *Simple + Simple + Simple/Complex*

אבי אבי רכב ישראל ופרשיו	2 Kgs 2:12; 13:14
אבשלום בני בני	2 Sam 19:1

3.3. Coordination

3.3.1. *Simple/Complex + waw + Simple/Complex*

איש הדמים ואיש הבליעל	2 Sam 16:7
אחי ועמי	1 Chr 28:2[12]

3.3.2 *Complex + waw + Complex + Simple*

אלהי אבי אברהם ואלהי אבי יצחק יהוה האמר אלי שוב לארצך ולמולדתך ואיטיבה עמך	Gen 32:10

---

[12] It is my view that both *ʔaḥay* "my brothers" and *ʕammi* "my people" in 1 Chr 28:2 refer to *kol-śɔre yiśrɔʔel* "all the officials of Israel" who gathered before David in Jerusalem in 1 Chr 28:1.

APPENDIX C:[1]
FREE FORMS OF ADDRESS: SEMANTIC CLASSIFICATION

1. *Addresses to Animate Beings*

1.1. *Humans*

1.1.1. *Simple/Complex Addresses Alone*

1.1.1.1. *PN*

אבנר	1 Sam 17:55; 26:14
אברם	Gen 15:1
אברהם	Gen 22:1
אהליבה	Ezek 23:22
אחזיה	2 Kgs 9:23
אחימלך	1 Sam 22:16
אליהו	1 Kgs 19:9, 13
אלישע	2 Kgs 2:4
אסא	2 Chr 15:2
ברוך	Jer 45:2
גוג	Ezek 38:16
גחזי	2 Kgs 5:25
גלעד	Judg 12:4
דוד	1 Kgs 12:16; 2 Chr 10:16
דניאל	Dan 9:22; 10:12; 12:4, 9
הגר	Gen 21:17
חנה	1 Sam 1:8
חנניה	Jer 28:15
יהוא	2 Kgs 9:22

---

[1] Abbreviations used in this appendix include the following: PN = personal name; KT = kinship term; T = title; GA = group address; ET = evaluative term; GN = geographical name.

יהודה	Jer 11:13; 2 Chr 20:17, 20
יונתן	1 Sam 14:44
יעקב	Gen 31:11
ירבעם	2 Chr 13:4
ירמיהו	Jer 1:11; 24:3
ישראל	Exod 32:4, 8; Deut 4:1; 5:1; 6:3, 4; 9:1; 10:12; 20:3; 27:9; Josh 7:13; 1 Kgs 12:16, 28; Ezek 13:4; 2 Chr 10:16
מואב	2 Kgs 3:23
מיכה	2 Chr 18:14
מיכיהו	1 Kgs 22:15
מפיבשת	2 Sam 9:6; 19:26
עזיהו	2 Chr 26:18
עמוס	Amos 7:8; 8:2
עשהאל	2 Sam 2:20
פשחור	Jer 20:6
קרח	Num 16:6
שמואל	1 Sam 3:6
שמשון	Judg 16:9, 12, 14, 20

1.1.1.2. KT

אבי	Gen 22:7; 27:18, 34, 38 (2x); 48:18; Judg 11:36; 1 Sam 24:12; 2 Kgs 5:13; 6:21; Isa 8:4
אחותי	2 Sam 13:11, 20
אחי	Gen 33:9; 2 Sam 13:12; 20:9; 1 Kgs 9:13; 13:30
אחי	Gen 19:7; 29:4; Judg 19:23; 1 Sam 30:23
אמי	1 Kgs 2:20; Isa 8:4
בני	Gen 22:7, 8; 27:1, 8, 13, 18, 20, 21, 26, 37, 43; 43:29; 48:19; Josh 7:19; 1 Sam 3:6; 4:16; 2 Sam 13:25; 18:22; 1 Chr 22:11
בני	1 Sam 2:24; 2 Chr 29:11
בנתי	Ruth 1:11, 12, 13
בתי	Judg 11:35; Ruth 2:2, 8, 22; Ruth 3:1, 10, 11, 16, 18

1.1.1.3. T

אדני	Gen 23:6, 11, 15, 18; 42:10; 43:20; 44:18; Num 12:11; Judg 4:18; 1 Sam 1:15, 26 (2x); 22:12; 25:24, 26; 1 Kgs 1:17; 3:17, 26; 2 Kgs 6:5, 15; Ruth 2:13
אדון	Jer 34:5
איש האלהים	1 Kgs 17:18; 2 Kgs 1:9, 11, 13; 4:40
בן המלך	2 Sam 13:4

חזה	Amos 7:12
מלך יהודה	2 Chr 35:21
מלך יהודה הישב על כסא דוד	Jer 22:2
מלכי יהודה	Jer 19:3
מלכי יהודה (הבאים בשערים האלה)	Jer 17:20
המלך	Judg 3:19; 1 Sam 17:55; 23:20; 26:22; 2 Sam 14:4; 15:34; 24:23; Esth 7:3; 2 Chr 25:7
נשיאי ישראל	Ezek 45:9
רעי ישראל אשר היו רעים אותם	Ezek 34:2
רעים	Ezek 34:7
רעים מאבדים ומפצים את צאן מרעיתי	Jer 23:1
הרעים	Ezek 34:9
השר	2 Kgs 9:5 (2x)

1.1.1.4 GA

בית ישראל	Jer 10:1; Ezek 11:5; 18:25, 29, 30, 31; 20:31, 39, 44; 33:11, 20; 36:22, 32; 44:6; Amos 3:1; 5:1
בנימן	2 Chr 15:2
בעלי שכם	Judg 9:7
ישבי ירושלם	Jer 19:3; 2 Chr 20:15, 20
כל הגולה אשר שלחתי מירושלם בבלה	Jer 29:20
כל יהודה	2 Chr 15:2; 20:15
כל יהודה הבאים בשערים האלה להשתחות ליהוה	Jer 7:2; 18:6 (2x)
כל ישבי ירושלם הבאים בשערים האלה	Jer 17:20
כל יהודה אשר בארץ מצרים	Jer 44:24
כל יהודה הישבים בארץ מצרים	Jer 44:26
כל ישראל	2 Chr 13:4
כל ישבי ירושלם הבאים בשערים האלה	Jer 17:20
כל עדתו	Num 16:6
עמי	Ezek 37:12, 13
עמי ישב ציון	Isa 10:24
צאני	Ezek 34:17
שארית יהודה	Jer 42:15, 19

1.1.1.5. ET

איבי	1 Kgs 21:20
איש חמדות	Dan 10:19
בית המרי	Ezek 12:25
בנים שובבים	Jer 3:14
בן נעות המרדות	1 Sam 20:30
ברוך יהוה	Gen 24:31

גבור החיל	Judg 6:12
זונה	Ezek 16:35
המרים	Num 20:10
עכר ישראל	1 Kgs 18:17
קרח	2 Kgs 2:23 (2x)
רשע	Ezek 33:8

1.1.1.6. *P/Matro/Andronymics*

אשת ירבעם	1 Kgs 14:6
בן אחיטוב	1 Sam 22:12
בני ישראל	Isa 31:6; 2 Chr 13:12; 30:6
בני לוי	Num 16:7, 8
בני צריה	2 Sam 16:10; 19:23
בן אדם	Ezek 2:1, 3, 6, 8; 3:1, 3, 4, 10, 17, 25; 4:1, 16; 5:1; 6:2; 7:2; 8:5, 6, 8, 12, 15, 17; 11:2, 4, 15; 12:2, 3, 9, 18, 22, 27; 13:2, 17; 14:3, 13; 15:2; 16:2; 17:2; 20:3, 4, 27; 21:2, 7, 11, 14, 24, 33; 22:2, 18, 24; 23:2, 36; 24:2, 16, 25; 25:2; 26:2; 27:2; 28:2, 12, 21; 29:2, 18; 30:2, 21; 31:2; 32:2, 18; 33:2, 7, 10, 12, 24, 30; 34:2; 35:2; 36:1, 17; 37:3, 9, 11, 16; 38:2, 14; 39:1, 17; 40:4; 43:7, 10, 18; 44:5; 47:6; Dan 8:17

1.1.1.7. *GN*

ירושלם	2 Chr 20:17
צר	Ezek 26:3
צידון	Ezek 28:22

1.1.1.8. *Gentilic*

פלשתים	1 Sam 4:9
הלוים	2 Chr 29:5

1.1.1.9. *Other*

הנער	1 Sam 17:58
כרוב הסכך	Ezek 28:16

1.1.2. *Compound Addresses*

1.1.2.1. *Honorific T + Occupational T*

אדני המלך	1 Sam 24:9; 26:17; 2 Sam 14:9, 19, 22; 16:4; 19:27; 1 Kgs 1:13, 18, 20, 24; 20:4; 2 Kgs 6:12, 26; 8:5; Jer 37:20; 38:9; 1 Chr 21:3
אדני איש האלהים	2 Kgs 4:16

Free Forms of Address: Semantic Classification

1.1.2.2. Honorific T + PN

אדני משה	Num 11:28
אדני אליהו	1 Kgs 18:7

1.1.2.3. Occupational T + PN

המלך יהושפט	2 Chr 20:15

1.1.2.4. PN + Occupational T

אסתר המלכה	Esth 5:3; 7:2
גוג נשיא ראש משך ותבל	Ezek 38:3; 39:1
הגר שפחת שרי	Gen 16:8
צדקיהו מלך יהודה	Jer 34:4

1.1.2.5. PN + PN

אברהם אברהם	Gen 22:11
יעקב יעקב	Gen 46:2
משה משה	Exod 3:4
שמואל שמואל	1 Sam 3:10

1.1.2.6. PN + KT

שלמה בני	1 Chr 28:9
שמואל בני	1 Sam 3:16

1.1.2.7. PN + ET

דניאל איש חמדות	Dan 10:11
זמרי הרג אדניו	2 Kgs 9:31

1.1.2.8. PN + KT + KT

אבשלום בני בני	2 Sam 19:1

1.1.2.9. KT + PN

בני דוד	1 Sam 24:17; 26:17, 21, 25

1.1.2.10. KT + KT + Other T

אבי אבי רכב ישראל ופרשיו	2 Kgs 2:12; 13:14

1.1.2.11. KT + GA

אחי ועמי	1 Chr 28:2

1.1.2.12. KT + PN + KT + KT + PN

בני אבשלום בני בני אבשלום	2 Sam 19:1

1.1.2.13. *KT + PN + KT + KT + PN*

בני אבשלום אבשלום בני בני   2 Sam 19:5

1.1.2.14. *ET + ET*

איש הדמים ואיש הבליעל   2 Sam 16:7

1.1.2.15. *ET + Occupational T*

חלל רשע נשיא ישראל אשר בא יומו בעת עון קץ   Ezek 21:30

1.1.2.16. *GA + GA*

עמים כלם   1 Kgs 22:28; 2 Chr 18:27

1.1.2.17. *GA + Patronymic*

כלכם בני ישראל   Judg 20:7

1.2. *Divine Beings*

1.2.1. *Simple/Complex Addresses Alone*

1.2.1.1. *PN*

1.2.1.1.1. *God*

אל	Num 12:13[2]
אלהים	1 Chr 17:17
האלהים	Judg 16:28
יהוה צבאות	1 Sam 1:11; Zech 1:12
יהוה	Exod 32:11; Num 10:35, 36; 14:14 (2x); Deut 21:8; 26:10; 1 Sam 3:9; 2 Sam 7:24; 15:31; 23:17; 24:10; 1 Kgs 18:37 (2x); 19:4; 2 Kgs 6:17, 20; 19:16 (2x), 17, 19; 20:3; Isa 37:17 (2x), 18; 38:3; Jer 11:5; Jer 51:62; Jonah 1:14 (2x); 4:2, 3; Dan 9:8; 1 Chr 17:19, 20, 22, 23, 26, 27; 29:11 (2x); 2 Chr 14:10 (2x)

1.2.1.1.2. *Messenger of God*

גבריאל   Dan 8:16

1.2.1.1.3. *Baal*

הבעל   1 Kgs 18:26

---

[2] Note that the reading *ʔel* in this verse is uncertain. The *BHS* editors suggest the vocalization *ʔal* "not" instead.

1.2.1.1.4. Satan

השטן	Zech 3:2

1.2.1.2. T

1.2.1.2.1. Divine T

אלהי	Dan 9:18, 19; Ezra 9:6 (2x); Neh 5:19; 6:14; 13:14, 22, 29, 31; 1 Chr 29:17; 2 Chr 6:40
אלהי ישראל	1 Kgs 8:26
אלהינו	Dan 9:17; Ezra 9:10, 13; Neh 3:36; 1 Chr 29:13; 2 Chr 20:7, 12

1.2.1.2.2. Honorific T (God)

אדני	Gen 18:3; 20:4; Exod 4:10, 13; 5:22; 34:9; Josh 7:8; Judg 6:15; 13:8; Dan 9:7, 16, 19 (3x); Neh 1:11
אדני	Dan 10:16; 12:8

1.2.1.2.3. Honorific T (Messenger[s] of God)

אדני	Gen 19:2, 18
אדני	Judg 6:13; Zech 1:9; 4:4, 5, 13; 6:4

1.2.2. Compound Addresses

1.2.2.1. PN + Divine T

אדני אלהינו אשר הוצאת את עמך מארץ מצרים ביד חזקה ותעש לך שם כיום הזה	Dan 9:15
אדני האל הגדול והנורא שמר הברית והחסד לאהביו ולשמרי מצותיו	Dan 9:4
אל אלהי הרוחת לכל בשר	Num 16:22
יהוה אלהי	1 Kgs 3:7; 8:28; 17:20, 21; 1 Chr 21:17; 2 Chr 6:19
יהוה אלהי אברהם יצחק וישראל	1 Kgs 18:36
יהוה אלהי אברהם יצחק וישראל אבתינו	1 Chr 29:18
יהוה אלהי אבתינו	2 Chr 20:6
יהוה אלהי אדני אברהם	Gen 24:12, 42
יהוה אלהי ישראל	Judg 21:3; 1 Sam 23:10, 11; 1 Kgs 8:23, 25; Ezra 9:15; 2 Chr 6:14, 16, 17
יהוה אלהי ישראל אבינו	1 Chr 29:10
יהוה אלהי ישראל ישב הכרבים	2 Kgs 19:15
יהוה אלהינו	2 Kgs 19:19; Isa 37:20; 1 Chr 29:16; 2 Chr 14:10
יהוה צבאות אלהי ישראל	2 Sam 7:27
יהוה צבאות אלהי ישראל ישב הכרבים	Isa 37:16

1.2.2.2. *PN + PN*

יהוה אלהים   2 Sam 7:25; 1 Chr 17:16, 17; 2 Chr 1:9; 6:41 (2x), 42

1.2.2.3. *PN + Divine T + Divine T*

יהוה אלהי השמים האל הגדול והנורא   Neh 1:5
שמר הברית וחסד לאהביו ולשמרי
מצותיו

1.2.2.4. *Honorific T + PN*

אדני יהוה   Gen 15:2, 8; Deut 3:24; 9:26; Josh 7:7; Judg 6:22; 16:28; 2 Sam 7:18, 19 (2x), 20, 22, 28, 29; 1 Kgs 8:53; Jer 1:6; 4:10; 14:13; 32:17, 25; Ezek 4:14; 9:8; 11:13; 21:5; 37:3; Amos 7:2, 5

1.2.2.5. *Divine T + Divine T + PN*

אלהי אבי אברהם ואלהי אבי יצחק יהוה   Gen 32:10
האמר אלי שוב לארצך ולמולדתך
ואיטיבה עמך

2. *Addresses to Inanimate Objects*

2.1. *Simple/Complex Addresses Alone*

הר הגדול	Zech 4:7
הרי ישראל	Ezek 36:1, 4, 8
עיר שפכת דם בתוכה לבוא עתה ועשתה גלולים עליה לטמאה	Ezek 22:3
העצמות היבשות	Ezek 37:4
הרוח	Ezek 37:9

2.2 *Compound Addresses*

מזבח מזבח   1 Kgs 13:2

APPENDIX D:
INDIRECT ADDRESSES: SEMANTIC CLASSIFICATION

1. *Honorific T*

אדני   Gen 31:35; 32:6; 33:8, 13, 14 (2x), 15; 44:7, 9, 16 (2x), 18, 19, 20, 22, 24, 33; 47:18 (3x), 25; Exod 32:22; Num 32:25, 27; Num 36:2 (2x); 1 Sam 16:16; 25:25 (2x), 26, 27 (2x), 28 (2x), 29, 30, 31 (3x), 41; 26:18; 2 Sam 1:10; 11:11; 13:32; 14:20; 19:20; 1 Kgs 18:13; 2 Kgs 2:19; 4:28; 8:12; 1 Chr 21:3 (2x); 2 Chr 2:14; Arad 21:3, 4; 26:2; 26:4; 40:6, 10; Lach 2:2, 4, 5–6; 3:3, 6, 8, 21; 4:1, 2, 4–5, 12; 5:1, 7; 6:2, 3, 8; 8:1, 7; 9:1–2; 12:1, 6; 17:2, 3; 18:2; KAjr 19A.9–10

2. *Honorific T + Occupational T*

אדני המלך   1 Sam 26:19; 29:8; 2 Sam 3:21; 4:8; 9:11; 13:33; 14:12, 17, 18, 19; 15:15, 21 (2x); 16:9; 18:28, 31, 32; 19:20, 21, 28 (2x); 29, 31, 36, 38; 24:3 (2x); 21, 22; 1 Kgs 1:2 (2x); 20, 21, 27 (2x), 36, 37; 2:38; 1 Chr 21:23

אדני השר   MHsh 1; Mous 2:2

3. *Honorific T + Occupational T + PN*

אדני המלך דוד   1 Kgs 1:31, 37

4. *Honorific T + PN*

לאדני לעשו   Gen 32:19
אֹדֹנִי יאוש   Lach 3:2

5. *Occupational T*

המלך   1 Sam 10:24; 19:4; 22:14, 15; 23:20; 24:15; 26:20; 2 Sam 6:20; 11:24; 13:24, 30, 32, 33, 35; 14:9, 11, 13 (2x), 22; 16:2, 16 (3x); 18:29; 19:20, 29, 35, 37 (2x), 42; 24:23; 1 Kgs 1:2, 19, 25; 22:6, 8, 12, 15; 2 Kgs 11:12; Esth 1:16, 18, 19 (2x), 20; 2:2, 3 (2x), 4; 3:8 (2x), 9 (2x); 5:4 (2x), 8 (4x); 6:7, 8 (2x); 9 (2x); 7:3, 4, 9; 8:5 (3x); 9:13; Neh 2:3, 5, 7, 8; 2 Chr 18:5, 7, 11; 23:11

6. Occupational T + Honorific T

| המלך אדני | 2 Sam 14:15 |

7. Occupational T + PN

| המלך שלמה | 1 Kgs 1:51 |
| המלך אחשורוש | Esth 1:16, 19 |

8. Other T

| פרעה | Gen 41:10, 16, 25 (2x), 28 (2x), 32, 33, 34, 35; Exod 8:25 (2x); 11:5 |
| משיח יהוה | 1 Sam 26:23; 2 Sam 19:22 |

9. PN

דוד	1 Sam 20:12, 15; 2 Sam 19:42
ירבעם	1 Kgs 14:10 (3x), 11
בעשא	1 Kgs 16:3, 4
אחאב	1 Kgs 21:21, 24
אלישב	Arad 16:2
מלכיהו	Arad 40:3

10. PN + Patronymic

| גדליהו [בן] אליאר | Arad 21:1–2 |

11. KT

| אבי | Gen 27:31 |

BIBLIOGRAPHY

Abba, Raymond. 1962. "Name." *IDB* 3:501–8.
Abbott, Edwin A. 1870. *A Shakespearian Grammar: An Attempt to Illustrate Some of the Differences between Elizabethan and Modern English, for the Use of Schools*. London: Macmillan.
Alford, Richard D. 1988. *Naming and Identity: A Cross-Cultural Study of Personal Naming Practices*. New Haven: HRAF.
Aliakbari, Mohammad, and Arman Toni. 2008. "The Realization of Address Terms in Modern Persian in Iran: A Sociolinguistic Study." *Linguistik Online* 35:3–12.
Alp, Sedat. 1991. *Hethitische Keilschrifttafeln Aus Maşat-Höyük*. Türk Tarih Kurumu Yayınları 6.34. Ankara: Türk Tarih Kurumu Basımevi.
Alter, Robert. 2013. *Ancient Israel: The Former Prophets: Joshua, Judges, Samuel, and Kings*. New York: Norton.
Andersen, Francis I. 1969. "Israelite Kinship Terminology and Social Structure." *BT* 20:29–39.
Andersen, Francis I., and A. Dean Forbes. 1983. "'Prose Particle' Counts of the Hebrew Bible." Pages 165–82 in *The Word of the Lord Shall Go Forth: Essays in Honor of David Noel Freedman in Celebration of His Sixtieth Birthday*. Edited by Carol L. Meyers and Michael O'Connor. Winona Lake: Eisenbrauns.
Andersen, Francis I., and David N. Freedman. 1989. *Amos: A New Translation with Introduction and Commentary*. AB 24A. New York: Doubleday.
Anderson, Arnold. A. 1989. *2 Samuel*. WBC 11. Dallas: Word.
Anderson, John M. 2004. "On the Grammatical Status of Names." *Language* 80:435–74.
Avigad, Nahman. 1975. "The Priest of Dor." *IEJ* 25:101–5.
———. 1978. "Baruch the Scribe and Jerahmeel the King's Son." *IEJ* 28:52–56.
———. 1986. *Hebrew Bullae from the Time of Jeremiah: Remnants of a Burnt Archive*. Jerusalem: Israel Exploration Society.
Avishur, Yitzhak, and Michael Heltzer. 2000. *Studies on the Royal Administration in Ancient Israel in the Light of Epigraphic Sources*. Tel Aviv-Jaffa: Archaeological Center Publication.
Avrahami, Yael. 2011. "Name Giving to the Newborn in the Hebrew Bible." Pages 15–53 in vol. 5 of *These Are the Names: Studies in Jewish Onomastics*. Edited by Aaron Demsky. Ramat-Gan: Bar-Ilan University Press.
Bakos, Ferenc. 1955. "Contributions à l'étude Des Formules de Politesse En Ancien Français I." *ALH* 5:295–367.

Baldick, Chris. 2008. *The Oxford Dictionary of Literary Terms*. Oxford: Oxford University Press.
Bar-Efrat, Shimeon. 1989. *Narrative Art in the Bible*. Sheffield: Almond Press.
Barkay, Gabriel. 1993. "A Bulla of Ishmael, the King's Son." *BASOR* 290/291:109–14.
Barr, James. 1989. "'Determination' and the Definite Article in Biblical Hebrew." *JSS* 34:307–35.
Barrick, W. Boyd. 2001. "Shaking of Jehoshaphat's Family Tree: Jehoram and Ahaziah Once Again." *VT* 51:9–25.
Başoğlu, Sylvia. 1987. *Anrede in Türkischer Gegenwartsliteratur: Eine Sprachvergleichende Untersuchung Türkischer Romane, Erzählungen Und Filme Und Ihrer Deutschen Übersetzungen*. Frankfurt am Main: Y. Landeck.
Bates, Elizabeth, and Laura Benigni. 1975. "Rules of Address in Italy: A Sociological Survey." *LiS* 4:271–88.
Baudissin, Wolf W. G. 1929. *Kyrios als Gottesname im Judentum und Seine Stelle in der Religionsgeschichte*. 4 vols. Giessen: A. Töpelmann.
Bauer, Hans, and Pontus Leander. 1962. *Historische Grammatik der Hebräischen Sprache des Alten Testamentes*. Hildesheim: Olms.
Biber, Douglas, Stig Johansson, Geoffrey Leech, Susan Conrad, and Edward Finegan. 2007. *Longman Grammar of Spoken and Written English*. Essex: Pearson Education.
Blau, Joshua. 2010. *Phonology and Morphology of Biblical Hebrew: An Introduction*. LSAWS 2. Winona Lake: Eisenbrauns.
Block, Daniel I. 1997. *The Book of Ezekiel: Chapters 1–24*. NICOT. Grand Rapids: Eerdmans.
———. 1999. *Judges, Ruth*. NAC 6. Nashville: B&H.
Blyth, Caroline. 2014. "When Raymond Met Delilah." *Relegere: Studies in Religion and Reception* 4:41–63.
Bordreuil, Pierre, and Dennis Pardee. 2009. *A Manual of Ugaritic*. LSAWS 3. Winona Lake: Eisenbrauns.
Bramwell, Ellen S. 2016. "Personal Names and Anthropology." Pages 263–78 in *The Oxford Handbook of Names and Naming*. Edited by Carole Hough. Oxford: Oxford University Press.
Braun, Friederike. 1988. *Terms of Address: Problems of Patterns and Usage in Various Languages and Cultures*. New York: de Gruyter.
———. 1998. "Terms of Address." Pages 1–18 in vol. 4 of *Handbook of Pragmatics: 1998 Installment*. Edited by Jef Verschueren, Jan-Ola Östman, Jan Blommaert, Chris Bulcaen. Philadelphia: John Benjamins.
Braun, Friederike, Armin Kohz, and Klaus Schubert. 1986. *Anredeforschung: Kommentierte Bibliographie zur Soziolinguistik der Anrede*. Tübingen: Narr.
Brettler, Marc Z. 1989. *God Is King: Understanding an Israelite Metaphor*. JSOTSup 76. Sheffield: JSOT Press.
Bridge, Edward J. 2010a. "Polite Language in the Lachish Letters." *VT* 60:518–34.
———. 2010b. "The Use of Slave Terms in Deference and in Relation to God in the Hebrew Bible." PhD diss. Sydney: Macquarie University.
Brin, Gershon. 1969. "The Title בן (ה)מלך and Its Parallels: The Significance and Evaluation of an Official Title." *AION* 29:433–65.

Brongers, Hendrik A. 1981. "Some Remarks on the Biblical Particle Halō?." Pages 177–89 in *Remembering All the Way: A Collection of Old Testament Studies Published on the Occasion of the Fortieth Anniversary of the Oudtestamentisch Werkgezelschap in Nederland*. OTS 21. Leiden: Brill.
Brown, Donald E. 1991. *Human Universals*. Philadelphia: Temple University Press.
Brown, Penelope, and Stephen C. Levinson. 1987. *Politeness: Some Universals in Language Usage*. Cambridge: Cambridge University Press.
Brown, Roger. 1965. *Social Psychology*. New York: Free Press.
Brown, Roger, and Marguerite Ford. 1961. "Address in American English." *JASPs* 62:375–85.
Brown, Roger, and Albert Gilman. 1960. "The Pronouns of Power and Solidarity." Pages 253–76 in *Style in Language*. Edited by Thomas A. Sebeok. Cambridge: The MIT Press.
———. 1989. "Politeness Theory and Shakespeare's Four Major Tragedies." *LiS* 18:159–212.
Brueggemann, Walter. 2000. *1 and 2 Kings*. Edited by R. Scott Nash. SHBC. Macon, GA: Smyth & Helwys.
Busse, Beatrix. 2006. *Vocative Constructions in the Language of Shakespeare*. Pragmatics and Beyond 150. Philadelphia: John Benjamins.
Byrne, Geraldine. 1936. "Shakespeare's Use of the Pronoun of Address: Its Significance in Characterization and Motivation." PhD diss. Washington, DC: Catholic University of America.
Chafe, Wallace. 1994. *Discourse, Consciousness, and Time: The Flow and Displacement of Conscious Experience in Speaking and Writing*. Chicago: University of Chicago Press.
Clermont-Ganneau, Charles. 1888. "Le sceau de Obadyahou, fonctionnaire royal israélite." *Recueil d'archéologie orientale* 1:33–36.
Clines, David J. A. 1972. "X, X Ben Y, Ben Y: Personal Names in Hebrew Narrative Style." *VT* 22:266–87.
Cohen, Simon. 1961. "Amos Was a Navi." *HUCA* 32:175–78.
Cole, Graham A. 2013. *The God Who Became Human: A Biblical Theology of Incarnation*. Downers Grove, IL: InterVarsity Press.
Conklin, Blane. 2011. *Oath Formulas in Biblical Hebrew*. LSAWS 5. Winona Lake: Eisenbrauns.
Contini, Riccardo. 1995. "Epistolary Evidence of Address Phenomena in Official and Biblical Aramaic." Pages 57–67 in *Solving Riddles and Untying Knots: Biblical, Epigraphic, and Semitic Studies in Honor of Jonas C. Greenfield*. Edited by Ziony Zevit, Seymour Gitin, and Michael Sokoloff. Winona Lake: Eisenbrauns.
Crenshaw, James L. 1971. *Prophetic Conflict: Its Effect upon Israelite Religion*. New York: de Gruyter.
Currie, Haver. 1980. "On the Proposal of Sociolinguistics as a Discipline of Research." *LiS* 9:407–11.
Dallaire, Hélène. 2014. *The Syntax of Volitives in Biblical Hebrew and Amarna Canaanite Prose*. LSAWS 9. Winona Lake: Eisenbrauns.

Dalman, Gustaf. 1889. *Studien Zur Biblischen Theologie: Der Gottesname Adonaj und Seine Geschichte*. Berlin: H. Reuther.
Daniel, Michael, and Andrew Spencer. 2009. "The Vocative—An Outlier Case." Pages 626–34 in *The Oxford Handbook of Case*. Edited by Andrej Malchukov and Andrew Spencer. Oxford: Oxford University Press.
Davidson, Andrew B. 1942. *Introductory Hebrew Grammar: Hebrew Syntax*. Edinburgh: T&T Clark.
Dehé, Nicole, and Yordanka Kavalova. 2007. "Parentheticals: An Introduction." Pages 1–22 in *Parentheticals*. Edited by Nicole Dehé and Yordanka Kavalova. LA 106. Philadelphia: Benjamins.
Demsky, Aaron. 1997. "Names and No-Names in the Book of Ruth." Pages 27–37 in vol. 5 of *These Are the Names: Studies in Jewish Onomastics*. Edited by Aaron Demsky. Ramat-Gan: Bar-Ilan University Press.
Dickey, Eleanor. 1996. *Greek Forms of Address: From Herodotus to Lucian*. Oxford: Clarendon.
———. 2002. *Latin Forms of Address*. Oxford: Oxford University Press.
———. 2004. "Literal and Extended Use of Kinship Terms in Documentary Papyri." *Mnemosyne* 57:131–76.
Dik, Simon C. 1997. *The Theory of Functional Grammar: Part 2 Complex and Derived Constructions*. Edited by Kees Hengeveld. FGS 21. Berlin: de Gruyter.
Diringer, David. 1934. *Le iscrizioni antico-ebraiche palestinesi*. Firenze: F. Le Monnier.
Dobbs-Allsopp, Frederick W., Jimmy J. M. Roberts, Choon-Leong Seow, and Richard E. Whitaker. 2005. *Hebrew Inscriptions: Text Form the Biblical Period of the Monarchy with Concordance*. New Haven: Yale University Press.
Domonkosi, Ágnes. 2018. "Metaphorical and Metonymic Motivations behind Hungarian Forms of Address." Pages 129–41 in *Polsko-Węgierskie Badania Hungarologiczne*. Edited by Bubak Grzegorz. Kraków: Wydawnictwo Uniwersytetu Jagiellońskiego.
Donner, Herbert. 1961. "Der 'Freund des Königs.'" *ZAW* 73:269–77.
Durkheim, Émile. 1912. *Les Formes Élémentaires de La Vie Religieuse*. Paris: F. Alcan.
Eichrodt, Walther. 1970. *Ezekiel: A Commentary*. OTL. Philadelphia: Westminster.
Eissfeldt, Otto. 1974. "אָדוֹן *'ādhôn*." *TDOT* 1:59–72.
El Guindi, Fadwa. 2012. "Milk and Blood: Kinship among Muslim Arabs in Qatar." *Anthropos* 107:545–45.
Emerton, John A. 1982. "New Light on Israelite Religion: The Implications of the Inscriptions from Kuntillet ʕAjrud." *ZAW* 94:2–20.
Ervin-Tripp, Susan M. 1972. "On Sociolinguistic Rules: Alternation and Co-occurrence." Pages 213–50 in *Directions in Sociolinguistics: The Ethnography of Communication*. Edited by John Gumperz and Dell Hymes. New York: Holt, Rinehart & Winston.
Esposito, Raffaele. 2009. "Kinship Terms as Forms of Address in Biblical Hebrew: Fictive and Literal Use." *AION* 69:127–40.
Estelle, Bryan. 2001. "Know Before Whom You Stand: The Language of Deference in Some Ancient Aramaic and Hebrew Documents." PhD diss. Washington, DC: Catholic University of America.
———. 2012. "Esther's Strategies of Becoming עבד משכיל." *HS* 53:61–88.

Exum, J. Cheryl. 2000. "Delilah." Pages 68–69 in *Women in Scripture: A Dictionary of Named and Unnamed Women in the Hebrew Bible, the Apocryphal/Deuterocanonical Books, and the New Testament*. Edited by Carol Meyers. Boston: Houghton Mifflin.
Falk, Avner. 1996. *A Psychoanalytic History of the Jews*. Madison: Fairleigh Dickinson University.
Fasold, Ralph. 1990. *Sociolinguistics of Language*. Oxford: Blackwell.
Fewell, Danna N. 1992. "Judges." Pages 73–83 in *The Women's Bible Commentary: Expanded Edition with Apocrypha*. Edited by Carol A. Newsom and Sharon H. Ringe. Louisville: Westminster John Knox.
Fitch, Kristine L. 1998. *Speaking Relationally*. New York: Guilford.
Fleming, Luke, and James Slotta. 2015. "Named Relations: A Universal in the Pragmatics of Reference within the Kin Group." *CLS* 51:165–79.
Fox, Michael V. 2000. *Proverbs 1–9*. AB 18A. New York: Doubleday.
Fox, Nili S. 2000. *In the Service of the King*. HUCM 23. Cincinnati: Hebrew Union College.
Franz, Wilhelm. 1900. *Shakespeare-Grammatik*. Halle: Niemeyer.
Freedman, David N. 1985. "Prose Particles in the Poetry of the Primary History." Pages 49–62 in *Biblical and Related Studies Presented to Samuel Iwry*. Edited by Ann Kort and Scott Morschauser. Winona Lake: Eisenbrauns.
Friedrich, Paul. 1966. "Structural Implications of Russian Pronominal Usage." Pages 214–59 in *Sociolinguistics: Proceedings of the UCLA Sociolinguistics Conference, 1964*. Edited by William Bright. The Hague: Mouton.
Frost, Stanley B. 1968. "The Death of Josiah: A Conspiracy of Silence." *JBL* 87:369–82.
Garr, W. Randall. 1985. *Dialect Geography of Syria-Palestine: 1000–586 B.C.E.* Winona Lake: Eisenbrauns.
Garrett, Duane A. 2008. *Amos: A Handbook on the Hebrew Text*. BHHB. Waco, TX: Baylor University Press.
Garsiel, Moshe. 1991. *Biblical Names: A Literary Study of Midrashic Derivations and Puns*. Ramat-Gan: Bar-Ilan University Press.
Gesenius, Wilhelm. 1960. *Gesenius' Hebrew Grammar*. Edited by Emil Kautzsch. Translated by Arthur E. Cowley. Oxford: Clarendon.
Gibson, John C. L. 1971. *Hebrew and Moabite Inscriptions*. Vol. 1 of *Textbook of Syrian Semitic Inscriptions*. Oxford: Clarendon.
Gilman, Albert, and Roger Brown. 1958. "Who Says 'Tu' to Whom." *ETC: A Review of General Semantics* 15:169–74.
Glušac, Maja, and Ana M. Čolič. 2017. "Linguistic Functions of the Vocative as a Morphological, Syntactic and Pragmatic-Semantic Category." *Jezikoslovlje* 18:447–72.
Goffman, Erving. 1967. *Interaction Ritual: Essays in Face-to-Face Behavior*. Chicago: Aldine.
Gogel, Sandra L. 1998. *A Grammar of Epigraphic Hebrew*. Atlanta: Scholars Press.
Goldsmith, Daena J. 2007. "Brown and Levinson's Politeness Theory." Pages 219–36 in *Explaining Communication*. Edited by Bryan B. Whaley and Wendy Samter. London: Lawrence Erlbaum Associates.
Golub, Mitka R. 2017. "Israelite and Judean Theophoric Personal Names in the Hebrew Bible in the Light of the Archaeological Evidence." *ANES* 54:35–46.

Gray, John. 1963. *I and II Kings: Commentary*. Philadelphia: Westminster.
Grayson, Albert K. 1975. *Assyrian and Babylonian Chronicles*. TCS 5. Locust Valley, NY: Augustin.
Greenstein, Edward L. 1992. "Wordplay, Hebrew." *ABD* 6:968–71.
Grice, H. Paul. 1975. "Logic and Conversation." Pages 41–58 in *Speech Acts*. Edited by Peter Cole and Jerry Morgan. Syntax and Semantics 3. New York: Academic Press.
Guttmacher, Adolf. 1903. "Friendship (ידידות, אהוה, רעות, אהוה)." *JE* 5:520–21.
Gzella, Holger. 2006. "Die Entstehung Des Artikels Im Semitischen: Eine 'phönizische' Perspektive." *JSS* 51:1–18.
Haddad, Youssef A. 2020. "Vocatives as Parenthetical Adjuncts: Evidence from Arabic." *Glossa* 5:1–37.
Halliday, Michael A. K. 1967. "Notes on Transitivity and Theme in English: Part 2." *JLg* 3:199–244.
———. 1968. "Notes on Transitivity and Theme in English: Part 3." *JLg* 4:179–215.
———. 2004. *An Introduction to Functional Grammar*. New York: Hodder Arnold.
———. 2014. *Halliday's Introduction to Functional Grammar*. New York: Routledge.
Hamilton, Victor P. 1995. *The Book of Genesis: 18–50*. NICOT. Grand Rapids: Eerdmans.
———. 2002. *A Brief History of Ancient Israel*. Louisville: Westminster John Knox.
Hartley, John E. 2000. *Genesis*. NIBCOT. Peabody, MA: Hendrickson.
Hayes, John H. 1988. *Amos, the Eighth-Century Prophet: His Times & His Preaching*. Nashville: Abingdon.
Hayes, John H., and Paul K. Hooker. 1988. *A New Chronology for the Kings of Israel and Judah and Its Implications for Biblical History and Literature*. Atlanta: John Knox.
Head, Brian F. 1978. "Respect Degrees in Pronominal Reference." Pages 151–211 in vol. 3 of *Universals of Human Language*. Edited by Joseph H. Greenberg. Stanford: Stanford University Press.
Hess, Richard S. 2015. "Personal Names in the Hebrew Bible with Second-Millennium B.C. Antecedents." *BBR* 25:5–12.
Higginbotham, Carolyn. 2009. "Pharaoh." *NIDB* 4:483–85.
Hijirida, Kyoto, and Ho-min Sohn. 1983. "Commonality and Relativity in Address-Reference Term Usages." *LR* 19:139–68.
Hillers, Delbert. 1983. "Hôy and Hôy-Oracles: A Neglected Syntactic Aspect." Pages 185–88 in *The Word of the Lord Shall Go Forth: Essays in Honor of David Noel Freedman in Celebration of His Sixtieth Birthday*. Edited by Carol L. Meyers and Michael O'Connor. Winona Lake: Eisenbrauns.
Hobbs, Trevor R. 1985. *2 Kings*. WBC 13. Waco: Word.
Hodson, Thomas C. 1939. "Socio-linguistics in India." *Man in India* 19:94–98.
Hoffmeier, James K. 1996. *Israel in Egypt: The Evidence for the Authenticity of the Exodus Tradition*. Oxford: Oxford University Press.
Hoffner, Harry A. 2009. *Letters from the Hittite Kingdom*. Edited by Gary M. Beckman. WAW. Atlanta: Society of Biblical Literature.
Holmstedt, Robert D. 2002. "The Relative Clause in Biblical Hebrew: A Linguistic Analysis." PhD diss. Madison: University of Wisconsin.
———. 2010. *Ruth: A Handbook on the Hebrew Text*. Edited by W. Dennis Tucker. BHHB. Waco, TX: Baylor University Press.

———. 2014. "Critical at the Margins: Edge Constituents in Biblical Hebrew." *KUSATU* 17:109–56.
Holtgraves, Thomas M. 2001. *Language as Social Action: Social Psychology and Language Use*. Mahwah, NJ: Lawrence Erlbaum Associates.
Huang, Yan. 2014. *Pragmatics*. Oxford: Oxford University Press.
Huehnergard, John. 2012. *An Introduction to Ugaritic*. Peabody, MA: Hendrickson.
Hwang, Juck-Ryoon. 1975. "Role of Sociolinguistics in Foreign Language Education with Reference to Korean and English Terms of Address and Levels of Deference." PhD diss. Austin: University of Texas, Austin.
Hymes, Dell. 1966. "Two Types of Linguistic Relativity." Pages 114–67 in *Sociolinguistics*. Edited by William Bright. The Hague: Mouton.
Jacob, Benno. 1992. *The Second Book of the Bible: Exodus*. New York: Ktav.
Jakobson, Roman. 1960. "Closing Statement: Linguistics and Poetics." Pages 350–77 in *Style in Language*. Edited by Thomas A. Sebeok. Cambridge: The MIT Press.
Jeremias, Joachim. 1997. "נָבִיא Nābî?." *TLOT* 2:697–710
Jucker, Andreas H., ed. 1995. *Historical Pragmatics*. P&BNS 35. Amsterdam: Benjamins.
Kambylis, Athanasios. 1964. "Anredeformen bei Pindar." Pages 95–199 in *Charis*. Edited by Anargyros Anastassiou and Athanasios Kambylis. Athens.
Keown, Anne S. 2004. "Metaphorical Motivations for Politeness Strategies: Linguistic Evidence from Russian, Polish, and Czech." PhD diss. Chapel Hill: University of North Carolina at Chapel Hill.
Keshavarz, Mohammad H. 1988. "Forms of Address in Post-revolutionary Iranian Persian: A Sociolinguistic Analysis." *LiS* 17:565–75.
Kiełkiewicz-Janowiak, Agnieszka. 1992. *A Socio-historical Study in Address: Polish and English*. New York: Lang.
Kim, Yoo-Ki. 2015. "Deferential Self-Reference in the Book of Samuel." *VT* 65:588–605.
Kimḥi, David. 2007. *The Commentary of Rabbi David Kimḥi to Chronicles: A Translation with Introduction and Supercommentary*. Translated by Yitzhak Berger. Providence: Brown University Press.
Krašovec, Jože. 2010. *The Transformation of Biblical Proper Names*. LHBOTS 418. New York: T&T Clark.
Kroger, Rolf O. 1982. "Explorations in Ethnogeny: With Special Reference to the Rules of Address." *AP* 37:810–20.
———. 1984. "Are the Rules of Address Universal? III: Comparison of Chinese, Greek, and Korean Usage." *JCCP* 15:273–84.
Kroger, Rolf O., Ken Cheng, and Ishbel Leong. 1979. "Are the Rules of Address Universal?: A Test of Chinese Language." *JCCP* 10:395–414.
Kroger, Rolf O., and Linda A. Wood. 1992. "Are the Rules of Address Universal? IV: Comparison of Chinese, Korean, Greek, and German Usage." *JCCP* 23:148–62.
Kroger, Rolf O., Linda A. Wood, and Thelma Beam. 1984. "Are the Rules of Address Universal? II: Greek Usage." *JCCP* 15:259–72.
Kugel, James L. 2007. *How to Read the Bible*. New York: Free Press.
Kuglin, Jörg. 1977. "Einige Bemerkungen zur Anrede im Deutschen und Türkischen." Pages 261–78 in *Korrespondenzen Festschrift Für Dietrich Gerhardt Aus Anlass Des 65*. Giessen: W. Schmitz.

Labov, William. 1972. "Some Principles of Linguistic Methodology." *LiS* 1:97–120.
———. 1994. *Principles of Linguistic Change*. 3 vols. Oxford: Blackwell.
———. 2006. *The Social Stratification of English in New York City*. Cambridge: Cambridge University Press.
Lambdin, Thomas O. 1953. "Egyptian Loan Words in the Old Testament." *JAOS* 73:145–55.
Lambert, Wallace E., and G. Richard Tucker. 1976. *Tu, Vous, Usted: A Social-Psychological Study of Address Patterns*. Rowley, MA: Newbury House.
Lande, Irene. 1949. *Formelhafte Wendungen der Umgangssprache im Alten Testament*. Leiden: Brill.
Landy, Francis. 1987. "Vision and Poetic Speech in Amos." *HAR* 11:223–46.
Layton, Scott C. 1990. *Archaic Features of Canaanite Personal Names in the Hebrew Bible*. HSM 47. Atlanta: Scholars Press.
Leeb, Carolyn S. 2000. *Away from the Father's House: The Social Location of Naʕar and Naʕarah in Ancient Israel*. JSOTSup 301. Sheffield: Sheffield Academic.
Leech, Geoffrey. 1999. "The Distribution and Function of Vocatives in American and British English Conversation." Pages 107–18 in *Out of Corpora: Studies in Honour of Stig Johansson*. Edited by Hilde Hasselgård and Signe Okselfjell. Amsterdam: Rodopi.
Leithart, Peter J. 2006. *1 and 2 Kings*. Grand Rapids: Baker.
Lemaire, Andre. 1979. "Note sur le Titre Bn Hmlk dans l'ancien Israël." *Semitica* 29:59–65.
Lemos, Tracy M. 2015. "Were Israelite Women Chattel?: Shedding New Light on an Old Question." Pages 227–41 in *Worship, Women, and War: Essays in Honor of Susan Niditch*. Edited by John J. Collins, Tracy M. Lemos, and Saul M. Olyan. Providence: Brown University Press.
Levinson, Stephen C. 1983. *Pragmatics*. Cambridge: Cambridge University Press.
Lévi-Strauss, Claude. 1966. *The Savage Mind*. Chicago: University of Chicago Press.
Listen, Paul. 1999. *The Emergence of German Polite Sie*. New York: Lang.
Longacre, Robert E. 2003. *Joseph: A Story of Divine Providence*. Winona Lake: Eisenbrauns.
MacDonald, John. 1976. "The Status and Role of the Naʕar in Israelite Society." *JNES* 35:147–70.
Macgowan, John. 1912. *Men and Manners of Modern China*. London: T. Fisher Unwin.
Marks, Herbert. 1995. "Biblical Naming and Poetic Etymology." *JBL* 114:21–42.
Mays, James L. 1969. *Amos: A Commentary*. OTL. Philadelphia: Westminster.
McCarthy, Michael J., and Anne O'Keeffe. 2003. "'What's in a Name?': Vocatives in Casual Conversations and Radio Phone-in Calls." Pages 153–85 in *Corpus Analysis*. Edited by Pepi Leistyna and Charles F. Meyer. New York: Rodopi.
McCawley, James D. 1998. *The Syntactic Phenomena of English*. Chicago: University of Chicago Press.
McClenney-Sadler, Madeline G. 2007. *Recovering the Daughter's Nakedness: A Formal Analysis of Israelite Kinship Terminology and the Internal Logic of Leviticus 18*. LHBOTS 476. New York: T&T Clark.
McFall, Leslie. 2010. "The Chronology of Saul and David." *JETS* 53:475–533.
McGivney, James. 1993. "'Is She a Wife or a Mother?' Social Order, Respect, and Address in Mijikenda." *LiS* 22:19–33.

Merwe, Christo H. J. van der. 2014. "The Challenge of Better Understanding Discourse Particles: The Case of לְכֵן." *JNSL* 40:127–75.
Merwe, Christo H. J. van der, Jacobus A. Naudé, and Jan H. Kroeze. 1999. *A Biblical Hebrew Reference Grammar.* Sheffield: Sheffield Academic.
———. 2017. *A Biblical Hebrew Reference Grammar.* 2nd ed. New York: Bloomsbury T&T Clark.
Mesthrie, Rajend., ed. 2001. *Concise Encyclopedia of Sociolinguistics.* New York: Elsevier.
Mettinger, Tryggve N. D. 1971. *Solomonic State Officials: A Study of the Civil Government Officials of the Israelite Monarchy.* ConBOT 5. Lund: Gleerup.
Meyer, Charles F. 2009. *Apposition in Contemporary English.* New York: Cambridge University Press.
Miller, Cynthia L. 1992. "Reported Speech in Biblical and Epigraphic Hebrew: A Linguistic Analysis." PhD diss. Chicago: University of Chicago Press.
———. 2003. *The Representation of Speech in Biblical Narrative: A Linguistic Analysis.* HSM 55. Winona Lake: Eisenbrauns.
———. 2010a. "Definiteness and the Vocative in Biblical Hebrew." *JNSL* 36:43–64.
———. 2010b. "Vocative Syntax in Biblical Hebrew Prose and Poetry: A Preliminary Analysis." *JSS* 55:347–64.
Miller, James M., and John H. Hayes. 2006. *A History of Ancient Israel and Judah.* Louisville: Westminster John Knox.
Miller-Naudé, Cynthia L. 2014. "Mismatches of Definiteness in Appositional Phrases." *JNSL* 40:97–111.
Milroy, Lesley. 1987. *Observing and Analysing Natural Language: A Critical Account of Sociolinguistic Method.* New York: Blackwell.
Moore, Rickie D. 2007. "The Prophet as Mentor: A Crucial Facet of the Biblical Presentations of Moses, Elijah, and Isaiah." *JPT* 15:155–72.
Moshavi, Adina. 2010. *Word Order in the Biblical Hebrew Finite Clause.* LSAWS 4. Winona Lake: Eisenbrauns.
———. 2011. "Rhetorical Question or Assertion?: The Pragmatics of הֲלֹא in Biblical Hebrew." *JANES* 32:91–105.
———. 2014. "What Can I Say? Implications and Communicative Functions of Rhetorical 'WH' Questions in Classical Biblical Hebrew Prose." *VT* 64:93–108.
Mühlhäusler, Peter, and Rom Harré. 1990. *Pronouns and People: The Linguistic Construction of Social and Personal Identity.* Oxford: Blackwell.
Müller, H.-P. 1974. "נָבִיא *nābî'*." *TDOT* 9:129–50.
Murdock, George P. 1945. "The Common Denominator of Cultures." Pages 123–42 in *The Science of Man in the World Crisis.* Edited by Ralph Linton. New York: Columbia University Press.
———. 1947. "Bifurcate Merging, a Test of Five Theories." *AA* 49:56–69.
Nathan, Norman. 1959. "Pronouns of Address in the 'Canterbury Tales.'" *MS* 21:193–201.
Naudé, Jacobus A. 1997. "חָזָה." *NIDOTTE* 2:56–61.
———. 1997. "רָאָה." *NIDOTTE* 3:1004–12.
———. 2004. "A Perspective on the Chronological Framework of Biblical Hebrew." *JNSL* 30:87–102.

Nida, Eugene A. 1949. *Morphology: The Descriptive Analysis of Words*. Ann Arbor: University of Michigan Press.

Noble, Paul R. 1998. "Amos and Amaziah in Context: Synchronic and Diachronic Approaches to Amos 7–8." *CBQ* 60:423–39.

O'Connor, Michael. 2002. "Discourse Linguistics and the Study of Biblical Hebrew." Pages 17–42 in *Congress Volume Basel 2001*. Edited by André Lemaire. Boston: Brill.

Oyetade, Solomon O. 1995. "A Sociolinguistic Analysis of Address Forms in Yoruba." *LiS* 24:515–35.

Pardee, Dennis. 1988. "An Evaluation of the Proper Names from Ebla from a West Semitic Perspective: Pantheon Distribution According to Genre." Pages 119–51 in *Eblaite Personal Names and Semitic Name-Giving*. Edited by Alfonso Archi. Roma: Missione archeologica italiana in Siria.

———. 2003. Review of *Ugaritische Grammatik*, by Josef Tropper. *AfO* 50:1–404.

Pardee, Dennis, S. David Sperling, J. David Whitehead, and Paul E. Dion. 1982. *Handbook of Ancient Hebrew Letters: A Study Edition*. Chico, CA: Scholars Press.

Parkinson, Dilworth B. 1982. "Terms of Address in Egyptian Arabic." PhD diss. Ann Arbor: University of Michigan.

———. 1985. *Constructing the Social Context of Communication: Terms of Address in Egyptian Arabic*. CSL 41. New York: de Gruyter.

Parpola, Simo, ed. 1987. *Letters from Assyria and the West*. Part 1 of *The Correspondence of Sargon II*. SAA 1. Helsinki: Helsinki University.

Parrott, Lillian A. 2010. "Vocatives and Other Direct Address Forms: A Contrastive Study." Pages 211–29 in *Russian in Contrast*. Edited by Alte Grønn and Irena Marijanović. Oslo: Oslo University Press.

Paul, Shalom M. 1991. *Amos: A Commentary on the Book of Amos*. Hermeneia 30. Minneapolis: Fortress.

Petersen, David L. 1981. *The Roles of Israel's Prophets*. JSOTSup 17. Sheffield: JSOT Press.

Philipsen, Gerry, and Michael Huspek. 1985. "A Bibliography of Sociolinguistic Studies of Personal Address." *AnL* 27: 94–101.

Pickett, Joseph P., ed. 2000. *The American Heritage Dictionary of the English Language*. 4th ed. Boston: Houghton Mifflin.

Polak, Frank H. 2010. "Forms of Talk in Hebrew Biblical Narrative: Negotiations, Interaction, and Sociocultural Context." Pages 167–98 in *Literary Construction of Identity in the Ancient World*. Edited by Hanna Liss and Manfred Oeming. Winona Lake: Eisenbrauns.

Porten, Bezalel. 1982. "Name, Personal Names in Israel." *EB* 7:33–51.

Portner, Paul. 2004. "Vocatives, Topics, and Imperatives." Talk delivered at the IMS workshop on Information Structure. Bad Teinach.

Provan, Iain W. 1995. *1 and 2 Kings*. NIBCOT. Peabody: Hendrickson.

Qin, Xizhen. 2008. "Choices in Terms of Address: A Sociolinguistic Study of Chinese and American English Practices." Pages 409–21 in *Proceedings of the 20th North American Conference on Chinese Linguistics*. Edited by Marjorie K. M. Chan and Hana Kang. Columbus: Ohio State University.

Quirk, Randolph, Sidney Greenbaum, Geoffrey Leech, and Jan Svartvik. 1985. *A Comprehensive Grammar of the English Language*. New York: Longman.
Rabinowitz, Louis I. 2007. "Apikoros." *EncJud* 2:255–56.
Radday, Yehuda T., and Moshe A. Pollatschek. 1980. "Vocabulary Richness in Post-Exilic Prophetic Books." *ZAW* 92:333–46.
Rainey, Anson. F. 1975. "The Prince and the Pauper." *UF* 7:427–32.
Redford, Donald B. 1992. "Pharaoh." *ABD* 5:288–89.
Replogle, Carol. 1973. "Shakespeare's Salutations: A Study in Linguistics Etiquette." *SP* 70:172–86.
Revell, Ernest J. 1996. *The Designation of the Individual: Expressive Usage in Biblical Narrative*. Kampen: Kok Pharos.
Romaine, Suzanne. 1982. *Socio-historical Linguistics: Its Status and Methodology*. New York: Cambridge University Press.
Rosenbaum, Michael. 1997. *Word-Order Variation in Isaiah 40–55: A Functional Perspective*. Assen: Van Gorcum.
Rudolph, Wilhelm. 1955. *Chronikbücher*. Tübingen: Mohr Siebeck.
Sarna, Nahum M. 2001. *Genesis*. Philadelphia: Jewish Publication Society of America.
Schegloff, Emanuel A. 1968. "Sequencing in Conversational Openings." *AA* 70:1075–95.
Schipper, Bernd U. 2010. "Egypt and the Kingdom of Judah under Josiah and Jehoiakim." *Tel Aviv* 37: 200–226.
Schloen, J. David. 2001. *The House of the Father as Fact and Symbol: Patrimonialism in Ugarit and the Ancient Near East*. Winona Lake: Eisenbrauns.
Schubert, Klaus. 1984. *Tilltal Och Samhällsstruktur*. Uppsala: Institutionen för nordiska språk vid Uppsala universitet.
Selms, Adrianus van. 1957. "The Origin of the Title 'The King's Friend.'" *JNES* 16:118–23.
Seymour, Timothy P. 1983. "Personal Names and Name Giving in the Ancient Near East." *UCLA Hist. J.* 4:108–20
Shiina, Michi. 2007. "Positioning and Functioning of Vocatives: Casework in Historical Pragmatics (1)." *BFL* 55:17–32.
———. 2008. "Positioning and Functioning of Vocatives: A Case Study in Historical Pragmatics (2)." *BFL* 56:29–48.
Siloni, Tal. 1995. "On Participial Relatives and Complementizer D0: A Case Study in Hebrew and French." *NLLT* 13:445–87.
Silverstein, Michael. 2003. "Indexical Order and the Dialectics of Sociolinguistic Life." *Language & Communication* 23:193–229.
Singerman, Robert. 2001. *Jewish Given Names and Family Names: A New Bibliography*. Edited by David L. Gold. Boston: Brill.
Slobin, Dan I. 1963. "Some Aspects of the Use of Pronouns of Address in Yiddish." *Word* 19:193–202.
Slobin, Dan I., Stephen H. Miller, and Lyman W. Porter. 1968. "Forms of Address and Social Relations in a Business Organization." *JPSP* 8:289–93.
Slocum, Poppy. 2016. "The Syntax of Address." PhD diss. Stony Brook, NY: Stony Brook University.
Smith, Arthur H. 1894. *Chinese Characteristics*. New York: Revell.

Spencer-Oatey, Helen. 1996. "Reconsidering Power and Distance." *JoP* 26:1–24.
Stager, Lawrence E. 1985a. "The Archaeology of the Family in Ancient Israel." *BASOR* 260:1–35.
Stähli, Hans-Peter. 1978. *Knabe-Jüngling-Knecht: Untersuchungen zum Begriff* נער *im Alten Testament*. Bern: Lang.
Stavrou, Melita. 2014. "About the Vocative." Pages 299–342 in *The Nominal Structure in Slavic and Beyond*. Edited by Lilia Schürcks, Anastasia Giannakidou, and Urtzi Etxeberria. Boston: de Gruyter.
Steiner, Richard C. 1979. "Review of 'An Adverbial Construction in Hebrew and Arabic: Sentence Adverbials in Frontal Position Separated from the Rest of the Sentence', by Joshua Blau." *AAL* 6:147–52.
———. 2003. *Stockmen from Tekoa, Sycomores from Sheba: A Study of Amos' Occupations*. CBQMS 36. Washington, DC: Catholic Biblical Association of America.
Svennung, Josef. 1958. *Anredeformen: Vergleichende Forschungen zur Indirekten Anrede in der Dritten Person und zum Nominativ Für den Vokativ*. Wiesbaden: Harrassowitz.
Taavitsainen, Irma, and Andreas H. Jucker, eds. 2003. *Diachronic Perspectives on Address Term Systems*. P&BNS 107. Amsterdam: John Benjamins.
Taglicht, Josef. 1984. *Message and Emphasis: On Focus and Scope in English*. New York: Longman.
Thomas, Benjamin. 2009. "The Language of Politeness in Ancient Hebrew Letters." *HS* 50:17–39.
Thomas, David W. 1953. "A Consideration of Some Unusual Ways of Expressing the Superlative in Hebrew." *VT* 3:209–24.
Thompson, John A. 1980. *The Book of Jeremiah*. NICOT. Grand Rapids: Eerdmans.
Torczyner, Harry. 1938. *The Lachish Letters: Lachish I*. London: Oxford University Press.
vanGemeren, Willem A. 1988. "?ABBĀ? in the Old Testament?" *JETS* 31:385–98.
Vaux, Roland de. 1965. *Ancient Israel: Social Institutions 1*. New York: McGraw-Hill.
Verhoef, Pieter A. 1997. "Prophecy." *NIDOTTE* 4:1065–76.
Wales, Kathleen M. 1983. "Thou and You in Early Modern English: Brown and Gilman Re-Appraised." *SL* 37:107–25.
Waterhouse, Ruth. 1982. "Modes of Address in Aelfric's Lives of the Saints Homilies." *SN* 54:3–24.
Webb, Barry G. 2012. *The Book of Judges*. Grand Rapids: Eerdmans.
Wegner, Judith R. 1988. *Chattel or Person?* New York: Oxford University Press.
Williams, James G. 1966. "The Prophetic 'Father': A Brief Explanation of the Term 'Sons of the Prophets.'" *JBL* 85:344–48.
Witherington, Ben. 1999. *Jesus the Seer: The Progress of Prophecy*. Peabody: Hendrickson.
Wolff, Hans W. 1977. *Joel and Amos: A Commentary on the Books of the Prophets Joel and Amos*. Hermeneia. Philadelphia: Fortress.
Yeivin, Shmuel. 1965. "בן המלך." *EB* 2:160.
Young, Ian. 1993. *Diversity in Preexilic Hebrew*. FAT 5. Tübingen: Mohr Siebeck.
———, ed. 2003. *Biblical Hebrew: Studies in Chronology and Typology*. JSOTSup 369. London: T&T Clark.
Young, Ian, Robert Rezetko, and Martin Ehrensvärd. 2008. *Linguistic Dating of Biblical Texts*. 2 vols. London: Equinox.

Zevit, Ziony. 1979. "Expressing Denial in Biblical Hebrew and Mishnaic Hebrew, and in Amos." *VT* 29:505–9.
Zimmermann, Frank. 1966. "Folk Etymology of Biblical Names." Pages 311–26 in *Volume Du Congrès: Genève 1965*. Edited by George W. Anderson et al. VTSup 15. Leiden: Brill.
Zwicky, Arnold. 1974. "Hey, Whatsyourname!" *CLS* 10:787–801.

ANCIENT SOURCES INDEX

Hebrew Bible/Old Testament
Genesis

Reference	Page(s)
3:10	129
3:12	127
3:16	73
3:19	69
4:7	131
4:11	150
4:23	74, 78
4:25	68
4:26	68
5:3	68
5:29	68–69
6:18	129
11:31	104
12	87
12:5	104
12:11	127
14:12	104
14:19	44
15:1	20, 28, 47, 136–37
15:2	134
15:8	134
16:7–8a	134
16:8	134
16:15	68
17:4	128
17:5	69
17:10	126
17:15	70
17:19	69
18:3	134
18:12	74
18:25	131
19:2	139
19:7	47, 110, 142
19:12	104
19:14	104
19:18	137
19:37–38	68
20	87
20:4	134
20:5	131
20:12	104
21:17	47, 136
22:1	47, 116, 132
22:7	21, 47, 107, 132, 136
22:7–8a	137
22:8	47, 107, 136
22:11	42, 132
23:4	87
23:6	48, 87, 136
23:11	21, 48, 86, 137
23:15	21, 48, 86, 134
24:2	87
24:10	87
24:12	134
24:18	23, 48, 86–87, 136
24:31	49, 136
24:42	134
25:29–34	11
25:30	69
27:1	47, 107, 132
27:8	47, 107, 139
27:13	47, 107, 136
27:18	47, 107, 132, 136
27:20	47, 107, 136
27:21	47, 107, 147
27:26	47, 107, 136
27:31	154

Genesis (cont.)

27:34	47, 107, 136
27:37	47, 136
27:38	47, 107, 136
27:43	47, 107, 139
28:2	104
29:4	47, 110, 134
29:10	77, 104
29:12	104
29:31–30:24	68
29:32	74
29:34	74
30:15	74
30:18	74
30:20	74
31:11	20, 30, 47, 132
31:35	155, 157
31:43	130
32:6	154, 157
32:10	39, 44, 134
32:19	154
33:8	155
33:9	47, 107, 136
33:13	155
33:14	19, 154–55, 157
33:15	155
34:23	131
35:10–12	69
35:18	68–69
37:2	89
38:3	68
38:4–5	68
38:8	104
38:9	104
38:11	104
38:13	104
38:16	104
38:24	104
38:25	104
41:10	7, 154–55, 157, 165
41:12	89
41:16	7, 154–55, 165
41:25	7, 154–55, 165
41:28	7, 154, 156, 165
41:32	7, 154, 165
41:33	7, 154–55, 165
41:34	7, 154–55, 165
41:35	7, 154, 165
41:45	69, 98
42:10	48, 137
42:12	126
43:20	48, 133
43:29	47, 112, 136
44:7	155
44:9	154
44:16	154
44:18	6, 48, 86, 133, 155, 157
44:19	155, 157
44:20	154
44:22	154
44:33	154
44:24	155
46:2	132
47:18	20, 27, 137, 154
47:25	155
48:18	47, 107
48:19	47, 107, 136
49	18

Exodus

2:6	89
2:10	69
2:22	68
3:1	98, 104
3:4	43, 132
4:10	133
4:13	133
4:18	104
5:18	131
5:22	134
7:7	73
7:27	128
8:25	7, 154, 157, 165
10:2	104
11:5	154–55, 157, 161–62, 165
18:1–2	104
18:5–8	104
18:12	104
18:14–15	104
18:17	104
18:24	104
18:27	104

32:4	47, 147	9:26	134
32:8	47, 147	10:12	47, 139
32:11	141–42	20:3	47, 136
32:22	73, 155, 157	21:8	136
34:9	139	22:20–21	73
		26:10	136
Leviticus		27:9	47, 136
18:9	104	27:22	104
18:10	104	27:23	104
18:12	104	32:6	53
18:13	104	33:1	95
18:14	104		
18:15	104	Joshua	
18:16	104	7:7	133
18:17	104	7:8	133
20:12	104	7:13	47, 136
20:17	104	7:19	47, 112, 134
20:19	104	14:6	95
20:21	104		
		Judges	
Numbers		3:19	48, 86, 136
10:29	104	4:14	131
10:35	136	4:18	48, 82, 86, 136
10:36	145	5	37
11:28	92–93, 134	6:12	49, 136
12:11	48, 73, 86, 133	6:13	133
14:14	145	6:15	133
16:6	47–48, 71	6:22	54, 133
16:7	49, 136	8:22	104
16:8	49	9:1	104
16:22	39, 54, 134	9:7	48, 136
20:10	30, 49	11:17	131
20:14–21	10	11:24	131
32:25	155	11:35	47, 107, 133
32:27	155	11:36	47, 107, 115, 126, 134
36:2	155–56	12:4	47, 145
		13:5	89
Deuteronomy		13:6	95
3:24	134	13:7	89
4:1	47, 139	13:8	89, 96, 133
5:1	47, 145–46	13:9	74
6:2	104	13:12	89
6:3	47, 136	13:24	68
6:4	47, 136	15:1	77
9:1	47, 136	15:6	104

Judges (cont.)		1:11	134
16:4	77	1:15	48, 86, 137
16:9	47, 77, 136	1:20	68
16:12	47, 77, 136	1:24	89
16:14	47, 77, 136	1:26	48, 86, 133, 139
16:20	47, 77, 136	2:24	47, 137
16:28	134, 136	2:27	95
18:29	69	3:6	47, 112, 132, 136, 150
19:5	104	3:9	136
19:23	47, 110, 137, 143	3:10	132
20:7	139	3:16	41, 72, 106, 132
21:3	141	3:20	95
21:21	128	4:9	36–37, 50, 147
		4:16	112, 136
Ruth		4:19	104
1:6	104	4:21	68, 104
1:6–8	105	5:5	98
1:7	104	9:6	95
1:8	104, 175	9:7	95
1:11	47, 136, 175	9:8	95
1:12	47, 136	9:9	95, 101
1:13	47, 137	9:10	95
1:14	104	10:5	89
1:22	104–5	10:10	89
2:2	47, 105, 112, 136	10:24	155
2:8	47, 112, 136	12:2	128
2:11	104	14:3	98
2:13	48, 86, 136	14:44	47, 72, 136
2:18	104	14:50	73, 82
2:19	104	15:1	130
2:20	104–5	15:17	131
2:22	47, 104–5, 112, 145	16:16	155, 158
2:23	104	17:43	151
3:1	47, 104–5, 112, 134	17:45	151
3:6	104	17:55	47
3:10	47, 112, 136	17:55	47–48, 67, 71, 73–
3:11	47, 112, 139		74, 82–83, 86 136, 139
3:16	47, 104–5, 112, 136	17:57	82
3:17	104	17:58	50, 136
3:18	47, 105, 112, 147	18:13	82
4:10	105	18:18	104
4:15	104–5	18:27	82
4:17	69	19:4	21, 74, 155
		19:20	89
1 Samuel		20:3	128
1:8	23, 47, 66, 72, 74, 78, 134	20:7	91

20:7–8	168	26:23	154
20:8	91	26:25	112, 136
20:12	92, 154, 157, 168, 174	29:3	166
20:13	168	29:8	154
20:15	92, 155, 168, 174	30:23	47, 110, 115, 145
20:29	17		
20:30	32, 39, 49, 134	2 Samuel	
22:1–2	82	1:10	154
22:12	48–49, 75, 82, 86, 136	1:26	110
22:14	75, 82, 104, 155	2:12–32	73
22:15	6, 82, 155, 157	2:20	47, 72, 136
22:16	47, 72, 125, 147	3:2	90
22:17	98	3:21	83, 154, 157
22:21	98	4:4	67
23:10	134	4:8	156
23:11	134	5:4	67
23:13	82	5:5	67
23:20	48, 144, 155	6:14	166
24:9	92, 132	6:16	166
24:12	47, 109, 134, 151	6:20	8, 155, 165, 174
24:15	155, 157, 166	7:14	53
24:17	112, 136	7:18	136
24:18	151	7:19	136
25:22	163	7:20	136
25:24	48, 86, 144	7:22	136
25:24–31	157	7:24	144
25:25	155, 157	7:25	54, 139
25:26	48, 86, 139, 140, 154	7:27	41, 144
25:27	154–55	7:28	139
25:28	154–55, 157	7:29	144
25:29	155, 158	9:6	47, 67, 71, 74, 132
25:30	154	9:8	74
25:31	154, 156–57	9:9–10	89
25:34	163	9:11	71, 155, 157
25:41	155	9:13	17, 67
25:44	109	11:1–4	67
26:14	47, 80, 136, 173	11:11	73, 82, 155
26:15–16	82	11:21	131
26:17	41, 92, 112, 136	11:24	155, 157
26:18	155, 157	11:26	74
26:19	150, 155, 157	12:1–15	78
26:20	155, 166	12:25	69
26:21	112, 136	13:3	91
26:22	48, 86, 136	13:4	48, 86, 91, 145
26:22–23	156	13:8	108

2 Samuel (cont.)

13:10	108	18:28	154
13:11	47, 107, 136	18:29	155
13:12	47, 67, 107, 137, 143	18:31	155, 157
13:20	47, 107, 139	18:32	155, 158
13:24	21, 74, 155, 158	18:42	155
13:25	30, 47, 107, 137, 143	19:1	72, 106–7, 134, 136
13:30	155	19:5	43, 107, 132
13:32	79, 155	19:13	111
13:33	155	19:18	89
13:34	136	19:20	6, 155–57
13:35	155, 157	19:20–21	157
14:4	48, 86, 93, 136	19:22	154, 156
14:5	74	19:23	49, 79, 147
14:7	74	19:26	47, 71, 136
14:9	92, 144, 155, 157	19:27	74, 92, 134
14:9–15	155	19:28	74, 154–55, 157
14:11	155, 158	19:29	74, 154, 157
14:12	154	19:31	74, 155
14:13	156–57	19:35	154
14:15	51, 154	19:36	154
14:17	155, 157	19:37	154–54
14:18	155	19:38	154, 157
14:19	92, 139, 155, 157	19:42	156–57, 167, 174
14:20	155	19:43	167
14:22	92, 147, 155, 157	20:9	47, 110, 136
14:29–32	66	20:23	73
15:15	155	23:17	147
15:21	155	23:24	73
15:31	136	23:39	73
15:34	48, 86	24:3	155
15:37	91	24:10	139
16:1	89	24:11	101
16:2	155	24:21	155
16:4	92, 115, 136	24:22	155
16:5	44	24:23	48, 86, 154, 157
16:7	39, 44, 136	1 Kings	
16:9	156	1:2	154
16:10	49, 79, 136	1:13	92, 144
16:16	88, 91, 155	1:13–21	74
17:16	154	1:16–17a	135
17:24–18:33	111	1:17	48, 86, 134
17:25	111	1:18	92, 139
18:12	91	1:19	155, 157
18:20	91	1:20	92, 139, 155, 157
18:22	47, 112, 136	1:20–21	166

1:21	156–57	14:29	131
1:24	81, 92, 134	15:19	166
1:25	81–82, 155	16:3	154, 157
1:27	81, 154–55, 157	16:3–4	163, 165
1:31	155	16:4	155, 157
1:36	155	16:8–16	73
1:37	154–55	16:11	163
1:51	79, 156	17–2 Kings 13	95
2:20	47, 107, 136	17:18	32, 48, 86, 95, 136
2:38	155, 157	17:20	134
3:7	139	17:21	134
3:17	48, 86, 133	17:24	95
3:26	48, 86, 133	18:3	93–94
4:5	91	18:7	92, 136
8:23	134	18:13	154
8:25	139	18:17	49, 136
8:26	53, 139	18:19	95–96
8:28	147	18:26	53, 134
8:53	136	18:36	96, 134
9:13	47, 79, 110, 136	18:37	136, 145
11:41	131	19:4	142
12:16	47, 136	19:9	47, 136
12:22	95	19:13	47, 136
12:28	47, 147	20:4	66, 79, 92–93, 144
13:1	95	20:28	95
13:2	30, 36–37, 55–56, 134	20:31	166
13:4	95	20:32	93
13:5	95	20:35	89
13:6	95	21:20	49, 136
13:7	95	21:21	154, 163
13:8	95	21:21–24	163, 165
13:11	95	21:24	154
13:12	95	22:1–28	3–5
13:14	95	22:31–32	166
13:21	95	22:6	81, 96, 155
13:26	95	22:8	25, 78, 79, 155, 161
13:29	95	22:12	81, 155
13:30	47, 110, 133	22:15	47, 72, 75, 81, 134, 155
13:31	95	22:26	91
14:6	49, 136	22:28	36–38, 136
14:7–9	164		
14:10	154–55	2 Kings	
14:10–11	163	1:9	48, 86, 95, 134
14:10–11a	163	1:10	95
14:11	154	1:11	48, 86, 95, 134

2 Kings (cont.)	
1:12	95
1:13	48, 86, 95, 134
2:3	89
2:4	7, 47, 72, 124, 134
2:5	89
2:7	89
2:12	33, 43, 52, 74, 106, 109, 132
2:15	89
2:19	155
2:23	31, 36–38, 49, 136
3:23	47, 136
4:1	74, 89
4:7	95
4:9	95
4:16	92–93, 95, 137, 143
4:21	95
4:22	95
4:25	95
4:27	95
4:28	154
4:38	89
4:40	48, 90, 95, 136
4:42	95
5	84
5:3	86
5:5	166
5:8	95
5:13	47, 82, 134
5:14	95
5:15	95
5:20	95
5:22	89
5:25	23, 47, 72, 136
6:1	87, 89
6:3	87
6:5	48, 86, 133
6:6	95
6:9	95
6:10	95
6:11–12	166
6:12	92, 96, 137
6:15	48, 86, 95, 133
6:17	134
6:20	134
6:21	25, 47, 65, 109, 136
6:26	92–93, 136
7:2	95
7:6	166
7:17	95
7:18	95
7:19	95
8:2	95
8:4	95
8:5	83, 92, 134
8:7	95
8:8	95
8:11	95
8:12	155
8:13	95
8:25	78
8:25–26	78
8:26	78
8:27	104
8:28	79
8:29	78
9:1	89
9:4	89
9:5	48, 82, 86, 88, 136
9:6	90
9:7	90
9:8	163
9:22	47, 71, 136
9:23	47, 77, 136
9:24	73
9:30–31	73
9:31	71, 75, 78, 136
11:4	91
11:12	155
11:18	98
13:14	33, 44, 52, 109, 132
13:19	95
15:5	91
16:7	166
19:15	39, 134
19:16	145–46
19:17	139
19:19	139, 145
20:3	133
20:19	131
23:16	95
23:17	95

23:33	153	6:17	139
24:17	69	6:19	147
25:29	17	6:40	142
		6:41	54, 144–45
1 Chronicles		6:42	54, 134
2:4	104	8:14	95
2:13	91	9:29	101
4:9	68	10:16	47, 136
7:16	68	11:2	95
7:23	68	12:15	101
16:5	94	13:1–22	75
17:13	53	13:4	47–48, 72, 79, 136
17:16	54, 136	13:5	75
17:17	54, 136	13:6–9	75
17:19	134	13:9	98
17:20	134	13:10	75
17:22	144	13:12	49, 134
17:23	139	14:10	134, 136
17:26	139	15:1	81
17:27	144	15:2	47–48, 80, 136, 173
21:3	79, 92, 141–42, 154–55	16:3	166
21:9	101	16:7	95
21:17	134	18:2	3
21:23	155, 157	18:5	81, 155
22:10	53	18:7	79, 155, 161
22:11	47, 107, 142	18:11	81, 155
23:14	95	18:14	47, 72, 134
25:5	95, 101	18:25	91
27:33	91	18:27	36–38, 136
28:2	110, 136	18:30–31	166
28:6	53	19:2	95, 101
28:9	72, 106, 144	20:6	134
29:10	34, 145	20:7	144
29:11	144	20:12	134
29:13	139	20:14	94
29:16	134	20:15	48, 68, 81, 92, 136
29:17	147	20:15–17	94
29:18	134	20:17	47, 50, 136
29:29	101	20:20	47–48, 136
		20:34	101
2 Chronicles		22:2	78
1:9	54, 142	23:3	91
2:14	79, 111, 155	23:11	91, 155
6:14	134	23:17	98
6:16	139	25:7	48, 81, 86, 95, 134

2 Chronicles (cont.)	
25:9	95
25:26	131
26:18	47, 81, 144
28:7	91
29:5	50, 135–36
29:10–11a	135
29:11	47, 134
29:25	101
29:30	101
30:6	49, 134
30:16	95
35:15	101
35:20	97
35:21	48, 79, 97–98, 136, 173
35:22	98

Ezra	
3:2	95
9:6	53, 134, 145
9:10	145
9:13	144
9:15	134

Nehemiah	
1:5	40, 42, 133
1:11	133
2:3	155
2:5	154, 157
2:7	154
2:8	154
3:36	136
5:19	145
6:18	104
12:24	95
12:36	95
13:14	145
13:22	136
13:28	104
13:29	145
13:31	145

Esther	
1:16	154–55
1:18	155
1:19	154, 157
1:20	155
2:2	154
2:3	155, 157
2:4	155
3:8	154–55
3:9	154–55
5:3	9, 25, 70, 78, 85, 136
5:4	74, 154–55, 166
5:8	74, 154–55
6:7	155
6:8	155
6:9	155
7:2	9, 25, 70, 78, 85, 136
7:3	9, 23, 48, 74, 85, 139, 154
7:4	74, 155
7:9	154
8:5	154–55, 157
8:7	78
9:13	154

Song of Songs	
1:9	78
2:10	78
4:8–12	105
4:9	78
5:1	105

Isaiah	
1:2	55
8:3	69
8:4	47, 107, 132
10:24	39, 48, 136
29:10	101
31:6	136
37:16	39, 134
37:17	145
37:18	139
37:20	139
38:3	133
40–55	175
41:1	55
61:6	98
63:16	53
64:8	53

Jeremiah		38:9	80, 92, 134
1:6	133	38:14	81
1:11	47, 136	38:16	81
3:4	52–53	42:15	48, 136
3:14	35–36, 39, 49, 136	42:19	48, 136
3:19	52–53	44:24	34, 40, 48, 136
4:10	133	44:26	40, 48, 136
6:13	96	44:30	81
7:2	40, 48, 136	45:2	47, 72, 136
10:1	48, 136	51:62	134
11:5	136	52:33	17
11:13	47, 136		
14:13	133	Ezekiel	
17:20	40, 48, 136	2:1	36, 134
18:6	48, 136	2:3	134
19:3	48, 136	2:6	144
20:6	47, 144	2:8	144
21:7	81	3:1	134
22:2	40, 48, 147	3:3	134
23:1	36, 39, 48, 133	3:4	134
24:3	47, 136	3:10	134
24:8	81	3:17	134
27:3	81	3:25	139
27:7	104	4:1	144
28:1	95	4:14	133
28:15	47, 72, 136	4:16	134
28:16	75	5:1	144
29:20	40, 48, 136	6:2	134
31:9	53	7:2	139
32:4	81	8:5	134
32:5	81	8:6	134
32:17	133	8:8	134
32:25	136	8:12	144
34:2	80	8:15	136
34:4	52, 80–81, 85, 136, 173	8:17	136
34:5	36, 48, 80, 133	9:8	133
35:1	96	11:2	134
35:4	95	11:3	133
36:26	91	11:4	136
37:3	81	11:5	48, 136
37:17	81	11:15	134
37:18	80–81	12:2	134
37:20	80–81, 92, 136	12:3	144
38:5	81	12:9	134
38:6	91	12:18	134

Ezekiel (*cont.*)		26:2	134
12:22	134	26:3	50, 136
12:25	49, 144	27:2	144
12:27	134	28:2	134
13:2	134	28:12	134
13:4	47, 144	28:16	36, 39, 50, 144
13:17	144	28:21	134
14:3	134	28:22	50, 136
14:13	134	29:2	134
15:2	134	29:18	134
16	73	30:2	134
16:2	134	30:21	134
16:35	31, 36, 49, 139	31:2	134
17:2	134	32:2	134
18:25	48, 136	32:18	134
18:29	48, 136	33:2	134
18:30	48, 136	33:7	139
18:31	48, 136	33:8	36, 49, 134
20:3	134	33:10	144
20:4	136	33:11	48, 136
20:27	136	33:12	144
20:31	48, 136	33:20	48, 136
20:39	48, 139	33:24	134
20:44	48, 136	33:30	139
21:2	134	34:2	39, 48, 133–34
21:5	133	34:7	36, 48, 139
21:7	134	34:9	48, 139
21:11	144	34:17	48, 139
21:14	134	35:2	134
21:24	144	36:1	55–56, 134, 144
21:30	36, 39, 139	36:4	55, 139
21:33	144	36:8	55, 144
21:34	36	36:17	134
22:2	139	36:22	48, 136
22:3	36, 38–39, 55–56, 134	36:32	48, 136
22:11	104	37:3	134
22:18	134	37:4	40, 55–56, 134
22:24	134	37:9	55–56, 136
23	73	37:11	134
23:2	134	37:12	48, 136
23:22	47, 139–40	37:13	48, 136
23:36	134	37:16	144
24:2	134	38:2	134
24:16	134	38:3	136
24:25	139	38:14	136
25:2	134	38:16	47, 136

39:1	136, 144	7:1–3	101
39:17	139	7:4	101
40:4	134	7:4–6	101
43:7	134	7:5	134
43:10	144	7:7	101
43:18	134	7:7–9	101
44:5	134	7:8	47, 136
44:6	48, 136	7:9	99
45:9	48, 136	7:10	98, 100
47:6	136	7:10–11	101
		7:10–17	101
Daniel		7:11	99
1:7	69	7:12	36, 48, 97, 99, 101, 134, 173
8:16	53, 134	7:12–13	98–99, 101
8:17	36, 147	7:14	99–100
9:4	39, 53–54, 133	7:15	99–100
9:7	144	8:1	101
9:8	134	8:1–3	101
9:15	40, 53–54, 139	8:2	47, 136
9:16	134	9:1	101
9:17	53, 145	9:1–6	101
9:18	145		
9:19	134, 136	Jonah	
9:22	47, 134	1:14	133, 144
10:11	36, 39, 134	4:2	133
10:12	47, 136	4:3	139
10:16	134		
10:19	33, 36, 39, 49, 136	Micah	
12:4	47, 144	1:2	38
12:8	134	3:7	101
12:9	47, 136	7:6	104
Hosea		Zechariah	
1:4	69	1:9	136
1:9	69	1:12	134
2:9	74	3:2	53, 136
2:18	74	4:4	136
Amos		4:5	137–38
1:1	99, 101	4:7	40, 55–56, 136
1:11–12	11	4:13	137
3:1	48, 145	6:4	136
3:8	99		
5:1	48, 136	Malachi	
7:1	101	1:6	53
7:2	134	2:10	53

Ancient Near Eastern Texts
Amarna Texts
EA

7:68	19	279–290	51
51	51	292–302	51
53	51	304–305	51
60	51	315	51
63–65	51	317–321	51
68	51	323–331	51
70	51	335	51
74–76	51	337	51
78–79	51	362–366	51
81	51	367:1	97
83–83	51	369:1	97
87–92	51	370:1	97
94	51	371	51
96	112	378	51

Aramaic Texts
VAT

102–109	51	8384:6	51
112	51		
114	51		

Egyptian Texts
Bentresh Stela

116–119	51	12	51
121–123	51		
125–126	51		

ANET

128–132	51	365	53

Hebrew Texts
Arad

135–144	51		
146–154	51	1–8	78
147–162	51	1:1	7, 152
150:18	51	2:1	7, 152
162:1	97	3:1	7, 152
164–166	51	4:1	7, 152
168	51	5:1	7, 152
171–172	51	6:1	7, 152
174–177	51	7:1	7, 152
179	51	8:1	7, 152
182–187	51	10–12	78
189	51	10:1	7, 152
191–209	51	11:1	7, 152
211–212	51	12:1	7, 152
214–217	51	14	78
221	51	14:1	7, 152
223–235	51	16	78
239–245	51	16:1–3	169, 174
248–262	51	16:2	7, 154, 158
264–265	51		
267–275	51		
277	51		

17	78	6:2	156
17:1	7, 152	6:3	155
18	78	6:8	154
18:1–2	7, 152	8	78
21	78	8:1	156
21:1–2	7, 154, 158	8:7	154
21:1–3	169, 174	9	78
21:3	7, 155	9:1–2	156
21:4	7, 154	12	78
24:1–2	7, 152	12:1	154
26:2	7, 154	12:6	154
26:4	7, 154	17	78
40	78	17:2	154
40:1–3	174	17:3	154
40:3	7, 154	18	78
40:6	7, 154	18:2	155
40:10	7, 154		

		Meṣad Ḥashavyahu	
Kuntillet ʔAjrud		1	90, 155
18:2	41	12	90
19A.9–10	154		
		Moussaïeff	
Lachish		2:2	155, 158
2	78		
2:1	152	**Hittite Texts**	
2:2	156	*ANET*	
2:2–3	157	397	53
2:4	155		
2:5–6	156	*HKM*	
3	78	46:15	51
3:2	154		
3:3	156	**Neo-Assyrian Texts**	
3:6	10, 155, 158	SAA	
3:8	155	1.1	51
3:21	154	1.29	51
4	78	1.31–39	51
4:1	156	1.41–60	51
4:2	155	1.62	51
4:4–5	155	1.64–67	51
4:12	155	1.70–78	51
5	78	1.80	51
5:1	156	1.82–83	51
5:7	154	1.87–94	51
6	78	1.96–102	51
6:1	152	1.104	51

SAA (cont.)	
1.106–110	51
1.112	51
1.115–119	51
1.121	51
1.124–125	51
1.128–139	51
1.143–144	51
1.146	51
1.148–150	51
1.152	51
1.155–156	51
1.158–161	51
1.163–165	51
1.171–177	51
1.179	51
1.181–186	51
1.188–190	51
1.192–202	51
1.204–208	51
1.210	51
1.212	51
1.216	51
1.219	51
1.222–224	51
1.226–227	51
1.229–231	51
1.233	51
1.235–243	51
1.245–246	51
1.249	51
1.251–252	51
1.256–260	51

Ugaritic Texts
CTU

1.2 iv 5	31
2.11:10	31
2.11:14	31

RS

18.040:1	51
18.113A:1	51
34.148:5	51
94.2391:1	51

COS

1.103:344	53

Mari Texts
ARM

27/1:1	51

Sumero-Akkadian Texts
ANET

385–386	53

Ancient Jewish Writers
Josephus, *Antiquities of the Jews*

9.28	89
9.106	89

Rabbinic Texts
Sanhedrin

100a	83

Rosh Hashanah

16b	70

Soferim

4:9	98

MODERN AUTHORS INDEX

Abba, Raymond 69
Abbott, Edwin A. 58
Alford, Richard D. 68
Aliakbari, Mohammad 93
Alter, Robert 33, 38, 91
Andersen, Francis I. 37, 98–100, 104
Anderson, Arnold. A. 43, 91
Anderson, John M. 117
Avigad, Nahman 91, 98
Avishur, Yitzhak 91
Avrahami, Yael 69
Bakos, Ferenc 15
Baldick, Chris 37
Bar-Efrat, Shimeon 43
Barkay, Gabriel 91
Barr, James 34
Barrick, W. Boyd 78
Başoğlu, Sylvia 14
Bates, Elizabeth 14, 62
Baudissin, Wolf W. G. 32
Beam, Thelma 62
Benigni, Laura 14, 62
Biber, Douglas 122, 126–29
Blau, Joshua 32
Block, Daniel I. 36, 49, 77
Blyth, Caroline 77
Bordreuil, Pierre 31
Bramwell, Ellen S. 68
Braun, Friederike 2, 6, 13–15, 19, 21–22, 27–28, 45, 47, 62–63, 106, 149
Brettler, Marc Z. 31
Bridge, Edward J. 10–11, 21, 25
Brin, Gershon 91
Brongers, Hendrik A. 143

Brown, Donald E. 68
Brown, Penelope 2, 8–10, 23–25, 58, 63–66, 83, 87, 102, 108, 111, 159–60, 171, 174
Brown, Roger 2, 11–15, 21–22, 58–63, 66, 74, 78–79, 81, 84, 100, 102, 113–15, 160, 171–73
Brueggemann, Walter 73, 78, 89
Busse, Beatrix 28
Byrne, Geraldine 58
Chafe, Wallace 126
Cheng, Ken 62
Clermont-Ganneau, Charles 91
Clines, David J. A. 36, 79
Cohen, Simon 101
Cole, Graham A. 54
Čolič, Ana M. 119
Conklin, Blane 127, 140, 168
Contini, Riccardo 47, 106
Crenshaw, James L. 101
Currie, Haver 11
Dallaire, Hélène 75, 77
Dalman, Gustaf 31–32
Daniel, Michael 47, 57
Davidson, Andrew B. 87
Dehé, Nicole 129
Demsky, Aaron 69
Dickey, Eleanor 13–17, 20–22, 27–29, 45, 47, 57, 62, 105–6, 117
Dik, Simon C. 127–29
Diringer, David 91
Dobbs-Allsopp, Frederick W. 10
Domonkosi, Ágnes 159, 165
Donner, Herbert 91
Durkheim, Émile 64–65

Ehrensvärd, Martin	18	Harré, Rom	1
Eichrodt, Walther	36	Hartley, John E.	43
Eissfeldt, Otto	31	Hayes, John H.	78, 88, 97, 99, 101, 162
El Guindi, Fadwa	102		
Emerton, John A.	41	Head, Brian F.	159
Ervin-Tripp, Susan M.	13–14	Heltzer, Michael	91
Esposito, Raffaele	9, 47, 106, 108, 111, 113	Hess, Richard S.	69
		Higginbotham, Carolyn	153
Estelle, Bryan	8–9	Hijirida, Kyoto	62
Exum, J. Cheryl	77	Hillers, Delbert	36, 187
Falk, Avner	97	Hobbs, Trevor R.	89
Fasold, Ralph	21, 57	Hodson, Thomas C.	11
Fewell, Danna N.	77	Hoffmeier, James K.	153
Fitch, Kristine L.	84	Holmstedt, Robert D.	18, 34, 128
Fleming, Luke	83, 108	Holtgraves, Thomas M.	63
Forbes, A. Dean	37	Hooker, Paul K.	78
Ford, Marguerite	2, 11, 13–14, 21, 22, 58, 61–63, 74, 78–79, 84, 102, 113–14, 171–73	Huang, Yan	117
		Huehnergard, John	31
		Huspek, Michael	1, 20
		Hwang, Juck-Ryoon	14
Fox, Michael V.	9	Hymes, Dell	57, 214
Fox, Nili S.	73, 88, 91, 94	Jacob, Benno	165
Franz, Wilhelm	58	Jakobson, Roman	43
Freedman, David N.	37, 99–100	Jeremias, Joachim	94–95
Friedrich, Paul	15	Kambylis, Athanasios	28–29
Frost, Stanley B.	97	Kavalova, Yordanka	129
Garr, W. Randall	37	Keown, Anne S.	159
Garrett, Duane A.	98, 101	Keshavarz, Mohammad H.	61
Garsiel, Moshe	69	Kiełkiewicz-Janowiak, Agnieszka	14–16, 22, 27
Gibson, John C. L.	10		
Gilman, Albert	2, 11–15, 21–22, 58–60, 62–63, 66, 74, 79, 81, 84, 100, 102, 113, 160, 171–73	Kim, Yoo-Ki	92
		Kim, Young Bok	57
		Kimḥi, David	98
Glušac, Maja	119–21	Kohz, Armin	14
Goffman, Erving	23, 63–65	Krašovec, Jože	69
Gogel, Sandra L.	19	Kroger, Rolf O.	57, 62
Goldsmith, Daena J.	24	Kugel, James L.	49
Golub, Mitka R.	69	Kuglin, Jörg	62
Gray, John	89	Labov, William	11
Grayson, Albert K.	97	Lambdin, Thomas O.	153
Greenstein, Edward L.	69	Lambert, Wallace E.	14
Grice, H. Paul	65	Lande, Irene	49, 71, 74, 79, 82, 87, 92–93, 105
Guttmacher, Adolf	91		
Gzella, Holger	34	Landy, Francis	101
Haddad, Youssef A.	117	Leeb, Carolyn S.	89
Halliday, Michael A. K.	120		
Hamilton, Victor P.	43, 87, 97		

Leech, Geoffrey	28, 117–18, 120, 122, 126, 136, 138, 174
Leithart, Peter J.	78
Lemaire, Andre	91
Lemos, Tracy M.	73, 77
Leong, Ishbel	62
Levinson, Stephen C.	2, 8–10, 23–25, 58, 63–66, 83, 87, 102, 108, 111, 117, 159–60, 171, 174
Lévi-Strauss, Claude	68
Listen, Paul	159–60
Longacre, Robert E.	7
MacDonald, John	90
Macgowan, John	63
Marks, Herbert	69
Mays, James L.	101
McCarthy, Michael J.	118–19
McCawley, James D.	126
McClenney-Sadler, Madeline G.	103–4
McFall, Leslie	67
McGivney, James	61
Merwe, Christo H. J. van der	141
Mesthrie, Rajend	11
Mettinger, Tryggve N. D.	91
Miller, Cynthia L.	6–8, 17, 19, 21, 28–29, 33, 35–36, 38–39, 45, 111, 124–26, 144–46, 159–61, 165–66, 175
Miller, James M.	88, 97, 162
Miller, Stephen H.	13
Milroy, Lesley	16
Moshavi, Adina	126
Mühlhäusler, Peter	1
Müller, H.-P.	94
Murdock, George P.	68, 103
Nathan, Norman	15
Naudé, Jacobus A.	18, 95
Nida, Eugene A.	11
Noble, Paul R.	98, 100
O'Connor, Michael	9, 31, 38
O'Keeffe, Anne	118–19
Oyetade, Solomon O.	61–62
Pardee, Dennis	7, 10, 31, 61, 78, 90, 169
Parkinson, Dilworth B.	14, 20, 57, 62, 105
Parrott, Lillian A.	123
Paul, Shalom M.	99–101
Petersen, David L.	98, 101
Philipsen, Gerry	1, 20
Pickett, Joseph P.	48
Polak, Frank H.	17
Pollatschek, Moshe A.	18
Porten, Bezalel	69
Porter, Lyman W.	13
Portner, Paul	117
Provan, Iain W.	78
Qin, Xizhen	57, 62
Quirk, Randolph	117
Radday, Yehuda T.	18
Rainey, Anson. F.	91
Redford, Donald B.	153
Replogle, Carol	15
Revell, Ernest J.	7–8, 27–28, 32, 45, 66, 71, 73–78, 82, 86–87, 90, 94, 96, 111, 124–25, 150, 152–53, 160–61, 166, 168
Rezetko, Robert	18
Romaine, Suzanne	16
Rosenbaum, Michael	175
Rudolph, Wilhelm	98
Sarna, Nahum M.	43
Schegloff, Emanuel A.	116, 132
Schipper, Bernd U.	97
Schloen, J. David	110
Schubert, Klaus	14–15, 27
Selms, Adrianus van	91
Seymour, Timothy P.	68
Shiina, Michi	122–23, 126, 138
Siloni, Tal	34
Silverstein, Michael	62
Singerman, Robert	69
Slobin, Dan I.	13, 62
Slotta, James	83, 108
Slocum, Poppy	123
Smith, Arthur H.	63
Sohn, Ho-min	62
Spencer, Andrew	47, 57
Spencer-Oatey, Helen	66

Stager, Lawrence E.	90	Waterhouse, Ruth	15
Stähli, Hans-Peter	90	Webb, Barry G.	54, 77
Stavrou, Melita	119	Wegner, Judith R.	73
Steiner, Richard C	99, 143	Williams, James G.	89
Svennung, Josef	25, 150	Witherington, Ben	89, 99
Taglicht, Josef	120–24, 131, 174	Wolff, Hans W.	99, 101
Thomas, Benjamin	9–10	Wood, Linda A.	62
Thomas, David W.	87	Yeivin, Shmuel	91
Thompson, John A.	78	Young, Ian	18
Toni, Arman	93	Zevit, Ziony	138
Torczyner, Harry	10	Zimmermann, Frank	69
Tucker, G. Richard	14	Zwicky, Arnold	15, 28, 45, 71, 94, 105, 116–17
vanGemeren, Willem A.	53		
Vaux, Roland de	91		
Verhoef, Pieter A.	89, 94		
Wales, Kathleen M.	62		

SUBJECT INDEX

address
  bound forms of, 2, 8, 15, 17–18, 20, 27, 51, 74–75, 88, 90, 111, 149–50, 152, 154, 160, 171
  complex, 29, 32–35, 39–42, 44–46, 52, 55–56, 171–72
  compound, 29, 32, 40–46, 50–56, 66, 70, 80, 84–85, 93–94, 106, 113, 161, 171–73
  definition of, 6, 7, 11, 14–15, 19, 27, 171
  direct, 22, 123, 150, 152, 160
  free forms of, 2, 11, 15, 17, 20, 27–29, 31–32, 35–39, 45, 47, 51–53, 56–58, 63, 70, 74–75, 85, 88, 106, 115–26, 130–34, 136–39, 141, 144–46, 148–49, 152–54, 159–61, 171–74. *See also* vocative
  group, 45, 154
  indirect, 25, 150, 152–63, 165–70, 174–75
  invariant norm of, 62
  nominal forms of, 1, 12, 14–15, 19, 27, 35–36, 58, 61, 63, 150, 154
  pronominal forms of, 4, 12, 14, 19, 27, 59, 61
  rules, 13, 20–22, 57–58, 63, 68, 78–79, 81, 84, 102, 152, 160, 162, 173
  simple, 29–31, 34, 39–40, 42–43, 45, 56, 113, 171–72
  switching, 1, 3, 60–61
  third-person, 159–60
  verbal forms of, 15, 19
address inversion, 62, 105
adjunct(s), 27–28, 117, 127–28, 130, 139
ʔªḏɔnɔy, 31–32, 53–55, 140, 144
ʔªḏoni, 6, 9–10, 19–21, 23, 25, 27, 31–32, 41, 51, 54, 56, 65, 70, 80, 82, 84–86, 93, 135, 138, 140, 142, 144, 150, 153, 157, 172
adverb(s), 125, 130
  clausal, 127–28, 131, 139–41, 143, 163
  demonstrative, 130–31, 140
  time, 130–31, 140–43
Amaziah, 81, 86, 97–101
Amos
  occupation of, 98–101. *See also* ḥoze
anaphoric, 6, 19, 157
anarthrous, 32, 35–39. *See also* definite article
andronymic, 45–47, 49–50
antecedent, 19, 158
apostrophe, 37, 55–56, 172. *See also* personification
apposition, 20, 33–34, 36, 40, 45, 56, 89, 172
article. *See* definite article
asymmetry, 12, 59
Babylonian Chronicle, 97
background information, 123, 129
baṯ, 78, 104–5, 134, 175
ben-ʔɔḏɔm, 8, 36–37, 46, 49
ben hammeleḵ, 90, 145–46
Bethel, 38, 95, 98–98, 100–101

Canaanite shift, 31
Chinese, 14, 62–63
clause, 99, 100, 117, 120, 124–25, 127–28, 130, 158, 174
    conditional, 127–28, 131, 139
    dependent, 117, 125–26, 129, 145, 147, 157
    finite, 126
    imperative, 146
    independent, 117, 126, 129
    infinitival, 147
    main, 123, 157
    matrix, 125, 129, 147–48
    nominal, 100
    participial, 129–30, 133
    relative, 29, 34, 40, 42, 45, 48
    subordinate, 123
    verbal, 129–30, 133, 144
    verbless, 100, 125, 133, 142, 144–46
close(ness), 66–68, 71, 76–80, 82–83, 91–92, 103, 108, 110–11, 113, 159–60, 173. *See also* solidarity
context
    role of, 21
communicative competence, 57
concord
    rule of, 157
condescension, 49, 61, 75, 97–98, 173
conversational maxims, 65
coordination, 40, 44–45, 56, 117, 126, 172
c-unit, 117, 122, 126–29, 131–34, 136–39, 141, 143, 146, 148
    body, 122, 124, 126–29, 131, 133, 138–39, 141, 143, 145–48, 174
    clausal, 117, 126, 133
    final, 131, 136–38
    initial, 131, 133, 136, 138
    medial, 131, 138
    nonclausal, 117, 126, 132–33
    preface, 122, 124, 126–28, 130, 133–34, 138–39, 141, 143, 148, 174
    stand-alone, 116, 131–33, 137–38, 148, 174
    tag, 122, 126–27, 129, 133, 139, 146–48, 174
    tail, 127, 129
data collection methods
    interviews, 13–15
    introspection, 15
    observation, 15
    questionnaires, 13–15
    text analysis, 15
deference, 6, 10, 24–25, 48, 61, 65, 74, 80–81, 84, 87, 90, 92–93, 109, 160–62, 165, 170, 173–74
deferential
    language/expression/term, 6–11, 19, 21, 61, 65, 80, 92, 102, 135, 142, 152, 159, 160–62, 166
definite article, 29–32, 34–39, 53, 89, 153, 172
    absence of, 29, 35–39, 56, 172. *See also* anarthrous
deictic, 6, 19
delay, 121, 141
detach(ment), 121–22, 124, 128, 131, 139, 141, 143–44, 146–48
dislocation
    left, 127–28, 130–31, 139
    right, 129, 147
distance, 1, 6, 10, 12, 23, 25, 36, 49, 53, 59, 61, 65–68, 76, 159–60, 162–63, 165–66, 170, 173–74
ego, 103–4, 108
emotion, 12, 22, 43, 61, 63, 77, 108, 133, 160, 162
    admiration, 61, 101
    anger, 12, 21, 61, 81–82, 87, 135, 142–43, 160, 164
    contempt, 12, 21, 61, 64, 102, 160, 173. *See also* face threatening acts: contempt
    disrespect, 16, 82, 84
    formality, 1, 14, 73, 160, 167–70, 174

insult, 32, 39, 48–49, 64, 73, 75, 82, 160, 166–68, 170, 174. *See also* face threatening acts: insult
irony, 61, 118
mockery, 31, 38, 61, 73, 101, 165–66
rejection, 101, 160, 163, 165–66, 168, 170, 174
respect, 9, 12, 24–25, 48, 61, 65, 75, 79, 84–85, 93–94, 98, 100–2, 106, 161, 173
evaluative terms, 38–39, 45, 71
expressive shift, 8, 57–58, 60–61, 63, 68, 79, 81–82, 84, 96, 98, 100, 102, 160, 162–63, 165–68, 173
extra-clausal constituents (ECCs), 127, 129
face, 23–24, 63–65
    positive, 23–24, 64
    negative, 23–24, 64, 118
face threatening acts, 23, 64, 109
    acceptance of offer, 64
    accusation, 64
    advice, 23
    apology, 64
    challenge, 64
    complaint, 23, 64, 111
    confession, 64
    contempt, 64. *See also* emotion: contempt
    criticism, 23, 64
    disagreement, 64
    excuse, 64
    imposition of, 23–25, 64–65
    insult, 32, 64. *See also* emotion: insult
    mitigation of, 64
    offer, 64
    order, 23, 64
    promise, 64
    request, 23, 64–66, 110
    suggestion, 64
    thanks, 64
    warning, 23, 64

    weightiness of, 23, 25, 65
face-work, 64. *See also* politeness
familiarity, 1, 66
focus, 123–24, 130, 139, 148, 174. *See also* function (of free forms of address): focusing
    contrastive, 125, 144–45
    intonation, 121–22
    information, 122, 124, 131, 141, 143–48, 174
folk etymology, 69
fronting, 121–22, 130, 144. *See also* preposing
function (of free forms of address)
    attention-getter, 20, 116–17, 120, 132–33, 135–38, 148, 174
    badinage, 118
    call, 28, 116, 119, 132
    clarifying, 129, 148
    conative, 119–20
    conversation management, 138, 148, 174
    emotive, 43, 119–20
    focusing, 123–24, 130, 139, 148, 174. *See also* focus
    giving the floor to the addressee, 138, 148, 174
    identifying the addressee, 28, 117, 136–38, 174
    information management, 122
    maintaining contact with the addressee, 22, 117, 119–20, 137–38, 148, 174
    mitigators, 118–19
    partition, 121, 139, 148, 174
    phatic, 119–20
    poetic, 119–20
    referential, 120
    metalinguistic, 120
    relational, 118–19
    signaling the beginning of a conversation, 138, 148, 174
    signaling the beginning of a turn, 148, 174

signaling the end of a turn, 137–38, 148, 174
signaling the end of a conversation, 137–38, 148, 174
summons 28, 116, 118–19, 132
topic management, 118–19
turn management, 118
geographic name, 45, 154
Georgian, 14, 62
gentilic, 37, 45–46, 50, 154
German, 1, 12–15, 58, 62, 119
Greek, 5, 13–16, 28–29, 32, 38, 62, 97, 119
h-, 34, 45
hannaʕar, 89
haśśɔr, 82, 85
Hebrew, Biblical, 1–2, 5, 7–8, 12, 16, 18–19, 27–29, 31, 35–36, 46, 48, 51, 56–58, 63, 66, 69, 83–84, 114–16, 124–31, 143, 146, 148–50, 152–53, 159–60, 162, 168–74
   dating, 18
   archaic, 18
   early,18, 22
   standard, 18
   classical, 18
   late, 18, 22
Hebrew, Epigraphic, 1–2, 5–6, 8, 12, 17, 19, 27–28, 51, 149–50, 152, 159–60, 162, 170–71, 174–75
Hezekiah, 97, 135, 140, 146
hoy, 36, 133, 187
ḥoze, 95, 98. *See also* Amos: occupation of
illocutionary force, 122–23, 143
indexical orders, 62
information structure, 120–21, 129
interjection, 43, 125, 133
interrogative, 124–25, 130–31, 141–43
intimacy, 12, 53, 61, 64, 66, 159, 173.
   See also solidarity
Iranian Persian, 61
ʔiš hɔʔelohim, 32, 90, 93–94
Italian, 12–14, 58, 62
Japanese, 62
Jehoram, 71, 73, 76–79, 88, 109

kallɔ, 104–5, 175
kinship, 16, 21, 102–3, 169
   consanguineal, 102–8
   affinal, 102–5
kinship terms, 2, 6–7, 9, 11, 14–16, 19, 21, 25, 29, 45, 58, 62, 67, 102, 125, 172–73
   ascending, 74, 82, 103–4, 108–10, 113, 125, 159–62, 173
   descending, 103–4, 106, 108, 111–13, 125, 161, 169, 173
   extended, 47, 52, 105–6, 108–11, 113, 173
   fictive, 9, 47, 106
   horizontal, 103–4, 108, 110–11, 113, 169, 173
   as in-group identity markers, 10, 24–25, 64, 108
   literal, 9, 52, 105, 107–8, 169
   primary, 103–8
   referential, 105, 107
   secondary, 103–5
   tertiary, 103
Korean, 14, 62
linguistic competence, 57
linguistic universal, 61–63, 84, 102, 113–14, 173
matronymic, 45–47, 49–50
messenger formula, 75, 80, 90, 98
metaphorical mapping, 108, 159
Mijikenda, 61
nɔḇiʔ, 89, 94, 99
Nabopolassar, 97
naming, 68–69
nomen rectum, 29, 32–35, 44, 155
nomen regens, 32
nonce epithets, 45
oath formula, 125, 127
   authenticating element, 127–28, 138, 140
onomastics, 69
particles
   presentative, 125
   prose, 37
   negative, 130–31

patronymic, 2, 7, 15, 19, 45–47, 49–50, 153–54
parenthetical, 117, 119–21, 123, 127
personal names, 2, 8–9, 15–16, 19, 22, 29, 36, 45, 47, 53, 57, 67–68, 125, 153, 172–74
   direct referentiality of, 83, 108
personification, 38, 55–56, 172. *See also* apostrophe
Pharaoh, 7, 79, 87, 97–98, 153–54, 156, 161–62, 165
   Psammetichus I, 97
plištim, 37
politeness, 1–2, 8–11, 23–25, 58, 63–65, 83, 87, 106, 108, 110–11, 113–14, 160–62, 170–71, 173. *See also* face-work
   negative, 24, 64–65, 87, 102, 109, 160, 162, 174
   positive, 24, 64–65, 108–11, 113
power, 10, 12–13, 16, 22–23, 25, 33, 48, 59–61, 63, 65–71, 74–77, 80, 82–85, 95, 100, 102, 106, 108–11, 113, 124–25, 159–62, 170, 173–75
praescriptio, 9, 17, 169
preposing, 130. *See also* fronting
proclamation formula, 80–81
Rab-shakeh, 97
reciprocity/non-reciprocity, 12–13, 22, 24, 59–61, 71, 73–75, 78–79, 88, 92, 108
reference, 86, 91, 94–96, 103–5, 175. *See also* self-referential
referent, 34, 83, 108, 148
repetition, 37, 40, 42–45, 55–56, 89, 132, 165, 172
   emotive function of, 43
Rheme, 120–21, 123
   marked, 121
rites
   negative, 64–65
   positive, 64–65
rituals
   avoidance, 64–65
   presentational, 64–65

roʔɛ, 43, 95
Romanian, 62
self-abasement, 10
self-referential, 74, 92, 123, 168–69, 175
Sennacherib, 97, 140
Sentence, 2, 15, 20, 27–28, 57, 115–17, 120–22, 124–26, 138, 143, 149, 154, 171
   complex, 123, 126
   compound, 117, 126
   declarative, 121
   host, 117, 120, 124, 126
sequence, 121. *See also* word order
   breaking of, 121
   marked, 121
   unmarked, 121, 124, 141, 143, 145–46
sociolinguistics, 1, 5, 11, 13, 15, 19, 23, 66, 93, 171
solidarity, 12–13, 22, 24, 59–61, 63–65, 108–11. *See also* close(ness) *and* intimacy
status, 5, 9–13, 19, 21, 25, 45, 48, 59, 61–62, 66, 68, 72–73, 75, 78, 80–81, 83–84, 87–93, 109–10, 113, 124–25, 150, 169, 174
   vertical dimension of, 12
   horizontal dimension of, 12
   equal, 62, 91, 110, 113
   unequal, 62
status emphaticus, 31
symmetry, 59
Theme, 120–21, 123, 127
   marked, 121, 123
titles, 1–2, 6–8, 13, 15–16, 19, 23, 29, 52, 57, 84, 98, 125, 166, 172–73
   divine, 53–55
   honorific, 1, 23, 25, 48, 50–56, 65, 74, 76, 80, 84–88, 92–94, 153–54, 172
   occupational, 46, 48, 50, 52, 65, 74, 80, 84, 88, 90, 92–94, 97–98, 100–1, 153–54
   other, 52, 153

topic
- contrastive 123

Turkish, 14, 62

T/V system, 12, 22, 58, 61–63, 84, 102, 113, 173

variation(s), 1, 5, 7, 10–11, 17, 19, 22, 171
- diachronic, 22
- stylistic, 5
- synchronic, 22

Via Maris, 97

vocative, 8, 9, 15, 20, 28, 36, 119, 124–26. *See also* address: free forms of

word order, 28, 56, 94, 126, 128–31, 172
   See also sequence

wordplay, 69

Yoruba, 61–62

zero-relative complementizer, 34

www.ingramcontent.com/pod-product-compliance
Lightning Source LLC
Chambersburg PA
CBHW021351300426
44114CB00012B/1173